DOMESTIC REGULATION AND SERVICE TRADE LIBERALIZATION

DOMESTIC REGULATION AND SERVICE TRADE LIBERALIZATION

Aaditya Mattoo and Pierre Sauvé, Editors

A copublication of the World Bank and Oxford University Press

© 2003 The International Bank for Reconstruction and Development / The World Bank
1818 H Street, NW
Washington, DC 20433
Telephone 202-473-1000
Internet www.worldbank.org
E-mail feedback@worldbank.org

1 2 3 4 5 06 05 04 03

A copublication of the World Bank and Oxford University Press.

Library of Congress Cataloging-in-Publication Data has been applied for.

Cover artwork done by Karine Anglade.

ISBN 0-8213-5408-6

Contents

PART III SECTORAL PERSPECTIVES

PART IV LOOKING AHEAD: THE GATS WORK PROGRAM

Acknowledgments

We would like to thank the British government's Department for International Development, the Organisation for Economic Co-operation and Development, and the World Bank for their generous financial and administrative support. We are grateful to Anders Ahlind, Dale Andrews, David Hartridge, Ken Heydon, Bernard Hoekman, and Abdel-Hamid Mamdouh for their guidance on different aspects of the project. Kamal Saggi and Maurice Schiff provided valuable comments on the manuscript. Julia Nielson made numerous contributions and played a central role in organizing the conference in March 2002 where the papers were first presented. Ann Katoh set up and managed the conference website with remarkable efficiency. Thanks are due to Susan Graham for being a superb production editor and Santiago Pombo-Bejarano for his wise guidance on the publication process.

This volume benefited greatly from the insightful comments of the discussants at the conference. Their contributions could unfortunately not be included in this volume for reasons of space but can be accessed through the OECD website. Our profound thanks are due to Johannes Bernabe, Roberto Bosch, Thomas Chan, Elbey Borrero Delgado, Ambassador Torbjorn Froysnes, Scott Gallacher, Ulriche Hauer, Ambassador Alejandro Jara, Hugo Cayrus Maurin, Malcolm McKinnon, Jan-Peter Mout, Jose F. Poblano, Vincent Sachetti, Sebastian Saez, Sergio Rodrigues dos Santos, Andrea Spear, and Pimchanok Vonkhorporn.

Aaditya Mattoo
Pierre Sauvé
June 18, 2003

DOMESTIC REGULATION AND TRADE IN SERVICES: KEY ISSUES

Aaditya Mattoo
Pierre Sauvé

Background

Trade in services, far more than trade in goods, is affected by a variety of domestic regulations, ranging from qualification and licensing requirements and procedures in professional services, procompetitive regulation in telecommunications, and other network services, to universal access requirements in health and education services. The quality of regulation may strongly influence the social and economic effects of trade and investment liberalization, as the recent experience in financial services so clearly demonstrated.

Members of the World Trade Organization (WTO) have agreed that a central task in the ongoing set of services negotiations will be to further develop rules to ensure that domestic regulations support rather than impede the opening of services markets to trade and investment. Because these rules are bound to have a significant effect on the evolution of domestic services policy, it is important that they be conducive to economically rational policymaking while preserving the regulatory autonomy required to pursue and achieve domestic policy objectives.

The General Agreement on Trade in Services (GATS) explicitly recognizes "the right of Members to regulate, and to introduce new regulations on, the supply of services within their territories in order to meet national policy objectives and, given asymmetries existing with respect to the degree of development of services regulations in different countries, the particular need of developing countries to exercise this right." Despite such language and the deference to regulatory autonomy and national preferences embedded in it, the interface between domestic regulation and trade and investment liberalization in services has spawned a lively public policy debate, particularly in developed countries.

The progressive liberalization, not deregulation, of services trade is the goal of the GATS. A common misunderstanding in the public policy debate over the GATS is use of the terms "liberalization" and "deregulation" interchangeably, as if they were synonyms. They are not, and it is simply wrong to equate regulations with trade restrictions. Services liberalization, indeed, often requires regulation or re-regulation, but such regulation, whether for

The authors are grateful to Anders Anhlid, Ken Heydon, and Julia Nielson for helpful comments and suggestions in drafting this chapter.

economic or social purposes, can be designed, implemented, or enforced in more transparent and efficient ways with positive overall effects in terms of democratic governance.

The principal concern linked to loss of sovereignty is the consequent loss of a nation's freedom to regulate its service sectors in the manner it deems appropriate. Many service sectors are highly regulated to ensure a certain level of quality, to protect consumers or the environment, and in the financial services sector, to ensure a country's financial stability. Governments are understandably cautious when agreeing to subject themselves to common rules in such areas. Such regulatory precaution is reflected in the GATS provisions that uphold the fundamental right of a government to regulate in order to pursue national policy objectives.

It is certainly true that, as with any other legally bound undertaking in the WTO (or any other international treaty), the GATS can affect the regulatory conduct of member countries. But countries accept such disciplines because they deem them necessary to reaping the full benefits from international cooperation in a rules-based system.

Commitments under the GATS to grant market access in sectors where domestic regulation plays an especially important role do not entail any changes—and certainly no compromises—to regulatory standards or preferences. Those commitments in force to protect the public or to achieve universal access (e.g., in telecommunications or water supply) apply regardless of the nationality of the supplier. Governments may also choose to impose additional requirements on foreign suppliers—something they typically do, for instance, in the case of professional licensing in medical services.

Purpose of Publishing this Book

This volume is the product of an ongoing collaborative project between the World Bank and the Organisation for Economic Co-operation and Development (OECD) Trade Directorate, and its objective is to contribute to the nascent policy debate by mobilizing leading expertise in academic, policymaking, and negotiating circles around what is widely seen as the most complex agenda item in services trade today. A greater degree of common understanding among key stakeholders is likely to prove particularly helpful in progressing negotiations under the GATS.

The book brings together a series of papers presented at the Third Services Experts Meeting organized by the OECD Trade Directorate and held in Paris in the spring of 2002. Its purpose is twofold. It aims, first, to provide analytical input, based on the considerable experience of the World Bank and the OECD and outside experts on trade-related regulatory issues, to the ongoing WTO round of services negotiations. Second, it seeks to generate greater awareness among sectoral specialists and policymakers of the opportunities offered by the services negotiations to promote and consolidate domestic policy reforms in key service sectors.

An important challenge of the ongoing services negotiations will be to achieve better bridge building and improve lines of communication among trade negotiators and the broad and diverse community of domestic regulators. The sheer novelty, near universality, and technical complexity of the GATS, coupled with the lack in most countries of established channels of policy dialogue and consensus building between trade negotiators and domestic regulators, contributed to an outcome that saw most WTO members err on the side of regulatory precaution during the Uruguay Round. This was generally true both of agreed framework rules and of liberalization undertakings under the GATS. The fundamental changes in technology and in approaches to regulation that have taken root in recent years in many parts of the world afford a more congenial setting in which to nurture constructive and forward-looking dialogue between these two policy communities. More often than not, such a dialogue will need to involve competition policy officials, as became clear during negotiations conducted in the telecommunications sector after the conclusion of the Uruguay Round.

Because regulatory policy in individual services sectors is constantly evolving, the analysis contained in this volume offers an in-depth look at the horizontal elements of the Article VI.4 work program and their implications across leading service sectors. Such research aims to develop training material for capacity-building purposes in the services field.

The Article VI.4 Work Program

GATS Article VI (Domestic Regulation) is provisional in nature. A central question then is how best to strengthen disciplines without unduly curtailing national regulatory freedom. Of related interest is the question of determining the extent to which government regulations can be based on principles of economic efficiency and good governance. From the GATS perspective, a key issue is the extent to which regulatory principles can, amidst considerable sectoral diversity, be pursued through the creation of meaningful horizontal (i.e., non-sector-specific) disciplines.

Given the importance of the regulatory dimension in the liberalization process, Article VI on domestic regulation plays a key role in the opening of services markets. Coupled with Article XVI on market access and Article XVII on national treatment, Article VI can indeed be seen as the third complementary dimension of a three-pronged approach to effective access to services markets. Whereas Article XVI primarily addresses all (i.e., discriminatory and nondiscriminatory) quantitative restrictions affecting services trade and Article XVII disciplines overtly discriminatory treatment of foreign services and service providers, Article VI aims to discipline more opaque forms of protection embedded in domestic regulatory conduct.

Article VI requires that "in sectors where specific commitments are undertaken, each Member shall ensure that all measures of general application are administered in a reasonable, objective and impartial manner." The article aims to create more transparent domestic regulatory decisionmaking, implementation, and administration. There is explicit recognition of the right of service suppliers to information on regulatory and administrative decisions and to judicial and administrative review and appeals processes. In both respects, the GATS champions principles of good governance.

Unable to complete all aspects of the incipient GATS framework before the Uruguay Round's conclusion, services negotiators agreed on language in Article VI.4 calling for further work on disciplines that would help ensure that regulatory measures affecting services trade are reasonable, objective, and impartial. Work in this area is designed to address the fact that nontransparent, unfair, or unduly burdensome regulations at the national level may undermine the value of market access commitments freely entered into by a WTO member. Article VI.4 spells out the objectives of possible new disciplines that would aim to ensure that regulatory requirements are, among other things:

a. Based on objective criteria, such as competence and the ability to supply a service
b. No more burdensome than necessary to ensure the quality of the service
c. In the case of licensing procedures, not in themselves a restriction on the supply of the service.

Pending the possible negotiation of disciplines called for in Article VI.4, GATS Article VI.5 applies those objectives to any new measures that may nullify or impair commitments made in member country schedules.

Recognition of the unfinished nature of existing framework provisions on domestic regulation led to sectoral experimentation after the conclusion of the Uruguay Round. This was the case in the accountancy and basic telecommunications sectors where complementary disciplines were developed that aimed at ensuring that trade and investment liberalization commitments were properly underpinned by procompetitive and market access–friendly regulatory environments.

Accountancy Disciplines

The draft disciplines on accountancy, which were adopted in December 1998 and are due to be integrated into the GATS at the conclusion of the current negotiations, would apply only to those countries that made commitments on accountancy services. The draft disciplines do not focus on the substantive content of qualifications in accountancy but seek to ensure procedural transparency in matters of licensing and qualification. One of the most important elements of the disciplines is the creation of a necessity test, which requires that measures relating to licensing, technical standards, and qualifications be no more trade restrictive than necessary to fulfill a legitimate public policy objective. With regard to standards, for instance, the disciplines require that they be prepared, adopted, or applied only to fulfill legitimate objectives, which are stated to include the protection of consumers, the quality of the service, professional competence, and the integrity of the profession. It bears noting that the list of objectives is illustrative in nature, and not closed. A key unanswered question is whether these or similar disciplines could be applicable to other professions and indeed to services more generally.

Telecommunications Reference Paper

The Agreement on Basic Telecommunications, which was concluded in February 1997 and entered into force one year later, saw the adoption of a reference paper that WTO members were free to include, in whole or in part, as legally binding additional commitments in their schedules. The reference paper features a negotiated set of regulatory principles, including competition safeguards (to guard against the abuse of market power by dominant suppliers), interconnection guarantees, transparency in licensing, independence of regulators, competition-neutral universal service mechanisms, and fairness in allocating scarce resources such as radio spectra or rights of way.

Both the accountancy and telecommunications experiments raise the still unresolved question of the desirability and feasibility of horizontal versus sectoral approaches to the domestic regulation/market access interface. Key questions confronting services negotiators today, therefore, are to what extent can focusing on the various rationales for regulatory intervention provide the basis for developing meaningful horizontal disciplines on domestic regulation under the GATS, and where may it be necessary to take a sector-specific approach?

Issues Considered in this Volume

To help address many of the challenges raised above and to launch a lively and fruitful policy debate among many of the key stakeholders of the ongoing set of GATS negotiations, the series of articles by leading international experts contained in this volume were commissioned and/or prepared by the World Bank and the OECD Trade Directorate. The first set of articles deals with a number of *horizontal* rulemaking issues that feature prominently in the GATS Article VI.4 work program or that have a central regulatory dimension that future services

negotiations will likely need to address. These articles focus on the following topics:

- How best to strengthen disciplines on transparency while acknowledging the administrative burden of potential new disciplines, particularly for developing countries
- The links between international standardization efforts and market openness, with particular emphasis on lessons arising from ongoing efforts in the financial sector
- Some of the lessons of the GATT's Technical Barriers to Trade and Sanitary and Phytosanitary Agreements and their relevance for services trade
- Lessons arising from the development and use of "necessity" tests in domestic regulatory practice.

The second set of articles takes a *sectoral* look at the interface between domestic regulation and services trade. In commissioning these articles, attention was given to choosing a sample of sectors that illustrate both the broad categories of rationales for regulatory intervention in services markets and the possible market access effects of such intervention. Attention was also paid to choosing sectors in which some of the lessons arising from the outcome of negotiations on basic telecommunications or accountancy may be most germane—and indeed possibly replicable—together with sectors that received relatively less attention in the Uruguay Round. The sectoral papers address accountancy, energy, finance, health, telecommunications, and transportation services. The broad aims of these articles are to:

- Identify current perceptions on optimal regulatory policy in each sector
- Examine the links between domestic regulation and trade, drawing on the experiences of selected countries
- Assess the degree to which and the manner in which the GATS can be harnessed to promote sound regulatory conduct while promoting a progressive, orderly opening of markets
- Assess the possible implications of the GATS disciplines on regulation for services that have to date been minimally traded and that have strong regulatory frameworks to meet public policy objectives.

The following lists outline a number of key policy questions that readers are encouraged to bear in mind as they deepen their understanding of the horizontal and sectoral dimensions of the interface between domestic regulation and trade in services. Although some questions will be more relevant for some horizontal issues or sectors than others, all of them represent key considerations in ensuring that the GATS promotes sound regulation in the context of trade and investment liberalization without impeding governments' ability to pursue national policy objectives.

Questions to ensure that the GATS maintains governments' regulatory freedom:

- How can the GATS rules promote regulatory reform without unduly limiting regulatory freedom?
- Are there any areas of services trade in which the GATS regulatory disciplines should not apply or should be minimal?

Questions to ensure that regulation does not nullify or impair the GATS commitments:

- Where do regulations create unnecessary impediments to trade?
- Is it possible to highlight broad, common characteristics of such impediments that could, in turn, inform the development of possible disciplines?

Questions to ensure that sound regulation underpins trade and investment liberalization:

- Where is improved regulation necessary for successful trade and investment liberalization?
- Is it possible to identify a hierarchy of procompetitive or market access–friendly regulatory measures? Can one speak of more or less economically or socially "efficient" forms of regulatory interventions based on their possible effects on trade and investment?
- How should countries approach the sequencing of regulatory reform and trade and investment liberalization? Does the need for sequencing vary across sectors?
- What service sectors are most likely to require procompetitive regulatory disciplines as a complement to trade and investment commitments? To what extent are the disciplines contained in

the reference paper negotiated in the context of the Agreement on Basic Telecommunications services replicable in other sectors?

Questions to promote internationally harmonized or recognized regulation:

- How much scope is there for eliminating regulatory barriers to trade and investment through mutual recognition and harmonization?
- Are weak regulatory frameworks and poor standards of service quality likely to legitimize external barriers to trade and investment in services?
- What are the links between GATS Article VI (Domestic Regulation) and Article VII (Recognition), and how can disciplines in both areas best be deployed in a complementary manner?

Questions to identify the constraints on regulatory reform and the needs of developing countries:

- What are the constraints on policy reform, and how do these differ according to development levels?
- What particular challenges does the Article VI.4 work program pose for developing countries?
- Does the administrative burden of possible new disciplines on domestic regulation call for special and differential treatment, progressivity in application, or variable geometry between WTO members at different levels of development?
- Have the procompetitive regulatory disciplines embedded in the reference paper on basic telecommunications services helped anchor regulatory reform efforts and the adoption of best regulatory practices in developing countries?
- Should developing countries be encouraged to embed internationally recognized standards in their regulation of services markets? What type of technical assistance may be required to this end?

Questions to determine the types of disciplines that should be developed under Article VI.4:

- Is the scope of potential Article VI.4 disciplines too broad?
- Should such potential disciplines apply solely to scheduled sectors?
- What are the limits of multilateral rules on domestic regulation?

- Does compliance by subnational governments raise particular difficulties?
- Would strengthened levels of regulatory transparency, including those that allow for prior comment in the development of regulation, be likely to heighten the political legitimacy of regulatory outcomes?
- How has the accountancy profession reacted to the regulatory disciplines adopted by the sector? Are such disciplines, including those on "necessity," generally applicable in other professions? Could they form the basis of possible horizontal disciplines?
- Where is an acceptable balance likely to be found between legislative (i.e., via positive rulemaking) and adjudicative (i.e., via dispute settlement) approaches to the interface between trade liberalization and domestic regulation?

- Which of the issues discussed in the first part of the Third Services Experts Meeting do participants see as particularly ripe for more detailed analysis?

Given the dearth of relevant policy research in this complex area, and the fact that discussions of this policy interface are still at an early stage in the WTO, this publication aims to generate useful input for ongoing discussions under the GATS Article VI.4 work program. It should also help further the goal of greater coherence in policy reform efforts—that is, to assist countries in designing domestic regulatory frameworks that fulfill national policy objectives while being complementary to, informed by, and supportive of trade and investment liberalization efforts, whether at the WTO or in regional settings.

2

TRANSPARENCY IN DOMESTIC REGULATION: PRACTICES AND POSSIBILITIES

Keiya Iida
Julia Nielson

Executive Summary

Transparency is an essential component in the openness of decisionmaking related to the introduction, administration, and enforcement of new or amended regulations. In both social and economic terms, it plays an important role in revealing the basis for, and the full range of possible costs and benefits of, regulatory decisions and their implementation. Regulatory transparency is also an important tool in preventing unnecessary barriers to trade for both goods and services, with open processes resulting in better regulation, greater compliance, and ultimately greater political legitimacy. Participation by foreign parties also may assist in disseminating international best practices and provide early warning of any trade dispute that may arise regarding a regulation. The chapter's aim is to synthesize and build on earlier Organisation for Economic Co-operation and Development (OECD) Trade Directorate studies of transparency in domestic regulation (see TD/TC/WP[99]43/FINAL and TD/TC/[2000]31/FINAL, available at www.oecd.org/ech) with a view to identifying good regulatory practices and options for enhancing transparency under the General Agreement on Trade in Services (GATS). The chapter both draws together a range of information from previous stud-

ies and includes additional material on disciplines in regional trade agreements and practices in developing countries. Proposals for enhancing transparency under the GATS, including via practices at the national level and notifications to the World Trade Organization (WTO), also are further developed. The chapter features the following elements:

- Benefits and costs of transparency in domestic regulation
- Regulatory disciplines at the multilateral level
- Regulatory disciplines at the regional level
- Regulatory practices at the national level
- Options for enhancing transparency under the GATS.

Detailed information on provisions in WTO agreements and regional trade agreements, as well as practices at the national level in both OECD and selected developing economies, can be found at www.oecd.org/ech.

Why Transparency Matters

Transparency is an essential component in the openness of decisionmaking related to the introduction, administration, and enforcement of new or amended regulations. Regulatory transparency is an important tool in preventing unnecessary barriers to trade for both goods and services. The cost and complexity of delivering services across borders or of establishing commercial presence in a market underscore the importance of regulatory transparency for trade in services.

Transparency in regulation is not static, but rather is part of the dynamic process of regulatory policymaking. In both social and economic terms, it plays an important role in revealing the basis for regulatory decisions and their implementation, and their full range of possible costs and benefits. Regulatory transparency is conducive to both more fair and more effective governance, improving public confidence in governmental and regulatory performance, and to economic efficiency, helping to remove distortions that might otherwise undermine domestic policy objectives. For trade policy, transparency in domestic regulation is a crucial tool in making policymakers, business, and civil society aware of the need for regulatory reform and trade and investment liberalization, and the full range of their social and economic costs and benefits.

In addition, transparency and openness in decisionmaking are essential parts of public governance in any democratic setting. Lack of transparency reduces the information available to interested parties and undermines their ability to participate meaningfully in policy processes (see Stiglitz 1999). The participation of various interests through open processes can lead regulatory authorities to reflect carefully on the full range of alternatives before introducing or modifying regulations, and that results in better regulation, greater compliance, and ultimately greater political legitimacy. If foreign parties also have opportunities to be informed and to participate, they may play a role in disseminating international best practices for achieving policy objectives and in providing an early warning system for trade disputes that may arise with respect to new or modified regulations.

Furthermore, transparent trade-related domestic regulatory processes provide firms with more predictable conditions in foreign markets. When trade-related regulatory decisionmaking is transparent, foreign firms are able to gain (a) information on the conditions and constraints they will encounter in a market; (b) information on the measures they could take to comply with regulatory requirements; (c) a more accurate picture of costs

and returns on their investment or commercial presence; and (d) time and flexibility to adjust to potential changes in regulation. Transparency also helps reveal hidden discrimination that can arise from administrative rules and procedures established by the regulatory authorities. Transparency enables foreign firms to find out whether these rules and procedures deviate from the founding, or enabling, legislation. Because transparency permits business and other parts of civil society to be better informed about such discretion, it creates additional incentives for bureaucrats to establish them within the mandate of legislation. Finally, regulatory transparency makes it more difficult for regulators to be captured by regulated firms, which helps protect the independence and autonomy that regulators need to do their jobs effectively.

Transparency in applying regulations also enhances predictability and accountability in the implementation of trade-related regulation. Although the focus tends to be on rulemaking, enhanced transparency (and thus predictability and accountability) in applying regulations would considerably facilitate trade in services by reducing unnecessarily burdensome administrative processes (e.g., in licensing processes, procedures for administrative actions and decisions, and review mechanisms for administrative decisions).

Disciplines at the Multilateral Level

This section of the chapter surveys existing regulatory disciplines in the various World Trade Organization (WTO) agreements with a view to providing the basis for discussion on possible enhancement of transparency disciplines under the GATS. Details of the provisions in each agreement can be found at www.oecd.org/ech.

Different terms describing regulations are found across the WTO agreements—laws, decrees, regulations, procedures, requirements, administrative guidelines, administrative ruling of general applications, administrative proceedings, decisions, or actions. To avoid any confusion and enable consistent usage in this chapter, we use "legislative measures" when referring to laws to be finally enacted by the legislative branch and "subordinate measures" when referring to decrees, regulations, procedures, requirements, administrative guidelines, and administrative rulings of general application established by regulatory authorities in the executive branch within the legislative mandate. "Administrative decisions" refers to any administrative proceedings, decisions, or actions by regulatory authorities in the executive branch within the legislative mandate. Although these distinctions are useful, they should be approached with some caution, given that these categories could vary among WTO members to reflect their differing legal and constitutional systems. It also should be recalled that the Reference Paper on Basic Telecommunications covers transparency on measures taken by nongovernmental entities.

The General Agreement on Tariffs and Trade (GATT) and the GATS already require members to publish legislative and subordinate measures before they are enforced. Disciplines in the GATT are more specific than in the GATS, requiring that measures be published promptly in a manner that enables relevant parties to become acquainted with them. Similarly the Sanitary and Phytosanitary (SPS) Agreement specifically mentions a "reasonable interval" between the publication of a measure and its entry into force, with consideration given to the difficulty developing countries may experience in adapting their products to the requirements of the importing members.

Notification and comment procedures via notifications to the WTO are found in both the Technical Barriers to Trade (TBT) and SPS Agreements, with exceptions for emergency situations. Notifications should include a brief indication of the objective of and the rationale behind the regulation. Notification and comment procedures are triggered when a technical regulation or a sanitary or phytosanitary measure is not based on an international standard or where no such standard exists. This is likely to be the case most of the time with regard to measures concerning services because there are few international standards. (Work to develop international standards has been concentrated thus far in such professional services as architecture.)

The GATS also requires an annual notification to the Council for Trade in Services on new or changed measures. An obligation to conduct prior consultation as a domestic procedure is only found in the Disciplines for the Accountancy Sector, but the obligation takes a best-endeavors form (that is,

"Members shall endeavour to provide an opportunity for comment, and give consideration to such comments, before adoption") and the disciplines have not yet entered into force (they are expected to come into force at the end of the current negotiations). The disciplines also require members to inform another member, upon request, of the rationale behind measures in the accountancy sector, in relation to legitimate objectives as referred to in paragraph 2 of the disciplines. These procedures in the TBT and SPS Agreements, the GATS, and the accountancy disciplines are only required for measures that significantly affect trade. In summary, three possible arrangements are identified in these agreements: (a) notification procedures through the WTO secretariat, (b) information exchanges upon request by members, and (c) prior consultation as a domestic procedure.

Regarding disciplines on administrative decisions, all agreements require uniform, impartial, and reasonable administration, an opportunity to appeal, and a review mechanism, with the degree of specificity varying among agreements. The GATS already incorporates some higher standard disciplines for "authorisation required for the supply of service," such as obligations to inform applicants of the decision concerning the application within a reasonable period of time and to provide information concerning the status of the application.

Enhanced requirements are found in the TBT and SPS Agreements and the Disciplines for the Accountancy Sector. These include (a) publishing the standard process period (TBT, SPS) or informing the applicant of the decision within, in principle, 120 days (Accountancy); (b) giving notice of the deficiencies in application (TBT, SPS, and Accountancy); and (c) transmitting results in a precise and complete manner so that corrective action may be taken (TBT, SPS) or providing information on the reasons for rejection of application (Accountancy). Although license procedures for trade in services are different from the conformity assessment in the TBT Agreement and from inspection or approval in the SPS Agreement, these key elements could be shared and applied to both procedures (see the section on options for enhancing transparency under the GATS).

Other types of disciplines on administrative decisions found in the SPS and TBT Agreements and the accountancy disciplines are not included in the GATS; for example, (a) nondiscriminatory processing of submission or application for both domestic and foreign parties, (b) avoidance of unnecessary information requirements for application, (c) nondiscriminatory treatment of confidential information, (d) reasonable application fees, and (e) reasonable requirement for authenticity of application materials. Although these disciplines also facilitate trade in services by reducing burdensome administrative process, they are more related to nondiscrimination and necessity in implementation than to transparency.

Regarding the measures taken by local governments and nongovernmental entities, WTO agreements generally require members to take such reasonable measures as may be available to them to ensure their compliance with the agreements.

Disciplines at the Regional Level

Disciplines on transparency are also found in regional trade agreements. It is particularly useful to examine these agreements because some countries, including developing countries, already make commitments to higher level disciplines on transparency in these regional frameworks than in the WTO. This section summarizes the situation regarding disciplines on transparency across a range of regional trade agreements. Information regarding disciplines on transparency in a range of regional trade agreements can be found at www.oecd.org/ech.[1]

Like the GATT and the GATS, all regional trade agreements require publication of legislative measures and subordinate measures at the time of their entry into force. They also incorporate basic disciplines on administrative decisions such as uniform, impartial, and reasonable administration, and opportunity for review and appeal of those administrative decisions. Generally speaking, in addition to the horizontal disciplines, more specific and detailed disciplines also are developed for specific sectors, such as telecommunications and financial services.

As for the GATS, obligations to inform applicants of the decision concerning the application within a reasonable period of time and to provide them with information concerning the status of the application are also included in the services provisions. It should be noted that some regional trade

agreements set a more specific period (120 days) in the provisions covering financial services, but this period could vary for other sectors (e.g., the European Union [EU] directive on telecommunication services sets the period at six weeks, with some exceptions).

Most regional agreements have more detailed disciplines on administrative decisions. They require that people directly affected by administrative decisions be provided a reasonable notice of the nature of these decisions and that such people are afforded a reasonable opportunity to present facts and arguments in support of their positions prior to any final decision. Regarding the review and appeal on administrative decisions and actions, some regional agreements require that each party establish or maintain judicial, quasi-judicial, or administrative tribunals or procedures and that such tribunals be impartial and independent of the office or authority entrusted with administrative decisionmaking. They also require that parties to the proceeding have the right to a reasonable opportunity to support or defend their respective positions; and a decision based on the evidence and submissions of record or, where required by domestic law, the record compiled by the administrative authority.

Most regional agreements also require prior notification bilaterally between governments or prior consultation with interested parties or prepublication as domestic procedures. For multilateral disciplines this takes three forms: notification among parties, information exchange upon request through inquiry, and prior consultation as a domestic procedure. Although the measures to be covered by these consultations are broad, they include some limiting wording, such as "to the (maximum) extent possible," "when so established by laws," or "make its best endeavours."

It is also interesting to note that further, weaker disciplines are found in regional agreements among developing countries. The agreement among Colombia, Mexico, and the República Bolivariana de Venezuela only requires an effort to publish any measures in advance and to offer the parties and any interested bodies a reasonable opportunity to formulate observations on the measure. Despite these reservations and some doubts about whether these provisions are fully implemented, it is significant that a few developing countries already make higher commitments on transparency than those commitments required by WTO agreements.

Regarding use of international standards, only the Free Trade Agreement between the EU and Mexico refers to international standards being developed by international financial regulatory organizations.

Regulatory Practices at the National Level

This section provides an overview of the range of practices on prior consultation on subordinate measures and legislative measures, and administrative decisions and actions in implementation of measures, found at the national level in OECD members and selected developing countries.[2] Detailed information on the regulatory processes found at the national level in OECD and selected developing countries can be found at www.oecd.org/ech.

Practices on Development of Subordinate Measures

Overall the case studies indicate a trend toward prior consultation for subordinate measures.[3] Across various country practices, the extent to which they incorporate three important elements in prior consultation practices can be identified for comparative analysis: transparency, nondiscrimination, and accountability.

- Transparency means that the consultation procedures themselves should be open and accessible.
- Nondiscrimination ensures that prior consultation procedures treat domestic and foreign parties equally in a nondiscretionary and impartial manner.[4]
- Accountability mandates that regulatory authorities explain the factual and logical basis for their decisions by giving due consideration to comments received, although they retain ultimate discretion in determining to what extent to consider and respond to a particular comment.

It can also be observed that prior consultation takes different forms depending on the different stages of preparation. When regulatory authorities introduce and modify measures, they first need to analyze the problems and explore possible solutions with experts and with their constituents. In earlier stages consultations tend to be limited to a relatively narrow range of interests; regulatory authorities may then build policies through progressive dialogues with strongly affected parties. In some cases they also set up forums for consultation, such as advisory councils or committees comprising selected interests. In other cases, they draft a policy recommendation, sometimes as a report of these forums, and set up notice and comment procedures for those reports to share their views with outside parties.

Regulatory authorities could make these preliminary consultations more transparent and nondiscriminatory by publishing reports on the substance of consultations or by collecting views of both domestic parties and foreign parties. These consultations should be as nondiscriminatory as possible, but it might be difficult for regulatory authorities to eliminate all discretionary aspects arising in the preparation process. As is already the case in some of the reviewed countries, however, regulatory authorities could notify draft measures for public comment at a later stage to ensure that all interested parties are informed and given equal opportunity to comment. This practice would provide an effective and credible safeguard against the possible abuse of selected participation in earlier stages of consultation and ensure transparency and nondiscrimination in prior consultation. In a few countries, draft texts are also prenotified with statements of regulatory impact analysis, which describe the objectives of, rationale behind, alternatives to, and benefits/costs of regulatory measures.

The studies also show that there are common types of measures excluded from prior consultation. The following measures are often excluded because prior consultation is perceived as impracticable, unnecessary, or contrary to the public interest:

- Measures to cope with urgent problems of safety, health, and environment arising or threatening to arise
- Measures dealing with military and foreign affairs, which are required in the interests of national security or which merely meet an obligation under an international agreement
- Measures of a minor nature, which do not substantially alter existing regulations.

Other categories of exceptions are found in some countries, but in most cases regulatory authorities are required to explain why they are exempted from the prior consultation requirements. Additionally, measures of a local government and other self-governing subentities are also typically carved out from prior consultation requirements.

Practices on Development of Legislative Measures

Unlike practices on subordinate measures, wider differences in practices for legislative measures can be observed in the country studies, reflecting different political systems or institutional structures. Although in parliamentary systems the executive branch proposes draft legislative measures and could conduct prior consultation before the measures are submitted to the legislative branch (as they do for subordinate measures), enactment of legislative measures may also be initiated from the legislative branch itself, based on political platforms or election commitments.[5] The draft of legislative measures is pre-announced in some countries to encourage the participation of citizens and other interested parties.

Whatever the political system, however, when the draft is submitted to the legislative branch, public consultation inevitably takes the form of political deliberation and citizens can participate in the discussion only through elected representatives (who usually must be nationals or citizens). Although in some cases public hearings could be held in the legislative branch to seek comments from external parties, including foreign interests, direct participation by foreign interested parties generally is limited.

Practice on Administrative Decisions

Some OECD members have enacted horizontal administrative procedures legislation to impose disciplines on administrative decisions. Basically they require that regulatory authorities make rules and procedures publicly known and make administrative decisions within a reasonable time. In some countries regulatory authorities are required to publish the standard period for processing applications as a benchmark for a "reasonable time" and to

inform applicants of the reason for denial of an application. The procedures also ensure that, in the case of suspension or revocation of license or other decisions adversely affecting a licensee, the licensee is given notice of the reasons by the regulatory authorities and the opportunity to demonstrate compliance with requirements or to defend his or her position. In other countries these disciplines are prescribed in specific statutes or guidelines but are not covered by horizontal regulations.

Developing Countries

Even in developing countries with limited administrative capacity there now are greater efforts to enhance transparency in policymaking, with public notice and comment procedures recently adopted to facilitate participation by citizens in the policymaking process. Developing countries also are adopting electronic means for these public notice and comment procedures as part of efforts to promote e-government. This can help ensure transparent and nondiscrimination processes in the presence of fewer administrative resources; however, access to information might be more limited in developing countries because of a lack of technical infrastructure. Although committees or other forums are set up to formulate regulatory measures in some cases, efforts also have been made to enhance transparency by publishing recommendations and inviting comments from external experts and other market participants. The study so far could not find any constitutional constraints on such consultations.

Public notice and comment procedures are not as widespread in developing countries as they are in some OECD members. Because the developing economies often do not have the capacity to implement horizontal schemes, those procedures are more frequently conducted for specific sectors, such as telecommunications and financial services. They also are conducted for specific issues considered to be more important in specific sectors, such as universal service obligations and spectrum management. This also reflects particular commitments to greater transparency undertaken in accordance with the GATS Reference Paper on Basic Telecommunications. In the context of their limited administrative capacity it is not altogether surprising that developing country regulatory authorities tend to narrow the scope of prior consultation to specific regulatory issues in specific sectors.

Options for Enhancing Transparency under the GATS

This section of the chapter explores some of the options open to WTO members for increasing transparency under the GATS. As indicated above, the GATS contains a number of provisions relating to transparency.

A threshold question may be to what extent are any further disciplines actually necessary or should the focus be on improving the implementation of existing obligations? A number of transparency issues arguably are more a matter of poor implementation of existing obligations than of the need for new obligations. But that also suggests there may be scope to improve the implementation of existing obligations—for example, via the development of standard form notifications. In other cases, the scope and content of existing obligations could be clarified—for example, by giving greater precision to the types of information that could be made available under Article III and to the means by which members could provide access to that information. A number of proposals in this section are focused on improving and facilitating adherence to existing transparency obligations.

New obligations could also be considered, however, including prior consultation and opportunity for comment before regulations are finalized. The suggestions in this section include options for increasing transparency via the WTO (e.g., for notifications and trade policy reviews) and through domestic procedures as part of national regulatory processes. Both means are necessary and can be mutually reinforcing. Finally, for all the options presented WTO members can choose from along the continuum of possibilities, from binding disciplines covering all sectors, to best-endeavors commitments adopted in full or in part only for some sectors.

Types of Measures Covered by the GATS

Before considering the possibility of enhanced disciplines, it is important to have a clear understanding of the scope of measures to which those disciplines could apply. In the GATS, "measure" is defined very broadly as any measure whether in the form of law, regulation, rule, procedure, decision, administrative action, or any other form (Article XXVIII). The following different types of measures are referred to in the GATS:

- Measures of general application that pertain to or affect the operation of this agreement (Article III.1 and III.4)
- Laws, regulations, or administrative guidelines that significantly affect trade in services *covered by . . . specific commitments* (Article III.3)
- Measures of general application affecting trade in services *in sectors where specific commitments are undertaken* (Article VI.1)
- Administrative decisions affecting trade in services (Article VI.2[a])
- Authorization required for the service *on which a specific commitment has been made* (Article VI.3)
- Measures relating to qualification requirements and procedures, technical standards, and licensing requirements (Article VI.4).

Whereas Article III.1 refers to "measures of general application," Article III.3 is limited to "laws, regulations or administrative guidelines" significantly affecting trade in services covered by a member's specific commitments. Although many of the measures of general application are likely to take the form of laws, regulations, and administrative guidelines, they need not directly regulate a particular service and need only affect or pertain to the operation of the agreement, rather than significantly affect trade in services. Such measures need only be published, not notified to the WTO (as is the case for measures under Article III.3). Article VI.1 also refers to measures of general application, but unlike Article III.1 it is limited to sectors where specific commitments are undertaken. Article VI.I requires that, for sectors where specific commitments are undertaken, measures of general application affecting trade in services must be administered in a reasonable, objective, and impartial manner; but a more detailed prescription is laid down for the narrower range of measures in Article VI.4. Qualification requirements and procedures, technical standards, and licensing requirements in Article VI.4 and Article VI.3 authorizations are related mainly to licenses for services. "License" in this context should be interpreted broadly, with basically the same meaning as "authorization," because it includes the whole part of an agency permit, certificate, approval, registration, or other form of permission.

Measures relating to restrictions on movement of natural persons are given further definition. The Annex on Movement of Natural Persons states that the agreement does not prevent a member from applying measures to regulate the entry or temporary stay of natural persons in its territory, provided that such measures do not nullify or impair the benefits accruing to any member under the terms of a specific commitment. Discriminatory visa requirements per se are not regarded as nullifying or impairing benefits under a specific commitment. General requirements for transparency under Article III apply to measures regulating the entry and temporary stay of natural persons. However, although regulations governing the issuance of work permits and defining foreigners' ability to work in individual areas fall under the GATS, general immigration legislation may not fall there.

Subnational Measures   "Measures" under the GATS also can be categorized by the level at which they are taken:

- Central government measures
- Local government measures
- Measures taken by nongovernmental entities.

As described above in the discussion of disciplines at the multilateral level, in recognition of members' different constitutional or institutional constraints, and while including regional and local government and nongovernmental bodies exercising delegated power in its definition of "measure" (Article I.3[a]), the GATS stipulates that each member shall take such reasonable measures as may be available to it to ensure observance by regional or local government bodies or nongovernmental bodies. It may be useful to examine whether transparency requirements should operate at the subnational level, given the difference in transparency practices between central government bodies and other bodies, the benefits of transparency for both governance and trade, and the fact that the locus of services regulation in many federal systems is at the subnational level

(where some difficulties for foreign traders can also arise). Exclusion of subnational measures may also result in any additional transparency obligations falling disproportionately on those WTO members with centralized political and regulatory systems. However, the additional administrative burden for WTO members with federal systems that include measures at the subnational level must also be considered; indeed, subnational measures are excluded from a number of these countries' prior consultation requirements. Nonetheless, transparency disciplines that require or encourage certain domestic practices or procedures could also encourage similar practices at the local or regional level.

Possible Types of Disciplines

Horizontal versus Sectoral Disciplines   Another threshold issue is the extent to which any new transparency obligations should be horizontal or sectoral in application, and whether any horizontal rules should apply across the board to all sectors or only to sectors where specific commitments have been made. Existing transparency disciplines apply both across the board and only in sectors where specific commitments have been made. Notwithstanding that fact, it may be worth considering whether any further disciplines on transparency should apply across all sectors, regardless of whether specific commitments have been undertaken. Given the benefits of transparency for both domestic governance and the development of efficient domestic services, it can be argued that all areas of the economy should benefit from greater transparency, not simply those sectors where international trade commitments have been made. Furthermore, transparency is increasingly recognized as a fundamental principle of the trading system (like most-favored-nation status), and lack of transparency is seen to be a major barrier to trade. Given the degree of unilateral liberalization being undertaken by countries outside of the GATS framework, an annex on transparency applying to all sectors could serve countries' own interests in developing sound transparency practices to assist with smoothly functioning and orderly market development at the same time that they liberalize. And having decided to open the market to foreign suppliers, it is in members' interests to provide their trading partners with the information needed to take advantage of the access granted.

There are also counterarguments, however—notably that members might be more willing to countenance additional transparency disciplines if they applied only in areas where commitments had been made. Similar arguments arise in relation to the question of whether any new transparency disciplines should apply horizontally or be developed on a sector-specific basis. Proponents of a horizontal approach to increased disciplines on transparency note that transparency is usually considered to be a cross-cutting issue, a fundamental principle of the trading system that is not dependent on sectoral specificities. They also point to the fact that, although services sectors themselves may be highly diverse, the fundamental requirements of transparency—such as making information available in a timely and readily accessible fashion—do not vary greatly among sectors. Similarly it is argued that there is little justification for treating one sector more favorably than another in terms of transparency, and that good regulatory practices should be encouraged across all of government, not simply in certain relatively easy or noncontroversial sectors. Horizontal disciplines also can prevent sectoral special interests from blocking progress. These arguments are underlined by the existence in a number of WTO members of national horizontal administrative procedures laws or regulations. Horizontal transparency rules also are argued to provide benefits in terms of an economy of negotiating effort and the legal clarity and simplicity of obligations by their avoidance of a proliferation of sector-specific disciplines.

However, those who favor sectoral disciplines point to the particularities of various services sectors—arguing that more detailed regulatory disciplines, especially those beyond transparency, cannot be uniform across sectors because of the nature of the sectors themselves and the administrative capacity of sectoral regulatory authorities. Given the need to develop sector-specific rules to address issues, such as interconnection, that arise only for certain types of sectors, it is argued that it is better to include tailored and specific transparency requirements in these rules—as was done in the Reference Paper on Basic Telecommunications and the accountancy disciplines—than to develop general transparency disciplines.

Proponents of a sectoral approach also argue that not all service sectors are traded to the same extent and not all encounter the same degree of problems with lack of transparency. Priorities for which measures should be addressed by what type of enhanced disciplines may also differ among sectors. Furthermore, because national regulatory practices vary among sectors it is argued that it may be difficult to develop a horizontal approach (e.g., administrative procedures laws or guidelines), especially for developing countries with limited administrative capacity. Members may be more willing to accept increased transparency disciplines if they are able to implement such disciplines gradually, starting with sectors and measures of priority interest, rather than by an "all or nothing" approach. Arguably, members may be less willing to convert unilateral liberalization into GATS commitments if they automatically assume additional obligations with regard to transparency.

Horizontal and sectoral approaches to enhanced transparency disciplines need not be mutually exclusive, however. Another option could be a basic set of horizontal rules on transparency that could be supplemented as necessary by sector- or mode-specific rules, as applicable. Additional sector-specific transparency requirements could be scheduled as additional commitments against the appropriate sector.

Another approach would be to give members the flexibility to inscribe standard new disciplines on transparency in their schedules against some sectors but not others. Alternatively, members could be allowed to accept common new rules in full or in part; that is, by selecting some of the disciplines to inscribe in their schedules and leaving others out. These last suggestions, however, also raise the issue of the extent to which any new disciplines should be binding.

Binding Disciplines versus Best Endeavors   New transparency obligations could take the form of mandatory disciplines or best-endeavor provisions. Mandatory provisions could be formulated as an annex applying horizontally to all sectors and binding on all members. Alternatively, members could choose to inscribe new transparency disciplines in their schedules in sectors where they have made specific commitments—that is, although the decision to adhere to the increased disciplines would be voluntary, once inscribed in the schedules (per Article XVIII additional commitments) they would have the status of binding commitments. Members could be given the flexibility not to include all sectors where they have made commitments, or not to include all disciplines. A further option—that could operate either for all sectors or only for those where specific commitments had been made—would be for any additional disciplines to be worded on a best-endeavors basis, providing members with a benchmark of best practice and with some flexibility in implementation. In any of these options, general transparency disciplines could be supplemented by additional sector- or mode-specific rules as appropriate. These options are summarized in box 1.

Reducing the Potential Administrative Burden

A key consideration in assessing whether, and to what extent, GATS transparency disciplines might be augmented or specific means for implementing current obligations might be developed is the need to balance the administrative burdens of new transparency requirements against the benefits of increased transparency. A number of options are open to WTO members with a view to ameliorating the administrative burden of increased transparency requirements while garnering the benefits for domestic efficiency and governance, as well as for trade.

Obviously the extent of the burden in terms of the timing and form of implementation will be determined by the type of disciplines that members choose (see box 1). And the administrative burden of increased transparency may be reduced to the extent that any new disciplines focus on developing procedures at the national level and on minimizing additional notification requirements to the WTO. Development of transparency practices at the national level still requires resources but it provides immediate and demonstrable domestic benefits, in addition to benefits for trading partners. Indeed, the nature of services trade suggests that many transparency procedures can be best operationalized at the national level, building on existing administrative structures and practices.

This flexibility can be further increased to the extent that any new obligations take the form of general objectives, leaving scope for members to implement them within their existing administrative structures. For example, specific time limits need not be set—timing requirements should be stated generally in terms of the objective they are designed to meet—that is, a specific time limit (e.g., six weeks) for prior consultation or application processing need not be mandated if the period meets the objective of being "sufficient to enable comments to be received and taken into account" or, in the case of applications, is "reasonable," "prompt," and "not an unnecessary barrier or restriction on the supply of the service." Ideally, transparency obligations should be objectives that members may achieve by a range of means appropriate to their domestic systems and levels of development.

The degree of administrative burden associated with increased transparency disciplines will also

---

BOX 1   Summary of Options for Possible Increased Transparency Requirements

- Binding general disciplines applying horizontally across all sectors.
- Binding general disciplines applying to all sectors where specific commitments have been made.
- Binding general disciplines applying only to those sectors where members have specifically scheduled them.
- Binding sector-specific transparency rules developed on a sector-specific basis.
- "Best endeavors" disciplines applying horizontally across all sectors.
- "Best endeavors" disciplines applying only in sectors where specific commitments have been made.
- "Best endeavors" disciplines applying only to those sectors where members have specifically scheduled them.
- Flexibility to apply only some of the disciplines (be they binding or "best endeavors") to only some sectors.
- Any of the above supplemented by additional sector- or mode-specific rules, as appropriate.

depend on the nature and scope of any provisions agreed to. Exceptions for measures of a relatively minor nature or related to security, for example, may reduce the burden, as could the carve-out of measures at the subnational level. In this regard it is also worth noting the different types of measures already referred to in the GATS and the different disciplines that apply to them. Additionally, as in the SPS and TBT Agreements, special transparency provisions could apply in emergency situations.[6]

Special and Differential Treatment Members also could consider whether special and differential treatment might be appropriate to address the particular concerns of developing countries in the context of their limited capacity to implement increased transparency requirements. Possible special and differential treatment could take a number of forms: the content of obligations could be different for developing countries, or, in the case of binding disciplines, those countries could be granted transition periods. Although it could be argued that, given the domestic benefits of transparency, there is little reason for differential levels of obligations, the limited administrative capacities of many developing countries need to be recognized.

Transition periods for binding disciplines could be set at a particular period (for example, 10 years) with countries expected to implement the requirements on a best-endeavors or "to the extent possible" basis in the interim. Were additional transparency obligations to be inscribed in schedules for sectors where specific commitments had been undertaken, developing countries might also take advantage of the flexibility already provided under the GATS to make "precommitments," that is, to precommit (in additional commitments) to the introduction of certain transparency practices in certain sectors at a later date.

In the context of binding disciplines, introducing a "peace clause" could provide some flexibility. A peace clause establishes a further period subsequent to the implementation deadline during which no dispute action can be brought. It may be questionable whether this would be necessary, given that dispute settlement procedures are unlikely to be brought against failure to implement transparency provisions; but such a clause may be helpful where failure to adhere to transparency obligations might arise in the context of a broader dispute, and in any

case may contribute to members' confidence in assuming additional obligations.

As noted above, however, the relative administrative burden of increased transparency provisions and the need for special and differential treatment are lessened in the context of obligations that are already best endeavors, or where members voluntarily opt to sign onto additional transparency obligations for certain sectors. Similarly, the need for special and differential treatment would also depend on how prescriptive any transparency obligations were. For example, if obligations specified exact time periods for processing of applications or responding to comments, there might be a case for allowing developing countries additional time in recognition of their more limited resources. However, obligations that are more general in nature— "a reasonable time"—arguably already contain sufficient flexibility. Equally, obligations could avoid containing specific technological requirements (e.g., requiring Internet publication) in the interests of flexibility for developing countries. One further possibility might be to include a general provision that members shall have regard to the level of development and administrative capacity of other members in interpreting "a reasonable period" or similar provisions.

Specific technical assistance and capacity-building provisions also could be considered in the context of any further transparency disciplines. Notwithstanding their link to and importance for trade, programs to increase domestic capacity for transparency in domestic regulation may be pursued most effectively and appropriately in the context of general development cooperation programs aimed at developing domestic institutions and frameworks for good governance.

Although any increased transparency involves resources, these must be set against the benefits gained for governance, the domestic economy, and trade by increasing the participation of stakeholders in regulatory decisionmaking. Additionally, resources devoted to increased transparency are more likely to heighten the legitimacy and "necessity" of regulatory measures. The more transparent the process of regulatory decisionmaking and the greater the opportunities for input by interested parties at an early stage, the less may be the likelihood that trading partners will bring WTO disputes over the necessity of a given regulation.

> **BOX 2   Summary of Ways to Reduce the Burden**
> **of Additional Transparency Provisions**
>
> - Express any obligations in terms of general objectives, with maximum flexibility for members to implement them in line with their level of development and with existing administrative and regulatory systems.
> - To the greatest extent possible, build on existing domestic structures and practices—for example, by implementing requirements at the national level rather than via notification to the WTO.
> - Consider exceptions provisions—for example, ones related to measures of a minor nature or those related to security. Consider special provisions for emergency situations.
> - Consider carving out certain types of measures or measures at a subnational level.
>
> - Consider special and differential treatment provisions for developing countries, including transition periods, a provision requiring members to consider another member's level of development and administrative capacity when interpreting "a reasonable period" or similar transparency requirements, or the extension of a "peace clause" subsequent to the deadline for implementation.
> - Encourage developing countries to make pre-commitments on transparency in specific commitments.
> - Encourage a focus on transparency in domestic regulation in general capacity building and development cooperation programs, including by drawing attention to the benefits for trade performance.

Box 2 summarizes the ways to reduce additional transparency burdens.

Transparency at Different Stages of the Regulatory Process

Transparency is required at a number of stages throughout the regulatory process—that is, not just after the measure has been adopted or the decision made but also in the decisionmaking process itself. These stages are recognized in existing GATS obligations, which refer to the need to publish measures before they come into force (Article III.1) and the need for prompt consideration of applications in the decisionmaking process (Article VI.3), as well as to procedures for the review of administrative decisions affecting trade in services (Article VI.2). The GATS also provides some guidance on how regulations should be implemented (Article VI.1 and VI.4). Proposals for increased transparency have tended to reflect these three different stages: the process of making the regulation; application procedures pursuant to a regulation; and review or appeals procedures subsequent to decisions having been made. The three stages are considered below.

Making the Regulation   The focus of transparency in the regulatory decisionmaking process has been on the opportunity for all interested parties—including foreigners—to be consulted and to pro-

vide comment on proposed new regulations. As the analysis of regulatory measures at the national level indicates, prior consultation as a domestic procedure could be implemented for subordinate measures in line with the key principles of transparency and nondiscrimination. The question arises whether it would be feasible for regulators to be transparent and nondiscriminatory throughout the process of developing a regulation, especially at the first stage where they tend to consult selectively with a relatively narrow range of strongly affected interests. It is more conceivable for regulatory authorities to ensure transparency and nondiscrimination in the notice and comment procedure for the draft texts of prospective regulation, which would usually occur later in the process of developing a regulation.

Another question arises whether it would be feasible for regulators to conduct prior consultation for all types of measures. Exceptions for emergency measures could be considered in the case of possible GATS prior consultation requirements, along with exceptions for measures dealing with military and foreign affairs and measures of a minor or mechanical nature. It would also be important to continue in all relevant WTO disciplines related to prior notification and opportunity for comment (the TBT and SPS Agreements and the accountancy disciplines) the current practice of focusing on measures that may significantly affect trade.[7] Although some of the regional trade agreements do not specifically exclude any particular type of measures from prior consultation, such obligations take a form ("to the extent possible") that gives the parties the flexibility to exclude measures. In developing countries and in some OECD members, prior consultation does not cover all measures and is applied to specific types of measures in specific sectors. Any discipline on prior consultation realistically needs to have some limits on the scope of its application, taking account of the limitations authorities may face and the need to avoid overly burdensome procedures, especially in developing countries.[8]

Compared with the practices for prior consultation on subordinate measures, there are wider differences among country practices for prior consultation on legislative measures. Because consultation is conducted in the legislative branch through elected representatives in any legislative framework, it is difficult to envisage effective WTO disciplines in this area.

Making Applications   Article VI.3 of the GATS requires authorities to make decisions within a reasonable time period and to provide information on the status of applications, but more detailed procedural transparency requirements could be developed for the GATS (as exist in the TBT and SPS Agreements, the accountancy disciplines, and some regional trade agreements). Such requirements could include:

- Making publicly available information on which activities require a license and the criteria for obtaining a license
- Publishing the standard processing period
- Providing information to applicants regarding all the documents and information they must supply in an application and notices of the deficiencies in application
- Explaining the reasons for rejection of an application
- Giving notice of the facts or conduct warranting disciplinary action or sanctions and the nature and extent of disciplinary actions, as well as providing a mechanism by which to respond to queries.

These requirements could be included in horizontal transparency disciplines or tailored to differ-

ent sectors to reflect the different needs and capacities of regulatory authorities in different sectors. Although license procedures for trade in services are different from the conformity assessment in the TBT Agreement and from inspection or approval in the SPS Agreement, these key elements could be shared and applied to both procedures.

Other types of disciplines on administrative actions or decisions are found in the SPS and TBT Agreements and the accountancy disciplines but are not found in the GATS. They include (a) nondiscriminatory processing of submission or application for both domestic and foreign parties, (b) avoidance of unnecessary information requirements for application, (c) nondiscriminatory treatment of confidential information, (d) reasonable application fees, and (e) reasonable requirement for authenticity of application materials. Although these disciplines also facilitate trade in services by reducing burdensome administrative processes, they are related more to issues of nondiscrimination and necessity than to issues of transparency.

Appealing and Reviewing   Many of the suggested disciplines relating to the appeals stage of the regulatory process similarly relate less to transparency per se and more to other aspects of good regulatory practice, such as nondiscrimination (e.g., the ability to file complaints about inconsistent treatment of foreign and domestic suppliers, nondiscriminatory sanctions in case of disciplinary procedures), fairness (e.g., disciplinary action may not be taken on the basis of violations of rules that were not in effect at the time the relevant activity took place), and the right of appeal (including against any sanctions imposed following a disciplinary hearing). However, elements related to transparency arise in the case of regulatory enforcement procedures, where the access of foreign suppliers to information can be particularly important. For example, requirements could include informing the affected party about any regulatory enforcement procedure; giving that party the opportunity to be heard; and ensuring that party the opportunity to submit and review evidence. Furthermore, procedures for disciplinary actions, including notification of violations, responses by the affected parties, explanation of decisions, and any procedures for appeal, could be made publicly available.

Options for Enhancing Transparency

This section examines some practical options for enhancing transparency under the GATS. It considers both ways in which the GATS disciplines might encourage the development of transparent procedures at the domestic level, and ways in which GATS transparency provisions requiring notification to the WTO might be made more effective. It considers both the introduction of new obligations and ways to enhance the implementation of existing obligations.

Improving Domestic Practices on Transparency: Reference Paper on Additional Transparency Requirements   Possible new transparency disciplines could establish a list of best practices to be implemented at the national level. Such a list could take the form of an annex, applying across all sectors, or a reference paper that could be voluntarily inscribed against individual service sectors under Article XVIII additional commitments and that could be accepted in full or in part. The more

extensive the list of proposed practices to enhance transparency, the more likely that members would take a voluntary approach to inscribing such additional disciplines in their schedules, and the more likely that they might seek additional flexibility regarding sectors and disciplines included.

Box 3 sets out examples of the sort of elements that could be included in a reference paper on transparency (the list is by no means exhaustive). They are suggested as horizontal disciplines, but without prejudice to the issue of whether sector-specific disciplines could be developed for some sectors.

As noted above, consideration could also be given to creating any necessary sector-specific disciplines to enhance the general reference paper approach. Further study of the regulatory experience at the sectoral level would be needed to determine the extent to which different sectors required sector-specific disciplines to enhance a horizontal reference paper.

Consideration could also be given to developing specific disciplines for mode 4, given the special sit-

---

BOX 3   Examples of Elements for a Reference Paper on Transparency

Prior consultation
- Prior comment procedures to be open to all interested parties, including non-nationals.
- Publication of the proposed measures along with any relevant background material.
- Explanation of the rationale behind measures on request.
- Time periods for prior consultation to be determined by national authorities; must be reasonable and sufficient to enable all interested parties to have input.
- Authorities must give consideration to all comments received.
- All comments received and responses to the comments will be made public.

Licensing and authorization
- Specify in writing the activities subject to licensing or authorization requirements and publish the criteria and conditions for such requirements.
- Inform applicants about all of the documents and information they must supply in an application.

- Provide notice of any deficiencies in an application.
- Publish the standard timeframe for the licensing and authorization process.
- Publish the names of competent authorities and contact points for complaints.
- Provide, upon request, the reasons for rejection of an authorization or application.
- Provide notice of the facts or conduct warranting disciplinary action or sanctions and the nature and extent of disciplinary actions, and provide a mechanism to respond to queries.
- In case of disciplinary action, inform the affected party about the procedure and provide the opportunity to be heard and to submit and review evidence.
- Make publicly available the notification of the violation, along with the responses by the affected party and the explanation of the decision.

uation of measures affecting trade in mode 4; that is, that they are closely linked to broader immigration policies and measures (as recognized by the Annex on Movement of Natural Persons). Arguably, however, most of the areas of interest to mode 4—such as provision of information on substantive requirements and criteria and procedures for applications; prior consultation on measures affecting mode 4 entry; timely responses for applications, or notification in the event of any delay; provision of statement of reasons for denial of application and availability of review/appeals procedures—could already be covered by a general reference paper on transparency. Given that general immigration legislation does not fall under the GATS (see note 5), the application scope of any transparency reference paper would have to be identified carefully. Nonetheless, it is worth noting that in some OECD countries public notice and comment procedures are applied to measures relevant to entry, stay, and work authorization of natural persons. For example, U.S. immigration rules and regulations are subject to the Administrative Procedures Act (5 U.S.C. 553), and the Japanese Ministry of Justice adopts public notice and comment procedures for its measures on immigration control.

Improving Transparency of Scheduled Commitments: Standard Forms for WTO Notifications, Economic Needs Tests, and Measures on Mode 4

The level of notifications under the GATS has been disappointing in general. In particular, there have been relatively few notifications under Article III.3 (annual notification to the Council for Trade in Services by a member of the introduction of any new, or changes to existing, laws, regulations or administrative guidelines that significantly affect trade in services covered by its specific commitments). Some developing countries also have pointed to the lack of notifications under Article VII.4 (notification of mutual recognition agreements, including those under negotiation, to provide adequate opportunity for other members to indicate their interest in participating in negotiations). In the case of Article III.3 it has been suggested that greater precision regarding the meaning of "significantly affect trade in services" could help generate a greater number of notifications. Similar calls for clarity have been made regarding the scope

of the general requirement that members publish "all relevant measures of general application pertaining to or affecting the operation of the Agreement" under Article III.1.

Furthermore, notifications received do not always provide the required information in an easy-to-use format. Standard form notifications (along the lines of the SPS and TBT Agreements) could be developed to ensure greater consistency of information provided, as well as to allow for comparability among members and to facilitate sharing of best practices. Standard form notifications do not add to existing obligations; rather, they facilitate their implementation and could be considered (or improved) for some (but not necessarily all) GATS notification requirements—for example, for Article III.3 and, in view of its importance for mode 4 trade, Article VII.4.

The standard form for Article III.3 notifications[9] could also include the name of the legislation/regulation or administrative guideline, a description of the purpose of the measure, and a contact point for further inquiries. Additionally, members could be asked to provide a brief assessment of the trade effects of the measure. A standard form for Article VII.4(b) could include the type of agreement, the parties to the negotiation, any industry advisory bodies involved or consulted, sectoral coverage, and a contact person for further information or to express interest in participating in the negotiations.

OECD work also has proposed the development of a standard form notification to provide additional useful information on the operation of economic needs tests (ENTs) (OECD 2001). A standard form notification for ENTs could include criteria,[10] duration of the measure, detail to relevant administrative procedures (including provision for explanation of decisions, review of applications), and review of the need to maintain the ENT in question. It could also include information on costs and approximate processing time (with appropriate caveats as to the possibility of change). A further useful inclusion might be the economic or social policy objective sought by the ENT. It should be noted, however, that standard form notifications under the TBT and SPS Agreements include only a brief and general description of regulatory objectives (e.g., health, safety, environment, and so forth). Alternatively, the approach in the accountancy disciplines (whereby, upon request, a member is required to inform another member of the rationale behind domestic regulatory measures in relation to legitimate objectives) could be considered. Indeed, some of the disciplines proposed in box 3 also could help make ENTs more transparent, especially because ENTs are often a feature of licensing regimes. For example, clarifying the rationale behind the ENT and providing reasons for the denial of an application or authorization could give potential service suppliers a better sense of the general regulatory environment of the sector in which the ENT applied and could flesh out the operation of the ENT in their specific instance. Further study could explore the linkages between achieving greater transparency for ENTs and the types of disciplines under consideration in the WTO Working Party on Domestic Regulation.

A system of standard form notifications also could be considered for mode 4 to cover the following elements for each type of entry program related to GATS mode 4 entry: documentation required, method of lodgment, processing time and application fees (if any), length and validity of stay, sectors where any special conditions apply, possibility of and conditions for extensions (including availability of multiple-entry visas), rules regarding accompanying dependents, review and appeal procedures (if any), and details of relevant contact points for further information. This notification requirement could also take the form of a requirement to contribute to a Web site dedicated to providing information on the conditions applying to temporary entry of service providers. Members would be responsible for the accuracy of their information and for ensuring that it is updated regularly.

Improving Inquiry Points   GATS inquiry points (mandated under Article III.4) are an avenue for providing to other members specific requested information on all measures of general application or international agreements pertaining to or affecting the operation of the agreement (per Article III.1) and all matters subject to notification under Article III.3 (laws, regulations, or administrative guidelines that significantly affect trade in services covered by a member's specific commitments). Additionally, Article IV.2 requires establishing contact points to facilitate the access of developing country service suppliers to information concern-

ing commercial and technical aspects of the supply of services; registration, recognition, and the obtaining of professional qualifications; and the availability of services technology in members' respective markets.

The WTO currently makes available on the WTO Web site the postal addresses and telephone and fax numbers of all GATS inquiry points that have been notified. Inquiry points appear to be little used, however, and often feature out-of-date information. Although such contact points are designed to serve as "one-stop shops" for information, in fact the range and diversity of services sectors make it difficult for them to fulfill that role. The contact point in the trade ministry (which normally has responsibility for WTO matters) is normally ill prepared to field questions on the transport or telecommunications sectors. One option may be for members to nominate sectoral contact points—that is, nominated persons in each of the relevant agencies at the domestic level who can provide information on particular service sectors. A comprehensive list of these inquiry points could be compiled by the WTO. Although any proposals to expand inquiry points would have to consider the potential costs for members, some countries currently provide such sector-specific inquiry points as part of regional arrangements (Asia Pacific Economic Cooperation [APEC] Individual Action Plans require individual inquiry points for each service sector). Alternatively, trade ministries with responsibility for GATS inquiry points could establish their own network of contacts in other relevant ministries at the national level to facilitate timely responses to sector-specific inquiries.

Additionally, a special inquiry point for mode 4 could be considered. Given the importance of immigration policy to mode 4, and the fact that for purposes of implementation the relevant ministry is often the immigration authorities (in combination with the labor market authorities), creating dedicated contact points within the trade or immigration ministries (or as a joint operation) could be considered. These contact points might also produce an annual report outlining any information received about problems relating to mode 4, with a view to the future refinement of procedures. Alternatively, members could simply be asked to create a one-stop information point (e.g., a Web site or government office) for information on mode 4 entry. Contact details for this point could be given to the WTO and perhaps listed on the WTO Web site, with links to members' electronic schedules.

The effectiveness of even the single inquiry point could be increased if members maintained a consolidated code of regulations. These typically cover all government regulations (beyond those affecting trade in services as required by the GATS) and are easily accessible to the general public—for example, via a Web site or government gazette. Consolidated codes at the national level can be useful in providing other WTO members and businesses with an accurate reading of measures in place at the market. Although perhaps less user friendly than an inquiry point, the information conveyed can be more comprehensive. A consolidated list of regulations also would allow readers to select for themselves the measures that may have an impact on trade rather than having that decision made by the agency responding to the query. Such consolidated codes may be resource intensive to construct, but information and communications technology is reducing the cost of preparing and maintaining such codes.

Improving the Breadth of Information Provided: Regulatory Transparency and the Trade Policy Review Mechanism In keeping with the function of the Trade Policy Review Mechanism (TPRM) as a way of exploring the general context for, and formulation of, members' trade policies without exploring their implementation of particular WTO commitments (the TPRM is not linked to the Dispute Settlement System), trade policy reviews could include a section on regulatory transparency. Although some might argue that domestic regulatory practices, strictly speaking, are not trade policies, such practices clearly affect trade, and their inclusion would give trading partners a better understanding of the context in which trade policy is made—one of the purposes of the TPRM. Furthermore, transparency underpins all WTO agreements and, indeed, the TPRM itself. Including a section on transparency in domestic regulation in the trade policy review report prepared by the WTO secretariat could disseminate information about best practices among WTO members, and the format of trade policy reviews would offer other members the

opportunity to ask questions about the operation of any domestic transparency mechanisms.

Concluding Remarks

This chapter has sought to identify good regulatory practices and options for enhancing transparency under the GATS. It began by outlining existing transparency requirements under WTO agreements for legislative measures, subordinate measures, and administrative decisions. The GATT and the GATS require members to publish legislative and subordinate measures before those measures are enforced, and the GATS requires annual notification of new or changed measures. WTO agreements also include three types of prior consultation: (a) via notification to the WTO (per the SPS and TBT Agreements); (b) via information exchange, upon request, among members; and (c) as a domestic procedure (per the Disciplines for the Accountancy Sector, although this obligation is hortatory in nature and the disciplines themselves have yet to enter into force). For administrative decisions, WTO agreements require uniform, impartial, and reasonable administration, as well as a review mechanism and an opportunity to appeal. Some agreements (e.g., the GATS, TBT/SPS Agreements, and the Disciplines for the Accountancy Sector) also include greater disciplines. WTO members usually are required to take such reasonable measures as may be available to them to ensure compliance with WTO disciplines by local governments and nongovernmental entities.

The chapter next turned its attention to disciplines on transparency in selected regional trade agreements. All the agreements studied require publication of legislative and subordinate measures at the time of entry into force. They also require uniform, impartial, and reasonable administration of administrative decisions, and an opportunity for review and appeal. Many agreements also include more detailed disciplines, including those for specific sectors (e.g., telecommunications). Most of the agreements studied also include prior notification between governments or prior consultation with interested parties as a domestic procedure; however, this is generally only required "to the (maximum) extent possible" or "when so established by laws." Although transparency disciplines in regional agreements among developing economies tend to be weaker than those in agreements among industrial countries, they sometimes exceed WTO requirements.

The chapter also examined a range of practices at the national level in both OECD and non-OECD countries. Overall there seems to be a trend toward prior consultation for subordinate measures, with practices taking different forms at different stages of preparation. Certain types of measures generally are excluded from prior consultation: those relating to urgent problems of safety, health, and environment or military and foreign affairs and national security; and those that merely meet an obligation under an international agreement or are of a minor nature. In most cases, regulatory authorities must explain any exceptions. Measures of local governments and other self-governing subentities also are often excluded from prior consultation. Practices vary more widely for legislative measures, reflecting different political systems or institutional structures. Whatever the political system, however, when a draft measure is before the legislative branch, consultation takes place only through elected representatives. Although public hearings are held in some cases, direct participation by foreign interested parties is generally limited.

Some OECD members have horizontal administrative procedures legislation that imposes disciplines on administrative decisions, but in other countries those disciplines are prescribed in specific statutes or guidelines. Developing countries are increasingly introducing public notice and comment procedures, but, given the countries' limited resources, the procedures tend to be focused on priority issues in specific sectors (e.g., universal service obligations and spectrum management in telecommunications) rather than horizontal.

The final section of the chapter considered a range of options for enhancing transparency under the GATS, including via the WTO or domestic procedures. The section drew attention to a continuum of possibilities, from binding disciplines covering all sectors, to best-endeavor commitments adopted in full or in part for some sectors only. Among the arguments raised in support of a horizontal approach are the facts that, whereas services sectors may be diverse, requirements for transparency are not and that transparency should be encouraged across all sectors, not just high-profile

sectors. Horizontal disciplines also can prevent sectoral special interests from blocking progress and can allow for economy of negotiating effort and clarity of obligations. Arguments for a sectoral approach include the facts that not all service sectors are traded to the same extent and that priorities for disciplines could differ. Moreover, developing countries with limited administrative capacity may wish to focus on priority sectors and measures, and may be more willing to accept increased transparency disciplines on a sectoral basis. Horizontal and sectoral approaches need not be mutually exclusive, however; a basic set of horizontal rules could be supplemented by sector- or mode-specific rules, as appropriate.

The administrative burden could be lessened, depending on the form of any further transparency disciplines. The disciplines could, for example, (a) be formulated as general objectives, allowing maximum flexibility for implementation in line with level of development and existing administrative and regulatory systems; (b) build to the greatest extent possible on existing domestic structures and practices; or (c) include appropriate exceptions and carve out subnational-level measures. Special and differential treatment for developing countries might also be considered—for example, through longer transition periods, a requirement that members consider another member's level of development and administrative capacity when interpreting "a reasonable period," or a "peace clause" subsequent to the implementation deadline.

Possible new transparency disciplines could establish a list of best practices to be implemented at the national level, taking the form of an annex, applying across all sectors, or a reference paper that could be inscribed voluntarily against individual sectors, in full or in part. Elements for inclusion in a horizontal reference paper are suggested in this chapter, without prejudice to the development of sector-specific disciplines. Options for improving the transparency of scheduled commitments were also considered, including the development of standard forms for notifications under GATS Articles III and VII.4, economic needs tests, and for mode 4; improvements to GATS inquiry points (either by the creation of sectoral inquiry points or in the context of a central code of regulations); and specific focus on transparency of domestic regulatory regimes in WTO trade policy reviews.

Notes

1. It could be noted that, in addition to specific disciplines on transparency, the structure of trade agreements can effect the overall level of transparency achieved. For example, in the case of services it can be argued that the "negative listing" approach to the scheduling of sector-specific commitments (found in the North American Free Trade Agreement and the Australia-New Zealand Closer Economic Relations Services Protocol) delivers more in terms of clarity and transparency than does a "positive listing" approach.

2. For countries that have been reviewed by the OECD, these studies of regulatory practices at the national level often draw on the country reviews conducted under the OECD Regulatory Reform Project. Reports are available at for the Czech Republic, Denmark, Greece, Hungary, Ireland, Italy, Japan, the Republic of Korea, Mexico, the Netherlands, Spain, and the United States, and reports on Poland and the United Kingdom are forthcoming. See www.oecd.org/regulatoryreform for additional information.

3. As noted previously, distinctions between subordinate and legislative measures may vary among WTO members in view of their differing legal and constitutional systems.

4. It may also be interesting to consider discrimination between stakeholders at the national level, such as between producer and consumer groups.

5. Note that this process is not limited to parliamentary systems. In Mexico both branches can propose draft legislative measures and the executive branch can conduct prior consultation before the measures are submitted to the legislative branch. Enactment of legislative measures also may be initiated by the legislative branch itself.

6. See Article 2.10 of the Technical Barriers to Trade Agreement and Annex B, Article 6, of the Sanitary and Phytosanitary Agreement for emergency cases.

7. Although both the TBT and SPS Agreements refer to regulations, which *may* have a significant effect on trade of other members, the accountancy disciplines refer to "measures, which significantly affect trade in accountancy services."

8. For a more detailed discussion of possible limits on the scope of potential disciplines on prior consultation, see OECD (2000).

9. A standard form is already in use for GATS notifications and it covers the following elements: member notifying; article under which the notification is made; date of entry into force and duration; agency responsible for enforcement of the measure; description of the measure; members specifically affected if applicable; and place from which texts are available.

10. Although the scheduling guidelines (MTN.GNS/W/164/Add.1) state that members should indicate the main criteria on which the ENT is based, few members have done so.

References

OECD (Organisation for Economic Co-operation and Development). 2000. Trade in Services: Transparency in Domestic Regulation: Prior Consultation. TD/TC/WP(2000)31/FINAL. Paris.

———. 2001. "The Scheduling of Economic Needs Tests in the GATS: Follow up Work," TD/TC/WP(2001)5/FINAL. Paris.

Stiglitz, Joseph E. 1999. "On Liberty, the Right to Know, and Public Discourse: The Role of Transparency in Public Life." Oxford Amnesty Lecture, January 27, Oxford, U.K.

3

ADDRESSING REGULATORY DIVERGENCE THROUGH INTERNATIONAL STANDARDS: FINANCIAL SERVICES

Joel P. Trachtman

Executive Summary

The member states of the World Trade Organization (WTO) must determine what types of actions, if any, to take pursuant to the Article VI.4 work program in order to discipline national regulation of financial services. One alternative is to defer to other organizational structures, including plurilateral or multilateral functional organizations such as the Basel Committee, the International Association of Insurance Supervisors (IAIS), the International Organization of Securities Commissions (IOSCO), or the Organisation for Economic Co-operation and Development (OECD); international financial organizations such as the International Monetary Fund; or regional organizations such as the European Community (EC) or the North American Free Trade Agreement. Organizations such as the Basel Committee, IAIS, and IOSCO (standard-setting bodies, or SSBs) articulate "soft" law; that is, law that is not binding in formal legal terms but that may nonetheless have substantial binding force.

A slightly different alternative to simply deferring to these organizations is to cooperate with and coordinate through them. Such a strategy could be analogous to the WTO approach to cooperation with the Codex Alimentarius and other organizations through the Sanitary and Phytosanitary Agreement of the General Agreement on Trade in Services. This type of cooperation would result in the hardening into semi-soft law of standards promulgated by organizations like the Basel Committee, IOSCO, and IAIS.

States must also determine whether to act vertically in specific sectors or horizontally across sectors. It appears that the first initiatives will be vertical until sufficient experience is gained to consider horizontal proposals. Of course, broader standards, such as "necessity," could be established on a horizontal basis, but they would adapt themselves to particular sectors and circumstances through dispute settlement. Furthermore, states must determine what types of specific rules, or what types of more general judicially applicable standards, to develop to enhance liberalization while adequately protecting regulatory values. Specific rules would include, for example, specific harmonized regulation, or specific

Many thanks to Dale Honeck, Gabrielle Marceau, Aaditya Mattoo, Julia Nielson, Joseph Norton, Pierre Sauvé, Marc Steinberg, and other participants in the OECD–World Bank Services Experts Meeting held in Paris, March 4–5, 2002, for their advice in connection with this chapter.

requirements of recognition. Judicially applicable standards range from national treatment to necessity to a balancing test.

Financial regulation is always an intervention—an interference—in the free market. Of course, such intervention may support the free market or may be designed to achieve other social goals. In domestic societies a central government decides about the scope of interference in the free market; this contrasts with the circumstance in international society, whereby a variety of functional organizations have responsibility for varying phases of the same question. Even in federal and quasi-federal systems like those of the United States and EC, a central government decides on the relationship between free trade in financial services and regulation of financial services. In the EC this decision is reflected in single-market directives such as the Second Banking Directive. In the multilateral system, institutions have not yet arisen that can make and enforce integrated binding law in this field. Although WTO law is somewhat more binding than many other types of international law, and is intended to be binding whereas SSB standards are not, WTO law has not integrated a full range of social policies.

Constructing the Article VI.4 Work Program for Financial Services

The member states of the World Trade Organization (WTO) must determine what types of actions to take pursuant to the Article VI.4 work program in order to discipline national regulation of financial services.[1] There are several parameters that must be evaluated in order to determine the WTO's action.

The first parameter is whether WTO action to discipline national regulation is required. Under current circumstances, the WTO should begin with a *laissez-regler* attitude, as expressed in the "prudential carve-out." However, as in other areas of regulatory standards, international discipline must be considered to address problems of hidden discrimination and of disproportionate regulation. Where discipline is needed, the WTO must compare its institutional capabilities with the alternatives.

One alternative is simple autonomous action by states, in the "market" of ad hoc diplomacy. Where states are not motivated by protectionism and

where they bear the consequences of their own inefficient regulation, it may be best to avoid multilateral legally binding action.

Another alternative is to defer to other organizational structures, including plurilateral or multilateral functional organizations such as the Basel Committee, the International Association of Insurance Supervisors (IAIS), the International Organization of Securities Commissions (IOSCO), or the Organisation for Economic Co-operation and Development (OECD); international financial organizations such as the International Monetary Fund (IMF); or regional organizations such as the European Community (EC) or the North American Free Trade Agreement (NAFTA). Organizations such as the Basel Committee, IAIS, and IOSCO articulate "soft" law—that is, law that is not formally binding but that may nonetheless have substantial binding force.

A slightly different alternative is to cooperate with and coordinate through these organizations, rather than simply deferring to them. Such a strategy could be analogous to the WTO approach to cooperation with the Codex Alimentarius and other organizations through the Sanitary and Phytosanitary (SPS) Agreement. This type of cooperation would result in the hardening of standards promulgated by organizations like the Basel Committee, IAIS, and IOSCO into semi-soft law.

A second parameter to evaluate is whether to act vertically in specific sectors or horizontally across sectors.[2] It appears that the first initiatives will be vertical until sufficient experience is gained to consider horizontal proposals. Of course, broader standards, such as "necessity," could be established on a horizontal basis but they would adapt themselves to particular sectors and circumstances through dispute settlement.[3]

Another parameter to evaluate is what types of specific rules, or what types of more general judicially applicable standards, should be developed to enhance liberalization while adequately protecting regulatory values (see Nicolaidis and Trachtman 2000). Specific rules would include, for example, specific harmonized regulation, or specific requirements of recognition. Judicially applicable standards range from national treatment to necessity to a balancing test.

It is obvious that action will not exclusively take one or the other of the above forms. Rather, it is to be expected that a work program will use specific tools, depending on specific circumstances, and that a combination of the types of devices described above will likely be selected in any particular circumstance. Although we must begin with vertical particularity, experience and negotiation will show the efficiency of horizontal disciplines of particular types. General judicially applicable standards are more conducive to horizontal application than are specific rules of recognition or harmonization.

At a deeper level, the choices made will reflect a degree of compromise of domestic regulatory values. It is neither unnatural nor inappropriate to compromise regulatory values, or perhaps domestic autonomy in implementing regulatory values, under some circumstances to achieve trade liberalization goals. The wisdom of doing so depends on a cost-benefit analysis of regulatory autonomy versus liberalization. Each circumstance will present a different cost-benefit profile, and so no overarching policy advice can be developed. However, it is important to construct institutions that can help set out the options, evaluate their costs and benefits, and enable states to negotiate or otherwise to work out suitable outcomes.[4]

Liberalization will require some degree of domestic deregulation, but it is essential to recall that international trade does not necessarily require deregulation. Rather, it will be useful under some circumstances to replace domestic regulation with international regulation in the form of harmonized standards and perhaps centralized coordination.

Thus coexisting and competing with the trade perspective on international movement of services, at least in the area of financial services, is a regulatory perspective. The regulatory perspective is concerned about the possibility of regulatory arbitrage, or simply of regulatory failure, because of the limitations of national regulation based on national jurisdiction. Firms such as BCCI, Daiwa, Barings, and now Enron have come to symbolize this type of failure. The regulatory perspective is concerned more with the goals of regulation than with the goals of free trade and competition in financial services, although free trade and competition may have important positive or negative effects on the ability to achieve regulatory goals. Geographic deregulation to provide market access may necessitate prudential re-regulation to ensure protection

of social values, such as accuracy in allocation of capital, mobilization of capital, and financial stability.[5] On the other hand, it must be understood that competition and broader markets can assist the regulator in achieving its goals in part by creating the prerequisites for profitability and, consequently, for sound financial services providers and stable markets.

Thus we recognize that there may be tensions between free trade goals on one hand and regulatory goals on the other hand. This is natural: all regulatory interventions are derogations from a hypothetical "free" market.[6] This tension exists regardless of the institutional form that it takes. In a rather imprecise way, we may understand the WTO as the institutional embodiment of the "free" market, whereas international financial regulatory organizations such as the Basel Committee, IAIS, and IOSCO are the avatars, or at least the representatives, of regulation. (I refer to these three organizations collectively as "standard-setting bodies" or "SSBs.")[7] This chapter will examine the tension between free trade and regulation in the context of the relationship, both actual and potential, between the WTO and the SSBs.

Although there is a tension between free trade goals and regulatory goals, both sets of goals are responsive to societal needs and may be pursued together in a synergetic relationship. Thus the EC provides an example of a system of separate jurisdictions that have permitted free trade in banking, securities, and insurance services on the basis of mutual recognition, predicated on a particular level of "essential" harmonization (see Trachtman 1995).

Regulatory Barriers to Trade in Services

As the types of regulatory barriers that impede trade in services generally, and financial services in particular, have already been catalogued, it will serve here simply to refer to them (see Sauvé and Steinfatt 2001):

- Licensing requirements
- Local ownership requirements
- Discriminatory regulation
- Inefficient regulation
- Quantitative/market access restrictions: stock exchange seats and the like.

Not all of these are subject to Article VI.4. Some must be addressed and scheduled under Articles XVI and XVII (see WTO Working Party on Domestic Regulation 2001).

Of course, most states reviewed their schedules of concessions to be sure that they did not require them to modify their regulatory structures: the General Agreement on Trade in Services (GATS) served more as an instrument of standstill than as an instrument of active liberalization, at least in connection with regulatory barriers to trade. Moreover, in the financial services field a prudential carve-out, contained in paragraph 2(a) of the Annex on Financial Services provides that:

> Notwithstanding any other provisions of [the GATS], a Member shall not be prevented from taking measures for prudential reasons, including for the protection of investors, depositors, policy holders or persons to whom a fiduciary duty is owed by a financial service supplier, or to ensure the integrity and stability of the financial system. Where such measures do not conform with the provisions of [the GATS], they shall not be used as a means of avoiding the Member's commitments or obligations under the Agreement.

Once this carve-out was negotiated, it was no longer thought necessary for financial services regulators to continue to participate in Uruguay Round negotiations. However, in theory this carve-out is overly broad; it leaves undisciplined certain prudential measures that may perpetuate regulatory barriers—in cases where the deadweight losses resulting from the barriers exceed the benefits of regulatory autonomy. Of course, its application depends on how the term "prudential" is defined, and how it is used.

The prudential carve-out may be interpreted to limit the scope of action under Article VI.4 in the field of financial services insofar as most action under Article VI.4 would address prudential measures. The scope of this prudential carve-out is unclear,[8] especially as Annex paragraph 2(a) continues to state, "Where such measures do not conform with the provisions of [the GATS], they shall not be used as a means of avoiding the Member's commitments or obligations under the Agree-

ment." This language seems to deny the exception where there is an *intent* to evade other GATS commitments. The regulatory exceptions included in the Telecommunications Annex do not include such a caveat (see Annex paragraph 5[e]).

In addition, one could expect that a measure might be attacked on the basis that it is not properly or sufficiently "for prudential reasons." It is difficult to predict how a WTO panel or the Appellate Body would approach this requirement. However, one possibility is that it might be treated the same as Article XX(g) of the GATT, which provides an exception from other GATT disciplines for measures "relating to the conservation of exhaustible natural resources." Earlier GATT dispute resolution jurisprudence required that measures sought to be justified under this provision be "primarily aimed" at such conservation. In *United States-Shrimp*, the Appellate Body appears to have abandoned the "primarily aimed at" test and focused instead on the means–ends relationship[9] between the measure and the goal pursued: "We must examine the relationship between the general structure and design of the measure here at stake, Section 609, and the policy goal it purports to serve, that is, the conservation of sea turtles."[10] By analogy, in order for a measure to benefit from the prudential carve-out of paragraph 2(a) of the GATS Annex on Financial Services, it would not need to be "primarily aimed" at prudential regulation, but would be required to be "reasonably related" to the regulatory goal. This is just one of several possible ways that a WTO panel might approach the prudential carve-out.

The WTO and the SSBs

At the 1996 Singapore Ministerial Meeting, the WTO stated that "[w]e encourage the successful completion of international standards in the accountancy sector by IFAC, IASC and IOSCO."[11] This signals the WTO's deference, and in effect delegation (at least in part and in political terms as opposed to legal terms), to these organizations. On the other hand, in 1998 the WTO adopted the Accountancy Disciplines. So the WTO has, to varying degrees and with varying degrees of formality, "delegated" to specific functional organizations the task of establishing standards to facilitate the free movement of accountancy services. This particular delegation is not inconsistent with prior practice in other particular areas, such as food safety standards (Codex Alimentarius Commission) and general product standards (International Organization for Standardization) (see Sykes 1995, pp. 58–60). We can begin to see some evidence of a common institutional solution to the "trade and . . . problem" using informal "delegation" to specialized functional international organizations. The further question, however, is how will the WTO ensure that these organizations reflect appropriately the trade perspectives that concern the WTO? This is an agency problem: to the extent that these functional organizations are acting as agents of the WTO, how can the WTO ensure that they are faithful and diligent agents whose incentives are congruent with those of the WTO? The WTO, or more correctly its member states, must review the structures and goals of these organizations before determining the scope of the delegation. Perhaps the best way to think of these problems is to recognize that the member states are the ultimate principals: these are multiple principal–multiple agent problems.

The GATS Process

This section relies considerably on, and provides an opportunity to particularize, the more general description of the GATS disciplines on domestic regulation contained in the author's "Lessons for the GATS" (Chapter 5 in this volume). Except for the prudential carve-out, paragraph 10 of the Understanding on Commitments in Financial Services, and certain less important differences, the treatment of nondiscriminatory regulation of financial services conforms with the general structure of Article VI.

Article VI.4 and the Accountancy Disciplines

Article VI.4, which appears to be applicable regardless of the member's commitments (although I understand this is the subject of debate), is forward looking, calling on the WTO's Council for Trade in Services to develop any necessary disciplines "with a view to ensuring that measures relating to qualification requirements and procedures, technical stan-

dards and licensing requirements do not constitute unnecessary barriers to trade in services. . . ." Such disciplines would ensure, among other things, that qualification requirements are "not more burdensome than necessary to ensure the quality of the service. . . ." This, of course, is not a proportionality requirement per se, but rather an agreement to develop disciplines based on a proportionality standard. Given the indefiniteness of the proportionality standard, it is difficult to see this provision as strongly binding in a legal sense.

The Uruguay Round Decision on Professional Services called for the work program under Article VI.4 dealing with professional services to be put into effect immediately, and called for the establishment of a Working Party on Professional Services (now the Working Party on Domestic Regulation) to develop "the disciplines necessary to ensure that measures relating to qualification requirements and procedures, technical standards and licensing requirements in the field of professional services do not constitute unnecessary barriers to trade." The Decision on Professional Services also established work in the accountancy sector of professional services as a priority, calling among other things for establishment of disciplines referred to in Article VI.4 and for the use of international standards. It further called on the Working Party on Professional Services to "encourage the cooperation with the relevant international organizations as defined under paragraph 5(b) of Article VI, so as to give full effect to paragraph 5 of Article VII."[12]

Limited Incentives for Article VI.4 Positive Integration Resulting from Weak Negative Integration under Article VI.5

As described in Chapter 5, "Lessons for the GATS," Article VI.5 provides little beyond a standstill to discipline nondiscriminatory regulation.[13] Thus one would not expect substantial judicially applied disciplines on disproportionate domestic regulation. Of course, in the area of financial services this is accentuated by the prudential carve-out. In some other contexts, such as the United States under the Commerce Clause, and the EC, judicial scrutiny of disproportionate measures has served as an incentive for more specific legislative action (see, e.g., Weiler 1991).

The Understanding on Financial Services

The GATS Understanding on Financial Services forms a template that some states have used for their financial services commitments. By its terms, the Understanding, where accepted in a member's schedule, only replaces Part III of the GATS, which includes only the national treatment and market access provisions (and not the domestic regulation provisions). Article 10 of the Understanding, regarding "nondiscriminatory measures," is hortatory, calling on each member to "endeavour" to remove or to limit significant adverse effects on financial service suppliers of nondiscriminatory regulatory measures. As such, it seems to add little to the provisions of the GATS itself and the Annex on Financial Services, recognizing that the prudential carve-out of paragraph 2(a) of the Annex would seem not to be overridden by this hortatory language.

Article VI, Article XIV, and the Line of Equilibrium

Thus there are three possible sources of a rule of necessity or proportionality that might be applied to a domestic regulation under the GATS. First, and least likely, is the "reasonableness" requirement, applicable to scheduled sectors, under Article VI.1 of the GATS. Second, is the weak discipline of Article VI.5 itself, but weakened further by the prudential carve-out. Finally, in the event of a finding of violation, a measure might be exempted under Article XIV. In the *Shrimp* case, the Appellate Body opined that determining whether a national measure complied with the textually similar *chapeau* of Article XX of the GATT required it to search for a "line of equilibrium" between trade values and other values (WTO Appellate Body Report 1998, para. 17).

The SSB "Soft Law" Process

During the past few decades we have observed the rise of several forums used by domestic regulators to coordinate their activities. These forums are characterized by the "soft" nature of the norms they produce and the uncertain domestic authority of the domestic regulators to make agreements. These forums have a number of functions, not least of which is to promote information exchange among regulators. This chapter addresses the Basel Committee on Banking Supervision, the IAIS, and the IOSCO. These organizations have much in common with the Codex Alimentarius Commission, the International Standards Organization, and other "soft" or "semi-soft"[14] norm generators in the goods sector.

This section will describe the standard-setting bodies, with particular attention to the kinds of norms they produce and the process by which they prepare these norms. It will also examine the extent to which these norms call for, substitute for, or are themselves barriers to trade. This description will prepare us to speculate regarding the types of relationships that the SSBs may have with the WTO.

As we begin, however, it is worth noting that at least the Basel Committee would not qualify as a "relevant international organization" under footnote 3 to Article VI.5(b) of the GATS as its membership does not appear to be open to all members of the WTO. Therefore its standards would not be taken into account in determining whether a member was in conformity with Article VI.5(a). IAIS and IOSCO may be more likely to qualify. Thus there may be a need to develop a multilateral bank regulatory organization to fulfill this role under Article VI.5(b). Of course, the prudential carve-out would obviate this need wherever it applies. Furthermore, recognition arrangements under Article VII would remain available.

The Basel Committee

The Basel Committee is the leading, and the exemplary, SSB in financial services. It has been developed principally to address the problem of adverse externalities resulting from contagion.

History, Membership, and Purpose   The Basel Committee was established by the central bank Governors of the Group of Ten countries at the end of 1974, in response to two large international bank failures. The committee's members are the central banks or other bank supervisory authorities of Belgium, Canada, France, Germany, Italy, Japan, Luxembourg, the Netherlands, Spain, Sweden, Switzerland, the United Kingdom, and the United States.

On its Web site (http://www.bis.org/bcbs/about bcbs.htm) the Basel Committee describes its formal role as follows:

> The Committee does not possess any formal supranational supervisory authority, and its conclusions do not, and were never intended to, have legal force. Rather, it formulates broad supervisory standards and guidelines and recommends statements of best practice in the expectation that individual authorities will take steps to implement them through detailed arrangements—statutory or otherwise—which are best suited to their own national systems. In this way, the Committee encourages convergence towards common approaches and common standards without attempting detailed harmonisation of member countries' supervisory techniques.

The committee reports to the central bank Governors of the Group of Ten countries and seeks the governors' endorsement for its major initiatives. In addition, however, because the committee contains representatives from institutions that are not central banks, the decisions it makes carry the commitment of many national authorities outside the central banking fraternity. These decisions cover a very wide range of financial issues. One important objective of the committee's work has been to close gaps in international supervisory coverage in pursuit of two basic principles: that no foreign banking establishment should escape supervision, and that supervision should be adequate. To achieve these objectives, the committee has issued a number of documents since 1975.[15]

Standards Promulgated by the Basel Committee The Basel Committee has taken a leading role in developing capital adequacy standards for financial institutions (the "Basel Accord"),[16] in organizing an understanding of the allocation of supervisory jurisdiction and responsibility with respect to international banking organizations (the "Basel Concordat"),[17] in developing minimum standards for regulation of international banking organizations (the "Basel Minimum Standards"),[18] and in developing core principles for bank supervision (the "Basel Core Principles").[19]

Decisionmaking in the Basel Committee We might describe the Basel Committee as a "network" that lacks its own formal legal authority, but which has the ability to coordinate and engage the formal legal authority of its members (and of other states as well).[20] Indeed, the Basel Committee has no formal constitution or by-laws and no staff of its own. It makes decisions by consensus (see Zaring [1998] *citing* Lichtenstein [1991]). When decisions are made by consensus, there is less reason to be concerned about compliance. There is also the possibility that one or a few states can delay agreement.

IOSCO

IOSCO is the leading SSB in the field of securities regulation. Securities regulation includes a number of types of regulation, principally regulation of securities offerings (transaction regulation) and of broker-dealers or investment banks (institutional regulation).

History, Membership, and Purpose IOSCO, presently based in Madrid, is the leading multilateral organization that addresses securities regulation (see Sommer 1996, p. 31; and Norton 1995). Like the Basel Committee, its members are not states per se but regulators charged with the relevant subject matter. IOSCO has broader membership than the Basel Committee, including a large number of developing countries. It has no charter or constitutive treaty but does have constitutive by-laws.

Like the Basel Committee, IOSCO differs from the GATS because of the specificity of its focus and by virtue of its emphasis on regulation rather than trade as a motivation. Its institutional character is similar to the Basel Committee with respect to bank regulation (see Norton 1995): it does not legislate (as the GATS may do under Article VI.4) in a legally binding sense but issues consensual recommendations that its members are bound, in an ethical or political sense, to implement. IOSCO functions to assemble comparative information regarding national securities regulation and to provide a forum for cooperation and coordination among securities regulators, culminating in annual meetings. The comparative information that it assembles can be used as a basis for efforts at harmonization, mutual recognition, or unilateral law reform.

IOSCO states its objectives as follows:

To cooperate together to promote high standards of regulation in order to maintain just, efficient and sound markets; to exchange information on their respective experiences in order to promote the development of domestic markets; to unite their efforts to establish standards and an effective surveillance of international securities transactions; to provide mutual assistance to promote the integrity of the markets by a rigorous application of the standards and by effective enforcement against offenses.[21]

Standards Promulgated by IOSCO   The 1998 Objectives and Principles of Securities Regulation[22] plays a role in securities regulation parallel to the Basel Core Principles. In 1998 IOSCO also issued International Disclosure Standards for Cross-Border Offerings and Initial Listings by Foreign Issuers.[23] This document deals with cross-border public offerings—an activity that broadly differs from cross-border banking because it is not subject to institutional regulation but to transaction regulation.

Of course, securities regulation and bank regulation differ and there are different motivations for regulatory cooperation in the two fields. These motivations, however, are largely based on (a) possibilities of adverse externalization resulting from lax regulation of foreign-based financial institutions, (b) avoidance of perceived regulatory competition (which is most problematic in cases of externalization),[24] (c) possibilities for regulatory economies of scale in supervision and in compliance for private actors, and (d) avoidance of protectionism. Factors (c) and (d) most engage the WTO.

Decisionmaking in IOSCO   IOSCO's work is done through two main committees: the Technical Committee and the Emerging Markets Committee (formerly the Development Committee). The Technical Committee was, until the admission of Mexico in 1993, the exclusive province of developed country securities regulators seeking to exchange information and coordinate their regulation. The Technical Committee has five working parties: (a) multinational disclosure and accounting, (b) regulation of secondary markets, (c) regulation of market intermediaries, (d) enforcement and the exchange of

information, and (e) investment management. The concerns of the Emerging Markets Committee, representing emerging securities market regulators, are increasingly dovetailing with those of the Technical Committee. IOSCO generally adopts standards by consensus (Guy 1992).

IAIS

History, Membership, and Purpose   The IAIS, established in 1994, comprises insurance regulators and supervisors from more than 100 jurisdictions, including all U.S. states and all EC member states.[25] These include both local and national authorities, as well as banking and other financial regulators, depending on the allocation of authority in the relevant state. For the United States it includes the National Association of Insurance Commissioners because insurance is regulated by the states. It includes the European Commission as well as the OECD.

The IAIS was formed for the following purposes:

- To promote cooperation among insurance regulators
- To set international standards for insurance supervision
- To provide training to members
- To coordinate work with regulators in the other financial sectors and international financial institutions.[26]

The IAIS issues papers and holds seminars on subjects related to insurance supervision. It is supported by a secretariat located at the Bank for International Settlements in Basel, is headed by an executive committee, and has three main committees: the Technical Committee, the Emerging Markets Committee, and the Budget Committee (IAIS 2000, p. 5). The Technical Committee is responsible for developing standards.

Standards Promulgated by IAIS   The IAIS issues principles, standards, and practices papers. In recognition of regulatory diversity among its members, these principles, standards, and practices are not mandatory, but members are expected to report on their level of compliance (Pooley 1998). The IAIS sets out principles that are fundamental to effective insurance supervision. These "principles" form the bases for "standards," which focus on particular issues and describe best or most prudent practices. Periodically, insurance supervisors carry out self-assessments and provide information on those self-assessments to the IAIS secretariat "so the IAIS can review the extent to which members are in compliance with the principles."[27] The Insurance Core Principles state that "[t]he Insurance Core Principles comprise essential principles that need to be in place for a supervisory system to be effective. Insurance Supervisors Should Apply the Insurance Core Principles in the supervision of all insurers within their jurisdiction" (IAIS 2000, para. 1.2). Principles address issues such as asset and liability risk, capital adequacy, supervision of cross-border operations, and cooperation with foreign regulators.

The IAIS has issued Principles Applicable to the Supervision of International Insurers and Insurance Groups and Their Cross-Border Business Operations (Insurance Concordat), December 1999. These principles are modeled on the Basel Concordat and the 1992 Minimum Standards for the Supervision of International Banking Groups and Their Cross-Border Establishments, and they provide, for example, that no foreign insurer shall go unsupervised. They allocate supervisory authority between host and home country authorities, depending in part on whether the entity is organized as a branch or a subsidiary. Although not requiring recognition per se, these statements are related to recognition because they allocate certain supervisory jurisdiction to the home country regulator. IAIS statutes provide that

> In deciding whether, and if so, on what basis, to license or to continue a license of a subsidiary or branch of a foreign insurer in its jurisdiction, the host supervisor may need to assess on a case-by-case basis the effectiveness of the supervision of the foreign insurer in its home jurisdiction, consulting the home supervisor as necessary. The assessment should take into account IAIS general supervisory principles and standards and the ability of the home supervisor to apply sanctions to prevent corporate structures that conflict with effective supervision.

Thus IAIS follows a similar pattern to that exhibited in the Basel Committee context: a range of "soft law" principles or standards combined with statements regarding international supervisory cooperation, including statements allowing home country regulatory quality to be assessed as a condition for licensing in a host country.

Decisionmaking in IAIS The IAIS develops standards through its Technical Committee. Once a standard is reviewed in the Technical Committee, it is sent to all members of IAIS for comment. The standard is then considered at an annual meeting (Pooley 1998).

A Critique of the Basel Committee, IAIS, and IOSCO from a Trade Standpoint

The Basel Committee, IAIS, and IOSCO, like the WTO, do not bring to bear the full range of societal preferences and values of each of their members. For example, the Basel Committee is fundamentally unidimensional, focusing on the safety, soundness, and stability of the banking system.[28] The WTO, on the other hand, is relatively unidimensional in another way, resulting in measures like the prudential carve-out.

The WTO is relatively ignorant of the subject matter and concerns of the SSBs, and, as shown in the trade and environment sphere, lacks the formal equipment to provide an integrated policy response. That is, an SSB might make policy in a way that insufficiently reflects concern for free trade in financial services, whereas the WTO might make policy in a way that insufficiently reflects concern for safety, soundness, and stability. Thus it is not enough simply to incorporate by reference the decisions of one forum in the other, nor is it acceptable any longer for these forums to ignore one another. There must be inter-forum negotiation and compromise.[29]

Of course, it might be argued in response that the negotiation, compromise, and policy integration take place at the level of the member state, and that each state will bring its integrated position to each forum in which it participates. However, these forums are not simply places of exchange; they must also be places of deliberation that can result in modified preferences. These forums lack the complete political system found in domestic society that allows for the full exercise of deliberative democracy (see Porter 2001).

The Trade Restrictive Impact of International Regulatory Standards

Greater policy integration has become necessary because it is clear that international regulatory standards can have trade-restrictive effects, and greater liberalization can have adverse regulatory effects. Thus the narrowly functional organizations that serve as avatars of these principles can harm one another's ability to achieve its goals—can create adverse "cross-functional" externalities (see Trachtman 2000).

For example, the Basel Core Principles are intended to serve as a basis for states to deny applications for branching or other entry from banking organizations based in states that fail to comply with the principles as a basis to restrain trade in financial services. This seems appropriate, but there may be a less trade-restrictive way to achieve the goals of financial integrity and stability. Furthermore, if the Basel Committee had considered the benefits of unencumbered trade in financial services, they might have decided on a different formulation of principles. In this sense we might say that the Basel Core Principles are not terribly different from the Basel Convention on the Control of Transboundary Movements of Hazardous Wastes and Their Disposal.[30] Both Basel emanations serve as bases for states to restrict trade for regulatory purposes, and both are valid expressions of public policy, which must be integrated commensurate with international trade public policy.

The Unilateral Use of SSBs

The SSBs may be used as a basis for unilateral measures by states. For example, in its review of foreign banking organizations under the Foreign Bank Supervision Enhancement Act (FBSEA),[31] the United States examines the extent to which the foreign banking organization's home jurisdiction regulates in compliance with the Basel Core Principles. Thus the SSBs may support unilateral action, and SSBs may be enforced and implemented through unilateral action. If Article VI.5(a) of the GATS provided substantial proportionality-type restrictions, unilateral measures that complied with SSB standards might be protected by virtue of an interpretation of the *Shrimp-Turtle* "line of equilibrium"

or through *Korea Beef*[32] or *Asbestos*[33] balancing that referred to the SSB standard.

In turn, it is important to note that the Basel Core Principles reflect, in substantial measure, prior U.S. regulatory policy (see Baxter and Freis 1999; Norton and Olive 2001). Thus we may understand SSBs as vehicles for the multilateralization and legitimation of unilateral policy.

The SSB Process and the International Financial Institutions

As the international financial institutions (IFIs), principally the IMF and World Bank, have sought to deal with recent financial crises, they have turned increasingly to microeconomic factors in the form of financial regulation, particularly bank regulation in the afflicted states. The IMF especially has grown concerned about compliance with SSB standards. "Consideration is being given to the gradual inclusion of standards in Fund conditionality" (Gianviti 2000, p. 110). The eligibility criteria for the IMF's Contingent Credit Lines include "a positive assessment of policies and progress toward adherence to internationally accepted standards."[34]

How the IMF Supports the Basel Core Principles

The IMF, the World Bank, and other international financial institutions have, during the past decade, increased their focus on regulatory standards as bases for sound financial sectors. They have developed the Financial Sector Assessment Program (FSAP) and the Reports on Observance of Standards and Codes (ROSC) to provide assessments of members' compliance with SSB standards among other things. In July 2001 the G7 made the following statements regarding the SSB standards:

> Authoritative information on observance of codes and standards should be fully integrated into enhanced IMF surveillance under Article IV, increasing its effectiveness as a tool for crisis prevention. This is a critical step, and the IMF should work expeditiously to implement it. The work being taken forward in the Fund on the modalities for using codes and standards information to guide and inform surveillance is an important step in this direction and we encourage its early completion.

Work to assess compliance with, and to implement, codes and standards needs to take full account of each country's unique development and reform priorities and institutional characteristics. We agree that countries and the Fund should continue to work, together with standard-setters as appropriate, to set priorities and establish action plans for compliance, within the framework of individual economic reform programs. The existing process for assessing compliance, which allows for progressive implementation of key codes and standards according to country-specific economic circumstances, provides an appropriate mechanism for facilitating prioritization.[35]

The IMF and World Bank are encouraging compliance with SSB standards. Although these initiatives do not make compliance mandatory per se, they provide some incentives for compliance. It might be worthwhile to compare the ROSC and FSAP programs with the WTO's Trade Policy Review Mechanism (TPRM). Both types of programs provide enhanced transparency and third-party assessment. However, the programs have differing motivations: financial stability on one hand and trade liberalization on the other. It would be useful to add market access to the concerns of ROSC and FSAP or, alternatively, for the WTO to add regulatory policy to the concerns of the TPRM or to create a "regulatory policy review mechanism."

The FSF and the WTO The Financial Stability Forum (FSF) recently prepared a report concerning incentives to foster implementation of its standards, which include the leading SSB standards (FSF 2001). It is significant that no mention is made in this report of the GATS. However, the FSF report shows that SSB standards are increasingly used as metrics for assessing foreign banks and insurance companies prior to permitting them market entry (FSF 2001, Annex IX).

Harnessing the SSB Process to Trade Liberalization and the WTO to Regulatory Effectiveness

The purpose of this section is to begin to analyze the utility and potential for greater integration in policymaking between the trade sector and the financial regulatory sector. As noted above, financial regulation is always an intervention, an interference in the free market. Of course, such intervention may support the free market or may be designed to achieve other social goals. In domestic societies, a central government decides about the scope of interference in the free market; contrast this with the circumstance in international society where a variety of functional organizations have responsibility for varying phases of the same question. Even in federal and quasi-federal systems like those of the United States and the EC, a central government decides on the relationship between free trade in financial services and regulation of financial services. In the EC, this decision is reflected in single-market directives such as the Second Banking Directive.

Soft Law, Hard Law, and Hardening Soft Law

In international society, institutions have not yet arisen that can make and enforce integrated, binding law in this field. Although WTO law is somewhat more binding than many other types of international law—and unlike SSB standards, is intended to be binding—WTO law has not integrated a full range of social policies.

The SPS and Codex Model

As illustrated by the discussion in "Lessons for the GATS," the SPS Agreement shows one possible way forward. It provides quasi-legislative authority to Codex Alimentarius, the International Plant Protection Center (IPPC), and the Office International des Epizootics (OIE)—the World Organization for Animal Health. It is possible that action under Article VI.4 could do the same for the SSBs. This would provide a way for SSB standards to attain quasi-legislative authority, in addition to that provided by the IMF and other IFIs. Do the SSB standards require greater authority? What is the trade interest in them? If the SSB standards could be agreed to as an *exclusive* basis for evaluation of the market access suitability of foreign financial service providers, this would presumably liberalize trade in financial services. Moreover, if the FSAP or ROSC process could be agreed to as an *exclusive* arbiter of compliance, it would further liberalize trade.

Bringing Trade Negotiators to the SSBs: Should the WTO Join the FSF?

Trade negotiators do not take direct part in the work of the Codex Alimentarius, the IPPC, or the OIE, although there are significant informal relations between these organizations and the WTO. Thus the standards promulgated by those organizations are not as likely to take account of trade concerns as they would be if trade negotiators participated. Of course, national representatives in these organizations may be briefed as to trade concerns of their states and may bring those concerns to bear. Thus it is possible to allow the cross-functional integration to take place in the member states. Under some circumstances, however, it may be more efficient to engage in more direct cross-functional integration, for example, by inviting trade negotiators to join in SSB meetings. This would allow them more directly to discuss market access issues relating to particular standards. Trade negotiators participating in SSB meetings could reflect on the trade incentives for harmonization, for recognition, or for allowing beneficial regulatory competition. Regulators often express concerns about a "race to the bottom," but from some standpoints it is a race to greater market access and greater efficiency (see, e.g., Kane 2001).

Alternatively, financial regulators could be invited to trade negotiations to bring a regulatory perspective. This would allow negotiators to move beyond a prudential carve-out and actually engage on issues of the relationship between free trade in financial services and regulatory reform. For example, more detailed work could be done on the role and extent of essential harmonization as a predicate for mutual recognition.

It is important to mention that the process of harmonization and recognition has both winners and losers. Not all states will benefit from every market liberalization measure, or every instance of regulatory reform. States may negotiate regulatory reform through a "request-offer" system.[36] This is one of the institutional advantages of the WTO: it is a place where states are able to trade to compensate one another for accepting a concession that will hurt the granting state less than it benefits the receiving state. These (presumptively) Kaldor-Hicks superior transactions result in enhanced aggregate welfare.

Until this type of treatymaking or other "legislative" action can be taken, it is still possible for SSB standards to have effects in GATS dispute settlement. How should the WTO's program under Article VI.4 of the GATS relate to the SSBs? There are several parameters that are worth mentioning.

First, if SSBs were judicially enforceable they might be held to supersede WTO law. This would be unlikely in WTO dispute settlement, as WTO dispute settlement does not directly apply non-WTO law. Alternatively, WTO law produced under GATS Article VI.4 might supersede SSB standards. General WTO law could also come into conflict with SSB standards—a WTO panel could find that compliance with SSB standards (e.g., rejection of a licensing application of a foreign bank) constitutes an illegal restriction on market access. Another possibility would be that the Article VI.4 process would incorporate SSB standards, possibly making them enforceable in WTO dispute settlement.

Concluding Remarks

It is important to ensure that the SSBs, the IMF, and the WTO do not work at cross purposes. Each of these organizations is intended to reflect a discrete set of social values. The question before us is to what extent, and how, it would be useful to integrate consideration of these values. Soft law and quasi-legislative processes may serve as an appropriate way to begin to address the problems of cross-functional integration. Managing the institutional intersection of the SSBs, the IMF, and the WTO is a proxy for managing the substantive intersection of the policy goals they represent.

Endnotes

1. This article uses the author's more general work on domestic regulation under the GATS contained in Chapter 5, "Lessons for the GATS from Existing WTO Rules on Domestic Regulation" (hereinafter, "Lessons for the GATS").

2. See Mattoo (2000): "a generic approach is to be preferred to a purely sectoral approach for at least three reasons: it economises on negotiating effort, leads to the creation of disciplines for all services rather than only the politically important ones, and reduces the likelihood of negotiations being captured by sectoral interest groups."

3. See WTO (2000), calling for a horizontal concept of necessity and for disciplines to expand and interpret necessity for application to specific sectors.

4. It is also important to note that the distributive consequences of particular arrangements must be addressed. The adoption of standards always helps some and hurts others.

5. OECD 2002, p. 3. Feketekuty (1988) argued that "[b]oth trade policy and regulatory policy have a contribution to make to the smooth and efficient functioning of the world economy." Consider the following 1993 exchange between U.S. Congressman Barney Frank and John P. LaWare, member, Board of Governors, Federal Reserve System, in hearings on the Free Trade in Financial Services Act, a law intended to impose a regime of specific reciprocity in connection with financial services liberalization in the U.S., and which was opposed by the board of governors. Congressman Frank is thinking of the proposed bill, which would impose a rule of reciprocal market access, as a trade issue, and Mr. LaWare is considering it from a regulatory perspective (U.S. House Committee on Banking, Financing, and Urban Affairs 1993, No. 103-96, p. 8).

   Congressman Frank: I am kind of taken aback when you say the thing is regulation. Where our financial institutions are restricted, is safety and soundness the reason? *Mr. LaWare:* It may very well be.

6. "There was nothing natural about laissez-faire; free markets could never have come into being merely by allowing things to take their course" (Polanyi 1944, p. 139). Polanyi identified the "re-regulation" that follows upon market expansion.

7. Of course, there are many potential standard-setting bodies to consider. The Financial Stability Forum (FSF) itself is one, and it refers to the following setters of financial standards: the Basel Committee on Banking Supervision, the Committee on the Global Financial System, the Committee on Payment and Settlement Systems, the Financial Action Task Force on Money Laundering, the International Association of Insurance Supervisors, the International Accounting Standards Committee, the International Federation of Accountants, the IMF, the IOSCO, and the OECD. Information is available at http://www.fsforum.org/Standards/WhoAre.html.

8. Australia has proposed clarification in the WTO Committee on Financial Services (see WTO Committee on Financial Services [2000], para. 4). Other states have questioned the utility or feasibility of clarification.

9. See WTO Appellate Body Report (1998), para. 137.

10. WTO Appellate Body Report (1998), para. 141: "In its general design and structure, therefore, Section 609—Focusing on the design of the measure here at stake, it appears to us that Section 609, *cum* implementing guidelines, is not disproportionately wide in its scope and reach in relation to the policy objective of protection and conservation of sea turtle species. The means are, in principle, *reasonably related to the ends*. The means and ends relationship between Section 609 and the legitimate policy of conserving an exhaustible, and, in fact, endangered species, is observably a close and real one, a relationship that is every bit as substantial as that which we found in *United States-Gasoline* between the EPA baseline establishment rules and the conservation of clean air in the United States."

11. See WTO (1996), para. 17. The IFAC is closely related to the IASB, but is concerned more with international auditing standards than with international accounting standards. The IASC is now the IASB. See http://www.iasc.org.uk/cmt/0001.asp.

12. Article VII.5, as discussed below, calls for recognition based on multilaterally agreed criteria, requiring that states "work in cooperation with relevant intergovernmental and nongovernmental organizations towards the establishment and adoption of common international standards and criteria for recognition...."

13. For a discussion of the application of the GATS to accounting standards, see Trachtman (1997, p. 63).

14. I use the term "semi-soft" to refer to the circumstance where the relevant norms are not formally binding in their originating organization but have taken on greater formal force in another organization—namely, the WTO—through the SPS Agreement. Although Codex Alimentarius standards are not fully binding in the SPS Agreement context, the SPS Agreement provides enhanced incentives for compliance.

15. From http://www.bis.org/bcbs/aboutbcbs.htm, visited December 23, 2001.

16. See Basel Committee on Banking Regulation and Supervisory Practices 1988. At the time of this writing, the Basel Accord is in the process of being revised.

17. Basel Committee on Banking Regulation and Supervisory Practices, Principles for the Supervision of Banks' Foreign Establishments, May 1983. The Basel Concordat has been revised and supplemented. See http://www.bis.org/publ/bcbsc004.htm#v3d2, visited December 23, 2001.

18. Basel Committee on Banking Regulation and Supervisory Practices, Report on Minimum Standards for the Supervision of International Banking Groups and Their Cross Border Establishments, June 1992.

19. Basel Committee on Banking Regulation and Supervisory Practices, Core Principles for Effective Banking Supervision, September 1997.

20. For a useful discussion and critique of the Basel Committee process, see Matthews (1995).

21. See http://www.iosco.org/gen-info.html.

22. See http://www.iosco.org/docs-public/1998-objectives.html.

23. See http://www.iosco.org/docs-public/1998-ntnl_disclosure_standards.html.

24. See Trachtman (2001a).

25. See www.iaisweb.org, visited December 22, 2001; and Pooley (1998).

26. See www.iaisweb.org, visited December 22, 2001; and Pooley (1998).

27. See the U.S. National Association of Insurance Commissioners ("NAIC") response at http://www.naic.org/1whatsnew/NAIC_IAIS_%20Response.doc.

28. But see Scott and Iwahara (1994), which shows the competitive aspects of the formulation of the Basel Accord.

29. In formulating the Accountancy Disciplines, SSBs submitted documentation and gave presentations on their activities to the WTO Working Party on Trade in Services. See Honeck (2000).

30. Done at Basel, March 22, 1989. Of course, we could also compare the Montreal Protocol on Substances That Deplete the Ozone Layer, or the Convention on International Trade in Endangered Species of Wild Fauna and Flora.

31. Foreign Bank Supervision Enhancement Act of 1991, Pub. L. No. 101-242, sections 201-215, 105 Stat. 2236-305 (codified at 12 U.S.C. sections 3101-3111). See Bhala (1994).

32. See WTO Appellate Body Report (2001a).

33. See WTO Appellate Body Report (2001a).

34. IMF Contingent Credit Lines: A Factsheet, available at http://www.imf.org/external/np/exr/facts/ccl.htm, visited

January 2, 2002. The IMF refers specifically to the Basel Core Principles.

35. G7 Statement on Strengthening the International Financial System, July 7, 2001.

36. For a similar argument relating to environmental regulation, see Trachtman (2000).

References

Baxter, Thomas C., and James H. Freis. 1999. "Fostering Competition in Financial Services: From Domestic Supervision to Global Standards." *New England Law Review* 34: 57–76.

Bhala, Raj. 1994. "Tragedy, Irony, and Protectionism after BCCI: A Three-act Play Starring Maharajah Bank." *Southern Methodist University Law Review* 48: 11–62.

Feketekuty, Geza. 1988. "International Trade in Services: An Overview and Blueprint for Negotiations." Washington, D.C.: Ballinger Press for the American Enterprise Institute.

FSF (Financial Stability Forum). 2001. "Final Report of the Follow-up Group on Incentives to Foster Implementation of Standards." August 21. <http://www.fsforum.org/Reports/Incentives.pdf>.

Gianviti, Francois. 2000. "The Reform of the International Monetary Fund (Conditionality and Surveillance)." *International Lawyer* 34: 107–16.

Guy, Paul. 1992. "Regulatory Harmonization to Achieve Effective International Competition." In Franklin R. Edwards and Hugh T. Patrick, eds., *Regulating International Financial Markets: Issues and Policies.* Boston: Kluwer Academic Publishing.

Honeck, Dale B. 2000. "Developing Regulatory Disciplines in Professional Services: The Role of the World Trade Organization." In Yair Aharoni and Lilach Nachum, eds., *Globalization of Services: Some Implications for Theory and Practice.* London: Routledge.

IAIS (International Association of Insurance Supervisors). Task Force on Core Principles Methodology. 2000. "Insurance Core Principles." October 10.

Kane, Edward J. 2001. "Relevance and Need for International Regulatory Standards." In Robert E. Litan and Richard Herring, eds., *Brookings-Wharton Papers on Financial Services.* Washington, D.C.: Brookings Institution Press.

Lichtenstein, Cynthia C. 1991. "Introductory Note to Bank for International Settlements: Committee on Banking Regulations and Supervisory Practices' Consultative Paper on International Convergence of Capital Measurement and Capital Standards." *International Legal Materials* 30: 967, 969.

Matthews, Barbara C. 1995 "Capital Adequacy, Netting and Derivatives." *Stanford Journal of Law, Business, and Finance* 2: 167.

Mattoo, Aaditya. 2000. "Developing Countries in the New Round of GATS Negotiations: Toward a Pro-Active Role." *The World Economy* 23: 471–84.

Nicolaidis, Kalypso, and Joel Trachtman. 2000. "From Policed Regulation to Managed Recognition in GATS." In Pierre Sauvé and Robert M. Stern, eds., *GATS 2000: New Directions in Services Trade Liberalization.* Washington, D.C.: Brookings Institution Press.

———. 1995. *Devising International Bank Supervisory Standards.* London: Graham and Trotman/M. Nijhoff.

Norton, Joseph J., and Christopher D. Olive. 2001. "A By-Product of the Globalization Process: the Rise of Cross-Border Bank Mergers and Acquisitions—the U.S. Regulatory Framework." *Business Law* 56: 591.

OECD (Organisation for Economic Co-operation and Development). 2002. "Open Services Markets Matter." Paris.

Polanyi, Karl. 1944. *The Great Transformation.* New York: Rinehart and Co.

Pooley, George. 1998. "The IAIS: A Progress Report and Some Thoughts for the Future." *Journal of Insurance Regulation* 16: 170–78.

Porter, Tony. 2001. "The Democratic Deficit in the Institutional Arrangements Governing Global Finance." *Global Governance* 7: 427–39.

Sauvé, Pierre, and Karsten Steinfatt. 2001. "Financial Services and the WTO: What Next?" In R. Litan, M. Pomerleano, and P. Masson, eds., *Open Doors: Foreign Participation in Financial Systems in Developing Countries.* Washington, D.C.: Brookings Institution Press.

Scott, Hal S., and Shinsaku Iwahara. 1994. "In Search of a Level Playing Field: The Implementation of the Basle Capital Accord in Japan and the United States." Group of Thirty, Occasional Paper 46.

Sommer, A. A. 1996. "IOSCO: Its Mission and Achievement." *Northwestern Journal of International Law and Business* 17: 15–29.

Sykes, Alan O. 1995. *Product Standards for Internationally Integrated Goods Markets.* Washington, D.C.: Brookings Institution Press.

Trachtman, Joel P. 1995. "Trade in Financial Services under GATS, NAFTA and the EC: A Regulatory Jurisdiction Analysis." *Columbia Journal of Transnational Law* 34: 37–122.

———. 1997. "Accounting Standards and Trade Disciplines: Irreconcilable Differences?" *Journal of World Trade* 31: 63–98.

———. 2000. "Assessment of the Effects of Trade Liberalization on Domestic Environmental Regulation: Toward Trade-Environment Policy Integration." In OECD, *Assessing the Environmental Effects of Trade Liberalisation Agreements: Methodologies.* Paris.

———. 2001a. "Institutional Linkage: Transcending Trade and. . . ." *American Journal of International Law* 96: 77–93.

———. 2001b. "Regulatory Competition and Regulatory Jurisdiction in International Securities Regulation." In Daniel Esty and Damien Gerardin, eds., *Regulatory Competition and Economic Integration: Comparative Perspectives.* Oxford, U.K.: Oxford University Press.

U.S. House Committee on Banking, Finance, and Urban Affairs, Subcommittee on International Development, Finance, Trade, and Monetary Policy. 1993. 103rd Cong., 1st sess., November 9.

Weiler, Joseph. 1991. "The Transformation of Europe." *Yale Law Journal* 100: 2403–83.

WTO (World Trade Organization). 1996. Singapore Ministerial Declaration. WT/MIN(96)/DEC, December 13.

———. 2000. Report of the Committee on Financial Services to the Council for Trade in Services. S/FIN/5, November 24.

———. 2001. Communication from the European Communities and Their Member States: Domestic Regulation: Necessity and Transparency. S/WPDR/W/14.

WTO Appellate Body Report. 1998. *United States—Import Prohibition of Certain Shrimp and Shrimp Products.* WT/DS58/AB/R, November 6.

———. 2001a. *European Communities—Measures Affecting Asbestos and Asbestos-Containing Products.* WT/DS135/AB/R, April 5.

———. 2001b. *Korea—Measures Affecting Imports of Fresh, Chilled and Frozen Beef.* WT/DS/161,169/AB/R, January 10.

WTO Committee on Financial Services. 2000. Report to the Council for Trade in Services. S/FIN/5, November 24.

WTO Working Party on Domestic Regulation. 2001. "Examples of Measures to Be Addressed by Disciplines under GATS Article VI.4." Informal Note by the Secretariat. Job (01)/62, May 10.

Zaring, David. 1998. "International Law by Other Means: The Twilight Existence of International Financial Regulatory Organizations." *Texas International Law Journal* 33: 281–330.

4

REGULATORY DISCRIMINATION IN DOMESTIC UNITED STATES LAW: A MODEL FOR THE GATS?

David W. Leebron

Executive Summary

This chapter examines, from an American legal perspective, the standards employed in domestic U.S. law to determine whether regulation unduly interferes with trade. The ultimate purpose of the chapter is to aid in the consideration of various legal tests that might be used to implement the requirements of Article VI of the General Agreement on Trade in Services (GATS). That provision requires that the Council for Trade in Services "develop necessary disciplines" to ensure that "qualification requirements and procedures, technical standards and licensing requirements do not constitute unnecessary barriers to trade in services," are "based on objective and transparent criteria," and are "not more burdensome than necessary to ensure the quality of the service." This chapter does not attempt to specify the test that should be adopted for application under the GATS, but rather seeks to discern whether U.S. practice might serve as one source for the appropriate tests.

The chapter proceeds in two parts. The first part presents the background and substance of American jurisprudence aimed at eliminating state (in the sense of the individual states of the union) interference with national commerce. The second part explores in general analytic terms the structure of legal tests for examining domestic regulation that burdens international trade, and further considers what lessons can be drawn for the GATS from the American experience and perspective.

The United States Jurisprudence of "Free Trade"

In many respects, the history of the American Union stands in sharp contrast to the history of the European Union. Although economic concerns played very prominently in the founding of the United States, it was foremost a political union. The American economy entered the Industrial Revolution—not to mention the growth in manufacture and trade of consumer products that followed it—after both political union and national identity had largely been forged through the Civil War. American states were not without their inclinations toward protectionism, but for the most part these were dwarfed by the rapid growth in the late 19th century of a truly national economy with powerful multistate enterprises. Compared with the European Union, this sequence of events resulted in a perhaps diminished role for law in creating and maintaining a national market.

As elaborated below, the legal regime in the United States for disciplining state[1] regulation of services is composed of three principle elements: the "dormant" Commerce Clause of the U.S. Constitution, the Privileges and Immunities Clause of the Constitution, and sectoral regulation establishing national regulatory frameworks that have been adopted by Congress (and elaborated by federal agencies). More than many might expect, U.S. markets for services remain fragmented by state regulation, although discriminatory regulation generally does not survive review by the courts.

The Commerce Clause

The key provision of the Constitution addressing the regulation of both international commerce and commerce among the states is the Commerce Clause of Article 1, Section 8: "[Congress shall have power] to regulate Commerce with foreign Nations, and among the several States, and with the Indian Tribes." Although explicitly only an affirmative grant of power to the Congress, the clause was ultimately interpreted to have a negative or "dormant" component that implicitly forbids the states from undertaking actions that discriminate or excessively burden such interstate or foreign commerce.[2] This dormant Commerce Clause restriction is in addition to other provisions of the Constitution that ban state treaties, state tariffs, state money, or state enactment of legislation or other actions that conflict with federal regulations. Loosely speaking, it serves roughly the same role as Articles III and XI of the General Agreement on Tariffs and Trade (GATT) (perhaps combined with Article XX) or Article 30 of the Treaty of Rome in ensuring that a state regulation or discrimination does not interfere with a regime of free trade.

Although widely accepted for more than a century, the dormant Commerce Clause is not without its critics today. At least three members of the current Supreme Court (Justices William Rehnquist, Antonin Scalia, and Clarence Thomas) have questioned the Constitutional authority for courts to review, in the absence of relevant federal regulation, the permissibility of general state regulation under the Commerce Clause.[3]

It is not an altogether easy task to reduce the Supreme Court's dormant Commerce Clause jurisprudence to the kind of simple test one might incorporate into an international agreement or statute. As one commentator (Lawrence 1998, p. 414) noted:

> As it stands today, it is difficult to know with any certainty what approach the Court will use in viewing a particular state measure potentially affecting interstate commerce. The nub of the matter is that the Court's current approach to dormant-commerce-clause cases is so scattered that nobody—not state legislators, not law students, not the academic authorities, not the lower courts, not, indeed, the Court itself—knows clearly what the Court's rules are concerning the Dormant Commerce Clause.[4]

Indeed, many commentators break down the Court's decisions not by analytical approaches but by subject matter areas. There are many reasons for this confusion, not least among them the usual difficulty in reconciling the notion of a national (or international) free market with the regulatory sovereignty of the constituent political units. And although the Commerce Clause has been acknowledged to be aimed at creating a single national free trade area, the Court has been reluctant to fully embrace the kinds of economic analysis that concept truly requires. Features of the European Union, and even of the GATT, that are aimed at eliminating barriers to trade are notably absent not only from the U.S. Constitution but also from the decisions of courts applying the Constitutional provisions. In many areas, state barriers to the national market remain substantial. Indeed, in some major areas, progress in creating the legal frameworks for a national market has been achieved only recently, and primarily through congressional legislation.

The positive aspect of the Commerce Clause has been understood as a sweeping[5] grant of power to the U.S. Congress to regulate commerce with foreign nations and among the states, and accordingly has been of much greater importance in achieving an economic union. In numerous areas, Congress has established comprehensive regulatory schemes and strong administrative agencies to promulgate detailed rules. Such agencies include, for example, the Food and Drug Administration, the Federal

Trade Commission, and the Securities and Exchange Commission. Under the Supremacy Clause,[6] federal statutes and regulations preempt any conflicting state regulation, and in many cases are held to preempt state action in an entire regulatory field.

Still, the courts'—in particular the Supreme Court's—interpretations of the negative Commerce Clause have played a substantial role in developing the legal framework for a national market. Most of the numerous decisions applying the dormant Commerce Clause address matters of state regulation and taxation, as states are clearly forbidden from applying the usual border measures.[7] The dormant Commerce Clause has been held to prohibit three basic kinds of state regulation: state regulation that is patently discriminatory, state regulation that "has the 'practical effect' of regulating commerce occurring wholly outside that State's borders,"[8] and state regulation that imposes "an undue burden on interstate commerce."[9]

Discrimination In general, the Court's analysis in such cases begins with an inquiry into whether the state or municipal[10] regulation at issue is discriminatory. Facially discriminatory regulation—that is, regulation that draws an explicit distinction between the treatment accorded local or in-state products or producers and out-of-state products or producers—is almost always invalidated. Statutes that discriminate "in effect" are, in theory, similarly disfavored, but the question of what constitutes such a "discriminatory effect" is often murky.[11]

The Court captured the essence of its approach to discriminatory regulation as follows:

> Discrimination against interstate commerce in favor of local business or investment is *per se* invalid, save in a narrow class of cases in which the municipality can demonstrate, under rigorous scrutiny, that it has no other means to advance a legitimate local interest.[12]

The strength of the state interest is unlikely to sustain facially discriminatory legislation.[13] As the Court stated, "However important the state interest at hand, 'it may not be accomplished by discriminating against articles of commerce coming from outside the State unless there is some reason, apart from their origin, to treat them differently.'"[14]

There are very few cases that survive such scrutiny, the only recent example being a prohibition by the state of Maine on imported baitfish in order to protect local Maine fisheries from parasites and other dangers.[15] In theory, a legitimate state interest might justify facial discrimination, but the interest would have to be compelling, the benefits of the measure would have to substantially outweigh the burden on interstate commerce, and there would have to be no alternative measure that would substantially achieve those benefits without facial discrimination. In short, the defender of such legislation must sustain the burden of proving that the measure at issue is virtually the only means by which the important legislative goals could be achieved, and that the impact on interstate commerce is small compared with the benefits to be realized by the regulation.

The Court has applied the prohibition on discrimination both to restrictions favoring in-state purchasers and to those favoring in-state sellers or producers. States may also not use unilateral measures to counteract discriminatory measures of other states.[16] Both export and import restrictions aimed at encouraging local processing are virtually per se unlawful.[17] States also cannot protect domestic producers by restricting the establishment of facilities owned by foreign producers.[18] In a major exception to these rules, the Court has repeatedly sustained the notion that a state may discriminate when it acts as a "market participant," purchasing products for its own use or selling products as owner or producer.[19] This deference to states has its ground in the particular conception of American federalism. The existence of the states, with their prerogative and duty to protect their citizens in numerous spheres of activity, operates as a check on the inclination under the Commerce Clause toward a national market unburdened by state regulation.

Nondiscriminatory Measures The Supreme Court's approach to facially neutral, nondiscriminatory legislation is different, and to a large extent reverses the burdens and presumptions applied in reviewing discriminatory legislation. The Supreme Court today applies to facially neutral regulation both a deferential balancing test and, in some cases, a least restrictive alternative test. On the former, the Court set forth the modern approach in the 1970 seminal case of *Pike v. Bruce Church, Inc.* The Court declared:

> Where the statute regulates even-handedly to effectuate a legitimate local public interest, and its effects on interstate commerce are only incidental, it will be upheld unless the burden imposed on such commerce is clearly excessive in relation to the putative local benefits.[20]

The *Pike v. Bruce Church* test thus potentially comprises four distinct inquiries in examining state regulation:

1. Is the purpose of the regulation a "legitimate" local public interest?
2. Is the regulation "even-handed," that is, nondiscriminatory?
3. Is the effect on interstate commerce "only incidental"?
4. Is the burden "clearly excessive" compared with the benefits?

Neither the Constitution nor the Court's jurisprudence list or limit the regulatory goals that are legitimate for purposes of Commerce Clause analysis. The only purpose that has generally been determined to be illegitimate under Commerce Clause analysis is straightforward economic protectionism.[21] Evidence that the regulation was motivated by protectionism might be supplied by the legislative history of the enactment of the regulation, including statements by public officials. However, it should be noted that some forms of state promotion of domestic industry have been upheld by the Court. In *Pike* itself, the Court declared that the state purpose "to protect and enhance the reputation of growers within the state" through packing and labeling requirements was legitimate, and that an equally legitimate interest is "maximizing the financial return to an industry within" a state. More important, over sharp academic criticism the courts have upheld state subsidies that favor their own industries,[22] although discriminatory taxes and tax credits are prohibited.[23] In short, a fine and uncertain line has been drawn between positive acts of promotion and encouragement of state industry on the one hand and protection of such industry and discrimination against out-of-state actors on the other.

Given the "strict scrutiny" applied to discriminatory legislation and the deferential approach taken with regard to nondiscriminatory regulation, the distinction between these is critical. However, the Court has been unable to provide very clear guidance on this issue. In one case, the Court found regulation that prohibited ownership of retail gasoline outlets by integrated petroleum companies to be nondiscriminatory even though there were no such companies in the state that were subject to the prohibition.[24] Similarly, the Court has not elaborated to any great degree the distinction between incidental and direct regulation, and rarely relies on that distinction in deciding whether to uphold or strike down state regulation. Two types of regulation appear to merit stricter scrutiny, however, perhaps because the effects are considered to be more direct. These are burdens on the means of interstate commerce and regulations with extraterritorial application or direct effects.

"Burdensome" Regulation The question of whether regulation impermissibly "burdens" interstate commerce is distinct from the question whether it "discriminates" against such commerce. Thus in recent years direct state regulation of the means of interstate commerce—highways and railways—has fared badly. For example, the Court invalidated a Wisconsin law prohibiting trucks longer than 55 feet,[25] an Iowa law banning 65-foot double tractor-trailers,[26] and an Arizona law forbidding trains longer than 14 passenger cars or 70 freight cars.[27] Although commentators and sometimes the Court itself explain such cases in terms of discrimination,[28] I believe the cases are better understood within the American context as cases involving direct regulation of the means of conducting interstate commerce. Where such a burden is substantial, the state regulation will be subjected to fairly strict scrutiny, rather than the more deferential approach taken with respect to other facially neutral regulation that does not directly affect the means of commerce. It is interesting to note that such cases typically involve what would be regarded on the international level as trade in services.

Occasionally, the Court's Commerce Clause jurisprudence has also emphasized the extraterritorial effects of state regulation. Where such regulation by intent or effect directly regulates out-of-state conduct, it will generally be invalidated. The

Court has treated extraterritorial impact as a particularly pernicious burden on interstate commerce that local benefits are unlikely to outweigh. This is especially so in circumstances where irreconcilable conflicts would arise if multiple states took such an approach. The Court has also stressed extraterritorial effect in striking down some forms of price regulation.[29]

The Weighted Balancing Test and Least Restrictive Alternatives The last element, the balancing test, has been severely criticized because such balancing is perceived to be a legislative rather than judicial function, and because it is not at all clear how one balances the benefits in achieving various public policy goals against burdens on interstate commerce. As Justice Scalia remarked, "both sides are incommensurate. It is more like judging whether a particular line is longer than a particular rock is heavy."[30] In fact, instead of the cost-benefit approach, many of the Court's decisions apply two closely related forms of analysis: regulatory fit and least restrictive alternative.

In reviewing state regulation under *Pike*, the Court often focuses on the question of regulatory fit—that is, how closely tailored the means chosen were to the articulated goals of the legislation. In that context, evidence that the statute is under-inclusive or over-inclusive sometimes appears to determine whether it will survive the balancing test. In many respects, the fit test is equivalent to a less restrictive alternative analysis, as making the regulation less discriminatory by either imposing the burdens more on in-state actors or less on out-of-state actors does seem less restrictive of interstate trade. However, the test seems more aimed at the issue of discrimination than the balancing of benefits and burdens; it thus calls into question the state's true purpose in regulating in the particular way chosen.

The Court also apparently applies a least restrictive alternative test in determining whether a burden is "clearly excessive" in relation to the local benefits. Following the quote above from *Pike v. Bruce Church, Inc.*, the Court added:

If a legitimate local purpose is found, then the question becomes one of degree. And the extent of the burden that will be tolerated will of course depend on the nature of the local inter-est involved, and on whether it could be promoted as well with a lesser impact on interstate activities.[31]

In most cases not dealing with the means of commerce, the least restrictive alternative test is a limited form of the balancing test. If there is an alternative means that would equally achieve the regulatory goals with a lesser burden on interstate trade, then *at the margin* the burdens of the measure outweigh its benefits. Thus the least restrictive alternative can be thought of as requiring a marginal analysis in addition to the basic balancing. A measure that, as a whole, might otherwise have been justified under the overall balancing test (because the benefits exceed the burdens) might still be invalidated under the least restrictive alternative approach.

Beyond extraterritorial effects and regulation of the means of commerce, however, there have been comparatively few cases in which nondiscriminatory regulation was found to burden commerce, and thus invoke the weighted balancing test. Some of the facially neutral statutes found to be discriminatory are those that effectively discriminate on the basis of distance from the locus of the regulation or transaction.[32] Such statutes, although not facially discriminatory, are more than merely discriminatory in effect; they are almost invariably found not to employ the least restrictive alternative. Perhaps the Supreme Court decision that comes closest to striking down a neutral state law regulating products was the invalidation of a North Carolina statute requiring apples sold in closed containers to display only official United States grades. The state of Washington believed that this regulation unfairly disadvantaged its apple growers, as they were not permitted to indicate the more rigorous Washington state grades. The Court essentially found that the North Carolina legislation deprived the Washington growers of the ability to make known their competitive advantage, and in that sense that the statute was discriminatory in effect. The case appears fairly unusual, and in fact emphasizes some requirement of discrimination if a law is to be invalidated. More typical perhaps was the case involving a Minnesota statute banning the sale of milk in plastic disposable containers, while allowing it in paper containers. In the absence of sufficient evidence of discrimination, the Court found that the burden was small compared with the substantial interests asserted by the legislature.[33]

Trade in Services under the American Constitution

Commerce Clause   Perhaps it is surprising that very few of the cases under the Commerce Clause, other than those involving regulation of transportation, have addressed the question of services. Decisions applying the dormant Commerce Clause make no distinction between goods and services in terms of the applicable legal standards. In a case involving Florida restrictions on out-of-state banks to establish Florida operations providing investment advisory services, the Court suggested that this fell within the per se rule against protectionist legislation, but ultimately ruled that the legitimate purposes of the legislation failed to justify the discriminatory burden. In the Court's view, the legislation was poorly tailored to achieve the asserted goals.[34] One of the Court's most recent Commerce Clause cases addressed property taxation of nonprofit enterprises. The state of Maine provided an exemption from such taxation for charitable enterprises operated primarily for people who resided in Maine. In effect this rule discriminated against out-of-state purchasers of services.[35] The Court's jurisprudence also makes clear that states cannot impose discriminatory restrictions on the establishment of business enterprises.[36]

In addition, an important group of cases in recent years has concerned state restrictions on waste disposal. On occasion, such restrictions have taken the form of limitations on the ability of waste disposal facilities to accept waste for disposal from out of state or outside the municipality.[37] Although some of these cases have been analyzed in terms of a restriction on trade in waste or hazardous materials,[38] they are better understood as involving discriminatory restrictions on out-of-state purchasers of services supplied by in-state waste disposal service providers or, conversely, as favoring in-state purchasers of scarce services over out-of-state purchasers. Despite the very strong public interest underlying such regulations, the Court has struck them down under the rubric of per se discrimination.

Privileges and Immunities Clause   With regard to services, an important restriction on states is their inability to regulate interstate immigration and emigration in any way, or to limit who may become a citizen of a state, or to discriminate on the basis of how long one has been a state resident or citizen.[39] State citizenship within the United States has long been little more than the choice and establishment of residence within a state by a resident of the United States. The open market for services is also protected by the Privileges and Immunities Clause of the Constitution,[40] which provides that "[t]he Citizens of each State shall be entitled to all Privileges and Immunities of Citizens in the Several States." The Court has declared that the purpose of both this clause and the Commerce Clause was "to create a national economic union."[41] Although what constitutes a privilege or an immunity is not altogether clear, the clause has often been applied to economic activities.[42] For example, the Supreme Court has repeatedly struck down state attempts to limit bar admission to residents.[43] The Privileges and Immunities Clause also protects residents of a state who wish to obtain medical services outside that state,[44] and limits the ability of a state through regulation to favor the employment of its own residents.[45] The impact of the Privileges and Immunities Clause on opening state markets, however, is limited by its inapplicability to artificial persons (e.g., corporations) or aliens.

When it has been determined that a regulation discriminates against a noncitizen of a state, the test to determine its validity is similar (but not identical) to that applied under the Commerce Clause:

> The [Privileges and Immunities] Clause does not preclude discrimination against nonresidents where (i) there is a substantial reason for the difference in treatment; and (ii) the discrimination practiced against nonresidents bears a substantial relationship to the State's objective. In deciding whether the discrimination bears a close or substantial relationship to the State's objective, the Court has considered the availability of less restrictive means.[46]

"Substantial" in this context means not only legitimate, but also plausible. Dubious factual assertions (e.g., that out-of-state lawyers would be less ethical than in-state lawyers or less likely to keep up to date on matters of state law) will be considered and rejected by the courts. The substantial relationship requirement is one of "fit," mandating that means chosen must be closely tailored to the ends sought, especially insofar as the means involve discrimination.

Legal Standards and the Emergence of National Markets in the United States

In many respects, those two clauses of the U.S. Constitution have turned out to be relatively weak tools for forging a national market and overcoming state regulation that burdens interstate commerce. One could certainly not conclude that the Commerce and Privileges and Immunities Clauses played the preeminent role in breaking down state regulatory barriers to internal trade within the American market. Rather, the United States has responded to the emergence or potential emergence of national markets for services with detailed sectoral regulation. In some circumstances, the federal government has acted aggressively to forge national markets, and in others it has explicitly allowed the states to maintain parochial legislation. Even today in such areas as insurance and legal practice, it could hardly be said that there is a national market in the United States, or that the judicial application of general constitutional restrictions will be the means to achieve it.

Instead, in such areas as telecommunications and financial services, the national government has vacillated between efforts to create national markets and efforts to ensure the power of local governments to regulate in the local interest. Both popular movements and major economic forces have influenced congressional approaches. National authority has been exercised through powerful administrative agencies, such as the Federal Communications Commission, the Securities and Exchange Commission, the Federal Reserve Banks, and the Federal Deposit Insurance Corporation.

These statutory and administrative schemes are too complex to describe in any detail here, but it was through the exercise of the positive Congressional power to regulate that state barriers were ultimately reduced. Financial services exemplify this story. Early in American history Congress created a national bank in the form of the Bank of the United States. The Supreme Court upheld the power of Congress to create such a banking corporation, but popular opposition and the rise of state banks led to a congressional decision to terminate the bank (twice) in the 19th century. A dual system of state and federal banking regulation was created at the time of the Civil War. Federal regulation seesawed between the creation of national banks and the protection of state banks and state regulatory policy. The Federal Reserve Bank and more comprehensive federal regulatory authority over banks were established early in the 20th century. Such regulation, however, was not used to create a national market in financial services. Even into the early 1990s, only six states allowed interstate branches. In 1994, however, Congress enacted legislation that effectively encouraged widespread interstate banking. In this historical context, the primary role of courts was in interpreting statutes enacted by Congress or administrative rules and decisions issued under statutory authority. General standards restricting state regulation, such as those under the dormant Commerce Clause, played little role.

A similar story played out in telecommunications, except that the trend toward a national market (at least in telephony) was aided in large part by the Bell System's early attainment of national monopoly. As another example of Congress' favoring dual systems of regulation, the 1984 Cable Act created an environment in which both the Federal Communications Commission and local franchise authorities exercised aspects of regulatory control over cable television. In some areas, such as broadcasting, Congress exercised its national authority specifically to prevent the emergence of a national market by creating ownership restrictions on broadcasting facilities. When Congress or federal agencies did choose to assert regulatory authority (albeit not always in furtherance of a national market), the courts generally sustained that authority.

In professional services as well, markets remained fragmented until relatively recently, with states continuing to exercise regulatory authority in licensing many such services. Both lawyers and accountants must qualify locally to practice in each state. Although, through a variety of measures, national firms have emerged in both fields, state regulatory barriers to the cross–state border provision of such services remain substantial.

In almost all of these cases it can fairly be said that Congress responded to economic forces (national and international) and events rather than actively leading the way in creating the necessary legal conditions for national markets in services. On the other hand, the prohibition on discriminatory restrictions on ownership or investment, or any restrictions based on state citizenship or residence, has undoubtedly helped maintain a more open environment for services.

Comparative Analysis

The Analytical Schema

Analytically, the task of examining regulatory burdens on international (or, in the case of domestic measures in the United States, interstate) trade can be separated initially into three steps. First, what is the "prima facie" case of violation triggering scrutiny of the regulation? Second, what defenses or justifications are available to justify the burdensome regulation? Third, are there, in effect, defenses to such defenses, that is, claims that undercut the validity of or otherwise limit the defense?[47] Although this structure suggests that the plaintiff has at least the burden of production (i.e., raising the issue and perhaps presenting some preliminary evidence) on the first and last issues, and the defendant has the burden on the second issue, this burden of production does not necessarily dictate who bears the burden of persuasion on that issue. Similarly, under the GATT the complaining country must first establish a violation—for example, that regulation or administrative action contravenes the national treatment requirement of Article III.[48] Then the country imposing the suspect rule can offer a legal justification, such as those contained in the Article XX exceptions. The complaining country, however, may assert that the justification is not "necessary," or is a "disguised restriction" on international trade.

Even when it is not explicit, it is important to keep this structure in mind because the acceptability of any legal test for trade-burdensome regulation will depend on each of these three elements, how they interact with each other, and who bears what burden of proof. The looser the requirements for what constitutes a violation or other triggering mechanism, the more countries are likely to demand that scrutiny of their measures be deferential. Conversely, the more narrowly drawn the threshold requirements are for applying such scrutiny, the more likely stricter scrutiny will be acceptable.

Although not articulated in these terms, this approach is at the heart of the Supreme Court's approach to reviewing state regulation under the dormant Commerce Clause. As discussed above, facially discriminatory regulation is subject to such strict scrutiny that the Court almost invariably regards such regulation as a per se violation of the Commerce Clause. Similarly, extraterritorial regulation and regulation that is likely to result in conflicting state rules applying to a single circumstance are subject to extremely strict scrutiny. Regulation that directly burdens the means of commerce or under which discriminatory effect is readily apparent, is subject to a demanding application of the cost-benefit and least restrictive alternative tests. Regulation that is neutral and only indirectly burdens commerce is subject to very deferential scrutiny. It will be sustained unless the burdens on interstate commerce are clearly excessive in relation to the benefit, or unless there is a less restrictive alternative.

The Commerce Clause and the Economic Principles of Free Trade

When one compares the situation within the United States with that of the European Union and the WTO, it is apparent why there are fundamental problems in achieving agreement on the appropriate standards for reviewing regulatory burdens on trade. The European Union began with a constitutive document aimed at achieving economic union, and provided the essential terms for quickly developing the legal framework of a free trade area and customs union. The Constitution of the United States is much more rudimentary in its economic provisions, and the Court has only hesitatingly embraced economic theory in elaborating those provisions. As Larry Tribe has noted, "behind the Court's analysis stands an important doctrinal theme: the negative implications of the Commerce Clause derive principally from a *political* theory of union, not from an *economic* theory of free trade. The function of the clause is to ensure national solidarity, not necessarily economic efficiency."[49] And "although the Court's Commerce Clause opinions have freely employed the language of economics, the decisions have not interpreted the Constitution as establishing the inviolability of the free market."[50] In some contexts, this leads to rather formalistic distinctions. Thus although a state cannot discriminate in taxation, it can choose to provide discriminatory subsidies.[51]

Still, the Court has identified the creation of a "national free market"[52] as one of the goals of the Constitution and the Commerce Clause, and the basic structure of analysis is certainly not unfamiliar to those who have studied international economic agreements such as the GATT or the Treaty of Rome. It would be a great mistake, however, to equate the issues within the United States with those facing the WTO, at least from a U.S. perspective. Tests for ensuring that regulatory actions do not "unnecessarily" burden international trade cannot be evaluated apart from the institutional context in which such tests are to be applied. It is one thing, for example, to adopt such a test for unilateral application by the relevant parties, and a completely different thing to suggest such a test for application by an international dispute settlement body. In evaluating alternatives, then, we should focus on the dangers perceived in assigning the judgments that must be made to an international dispute settlement body. Legal tests that are accepted for application by the judiciary of a federal state raise very different problems for international tribunals.

The jurisprudence of the dormant Commerce Clause must be understood in the overall scope of the Commerce Clause, that is, along with the positive grant of legislative power to the United States. It is a question of jurisdictional allocation and not simply one of supervising potential protectionism. When state action is invalidated under the Commerce Clause, for the most part the Court is simultaneously saying that such action should be undertaken, if at all, by the federal government, or possibly that the federal government should if it so desires specify the conditions under which the states can properly exercise such authority. More broadly, in comparing the WTO context with the United States, an important distinction is that under the dormant Commerce Clause democratic or local choice can be restored by Congressional action, whereas under the WTO the only means of recourse are continued violation subject to some form of retaliation or compensation, or renegotia-

tion (Farber and Hudec 1994).[53] On the other hand, the WTO lacks the ability to invalidate national or state regulation in the way the Supreme Court can. Although this point is often misrepresented by opponents of the WTO, it is crucial to understanding and accepting the WTO's ability to scrutinize national legislation for trade-restrictive effects.

Lessons from the American Approach

With these caveats in mind, important lessons can be drawn from the American approach. First, the threshold question of discrimination has played an essential role in the Supreme Court's approach. The complication posed by the WTO agreements is the role of negotiated market opening commitments that could easily be undermined by both discriminatory regulation and nondiscriminatory regulation that results in differential burdens (or, in the words of the General Agreement on Trade in Services [GATS], "modifies the conditions of competition.")[54] It is doubtful, for example, that most of the market access commitments contained in Article XVI of the GATS would be imposed on states by the courts under the rubric of the Commerce Clause.

GATS Article VI, on domestic regulation, is not explicitly limited to the context of negotiated commitments. Article VI.4 in particular is aimed at achieving in the services sector the broad kind of "horizontal" discipline provided with respect to goods by GATT Articles III, XI, and XX. The basic problem with services, of course, is that, in contrast to goods, regulation of providers and their qualifications is generally regarded as necessary to achieve regulatory aims of safety and consumer protection. For this reason, in addition to technical standards, "qualification requirements and procedures" and "licensing requirements" are regarded as completely acceptable tools for achieving regulatory aims.

How, then, can we ensure that such requirements are "no more burdensome than necessary to assure the quality of the service." From a U.S. perspective, this test immediately appears to be overbroad. Its literal terms do not require any threshold showing of harm or discrimination. Such a broad reading would enable an international tribunal to determine that domestic regulations were "unduly burdensome" for market participants or potential entrants apart from a particular impact on international trade. The European Communities in their submission on this issue took the position that "[d]omestic regulation measures under Article VI are non-discriminatory."[55] Under the introductory clause of Article VI.4, however, the aim is to discipline "unnecessary barriers to trade." In my view, merely demonstrating that a regulation is inefficient or burdensome would not be a sufficient basis for invoking disciplines adopted under Article VI.4.[56] Rather, the challenged regulation must in some sense be more specifically a barrier to trade. This might be demonstrated by showing that the regulation is discriminatory in effect or purpose, and the question then becomes what the legal requirements for demonstrating such effect or purpose ought to be.

As noted above, burdens on the *means* of interstate commerce appear to be subjected to stricter scrutiny under U.S. law. This principle is probably not precisely applicable to the international context, or to the GATS in particular, unless such means are themselves the subject of international commitments (as they might be under the GATS agreements on telecommunications and transport). However, it might be worthwhile to focus special attention on national regulation that directly burdens the *modalities* of trade in services under the GATS. Restrictions on investment, for example, or on travel to purchase or supply services, or on telecommunications used as a means of delivering services, ought to be particularly disfavored when the result is a burden on trade. Such restrictions, therefore, could be a basis for invoking disciplining tests adopted pursuant to Article VI.4.

This point about threshold requirements for invoking tests that rely on balancing (proportionality), fit, or least restrictive alternative is critical. The more demanding the threshold, the more exacting the legal test for reviewing the regulation should be. For the most part, then, the threshold requirement to invoke the scrutiny of a horizontal discipline should be a demonstration of discrimination (on either a national treatment or most-favored-nation basis), and not simply the exclusion of a potential provider from a market. Such discrimination could be either de jure (i.e., "facial") or de facto. As suggested by the United States' domestic approach to these issues, the level of scrutiny applied to the two cases should not be the same.

With regard to the standard that regulations not be "more burdensome than necessary to ensure the quality of the service," two preliminary observations are in order. First, the part of the provision regarding the purpose of such regulation—"to ensure the quality of service"—ought to be interpreted broadly. Quality in some circumstances is not only to be determined with regard to the service delivered to the consumer, but also with regard to externalities and public-regarding goals.[57] To take one of the simpler examples, shipping services might be regulated to ensure environmental quality or to ensure that the means of transport are not overburdened or damaged. Financial services might be regulated not only to ensure the quality of the service to the customer, but also to ensure the responsiveness of service providers to monetary policy and other government goals.

Second, the clause does not by its terms incorporate the kind of weighted balancing analysis found in the U.S. jurisprudence under the Commerce Clause. Although the provision in effect speaks to "burdens," those burdens are not to be compared with the benefits of open trade, but rather with what is necessary to achieve the regulatory goals. If an alternative regulation would equally achieve the goals but with less burden on trade, then the less burdensome regulation must be used.

There is therefore, in my view, no meaningful distinction between the notion of "no more burdensome than necessary" and "least trade restrictiveness." If a measure is more burdensome than necessary, then by hypothesis there must be some measure that would be less burdensome, and by definition that would be a less restrictive alternative. Or perhaps put somewhat more conservatively, any formal or literal distinctions between the two tests are overwhelmed by the ambiguity that leaves a great deal of space for interpretation. Whereas under United States jurisprudence[58] such a test appears to be part of the overall cost-benefit approach, under the GATS it is a separately defined requirement whose terms appear to preclude such balancing. It would be possible (particularly in light of some GATT panel jurisprudence interpreting "necessary" in other contexts) to read "necessary" as meaning "reasonable in relation to the benefits," but there is no reason that "least trade restrictiveness" could not also be read in some broader fashion.

At first blush, a least restrictive alternative test appears to impinge very little on a state's ability to pursue its regulatory goals. A state is required to use an alternative regulatory strategy only if that strategy would equally achieve those goals while burdening or restricting trade to a lesser degree. A problem arises, however, when the alternative strategy poses costs other than the ability to achieve the original policy goals. For example, the alternative strategy might be considerably more expensive. One formulation limits this situation by requiring that the alternative be "reasonably available."[59] This puts one back in the realm of balancing tests in which one of the factors to be balanced is no longer zero. The distinction between this and the overall balancing test (or proportionality test) is that only marginal collateral costs are weighed.[60] It is not entirely clear what those marginal collateral costs are to be weighed against. If a purely marginal analysis is to be applied, then they would be weighed against the benefits of the marginal diminution of trade restrictiveness resulting from adopting the alternative measure.

Conclusion

Many people may find it surprising that the legal norms for enforcing the American common market are so undeveloped and uncertain. They are also, in some respects, less demanding and less sweeping than the corresponding legal standards for the European Union, and even to some extent than the GATT. This is the result of many factors, including the availability of federal regulation whereby Congress chooses to take positive action to create national markets.

Still, the basic tests applied within the United States will be familiar to those who study WTO or European Union law. These include balancing (cost-benefit or proportionality) tests, least restrictive alternative requirements, and regulatory fit analysis. The main thrust of the U.S. approach is to ferret out discrimination, and not to independently impose requirements for the most open or efficient markets. The three primary exceptions to the discrimination requirement (even if proved by indirect means) are burdens on the means of commerce, potential for irreconcilable conflict among applicable state rules, and extraterritorial effect.[61] Each of these three potential or actual consequences will

trigger a more searching scrutiny than nondiscriminatory regulation without these characteristics. Even when the U.S. courts do apply a balancing test, it is strongly weighted in favor of the regulation when there is no discrimination. Regulation will be invalidated only if the burden on commerce is "clearly excessive" compared with the local benefits.

The U.S. approach has been described as confused and unpredictable. This may be true, and it is probably not possible to reconcile all of the conflicting values in a clear and certain test. Despite the carping of judges and academics alike, the Supreme Court has created a sufficiently clear and stable legal framework to support the development of national markets in both goods and services without unduly undermining the values of federalism and the advantages of local regulation. The jurisprudence appears confused precisely because it is nuanced. The Court's decisions require stricter scrutiny when the core elements of a national market are clearly threatened.

In many respects, the circumspect U.S. approach on the domestic front is a caution to the drafters of international treaty obligations. It seems unlikely that the United States would be willing to accept disciplines on local regulation greater than those it has applied within its own borders to local regulation by the states. However, tests such as "least restrictive alternative" and "no more burdensome than necessary" should certainly be acceptable from an American perspective, because these are the familiar vocabulary through which regulatory obstacles to free trade are disciplined in the domestic context. And although legal tests used by domestic courts in the domestic context are not always appropriate in the international context, the United States has accepted standards such as these in both regional and international trade agreements, including those under the World Trade Organization.

As always, the devil is in the details. Here the challenge is to adapt the varying levels of scrutiny and burdens of proof that have been part of the U.S. approach to the specific context of the GATS. But, as suggested here, at least as much thought needs to be given to the threshold violations, the "prima facie" case, that must be established before such disciplining rules can be invoked. These might include not only facial discrimination, but also clear demonstrations of significant discriminatory effect and burdens on the means by which services can be delivered across borders. Care in drafting such "triggering" requirements and the burden of proof to be met by a complaining country should produce greater willingness to adopt serious scrutiny of domestic regulation that interferes with international trade in services.

Endnotes

1. For clarity in this chapter, unless explicitly stated otherwise, "state" is always used in the sense of the individual states of the United States.

2. The Supreme Court first struck down action as violative of the Clause in the absence of a pertinent federal statute in 1849. See Tribe (2000, p. 1047, n. 6) citing The Passenger Cases, 48 U.S. (7 How.) 283 (1849). Shortly thereafter, in *Cooley v. Board of Wardens,* 53 U.S. (12 How.) 299 (1851), the Court adopted a test that attempted to categorize the subject matter of regulation as "local" or "national," depending on whether state diversity or national uniformity was required.

3. See *Camps Newfound/Owatonna, Inc. v. Town of Harrison,* 520 U.S. 564, 607 (1997) (Thomas, J., dissenting, joined by Chief Justice Rehnquist and Justice Scalia); *Bendix Autolite Corp. v. Midwesco Enterprises, Inc.,* 486 U.S. 888, 895 (Scalia, J., concurring in the judgment).

4. This view is not new. See also Eule (1982): "the only thing consistently predictable about the Court [in its Dormant Commerce Clause decisions] is its continued unpredictability."

5. At one time, the ability of Congress to exercise power under the Commerce Clause was thought to be nearly unlimited because virtually every aspect of daily life could be viewed cumulatively as affecting or being affected by interstate commerce in some way. In 1995, however, the Supreme Court inaugurated a series of decisions that ultimately defined some limits to congressional power under the Commerce Clause. *United States v. Lopez,* 514 U.S. 549 (1995) (striking down federal law making it a criminal offense to possess a firearm in a school zone).

6. United States Constitution, Art. 6, clause 2: "This Constitution, and the Laws of the United States which shall be made in Pursuance thereof; and all treaties made, or which shall be made, under the Authority of the United States, shall be the supreme Law of the Land; and the Judges of every State shall be bound thereby, any Thing in the Constitution or Laws of any State notwithstanding."

7. A few cases have, however, upheld the power of the states to exclude diseased or potentially diseased products. See, for example, *Mintz v. Baldwin,* 289 U.S. 346 (1933); *Maine v. Taylor,* 477 U.S. 131 (1986). A state cannot, however, discriminate between in-state and out-of-state products in its restrictions on "noxious" articles.

8. *Healy v. Beer Institute, Inc.,* 491 U.S. 324 (1989).

9. *Dean Milk Co. v. City of Madison,* 340 U.S. 349 (1951).

10. Many of the cases involve regulations not at the state level but at more local levels, such as county or municipality.

11. The Court has, however, ruled that municipal regulation that discriminates against both in-state and out-of-state commerce from outside the municipality is discriminatory under the Commerce Clause. See *Fort Gratiot Sanitary*

Landfill, Inc. v. Michigan Dept. Natural Resources, 504 U.S. 353 (1992); *C&A Carbone, Inc. v. Town of Clarkstown,* 511 U.S. 383 (1994).

12. *C&A Carbone, Inc. v. Town of Clarkstown,* 511 U.S. 383, 392 (1994).

13. In one case the Court noted that the burden of justification in the presence of facial discrimination is "so heavy that 'facial discrimination by itself may be a fatal defect,'" *Oregon Waste Systems, Inc. v. Dept. Environmental Quality,* 511 U.S. 93, 101 (1994) (quoting *Hughes v. Oklahoma,* 441 U.S. 322, 337 (1979).

14. *Lewis v. BT Investment Managers, Inc.,* 447 U.S. 27, 36 (1980) (quoting *Philadelphia v. New Jersey,* 437 U.S. 617, at 626-627 (1978).

15. *Maine v. Taylor,* 477 U.S. 131 (1986).

16. *Great Atlantic & Pacific Tea Co., Inc. v. Cottrell,* 424 U.S. 366 (1976) (striking down a state statute restricting milk market access to producers from states that provided reciprocal access). See also *New Energy Co. of Indiana v. Limbach,* 486 U.S. 269, 274–275 (1988).

17. *Pike v. Bruce Church, Inc.,* 397 U.S. 137, 145 (1970) (export restriction in the form of a packing requirement). See also *Dean Milk Co. v. City of Madison,* 340 U.S. 349 (1951) (ordinance requiring local pasteurizing and bottling of milk).

18. *H.P. Hood & Sons v. Du Mond,* 336 U.S. 525 (1949).

19. *Reeves, Inc. v. Stake,* 447 U.S. 429 (1980) (upholding the policy of a cement plant owned by South Dakota of selling preferentially to state residents during times of cement shortage).

20. *Pike v. Bruce Church, Inc.,* 397 U.S. 137, 142 (1970). See also *Brown-Forman Distillers Corp. v. New York State Liquor Authority,* 476 U.S. 573 (1986) (regulation will be struck down "if the burden on interstate commerce clearly exceeds the local benefits"). Justice Scalia has expressed particular criticism for the cost-benefit strand of analysis under the dormant Commerce Clause. See *CTS Corp. v. Dynamics Corp.,* 481 U.S. 69, 95 (1987) (Scalia, J., concurring); *Bendix Autolite Corp. v. Midwesco Enterprises, Inc.,* 486 U.S. 888, 897.

21. *Philadelphia v. New Jersey,* 437 U.S. 617, 624 (1980) ("where simple economic protectionism is effected by state legislation, a virtually *per se* rule of invalidity has been applied").

22. However, a state may not use a nondiscriminatory tax to fund a discriminatory subsidy. *West Lynn Creamery, Inc. v. Healy,* 512 U.S. 186 (1994).

23. *New Energy Co. of Indiana v. Limbach,* 486 U.S. 269 (1988); *Camps Newfound/Owatonna, Inc. v. Town of Harrison,* 520 U.S. 564, 589 (1997). However, it should be noted that the Court has "never squarely confronted the constitutionality of subsidies" (*New Energy v. Limbach* at 589), quoting *West Lynn Creamery v. Healy,* 512 U.S. 186, 199 (1994).

24. *Exxon Corp. v. Governor of Maryland,* 437 U.S. 117 (1978).

25. *Raymond Motor Transportation, Inc. v. Rice,* 434 U.S. 429 (1978).

26. *Kassel v. Consolidated Freightways Corp.,* 450 U.S. 662 (1981).

27. *Southern Pacific Co. v. Arizona,* 325 U.S. 761 (1945).

28. See, for example, Tribe (2000, p. 1073).

29. See, for example, *Brown-Forman Distillers Corp. v. New York State Liquor Authority,* 476 U.S. 573 (1986) (striking down state regulation requiring liquor producer selling to wholesalers to affirm sales price was no higher than lowest price sold in other states); *Healy v. Beer Institute, Inc.,* 491 U.S. 324 (1989) (similar regulation regarding beer).

30. *Bendix Autolite Corp. v. Midwesco Enterprises,* 486 U.S. 888, 897 (1988) (Scalia, J., concurring).
31. *Pike v. Bruce Church, Inc.,* 397 U.S. 137, 142 (1970).
32. See, for example, *Minnesota v. Barber,* 136 U.S. 313 (1890) (striking down a law requiring meat to be inspected by a local inspector 24 hours before slaughter); *Dean Milk Co. v. Madison,* 340 U.S. 349 (1951) (invalidating municipal ordinance requiring pasteurization within five miles of the town center).
33. *Minnesota v. Clover Leaf Creamery Co.,* 449 U.S. 456 (1981). The decision stands in sharp contrast to the European decision striking down aspects of Denmark's law on returnable bottles. *Commission v. Denmark,* Case 302/86, [1988] ECR 4607.
34. *Lewis v. BT Investment Managers, Inc.,* 447 U.S. 27, 43–44 (1980).
35. *Camps Newfound/Owatonna, Inc. v. Town of Harrison,* 520 U.S. 564 (1997). The Court rejected the argument that "campers are not 'articles of commerce.'" It concluded that the "services that petitioner provides to its principally out-of-state campers clearly have a substantial effect on commerce, as to state restrictions on making those services available to nonresidents" (at 574). The Court recognized that the discriminatory tax "functionally serves as an export tariff that targets out-of-state consumers by taxing the businesses that principally serve them" (at 580–81).
36. *H.P. Hood & Sons v. Du Mond,* 336 U.S. 525 (1949).
37. *Fort Gratiot Sanitary Landfill, Inc. v. Michigan Dept. of Natural Resources,* 504 U.S. 353 (1992); *Philadelphia v. New Jersey,* 437 U.S. 617 (1978).
38. In *Philadelphia v. New Jersey,* for example, the Court based its decision on the discrimination against "articles of commerce coming from outside the State." 437 U.S. at 627.
39. *Zobel v. Williams,* 457 U.S. 55 (1982).
40. United States Constitution, Article 4.
41. *Supreme Court of New Hampshire v. Piper,* 470 U.S. 274, 280 (1985).
42. *Toomer v. Witsell,* 334 U.S. 385, 396 (1948) ("one of the privileges which the Clause guarantees to citizens of State A is that of doing business in State B on terms of substantial equality with the citizens of that State.") On the other hand, the Court has held recreation not to be one of the privileges so protected. *Baldwin v. Montana Fish & Game Comm'n,* 436 U.S. 371 (1978).
43. *Supreme Court of Va. v. Friedman,* 487 U.S. 59 (1988); *Barnard v. Thorstenn,* 489 U.S. 546 (1989).
44. *Doe v. Bolton,* 410 U.S. 179 (1973) (involving abortion services).
45. *Hicklin v. Orbeck,* 437 U.S. 518 (1978).
46. *Supreme Court of New Hampshire v. Piper,* 470 U.S. 274, 284 (1985).
47. This is a common legal structure. For example, in a case of battery, the plaintiff must first prove that the defendant intentionally touched the plaintiff. Then the defendant can offer a justification, such as consent. In response, the plaintiff might prove the consent was invalid, perhaps because the plaintiff was incapacitated or under age.
48. As at least a technical matter, the complaining party must demonstrate nullification and impairment of benefits under the agreement, but such nullification and impairment are presumed in the case of a violation. Under the GATT, a party can also seek redress for nonviolation nullification and impairment, and it is proof of that that consti-

tutes the prima facie case in the absence of a violation of GATT obligations.
49. Tribe (2000, p. 1057), citing *Baldwin v. G.A.F. Seelig, Inc.,* 294 U.S. 511 (1935).
50. Tribe 2000, p. 1058.
51. See, for example, *New Energy Co. of Indiana v. Limbach,* 486 U.S. 269, 278 (1988).
52. *General Motors v. Tracy,* 519 U.S. 278, 298 (1997).
53. The Farber and Hudec article provides an excellent overview of the relationship between the legal approaches to disciplining discriminatory regulation under the Commerce Clause and the GATT.
54. General Agreement on Trade in Services, Article XVII.3.
55. WTO doc. S/WPDR/W/14, 1 May 2000, paragraph 8.
56. I do not, however, take this position with regard to sectoral disciplines, where it seems to be that the narrowing of focus and greater detail of obligations raises very different issues.
57. Compare the GATS Annex on Telecommunications, paragraph 5(e); WTO Working Party on Professional Services, Disciplines on Domestic Regulation in the Accountancy Sector, S/L/64, December 17, 1998. It is not clear from the text of the GATS how the general exceptions of Article XIV should apply to measures adopted pursuant to Article VI.4. One could read Article VI.4 narrowly and allow the specific requirements mentioned in Article VI.4 to be justified under Article XIV as well. Because Article XIV also adopts a "necessity" for its more general provisions, the consequences of a broad or narrow reading of "quality of service" under Article VI.4 (and measures adopted thereunder) may be small. One important difference may be in the burden of proof. If Article VI.4 is read narrowly, then an effective violation would occur if a licensing or qualification measure was not aimed at ensuring the quality of service. The burden would then shift to the respondent to justify the measure under the broader criteria of Article XIV.
58. See *Pike v. Bruce Church, Inc.* discussed above.
59. See Trachtman (2002) and compare the GATT Agreement on the Application of Sanitary and Phytosanitary Measures, article 5.6.
60. If such collateral costs are to be considered in determining whether a state is required to implement an alternative but in some respects more costly measure, it is unclear whether both private and public costs are to be taken into account.
61. In nearly all cases, whenever one of these exceptions applies it can also be argued that there is a discriminatory effect.

References

Eule, Julian N. 1982. "Laying the Dormant Commerce Clause to Rest," *Yale Law Journal* 91: 425–85.

Farber, Daniel A., and Robert E. Hudec. 1994. "Free Trade and the Regulatory State: A GATT's-Eye View of the Dormant Commerce Clause." *Vanderbilt Law Review* 47: 1401–40.

Lawrence, Michael A. 1998. "Toward a More Coherent Dormant Commerce Clause: A Proposed Unitary Framework." *Harvard Journal of Law and Public Policy* 21: 395–465.

Trachtman, Joel P. 2002. "Lessons for GATS Article VI from the SPS, TBT and GATT Treatment of Domestic Regulation." Paper prepared for OECD–World Bank Services Experts Meeting, Paris, March 4–5.

Tribe, Laurence H. 2000. *American Constitutional Law.* Vol. 1. New York: Foundation Press.

5

LESSONS FOR THE GATS FROM EXISTING WTO RULES ON DOMESTIC REGULATION

Joel P. Trachtman

Executive Summary

One of the most important and difficult issues in international trade is the relationship between international trade liberalization and domestic regulatory autonomy. This issue has been addressed in a variety of ways in the goods sector, and is still being worked out according to a dynamic process of substantive and institutional change. Although regulatory autonomy is needed to allow local regulation to respond to local conditions, there are times when regulatory autonomy is abused as concealed protectionism or is not sufficiently motivated to provide efficient regulation. Transparency can help to reduce concealed protectionism, but it cannot alone eliminate the more persistent and the more deeply embedded inefficiencies.

In relation to this tension between trade liberalization and domestic regulatory autonomy, services trade is at least comparable to goods trade. Of course there are significant differences between goods and services trade, and among services trade sectors, but there are sufficient similarities to make it worthwhile to study the approaches to domestic regulatory autonomy in goods in connection with discussions of intensified approaches to domestic regulatory autonomy in services.

Under the Sanitary and Phytosanitary (SPS) Agreement, the Technical Barriers to Trade (TBT) Agreement, and the General Agreement on Tariffs and Trade (GATT), regulatory autonomy is constrained. This chapter compares these three sources of WTO law relating to goods, and compares them with the General Agreement on Trade in Services GATS, in order to advance an array of options for services negotiators and to suggest how negotiators might discriminate among these options.

There seem to be no general, or *horizontal*, reasons to treat services regulation, as a whole, differently than goods regulation. It may be that certain areas of services regulation merit special treatment of one kind or another. For example, the fact that much of financial regulation takes the form of *institutional* regulation accentuates the kind of jurisdictional problem associated with the product–process distinction in the goods field. That is, the institution offering cross-border banking services may be

Many thanks to Dale Honeck, Gabrielle Marceau, Aaditya Mattoo, Julia Nielson, Joseph Norton, Pierre Sauvé, Marc Steinberg, and other participants in the OECD–World Bank Services Experts Meeting held in Paris on March 4–5, 2002, for their advice in connection with this chapter.

located (at least in formal terms) in Luxembourg, although it offers services in the United Kingdom. Although trade may be facilitated by a regime of mutual recognition (which in fact exists in the European Communities), and although it may seem natural to allow a Luxembourg bank to be regulated by Luxembourg, there is the possibility for adverse externalization (e.g., Bank of Credit and Commerce International [BCCI]). There are also possibilities for races to the bottom, accentuated by possibilities for externalization.

Therefore, it seems worthwhile to evaluate the range of disciplines offered by the SPS Agreement, the TBT Agreement, and the GATT for horizontal adoption in the field of services. This can initially be accomplished in selective sectors, on a trial basis, as in the field of accountancy. Where standards like "necessity" or "proportionality" are to be used, it would be wise to use consistent language, unless a different meaning is desired. However, in this field, there seems little reason to use different formulations for the same concept in different sectors. This would appear to apply to areas like discrimination, necessity, proportionality, performance regulation rather than design regulation, requirements of recognition, reference to international standards, and other, more general disciplines. More specific rules, such as harmonization of regulation, either alone or as a prerequisite for specified types of recognition, obviously must be accomplished on a sectoral or even an issue-by-issue basis. The European Union provides a rich source of experience in this area. Some more specific recommendations follow:

1. Consider replacing the national treatment language of GATS Article XVII with language that specifically allows for justification of differential treatment, such as that of Article 2.3 of the SPS Agreement.
2. It is difficult to understand why the proportionality requirement of GATS Article VI.5 is so weak. Consider horizontally applying language such as that in paragraph 2 of the Accountancy Disciplines. It is worthwhile to explore the proposal made by the EC in its Communication on Necessity to provide a necessity test, with an additional proportionality defense. The weakness of Article VI.5 places a premium on action under VI.4.

3. Article XIV of the GATS contains inappropriately restricted regulatory goals (e.g., it does not refer to "exhaustible natural resources," as does Article XX[g] of GATT), and should be expanded along the lines of paragraphs 2 and 25 of the Accountancy Disciplines to refer more broadly to "legitimate objectives." The regulatory goals referred to in Article VI.4(b) should also be expanded beyond "quality of the service."
4. In the matter of "scientific basis"/risk assessment, the SPS innovation of requiring states to go through a process of risk assessment to validate their regulation could be considered for extension beyond the SPS area. If an explicit "rational regulatory basis" requirement is imposed, a provisional "precautionary principle"–type authority should also be provided, along the lines of Article 5.7 of the SPS Agreement.
5. The "prudential carve-out" in financial services seems too broad, although I recognize that it has been popular with member states.
6. With regard to the equivalence/recognition requirement, Article VI.4 should be used to provide for either horizontal or vertical requirements of equivalency. For example, paragraph 19 of the Accountancy Disciplines requires some level of equivalency.
7. Both the SPS Agreement and the TBT Agreement provide incentives for compliance with certain international standards. This also could be provided in services on either a horizontal or vertical basis.

This chapter provides a comparison among the SPS, TBT, GATT, and GATS agreements that is organized by reference to different types of general disciplines. Although these disciplines often work in synergy with one another, and so should not simply be compared on their own, this is a first step toward developing a taxonomy of disciplines.

Lessons for Services Trade Negotiations from the SPS, TBT, and GATT Agreements

One of the most important and difficult issues in international trade is the relationship between international trade liberalization and domestic regulatory autonomy. This issue has been addressed in a variety of ways in the goods sector, and is still being worked out according to a dynamic process of substantive and institutional change. Although regulatory autonomy is needed to allow local regulation to respond to local conditions, there are times when regulatory autonomy is abused as concealed protectionism or is not sufficiently motivated to provide efficient regulation. Transparency can help reduce concealed protectionism but it cannot alone eliminate the more persistent and more deeply embedded inefficiencies.

In relation to this tension between trade liberalization and domestic regulatory autonomy, services trade is at least comparable to goods trade. Of course there are significant differences between goods and services trade and among services trade sectors, but there are sufficient similarities to make it worthwhile to study the approaches to domestic regulatory autonomy in goods in connection with discussions of intensified approaches to domestic regulatory autonomy in services (see WTO Working Party on Domestic Regulation 1996).

Under the Sanitary and Phytosanitary (SPS) Agreement (WTO 1994a), the Technical Barriers to Trade (TBT) Agreement (WTO 1994b), and the General Agreement on Tariffs and Trade (GATT), national regulatory autonomy is constrained. This chapter compares these three sources of WTO law relating to goods, and compares them with the General Agreement on Trade in Services (GATS) to advance an array of options for services negotiators and to suggest how negotiators might discriminate among these options.

First, there seem to be no general, or *horizontal*, reasons to treat services regulation, as a whole, differently from goods regulation. It may be that certain areas of services regulation merit special treatment of one kind or another. For example, the fact that much financial regulation takes the form of *institutional* regulation accentuates the kind of jurisdictional problem associated with the product-process distinction in the goods field. That is, the institution offering cross-border banking services may be located (at least in formal terms) in Luxembourg, although it offers services in the United Kingdom. Whereas trade may be facilitated by a regime of mutual recognition (which in fact exists in the European Union [EU]), and whereas it may seem natural to allow a Luxembourg bank to be regulated by Luxembourg, there is the possibility

for adverse externalization (e.g., Bank of Credit and Commerce International [BCCI]). There are also possibilities for races to the bottom, accentuated by possibilities for externalization (Trachtman 2000).

Therefore, it seems worthwhile to evaluate the range of disciplines offered by the SPS Agreement, the TBT Agreement, and the GATT for adoption in the field of services. This can be accomplished initially in selected sectors, on a trial basis, as in the field of accountancy. Where standards like "necessity" or "proportionality" are to be used, it would be wise to use consistent language unless a different meaning is desired. The WTO's Appellate Body has incorporated the doctrine of *effet utile* in its jurisprudence and will seek meaning in any differences of language. In this field, however, there seems little reason to use different formulations for the same concept in different sectors, although evidently there may be reasons to treat different sectors differently. This would appear to apply to areas like discrimination, necessity, proportionality, performance regulation rather than design regulation, requirements of recognition, reference to international standards, and other more general disciplines. More specific rules, such as harmonization of regulation, either alone or as a prerequisite for specified types of recognition, obviously must be accomplished on a sectoral or even an issue-by-issue basis. The EU provides a rich source of experience in this area.

This chapter provides a comparison, organized by reference to different types of general disciplines. Although these disciplines often work in synergy with one another and so should not simply be compared on their own, this is a first step toward developing a taxonomy of disciplines.

Comparison of the Disciplines of the SPS, TBT, and GATT with the Disciplines of the GATS

To take advantage of the experience in goods, we first must develop a taxonomy of the instruments available there.[1] Sources of discipline on domestic regulation include the SPS Agreement, the TBT Agreement, and the GATT itself. The original 1979 Standards Code, the predecessor to the TBT Agreement, was developed to provide disciplines on national technical regulations and nonbinding standards that were more specific than those provided under the GATT.

In the decade following the 1979 Tokyo Round, a consensus emerged that "the Standards Code had failed to stem disruptions of trade in agricultural products caused by proliferating technical restrictions" (Roberts 1998, pp. 377, 380). Furthermore, of course, one of the great advances of the Uruguay Round was to introduce greater disciplines on other types of agricultural protectionism, including quotas and domestic price supports. To protect this advance from potential regulatory defection, it was viewed as necessary to establish the SPS Agreement and to have it apply universally, not plurilaterally (Roberts 1998). Of course, enforcement of the original Standards Code was weakened by the requirement of consensus to establish a panel and to adopt a panel report—a weakness that was remedied by the Uruguay Round's Dispute Settlement Understanding. Finally, the original Standards Code failed to address measures regulating production and processing methods (PPMs).[2] It is noteworthy that the SPS Agreement imposes stronger disciplines than the TBT Agreement precisely because it was perceived that sanitary and phytosanitary standards were used more frequently for protectionist purposes, and/or the value in trade liberalization was perceived as greater in the SPS field than in the TBT field. It would be worthwhile to consider whether domestic regulation of services is more like the TBT field or the SPS field in these terms.

The GATS was negotiated separately from the goods agreements, and neither the TBT Agreement nor the SPS Agreement applies to services,[3] because negotiators thought the services sphere too heterogeneous for the application of general disciplines on standard-setting (see Self 1996). It is perhaps worth noting that Chapter 9 of the North American Free Trade Agreement (NAFTA) contains an integrated standards "code" that applies to both goods and services, but only to a limited range of services.[4]

Therefore, the SPS, TBT, and GATT agreements on one hand and the GATS on the other hand each contain a number of *different* disciplines on national regulation. In general, these disciplines apply cumulatively: whereas application of the SPS Agreement excludes application of the TBT Agreement, and an SPS measure that is permitted under the SPS Agreement will be presumed to comply with the GATT, other measures must generally meet the requirements of all applicable agreements. In the *Bananas* case, the Appellate Body found that the GATS could apply to the same set of circumstances to which the GATT applied (WTO Appellate Body Report 1997). This section discusses selected disciplines under the following categories:

- National treatment or most-favored-nation (MFN)–based antidiscrimination rules[5]
- Necessity, least trade-restrictive alternative, or proportionality requirements
- Requirements for national measures to conform to international standards
- Other requirements of harmonization
- Regulation of regulatory goals and preservation of national autonomy in goal setting
- Requirements for a scientific or other prudential basis for regulation
- Requirements for internal consistency across regulatory subjects
- Permission for "precautionary" action
- Balancing tests
- Requirements of recognition
- The distinction between regulation of products (or services) as such, and regulation of their production processes, and related issues of the scope for regulation intended to protect extraterritorial values.

These disciplines work in varying combinations within each of the various sources of World Trade Organization (WTO) law. They also work together from the broader perspective of general WTO law. They may best be understood as addressing, to varying degrees, one (or both) of two fundamental questions: first, are the regulatory benefits sufficient to justify the costs in terms of restraint of trade,[6] and, second, is the restraint of trade intentional? The first question is the most difficult and requires, in each case, the application of comparative institutional analysis (see, for example, Abbott and Snidal 2001).

Nondiscrimination: National Treatment and MFN

Obligations of nondiscrimination in internal regulation, including the application of internal regulation at the border, occupy a primary position in the GATT, and the SPS and TBT Agreements although each document has slightly different formulations. These obligations, although also important in the

GATS, are relatively untested as applied to services. It might be argued that nondiscrimination is adequately addressed under Article XVII of the GATS, and requires no further evaluation here (see WTO Working Party on Professional Services 1998). The border between Article VI on one hand and Articles XVI and XVII on the other hand is expected to be based on the fact that Article VI deals with bona fide regulatory measures (see Low and Mattoo 1999). As will be seen, nondiscrimination is not by itself an easily applied test, and its application requires elements of evaluation associated with necessity or proportionality tests, including implicit determinations of the bona fide nature of regulation.

GATT Article III.4 It is appropriate to begin with Article III.4 of the GATT, which provides as follows:

> The products of the territory of any contracting party imported into the territory of any other contracting party shall be accorded treatment no less favorable than that accorded to like products of national origin in respect of all laws, regulations and requirements affecting their internal sale, offering for sale, purchase, transportation, distribution or use.

This language has been interpreted in a number of GATT and WTO cases. Most recently, in the *Asbestos* case, the Appellate Body emphasized the fact that differential treatment may be acceptable so long as it is "no less favorable" (WTO Appellate Body Report 2001a, para. 100). Article XVII.3 of the GATS specifically provides that "[f]ormally identical or formally different treatment shall be considered to be less favorable if it modifies the conditions of competition in favor of services or service suppliers of the Member compared to like services or service suppliers of any other Member." This is one way in which the bona fide nature of regulation may be implicitly evaluated.

To apply any nondiscrimination test it is necessary to determine that two goods are in a similar category (similar enough to deserve treatment "no less favorable"): in WTO parlance, that the two goods are "like products." Discrimination consists of treating like things differently, or different things alike. In the *Asbestos* case, the Appellate Body found that "likeness" under Article III.4 is, "fundamen-

tally, a determination about the nature and extent of a competitive relationship between and among products" (WTO Appellate Body Report 2001a, para. 99). The Appellate Body rejected the panel's finding that the goods that contained asbestos were like products with the goods that did not contain asbestos. The Appellate Body examined the evidence under four basic criteria: physical properties, end uses, consumer tastes and habits, and tariff classification. The Appellate Body determined that panels must examine the physical properties of products that affect the competitive relationship in the marketplace, including health risks.[7] The Appellate Body resoundingly concluded, "carcinogenicity, or toxicity, constitutes, as we see it, a defining aspect of the physical properties of chrysotile asbestos fibres" (WTO Appellate Body Report 2001a, para. 114).

This type of "like-products" analysis is necessary in any case of alleged discrimination. There is little reason to believe it would not be necessary to engage in like-products analysis under the antidiscrimination provisions of the SPS and TBT Agreements, or under Article XVII of the GATS.

SPS Article 2.3 of the SPS Agreement provides as follows: "Members shall ensure that their sanitary and phytosanitary measures do not arbitrarily or unjustifiably discriminate between Members where identical or similar conditions prevail, including between their own territory and that of other members. Sanitary and phytosanitary measures shall not be applied in a manner which would constitute a disguised restriction on international trade."

This language evidently departs from that of Article III of the GATT, adapting its operative language from the *chapeau* of Article XX of the GATT.[8] Recall that under the GATT these requirements of Article XX would only apply where a violation of Article III (or another provision of the GATT, such as Article XI) was already established. The SPS Agreement lacks a more basic prohibition of discrimination among *products*, along the lines of Article III of the GATT. Notably, Article 2.3 does not contain a reference to "like products," but rather simply prohibits discrimination among member states, including the importing state. Note that Article 5.5 of the SPS Agreement restricts "arbitrary or unjustifiable distinctions" between "different situations, if such distinctions result in discrimination or a disguised restriction on international trade."

In the *Australian Salmon* decision (WTO Appellate Body Report 1998a; see also Pauwelyn 1999), the Appellate Body found that an unexplained distinction in the levels of protection imposed by Australia resulted in disguised restriction on international trade, in violation of Article 5.5 of the SPS Agreement and, by implication, of Article 2.3. It is interesting that in the *Australian Salmon* decision the Appellate Body did not adopt the kind of balancing test it had used in the *Shrimp* decision (WTO Appellate Body Report 1998c) to determine whether the U.S. measure in the latter case constituted arbitrary or unjustifiable discrimination pursuant to the *chapeau* of Article XX. We discuss below the balancing test developed by the Appellate Body in *Asbestos* and *Korea-Beef* in connection with the application of the "necessity" test of Articles XX(b) and (d).

TBT Article 2.1 of the TBT Agreement, following much more closely Article III (and the MFN requirement, Article I) of the GATT, requires "treatment no less favorable than that accorded to like products of national origin and to like products originating in any other country." However, it is worth noting that the TBT Agreement has no equivalent of Article XX, providing an exemption under certain circumstances.

GATS Article XVII.1 of the GATS provides that:

> In the sectors inscribed in its schedule, and subject to any conditions and qualifications set out therein, each Member shall accord to services and service suppliers of any other Member, in respect of all measures affecting the supply of services, treatment no less favorable than that it accords to its own like services and service suppliers.

Thus national treatment under the GATS is not universal but is subject to the positive listing of the relevant service sector in the relevant state's schedule (see Mattoo 1997). In addition, it is subject within each listed sector to the negative listing of any exception to the national treatment obligation in that schedule. Deciding that national treatment should not be a general principle, as in the GATT,

but rather a concession to be bargained over is one of the distinctive features of the GATS. The core of a nondiscrimination obligation such as national treatment is the comparison between the favored good, service, or service supplier and the disfavored one. Article XVII sets up the comparison as being one between "like" services or service suppliers, referring on its face to the "like-products" concept articulated pursuant to Article III of the GATT.

What makes two services "like"? For example, is the underwriting of a bond issue "like" a bank lending transaction? If so, why are different reserve requirements and capital requirements applicable? Does it matter for regulatory purposes that one transaction is effected by a bank that accepts insured deposits? Similarly, is Internet telephony "like" standard telephone service? More fundamentally, is it permissible to make distinctions between services on the basis of the identity and structure of the service supplier as well as the way the service appears to the consumer? Although it would be possible to apply to services something analogous to the Border Tax Adjustments factors, it is not clear that these parameters of likeness make sense even in the GATT.

The Border Tax Adjustments report adumbrated the following basic (but not exhaustive) parameters of likeness: (a) the properties of the products, (b) the end uses of the products, (c) consumer tastes, and (d) tariff classification (GATT Working Party Report 1970). This approach is intended to approximate the competitive relationship between the relevant goods—it is not as accurate or refined as simply testing cross-elasticity of demand. But the point is that this test is relatively ignorant of factors that motivate regulation. The economic theory of regulation suggests that regulation is necessary precisely where consumers cannot adequately distinguish relevant goods—where the goods are in close competitive relation. Thus a competitive relationship test for likeness will often result in a finding that goods that differ by the parameter addressed by regulation are indeed like and should be treated the same.

Under GATT Article III jurisprudence, regulation of production processes may not be "subject to" Article III, and therefore would be an illegal quantitative restriction under Article XI, unless an exception applies under Article XX. This "strong" version of the product-process distinction is disputed; another version suggests that regulation of production processes remains "subject to" Article III, but that differing production processes would not ordinarily be sufficient to render two otherwise similar goods not "like" and that, therefore, less favorable treatment of one of these "like" goods would violate Article III.

In either version, the product-process distinction serves as a kind of territorially based allocation of jurisdiction in which the product, which travels to the importing state, is permitted to be regulated by the importing state. On the other hand, regulation of the production process, which is assumed to take place in the exporting state, is either not "subject to" Article III, and therefore unprotected from the strict scrutiny of Article XI, or violates Article III (and regulation by the host state is only permitted if justified under Article XX). In *Asbestos* the Appellate Body was careful to point out that in addition to the need to determine the existence of like products under Article III.4 (which is, as pointed out above, a question of market competition) it is necessary to find that the imported product is treated "less favorably." How this language would apply to an otherwise origin-neutral process regulation has not yet been addressed.

The situation is quite different in the GATS, where regulation of service providers is expressly validated and subjected to the national treatment criterion (see Mattoo 1997). Because in many services service provider—person or firm—may itself be a part of the continuing nature of the service, a different arrangement seems appropriate. That is, it seems less obvious (if it is at all obvious in the goods sector) that the service-importing state should not have equal rights to regulate the service provider itself, even though on the territory of the home country. In other words, the process by which a service is "produced" (a loan issued, a professional trained) may determine the actual characteristics of the ultimate service "product" (the loan, the training, the advice, the treatment). This would validate traditional institutional regulation of most types of financial institutions, as well as regulation of the structure of law firms or other types of service providers.

Furthermore, we must distinguish between the two main vehicles for trade in services: cross-border provision (including consumption abroad) and commercial presence.[9] In cases of commercial presence, the foreign service provider would be present,

at least to some extent, in the territory of the service-importing state, and thus would more naturally be subject to the full territorial jurisdiction of that state.[10] The need for commercial presence indeed reflects the fact that a service is often "produced" and "consumed" simultaneously and in the same place. We have a much less "natural"—and more difficult—problem of allocation of regulatory jurisdiction in connection with cross-border provision of services, whereby production and consumption need not happen in the same place. However, as seems to be recognized in Article XVII, the importing state should not be prevented, prima facie, from regulating the service provider in such cases.

The structure of Article XVII seems, on its face, to indicate that a national service regulation imposed on a foreign service provider must meet two tests: it must provide treatment no less favorable than that accorded domestic like services, and it must provide treatment no less favorable than that accorded domestic like service providers. Therefore, even if the service providers are not "like," and there is thus no possible basis for finding illegal discrimination between them, it is still possible that the services they provide may be "like," giving rise to a claim of violation of the requirement of national treatment. On its face this might seem an absurd result and might invalidate, for example, a regulation that requires a bank to maintain reserves different from those maintained by an insurance company prior to making a loan, because although the service providers are not "like," the services are.

Thus a better reading would separate the evaluation of treatment of services from the evaluation of treatment of service providers. It simply would evaluate regulation of services as services, by determining whether the regulation treats "like" services alike, period. If this were the case, regulation of service providers would be evaluated to determine only whether like service providers, as service providers, are treated alike.[11] Using this interpretation there would be no violation of national treatment if like services were treated differently where the reason for the difference in treatment is the regulation of the service provider as service provider. This is likely to be the interpretation that a WTO panel or the Appellate Body would apply.

In effect, such an approach would replicate a kind of product-process distinction as a service-service provider distinction. But contrary to the more doubtful case of products, host state regulation of the "process" or the service provider—often geographically located in the host state—would be validated (subject only to a strict national treatment constraint). Regulations applying to the service, as such, would only be evaluated to determine whether like services are treated alike, whereas regulations applying to the service provider, as such, would only be evaluated to determine whether like service providers are treated alike.[12] The WTO Dispute Settlement Body would be required to distinguish between regulation of services and regulation of service providers. In addition, the analogy to products might be taken one step further to suggest stronger constraints on host state regulation of the service provider than on the service. Of course, there is nothing in the GATS that would support this treatment.

As noted at the beginning of this section, GATT/WTO dispute resolution has been unable to provide a predictable, consistent approach to determining when products are "like." We cannot expect GATS dispute resolution to do better. Thus, for example, we might ask whether two accountants with advanced university degrees from universities in different states are "like service providers"? Are two banks from different states in which they are required to establish different levels of reserves "like service providers"? Similarly, are the loans provided by these two banks "like services"? Under GATT jurisprudence these questions cannot be answered predictably or in the abstract but must be determined on a case-by-case basis. Although this jurisprudence results in a degree of unpredictability, the Appellate Body has now addressed several cases, thus providing experience in how these multiple factors are likely to be viewed and applied. The question for us is whether this situation of case-by-case analysis by the dispute settlement mechanism is superior to a more discrete, ex ante specification that could be provided by treatymaking or other quasi-legislative process?

Given the broad definition of "like products" provided by the Appellate Body in the area of goods, it is likely that WTO dispute settlement will place increasing emphasis on the "no less favorable" component of national treatment obligations. This component may be interpreted as containing some element of judgment, based on balancing or proportionality concerns, as to whether the domestic regulatory categories are appropriately justified by nonprotectionist regulatory policy objectives— hence, the relationship between national treatment and necessity. On the other hand, Article XVII.3 of the GATS, defining "no less favorable" in terms of the conditions of competition, may limit this type of flexibility in the services context.

Necessity/Least Trade-Restrictive Alternative/Proportionality

Aside from antidiscrimination rules, the most important general discipline on domestic regulation in WTO law is the necessity test, which is generally interpreted as requiring the domestic regulation to be the least trade-restrictive alternative method of achieving the desired policy objective. "Proportionality" may include least trade-restrictive alternative analysis, but includes other tests as well. To provide the context for "necessity" and proportionality in the GATS it is necessary briefly to outline the way these concepts present themselves in the GATT, the TBT Agreement, and the SPS Agreement.

GATT XX(b) and (d)   Of course, the exceptional provisions of GATT Article XX only become relevant after a violation of another provision of the GATT is found. This is a significant distinction from both the SPS and the TBT Agreements, which apply requirements of least trade restrictiveness independently. Under the GATT, of course, the least trade-restrictive alternative requirement of Articles XX(b) and (d) is a part of a defense to be made out by the respondent with the burden of proof on the respondent. Under the SPS and TBT Agreements, on the other hand, the same standard is framed as an obligation of the defendant, with the complainant required to make out an affirmative case. Thus the choice between these norms will have an effect on the allocation of the burden of proof (see Howse and Mavroidis 2000).

Recall that the "necessity" qualifications contained in Articles XX(b) and (d) of the GATT have been interpreted to require the national measure to be the least trade-restrictive alternative *reasonably available*.[13] What is reasonable?[14] If the reasonableness test amounts to a requirement that the least trade-restrictive alternative not be so costly as to countervail the benefits of the regulatory measure, then it bears some resemblance to a truncated cost-benefit analysis, excluding from its maximizing analysis precise measurement of the benefits of the regulatory measure. If, alternatively, it amounts to a comparison that requires that the regulatory costs not be disproportionately greater than the trade benefits, then it is a kind of proportionality testing.

TBT Agreement   Article 2.2 of the TBT Agreement adds a curious phrase to the necessity test: it provides that "technical regulations shall not be more trade-restrictive than necessary to fulfill a legitimate objective, *taking account of the risks non-fulfillment would create*."[15] On its face, the italicized language appears nonsequacious: what part of necessity test analysis would consider the risks of nonfulfillment of the regulatory goals? However, if the necessity test is thought of as a balancing or cost-benefit analysis test,[16] considering the potential costs of regulatory failure as part of its calculus, then this language may make sense. Cost-benefit analysis ordinarily would discount a risk by its probability in order to calculate its "cost." In addition, if the necessity test under this provision is thought of as proportionality testing, the magnitude and probability of risk become relevant.

SPS Agreement   On the other hand, the SPS Agreement contains a necessity test subject to a "reasonable availability" qualification, which requires that sanitary and phytosanitary measures be "not more trade restrictive than required to achieve their appropriate level of protection, taking into account technical and economic feasibility."[17] The related footnote indicates that this standard disciplines two of the three components of regulatory cost and benefit. First, it asks whether there is a regulatory alternative that is significantly less restrictive to trade. Second, it asks whether that regulatory alternative is reasonably available. It declines to discipline the extent to which the measure maintains its ability to meet the appropriate level of protection; that is, it does not on its face require any reductions in protection, no matter how costly in trade terms.[18] Given the Appellate Body's willingness to do so, made evident in the recent *Asbestos* and *Korea-Beef* decisions, in the context of Article XX, the Appellate Body also might find a basis for doing so under the SPS Agreement.

Article 2.2 of the SPS Agreement requires members to ensure that any measure is applied only to the extent necessary to protect human, animal, or plant life. The interpretive question here relates to the significance of the term "applied." This term appears here, but also in the *chapeau* of GATT Article XX. In the *Shrimp* case and the *Gasoline* case, the Appellate Body suggested that the *chapeau*'s requirements relate not to the substance of the measure itself but to the way in which it is applied—for example, whether it is applied in a way that constitutes arbitrary or unjustifiable discrimination (see Howse 2000, citing Barcelo 1994). On the other hand, at least in the SPS Agreement, Article 5.6, also imposing a "least trade-restrictive alternative" requirement, does not limit itself to the manner in which a measure is *applied*, but addresses measures themselves. The operation of this distinction is unclear and its relationship to jurisprudence, as in the *U.S. Section 301* case and the *U.S. Countervailing Duties in Respect of Export Restraints* case (holding that measures may violate WTO law even if they are not yet *applied* in a way that violates a specific provision of WTO law), is also unclear.

GATS Proportionality   It is important to note that even if a state is otherwise found to violate the national treatment obligation of Article XVII (or other provisions of the GATS, such as Article VI.5), its regulation might be permitted under the exceptional provisions of Article XIV. Of course, Article XIV would only apply where there was an original violation of another provision of the GATS for nondiscriminatory regulation. *We* will see that there are few possibilities for finding an original violation. Article XIV parallels Article XX of the GATT, providing certain domestic policy exceptions from the otherwise applicable GATT obligations. The most relevant bases for exceptions under Article XIV are for measures:

- Necessary to protect human, animal, or plant life or health
- Necessary to secure compliance with laws or regulations that are not inconsistent with the provisions of the agreement including those relating to:
  (a) the prevention of deceptive and fraudulent practices or to deal with the effects of a default on services contracts
  (b) safety

Both of these clauses incorporate a "necessity" test, which has been interpreted in the GATT context to require that the national measure be the least trade-restrictive alternative reasonably available to achieve the regulatory goal. As noted above, and as described in more detail below, in the *Korea-Beef* and *Asbestos* cases the necessity test has been interpreted by the Appellate Body to require substantial balancing. Least trade-restrictive alternative analysis in the EU has often turned to labeling requirements, which might be less applicable in some service areas than they are in goods. However, in areas such as consumer finance or insurance, required notices to consumers are somewhat analogous to labels.

Furthermore, the exceptions under Article XIV would only be available if the national measures also met the requirements of the *chapeau* of Article XIV, which requires that such measures "are not applied in a manner which would constitute a means of arbitrary or unjustifiable discrimination between countries where like conditions prevail, or a disguised restriction on trade in services. . . ." The *Gasoline* and *Shrimp/Turtle* decisions of the WTO Appellate Body have interpreted the same language in the context of Article XX of the GATT in a fairly restrictive manner. In the *Shrimp/Turtle* case the Appellate Body applied a balancing test, evaluating whether the national measure is appropriate to achieve the regulatory goal, whether it is the least trade-restrictive alternative reasonably available to achieve the regulatory goal, and whether it is applied equally to all member states. Given that the *chapeau* of Article XIV is identical to that of Article XX, one would expect similar scrutiny to be applied in services cases.

Nullification or Impairment and the Necessity Test under Article VI.5 Article VI (domestic regulation) primarily spells out general obligations for service sectors that have been included by contracting parties in their national schedules,[19] except for measures that are covered by reservations in these schedules under Article XVII (national treatment) and XVI (market access).

In vague terms, Article VI.1 provides that domestic regulations, applied in a sector that a member has agreed to include under specific liberalization commitments, must be administered in a "reasonable, objective, and impartial manner." It is possible that this requirement—especially its reasonableness prong—may be employed and developed in WTO dispute settlement to impose substantive obligations of proportionality in connection with domestic regulation. It is interesting that the relevant portions of the New Shorter Oxford English Dictionary definition of "reasonable" includes "in accordance with reason; not irrational or absurd," "proportionate," and "within the limits of reason; not greatly less or more than might be thought likely or appropriate."[20] On the other hand, it must be noted that Article VI.1 disciplines the "administration" of domestic regulation rather than the regulation itself. It is difficult to predict how this distinction will develop, especially in relation to the goods jurisprudence under the *chapeau* of GATT Article XX, in some cases relating to the manner in which measures are *applied*.

Article VI also includes procedural guidelines requiring that decisions in cases where the supply of a service requires authorization in the host country must be issued "within a reasonable period of time," and that signatories establish tribunals and procedures to process potential complaints by foreign service suppliers.

Article VI.4 of the GATS calls on the Council for Trade in Services (CTS) to develop any necessary disciplines to ensure that measures relating to qualification requirements and procedures, technical standards, and licensing requirements[21] do not constitute unnecessary barriers to trade in services. Prior to the agreement and entry into force of more specific rules under Article VI.4, supervision on national measures is available under Article VI.5 in sectors in which the importing member has undertaken specific commitments. For these disciplines to apply, two criteria must be satisfied:

1. The licensing or qualification requirements or technical standards must nullify or impair specific commitments in a manner that could not reasonably have been expected at the time the specific commitments were made.
2. The measure must be (a) not based on objective and transparent criteria; or (b) more burdensome than necessary to ensure the quality of the service; or (c) in the case of licensing procedures, in itself a restriction on the supply of the service.

Let us examine each of these criteria in turn.

Nullification or Impairment Nullification or impairment (N/I) has served as a central feature in GATT and WTO dispute resolution. Under GATT Article XXIII redress pursuant to the dispute resolution system of the GATT is only available in the event of N/I. Where a provision of WTO law is violated, nullification or impairment is presumed.[22] On the other hand, it is possible, although infrequent, for N/I to serve as the basis for a successful complaint in the absence of an actual violation of the GATT: so-called "non-violation nullification or impairment." Article VI.5 of the GATS incorporates this concept.

In the leading nonviolation nullification or impairment case, *Film* (WTO Report of the Panel 1998), the panel reviewed in detail the basis for certain U.S. expectations in order to decide whether the United States had "legitimate expectations" of benefits after successive tariff negotiation rounds. As the complaining party, the United States was allocated the burden of proof of its legitimate expectations. For the United States to meet this burden it was required to show that the Japanese measures at issue were not reasonably anticipated at the time the concessions were granted (WTO Report of the Panel 1998, para. 10.61). Where the measure at issue was adopted after the relevant tariff concession, the panel established a presumption, rebuttable by Japan, that the United States could not reasonably have anticipated the measure.

The import of this approach in the services context is clear. The complaining party must show that the measures attacked were not reasonably anticipated. Thus longstanding regulatory practices or circumstances are protected. This means that the domestic circumstances as they are form a background for all concessions; as a matter of negotiation strategy, members of the GATS must recognize this and bear the burden of negotiating an end to existing measures that reduce the benefits for which they negotiate. It is also clear, as described in more detail below, that Article VI.5 will not impose substantial discipline on domestic regulation, which will place a greater burden on Article VI.4 as a source of discipline.

It is worthwhile to compare this structure with that applicable to goods under the GATT and under the two WTO agreements applicable to regulatory standards—the Agreement on Technical Barriers to Trade and the Agreement on the Applica-tion of Sanitary and Phytosanitary Measures. Neither the GATT nor these agreements include the N/I requirement in the prohibition itself. Therefore, in connection with trade in goods, determination that a provision of a covered agreement has been violated results in prima facie N/I under Article 3(8) of the DSU, and places the burden of rebutting the existence of N/I on the respondent. In the context of Article VI.5 of the GATS, without N/I there is no violation. Without a violation there is no prima facie N/I. Consequently, it will be for the complaining party to show nullification or impairment. This will make it more difficult for national services regulation to be addressed under Article VI.5.

We may speculate as to why the GATS relies so heavily on the N/I concept in this context. Nonviolation N/I is an extremely vague standard, but one that by itself has been difficult to meet. Thus, in the absence of an ability to negotiate more specific disciplines on national regulation, nonviolation N/I provides a modicum of more general discipline. It might be viewed as a "least common denominator" insofar as the parties could agree not to nullify or impair concessions earnestly made, but could not agree on more pervasive, blanket restrictions on their national regulatory sovereignty. Thus Article VI.5 is first and foremost merely a standstill obligation in the sense that only new regulatory measures subsequent to scheduling are likely to be disciplined.

The Necessity Test Under this additional component of the GATS Article VI.5 test we focus on the requirement (incorporated from Article VI.4[b]) that the national measure not be more burdensome than necessary to ensure the quality of the service. Even if it is possible to show that a national measure nullifies or impairs service commitments, a complainant would be required to show that the national measure does not comply with the criteria listed in Article VI.4, the most likely of which is the necessity test examined here.

As described above, GATT dispute resolution panels have taken a narrow view of what is "necessary" under Article XX of the GATT, which contains language upon which GATS Article VI.5 is modeled (*Thailand* 1990). To be deemed necessary according to the traditional test the measure must be the least trade-restrictive measure reasonably available to achieve the regulatory goal. In the context of Article VI.4(b), the reference is to measures "not more burdensome than necessary to ensure the quality of the service." The last clause could be very interventionist. It could restrict not just the means to attain a given regulatory goal but even the types of regulatory goals that might be achieved, as when the regulatory goal is not to maintain the quality of the service but to avoid some other externalization or regulatory harm by the service provider. For example, ignoring for a moment the prudential carve-out, if a bank is required to maintain a particular reserve in relation to a loan, is that necessary to ensure the quality of the service? Many types of service regulation might be subject to similar, inappropriate attack. This provision should be revised.

Furthermore, in a placement comparable to the inclusion of the N/I criterion in the substantive prohibition, here the necessity criterion is included as a parameter of the substantive prohibition, in addition to being included in the exceptional provisions of Article XIV(c).[23] Therefore, in order to make out a violation of Article VI.5 under this clause, the national measure must be shown to be unnecessary in the sense described above. Then, for the respondent to claim an exception under XIV(c) it will be required to show that it is necessary in the broader sense defined there. One interesting question involves the burden of proof. Under the products jurisprudence of the Appellate Body it appears that the complainant will be required to show the lack of necessity under Article VI.5, whereas the responding state would ordinarily be required to prove the affirmative defense of necessity under Article XIV(c). This is at least an odd legal circumstance in which each side is allocated the burden of proof on the same issue at different phases. The complaining state would be required to show that the responding state's regulatory approach is "unnecessary" under Article VI.5, and the responding state would be required to demonstrate its necessity under Article XIV(c).

In 1998 the CTS adopted the *Disciplines on Domestic Regulation in the Accountancy Sector* (the "Accountancy Disciplines") (WTO 1998, pp. 10–11)[24] developed by the GATS Working Party on Professional Services (now the Working Party on Domestic Regulation). These disciplines apply to all member states that have made specific commitments in accountancy (positive list) but do not

apply to national measures listed as exceptions under Articles XVI and XVII (negative list). They generally articulate further and tighten the principle of necessity: that measures should be the least trade-restrictive method to effect a legitimate objective. In fact, these provisions replicate requirements that have been imposed in the EU pursuant to European Court of Justice (ECJ) single-market jurisprudence.[25] They also replicate the approach of the EU's General System Directives on professions, codifying principles of proportionality[26] or necessity. They have the following features relevant to this chapter:

- **Necessity.** Member states are required to ensure that measures relating to licensing requirements and procedures, technical standards, and qualification requirements and procedures are not prepared, adopted, or applied with a view to or with the effect of creating unnecessary barriers to trade in accountancy services. Such measures may not be more trade restrictive than necessary to fulfill a legitimate objective, including protection of consumers, the quality of the service, professional competence, and the integrity of the profession. As will be clear from the discussion above, this necessity requirement is substantially stronger than that contained in Article VI.5 of the GATS.

- **Qualification Requirements.** Member states must take account of qualifications acquired in the territory of another member state on the basis of equivalency of education, experience, and/or examination requirements. Examinations or other qualification requirements must be limited to subjects relevant to the activities for which authorization is sought.

- **Technical Standards.** Technical standards must be prepared, adopted, and applied only to fulfill legitimate objectives. In determining conformity with this requirement of a member state's measures, account must be taken of internationally recognized standards applied by that member. This is an extension of GATS Article VI.5(b).

It is worth noting that the EU has stated that the following should be considered in defining necessity under Article VI.4: "A measure that is not the least trade restrictive to trade will not be considered more burdensome/more trade restrictive than necessary so long as it is not disproportionate to the objective stated and pursued" (WTO 2001, summary after para. 22). This is substantially more lenient in respect to domestic regulation than the definition of "necessity" developed in GATT/WTO jurisprudence. It would provide an additional defense for regulation that is not the least trade-restrictive alternative but is nevertheless "proportionate." The Appellate Body's jurisprudence in *Korea-Beef* and *Asbestos* may be understood as somewhat consistent with this approach, adding additional factors to the least trade-restrictive alternative test. However, it is not clear precisely what "disproportionate" means in this context. It is likely that the EU meant to refer to proportionality stricto sensu (Emiliou 1996; Trachtman 1998), which asks whether the means are "proportionate" to the ends—whether the costs are excessive in relation to the benefits. Proportionality stricto sensu might be viewed as cost-benefit analysis with a margin of appreciation because it does not require that the costs be less than the benefits. A wider definition of proportionality developed in the EU internal market context includes three tests: (a) proportionality stricto sensu, (b) a least trade-restrictive alternative test, and (c) a simple means-end rationality test. At the same time that it adds proportionality to a least trade-restrictive alternative test, the EU seems to suggest that "the validity, or rationale, of the policy objective[s] must not be assessed" (WTO 2001, para. 17). The EU may intend that the "appropriate level of protection" selected by a member state should not be questioned.

Recognition and Necessity Necessity has a complex relationship with recognition. That is, a necessity test, interpreted as a requirement that the national measure be the least trade-restrictive alternative reasonably available to address the regulatory concern, can either be an absolute requirement or a relative requirement. Thus a less restrictive option might make sense irrespective of the home regime, or conversely might only be justified in reference to the home country regulatory regime, as a *complementary* measure. Judgments based on the former assessment reflect a high degree of judicial activism and are unlikely to be found legitimate.

In the latter case, where the home country regulatory regime satisfies the host country concerns, necessity may require recognition. This would be

an extreme interpretation of necessity as least trade-restrictive alternative analysis, stating in effect that *no* regulatory intervention on the part of the importing country is necessary at all. The least restrictive alternative is to do nothing. We have seen this in the ECJ jurisprudence,[27] and there are treaty provisions reflecting this concept in Article 4 of the SPS Agreement[28] and Article 2.9 of the TBT Agreement.[29] Under this interpretation recognition may be mandated by *judicial fiat.*

Note that Article VII of the GATS and paragraph 3 of the Annex on Financial Services, in contrast, do not require recognition but merely authorize it. Although a strong GATS standard of necessity might eventually lead to such judicially required recognition, this is unlikely to be the case under current treaty language. But the necessity test might nevertheless mandate partial recognition of some regulations and not others, whereby partial recognition becomes the operational consequence of the principle of proportionality. It is important to note that the Accountancy Disciplines require recognition of professional qualifications in accountancy.

As noted above, the Accountancy Disciplines include a substantially enhanced necessity test, applicable within that sector.

Other Requirements of Harmonization

GATT The GATT contains no specific requirements of harmonization. Before moving on, however, it is important to note that under certain circumstances necessity or least trade-restrictive alternative tests will require acceptance of either another state's standard (recognition) or an international standard (harmonization). That is, the other standard may be the least trade-restrictive means to achieve the regulatory goal. For example, Article XX of the GATT, in connection both with its *chapeau* and with clauses (b) and (d), seems to provide some incentives for harmonization. In the *Shrimp* case, the Appellate Body suggested that for a national measure to be eligible for exemption under the *chapeau* of Article XX, a state might be required first to attempt to achieve its regulatory goals through multilateral (or other non-unilateral) means.

SPS and TBT Article 3.4 of the SPS Agreement requires member states, within the limits of their resources, to play a full part in relevant international organizations in order to promote the development of international standards. Similarly, Article 2.6 of the TBT Agreement provides that:

> With a view to harmonizing technical regulations on as wide a basis as possible, Members shall play a full part, within the limits of their resources, in the preparation by appropriate international standardizing bodies of international standards for products for which they either have adopted, or expect to adopt, technical regulations.

GATS on Harmonization   Article VI.4 of the GATS provides a facility for harmonization but does not require it. Moreover, because of the weak negative integration under Article VI.5, there are fewer incentives for harmonization under the GATS than under the SPS or TBT Agreements. As discussed more fully below, Article VI.5(b) of the GATS requires that applying the disciplines of Article VI.5(a) take into account relevant standards of international organizations applied by the relevant member state.

Article VII.5 of the GATS states, "In appropriate cases, Members shall work in cooperation with relevant intergovernmental and non-governmental organizations towards the establishment and adoption of common international standards and criteria for recognition and common international standards for the practice of relevant services trades and professions."

Conformity with International Standards: Rules and Standards; Adjudication at WTO and Legislation Elsewhere

One of the core problems facing the WTO is the imbalance between its new (since 1994) dispute resolution authority on one hand and its extremely limited legislative capacity on the other. The legislative capacity of the WTO is limited by virtue of both legal constraints and a network of informal expectations and attitudes. Moreover, there are substantial questions about the subject matter competence of the WTO—the extent to which the WTO can or should address areas outside of its "core competency" of international trade. Increasingly, the core of international trade is inseparable

from its penumbra of traditionally domestic regulatory prerogatives in environment, health, labor, culture, tax, and so forth.

At the Singapore Ministerial Meeting in 1996, the WTO (informally) referred certain trade-related labor issues to the International Labor Organization; this referral was reaffirmed more recently at Doha. Not to decide is to decide, however, and the WTO's abdication of authority has certain substantive results. Although this chapter points to certain *negative integration* powers available in WTO dispute settlement to be exercised through the application of general standards, the WTO has much more limited powers of *positive integration* available to be exercised through the legislation of specific rules. Article VI.4 is a partial exception.

SPS   It is interesting to note that in the Uruguay Round, in the area of sanitary and phytosanitary measures, the WTO formally referred certain quasi-legislative authority to certain other functional organizations. That is, the definition of "international standards" contained in Annex A to the SPS Agreement appoints Codex Alimentarius (Codex), the International Office of Epizootics (OIE), and the International Plant Protection Convention (IPPC) as quasi-legislators of these standards in relevant areas. What do I mean by "quasi-legislators"?

First, under the terms of their own constitutive documents, the standards developed by Codex, OIE, and IPPC for human, animal, and plant health, respectively, are nonbinding. Article 3.1 of the SPS Agreement, however, provides that "Members shall base their sanitary or phytosanitary measures on international standards, guidelines or recommendations, where they exist, except as otherwise provided for in this Agreement, and in particular in paragraph 3." Moreover, Article 3.2 states that SPS measures of WTO members that are in conformity with international standards, guidelines, or recommendations shall be "presumed to be consistent with the relevant provisions of this Agreement." In its *Hormones* decision the Appellate Body found that the terms "based on" in Article 3.1 and "in conformity with" in Article 3.2 have different meanings. "Based on" means simply derived from, and provides greater flexibility to members.[30] On the other hand, reversing the panel, the Appellate Body found that Article 3.2

was a safe harbor but did not establish the converse presumption: the panel erred in presuming that measures that did not conform to international standards were inconsistent with the SPS Agreement.

So, although Codex, OIE, and IPPC do not by any means legislate in the normal, or full, sense, the norms that they produce have certain lesser binding force—they provide incentives that guide conduct. They are safe harbors with characteristics similar to those used to guide conduct, for example, in U.S. tax or securities law regulations. The SPS Agreement provisions mentioned above provide important incentives for states to base their national standards on or conform their national standards to the Codex, OIE, and IPPC standards. Article 3.3 provides an important exception in certain circumstances, including situations in which a state adopts a higher "appropriate level of sanitary or phytosanitary protection." This is a refined system of applied subsidiarity, subtly allowing national autonomy subject to certain subtle constraints, or incentives.

Before the SPS Agreement, Codex standards had no particular binding force unless accepted for application by national legislation.[31] Given the new quasi-legislative character of standards set by Codex, OIE, and IPPC (and other organizations), it is worthwhile to examine how these organizations adopt standards (Stewart and Johanson 1998). It may be that the phenomenon of strengthened enforcement of standards by virtue of the SPS Agreement will give rise to modified standard-setting procedures.[32]

Codex Alimentarius standards are developed by committees of government representatives under one of two stepwise approaches: an eight-step full procedure, and a five-step accelerated method. In the final, adoption stage of both approaches, the Codex Commission makes "every effort to reach agreement on the adoption of standards by consensus" (Ontario Ministry of Agriculture, Food, and Rural Affairs 2000). However, when "efforts to reach a consensus have failed" (Ontario Ministry of Agriculture, Food, and Rural Affairs 2000), voting does occur and decisions of the Commission are "taken by a majority of the votes cast."[33]

Article 3.5 of the SPS Agreement requires the WTO Committee on Sanitary and Phytosanitary Measures to monitor international harmonization activities and to coordinate with the "relevant international organizations."

TBT Article 2.4 of the TBT Agreement requires members to use international standards as a basis for their technical regulations, unless the international standards are an inappropriate or ineffective means to achieve legitimate objectives. This requirement is less complex, and less subtle, than that under the SPS Agreement. Article 2.5 provides a presumption of compliance for standards that conform to relevant international standards.

GATT The GATT does not specifically require the use of international standards at all, although the least trade-restrictive alternative requirements under Article XX may include a requirement to try to create or use an international standard before applying a unilateral one (WTO Appellate Body Report 1998c).

GATS The GATS, like the GATT, does not specifically require the use of international standards and provides weaker incentives for the use of such standards than does the SPS Agreement or the TBT Agreement. As noted above, Article VI.5(b) requires that account be taken of compliance with international standards where a member state's compliance with Article VI.5(a) is being evaluated. This is a nod toward a safe harbor for states that comply with international standards, although it should provide only very modest incentive effects because of the weakness of Article VI.5(a). It does not provide a presumption of compliance, as do Article 2.5 of the TBT Agreement and Article 3.2 of the SPS Agreement.

The Accountancy Disciplines require that technical standards be prepared, adopted, and applied only to fulfill legitimate objectives. In determining conformity with this requirement of a member state's measures, account must be taken of internationally recognized standards applied by that member. This is an extension of GATS Article VI.5(b).[34]

Rules and Standards: Relating Legislative Capacity to Judicial Scrutiny In different legal systems and in different historical moments it may be better for legislators or treatymakers to engage in more specific negotiations toward more specific rules, or to engage in more general negotiations toward more general "standards," for subsequent application by a court (Trachtman 1999). It is possible for a "legislative" act to provide either a broad or a narrow mandate to a court. A narrow mandate will call for less discretion to be exercised by the court.[35]

Not only do treatywriters delegate authority to dispute resolution tribunals; they also maintain complex relationships with the dispute resolution process, both formal and informal. First, of course, is the possibility of legislative reversal: if the authors of the treaty become discontented with the manner of its application, they may change the treaty. Furthermore, they may restrain dispute resolution. Second, and relatively unusual in general international law, is a formal "political filter" device. This political filter was much more important prior to the 1994 changes to WTO dispute resolution, but it still exists in attenuated form.

The fact that the "legislative" act in connection with sanitary and phytosanitary standards takes place *outside* the WTO provides some interesting features. First, it may lend the WTO a degree of insulation from criticism. Second, it offers a legislative device that may evade the need for unanimity, or at least consensus, within the WTO.[36] Amendments and decisions within the WTO have varying formal requirements, up to and including effective unanimity for states to be bound by amendments, but these formal requirements form the background for informal consensus-based practices. Codex and other standard setters may provide opportunities for less rigorous adoption of measures. Third, it may be possible, subject to the difficulty of changing WTO law, to legislatively override Codex or other outside sources of standards. Fourth, this structure provides an opportunity for subject matter specialists rather than trade specialists to take a leading role in formulating the standards.

Finally, we may consider standard setting, or positive integration, and its relationship to "adjudicative" scrutiny of national measures, or negative integration. Negative integration provides some incentives for states, including the direct incentive arising from the fact that an international standard may be viewed as the least trade-restrictive alternative or may be privileged under the SPS or TBT Agreement. We have seen this type of effect in connection with the EU's so-called "new approach to harmonization." In that context, the EU relied on substantial judicial scrutiny, including judicially required recognition under *Cassis de Dijon* and other precedents, while engaging in "essential" harmonization to establish the further prerequisites for mutual recognition. Of course, in the trade area recognition is consistent with complete regulatory market access.

These considerations apply in the GATS, although they are ameliorated by the limited possibilities under Article VI.5 for judicial scrutiny of nondiscriminatory regulation.[37] It is at least possible, however, that Article VI.1 might be interpreted as a broad standard that could have the effect of invalidating domestic regulation. Conversely, Article VI.1 seems intended to apply to the manner of administration rather than to the substance.

It is worthwhile to note that in the Accountancy Disciplines the CTS elaborated the standards of necessity and recognition rather than applying more specific rules for accountancy qualifications.

Appropriate Level/Scientific Basis/Regulation of Regulatory Goals

Article 2.2 of the SPS Agreement provides that sanitary and phytosanitary measures must be based on scientific principles and may not be maintained without sufficient scientific evidence, except under Article 5.7. This is possibly the greatest difference between the SPS Agreement and the TBT Agreement (not to mention the GATT): the TBT Agreement does not explicitly regulate risk assessments or require scientific bases for regulation. While proportionality or other standards applicable under the TBT Agreement, the GATT, or the GATS may *implicitly* require some scientific basis, this implicit requirement can be expected to be significantly less *rigorous* than the explicit requirements of the SPS Agreement.

Article 3.3 of the SPS Agreement permits states to introduce measures that result in a higher level of protection than do international standards if there is scientific justification or as a consequence of a Member's appropriate level of protection. Note 2 to this provision explains that a scientific justification exists if, on the basis of scientific evidence, the regulating state determines that international standards are insufficient to achieve the appropriate level of protection.

Articles 5.1 and 5.2 of the SPS Agreement impose a requirement of risk assessment, taking into account available scientific evidence. These requirements were interpreted in each of the three cases under the SPS Agreement: *Hormones*, *Australia-Salmon*, and *Japan-Agricultural Products*. A "risk assessment" is defined in Annex A to include not just scientific evidence but also evaluation of potential biological and economic consequences (see Howse 2000, citing Barcello 1994). Furthermore, Article 5.4 of the SPS Agreement exhorts member states, when determining an appropriate level of protection, to take into account the objective of minimizing negative trade effects. Although Annex A specifies that the "appropriate level of sanitary or phytosanitary protection" is that deemed appropriate by the regulating state, this is a requirement for member states to engage in a rather complete balancing test when establishing and maintaining SPS measures. However, it is not itself a balancing test for application by panels or the Appellate Body. These types of measures might be supervised more politically, for example, through the Trade Policy Review Mechanism.

The GATS does not have any explicit requirements relating to bases for regulation or appropriate levels of regulation. As noted elsewhere, the "reasonableness" requirement of Article VI.1 could be interpreted to do so if the reference to "administration" were read broadly. Also, in the leading sector of financial services the Annex on Financial Services specifically provides that nothing in the GATS shall prevent a state from taking measures for prudential reasons.[38] Although this contains an implicit requirement that the measure be for "prudential reasons," the only consequence of a failure of a measure to satisfy this requirement is that it is not eligible for blanket protection from scrutiny.

Internal Consistency

Article 5.5 of the SPS Agreement addresses an interesting theoretical issue: why do people accept greater risk in some circumstances than in others? It requires a regulating state to "avoid arbitrary or unjustifiable distinctions in the levels it considers to be appropriate in different situations, if such distinctions result in discrimination or a disguised restriction on international trade." This provision adds marginally, if at all, to the prohibition of Arti-

cle 2.3 (see WTO Appellate Body Report 1997, para. 212). Because it requires discrimination or a disguised restriction it is not clear that it adds much beyond the requirement of national treatment in Article III of the GATT or in Article 2.1 of the TBT Agreement. The GATS does not contain any similar language.

Precautionary Principle

The precautionary principle (see Geistfeld 2001), of course, has been the subject of extensive debate that cannot be recounted here. It is worth pointing out, however, that the precautionary principle is stated in a very specific and limited form in Article 5.7 of the SPS Agreement. It is available to allow provisional measures where scientific evidence is insufficient, where the member acts on the basis of available information, and where the member seeks to obtain the additional information needed for a more objective assessment of risk within a reasonable period of time (WTO Appellate Body Report 1999). There is nothing similar in the GATT, the TBT Agreement, or the GATS, presumably in part because they lack a specific requirement for a risk assessment taking into account scientific evidence. Lacking the specific requirement, they do not need an exception for emergent circumstances. However, this leaves a degree of uncertainty because a measure taken without sufficient scientific basis might otherwise be found to be unnecessary or disproportionate under applicable standards.

Balancing

To many commentators, the idea of balancing tests in contexts where domestic regulation is subject to international scrutiny has been anathema. There are two likely reasons. First, balancing tests seem to some to accord too much power to courts. At least in the United States, however, it is not unusual for courts to be assigned, explicitly or implicitly, to balance under specified circumstances. Second, and even more intractable, balancing tests seem to intervene too greatly in national regulatory autonomy.[39] This intervention is considered excessive not because it might strike down domestic regulation but because it might involve an international tribunal in too extensive an inquiry into the costs and benefits of domestic regulation.

The GATT has no specific language authorizing a balancing test in connection with domestic regulation. The SPS Agreement and the TBT Agreement, while providing for least trade-restrictive alternative analysis, also avoid specific reference to balancing tests. Note that a necessity or least trade-restrictive alternative test, at least as conceived before *Korea-Beef* and *Asbestos*, avoids evaluation of the goal sought by the relevant domestic regulation, as well as comparison between that value and the detriment to international trade caused by the domestic regulation.

In *Korea-Beef*, the Appellate Body first examined the definition of "necessity" under Article XX(d) of the GATT and found that it could be something less than absolute indispensability. It is interesting that the Appellate Body stated that "a treaty interpreter assessing a measure claimed to be necessary to secure compliance of a WTO-consistent law or regulation may, in appropriate cases, take into account the relative importance of the common interests or values that the law or regulation to be enforced is intended to protect" (WTO Appellate Body Report 2001b, paras. 162, 163). This statement would involve the Appellate Body in assessing the importance of national goals to a degree not seen, at least explicitly, before (see Trachtman 1999). Moreover, it is potentially inconsistent with the principle, expressed in the SPS Agreement (and referred to in the *Asbestos* case) that member states are permitted to set their own appropriate levels of protection. Finally, it is interesting that the Appellate Body refers to "common interests or values." Does this require, or prefer, a degree of homogeneity of purpose?

Indeed, the Appellate Body sets up, rather explicitly, a balancing test. It considers the degree to which the measure contributes to the realization of the end pursued: "the greater the contribution, the more easily a measure might be considered to be 'necessary'" (WTO Appellate Body Report 2001b, para. 163). It would also consider the "extent to which the compliance measure produces restrictive effects on international commerce" (WTO Appellate Body Report 2001b). The Appellate Body's statement will be breathtaking to some:

In sum, determination of whether a measure, which is not "indispensable," may nevertheless be "necessary" within the contemplation of Arti-

cle XX(d), involves in every case a process of weighing and balancing a series of factors which prominently include the contribution made by the compliance measure to the enforcement of the law or regulation at issue, the importance of the common interests or values protected by that law or regulation, and the accompanying impact of the law or regulation on imports or exports [WTO Appellate Body Report 2001b, para. 164].

This statement constitutes a significant shift toward a greater role for the Appellate Body in weighing regulatory values against trade values. It appears to be intended to speak beyond the Article XX(d) context to all necessity testing, including that under Article XX(b) and presumably under the SPS Agreement, the TBT Agreement, and the GATS.

The Appellate Body found that the panel was justified in examining enforcement measures in similar circumstances without, as Korea complained, imposing a "consistency" requirement. "Examining such enforcement measures may provide useful input in the course of determining whether an alternative measure which could 'reasonably be expected' to be utilized, is available or not" (WTO Appellate Body Report 2001b, para. 170). The application of WTO-compatible measures to the same kind of illegal behavior suggested to the Appellate Body that a reasonably available alternative measure might exist (WTO Appellate Body Report 2001b, para. 172). The Appellate Body confirmed the panel's conclusion that Korea failed to demonstrate that alternative measures were not reasonably available.

It is interesting that in its decision regarding *Asbestos*, the Appellate Body referred to its decision in *Korea-Beef* to the effect that in determining whether another alternative method is reasonably available it is appropriate to consider the extent to which the alternative measure "contributes to the realization of the end pursued" (WTO Appellate Body Report 2001a, para. 172, citing Appellate Body Report 2001b, paras. 163, 166). This is a significant (and explicit) departure from the conventional understanding of "reasonably available," which would consider the costs of the alternative regulation but not the degree of its contribution to the end. In fact, the degree of contribution to the end seemed before to be inviolable: states were entitled to *complete* accomplishment of the end reflected in their regulation. This is not the ordinarily understood meaning of necessity as a search for the least trade-restrictive alternative reasonably available: that formulation would not ordinarily involve an evaluation, or any compromise, of the end pursued (Trachtman 1999). Furthermore, the Appellate Body referred to *Korea-Beef* for the proposition that the more important the common interests or values pursued, the easier it would be to accept the national measure as necessary (WTO Appellate Body Report 2001a, para. 172).

The balancing test for determining "necessity" under Article XX(b) and (d) developed in these opinions will stimulate much discussion and controversy.

Under the GATS a necessity criterion is applied in two places. First, Article VI.5(a) includes "necessity" as one of several tests for invalidation of domestic regulation. As noted above, it will be difficult to satisfy all of these tests in real cases. Second, Article XIV(a), (b), and (c) each include the "necessity" qualifier, as a prerequisite for eligibility for an exception to GATS prohibitions. It is possible that the Appellate Body would extend its balancing jurisprudence to the "necessity" tests in the GATS. As suggested above, however, there are few significant GATS prohibitions that would apply to invalidate nondiscriminatory domestic regulation. Even the product-process distinction does not seem to apply in the GATS in a way that would indiscriminately invalidate process-based regulation. Therefore, there will be little need for exceptions. Under these circumstances (except in connection with the Accountancy Disciplines) it cannot be said today that "necessity" is an important discipline for domestic regulation under the GATS.

Recognition/Equivalence

Another discipline on domestic regulation that may serve as a parameter by which to distinguish among GATT, the SPS Agreement, the TBT Agreement, and the GATS is the requirement of recognition. The GATT contains no explicit requirement or facility of recognition. As noted above, however, it is possible that least trade-restrictive alternative requirements under Article XX(b) or (d) could require recognition. Article 4.1 of the SPS Agreement does require recognition: "Members shall accept the sanitary or phytosanitary measures of

other Members as equivalent, even if these measures differ from their own or from those used by other Members trading in the same product, if the exporting Member objectively demonstrates to the importing Member that its measures achieve the importing Member's appropriate level of sanitary or phytosanitary protection."

The requirement of the SPS Agreement is stronger than the more hortatory obligation of Article 2.7 of the TBT Agreement, which simply requires members to give positive consideration to accepting foreign regulation as equivalent if it fulfills the importing state's objectives.

The GATS contains no explicit requirements of recognition. Article VII authorizes and regulates plurilateral recognition regimes but imposes no requirement of recognition. Articles VI.1 and VI.5 may be viewed as containing potential implicit requirements of recognition as set forth above but they are quite uncertain in their operation. As noted above, the Accountancy Disciplines require a degree of recognition of qualification requirements.

Article VII, however, does not exist in isolation from Article VI. These provisions work together to provide a complex system for managed mutual recognition (see Nicolaïdis 1996, 1997). That is, the weak disciplines of Article VI.5, combined with potentially strengthened disciplines developed under Article VI.4, can provide incentives for recognition under Article VII, or under other circumstances they can accomplish the same goals as those sought under Article VII.

Product-Process Issues and Extraterritorial Protection Issues

Finally, an area of great importance is the territorial scope of application of the various exceptional measures: that is, to what extent can a state take action under its domestic law to protect health or other "domestic" regulatory values *outside* its own territory? In substance this is a choice of law or prescriptive jurisdiction issue. It has arisen explicitly in connection with the application of Articles XX(b) and XX(g), and implicitly in the form of the product-process distinction. That is, the product-process distinction tends to serve as a proxy for a territorial-extraterritorial regulation distinction: production processes occur in the exporting state and the product arrives in the importing state.

GATT The territoriality-extraterritoriality and product-process issues have been important in the *Tuna* and *Shrimp* cases. They arise in connection with the relationship between Article III and Article XI of the GATT on one hand and in connection with the exceptional provisions under Article XX on the other hand. As discussed above, the product-process distinction can be seen as a proxy for a rule of territoriality. In the *Shrimp* case it is important that the Appellate Body specifically declined to rule on whether there is a territorial or jurisdictional limitation in Article XX(g)—whether the "extraterritorial" nature of the U.S. measure removed it from eligibility for an exception under that provision. The Appellate Body was able to do so because the sea turtles at issue were migratory, migrating to and from U.S. waters (WTO Appellate Body Report 1998c, para. 133).

SPS Annex A to the SPS Agreement contains a definition of "sanitary and phytosanitary measures" that includes only measures that protect health *within the territory* of the regulating member. It therefore excludes from its coverage measures addressing health outside the regulating member's territory. It is curious that Article 1.5 of the TBT Agreement excludes from its scope of application only sanitary and phytosanitary measures as defined in Annex A of the SPS Agreement. This leaves importing state regulation seeking to regulate processes and production methods in the exporting state, with the goal of protecting health outside the territory of the importing state, outside the coverage of the SPS Agreement, but potentially subject to either the strict scrutiny of Article XI of the GATT and/or the somewhat less strict scrutiny of the TBT Agreement.

TBT Annex 1 of the TBT Agreement defines "technical regulation" as a "[d]ocument which lays down product characteristics or their related processes and production methods, including the applicable administrative provisions with which compliance is mandatory." Early debates about this definition were motivated by a desire to *include* processes and production methods within the disciplines of the TBT Agreement to prevent them from becoming barriers to trade (WTO Secretariat 1995). These discussions assumed that PPMs would not be subject to strict scrutiny under GATT

Article XI, as occurred in the unadopted *Tuna* cases. However, given the interpretation that PPMs are not "subject to" Article III and therefore are not protected from the strict scrutiny of Article XI, it might be argued that PPMs would be subject to lesser scrutiny if they are covered by the TBT Agreement. On the other hand, Article 2.1 of the TBT Agreement may be viewed as incorporating the jurisprudence of GATT Article III.

GATS, the Product-Process Distinction, and Territoriality The problem of allocating territorial jurisdiction is even more difficult in connection with services than with goods. The service supplier and the service production often are inextricably embedded in the service. Therefore, the product-process distinction is less natural in services than in goods. As discussed above, Article XVII of the GATS overcomes this problem by referring to like services and like service suppliers. Although it does not provide the possibility for discrimination based on the way the service is produced per se, that would seem to be included in its review of discrimination on the basis of the identity of the service supplier.

Conclusion

The purpose of this chapter has been to outline certain critical rules applicable under the GATT, the SPS Agreement, and the TBT Agreement so as to compare them with coordinate provisions of the GATS.

This chapter has shown that the GATT is more *laissez-regler* than the SPS and TBT Agreements, at least for most purposes. The GATT's primary discipline is nondiscrimination. Article XX is only invoked *after* a finding of violation of, for example, Article III or Article XI. An exception to this observation exists in the case of PPMs: the GATT has been interpreted to be subtly stricter in its scrutiny—at least with regard to allocation of burdens of proof—than might be the case under the SPS or TBT Agreement, to the extent that PPMs are subject to either of those agreements.

Furthermore, the TBT Agreement is generally less strict in its scrutiny of domestic regulation than is the SPS Agreement. For example, the TBT Agreement lacks an explicit requirement of a risk assessment.

TABLE 5.1 Applicability of Disciplines on Domestic Regulation under WTO Agreements

	GATT	TBT	SPS	GATS	GATS Accountancy Disciplines
National Treatment	✓	✓	✓	If scheduled; like services and like service providers	No change
Proportionality/necessity	✓ (under XX)	✓	✓	Weak	Strengthened
International standards	Weak (under XX)	✓	✓ strong	Very weak	Strengthened
Other harmonization	n.a.	✓	✓	Weak	No change
Recognition	Weak (under XX)	✓	✓	Weak	Strengthened
Goals	✓ (under XX)	n.a.	✓	Weak	No change
Scientific basis	n.a.	n.a.	✓	n.a.	No change
Consistency	n.a.	n.a.	✓	n.a.	No change
Precautionary	n.a.	n.a.	✓	n.a.	No change
Balancing	✓ (under XX)	✓	✓	Very limited	Strengthened
Product/process; territoriality	✓ (III)	✓	✓	Service/service supplier	No change

Note: n.a. = Not applicable; ✓ = the relevant discipline applies; XX refers to Article XX of GATT.

But the greatest differences are between the provisions relating to goods on one hand and those relating to services on the other. See table 5.1 above for a summary comparison. Along a number of dimensions the GATS appears much more *laissez-regler* than the goods agreements. Although this chapter does not provide the empirical support necessary to develop a list of "best practices" from the goods agreements to adapt to services, what follows is a list of goods disciplines worth considering for adaptation to the GATS. Some of them might be adopted pursuant to Article VI.4; others may require amendments to the GATS itself.

- *"Softer" antidiscrimination norms.* Consider replacing the national treatment language of GATS Article XVII with language that allows for justification of differential treatment, such as that of Article 2.3 of the SPS Agreement. This change would respond to some of the concerns expressed by the Appellate Body in paragraph 100 of the *Asbestos* decision. Of course, given that application of Article XVII depends on scheduling, states can establish appropriate exceptions in the scheduling process.
- *Stronger necessity/proportionality discipline.* It is difficult to understand why Article VI.5 is so weak. Consider applying language such as that in

paragraph 2 of the Accountancy Disciplines horizontally. This is the role of the Working Party on Domestic Regulation. Member states may decide to respond to the recent *Korea-Beef* and *Asbestos* jurisprudence to restrict the scope of a balancing test under these provisions. It is worthwhile to explore the proposal made by the EU in its Communication on Necessity to provide a necessity test, with an additional proportionality defense. In addition, it would be worthwhile to explore the role of labeling, or notifications to service consumers, in connection with necessity or proportionality analysis. The weakness of Article VI.5 places a premium on action under VI.4.

- *Permissible regulatory goals.* Article XIV of the GATS contains inappropriately restricted regulatory goals (for example, it does not refer to "exhaustible natural resources," as does GATT Article XX(g)) and should be expanded along the lines of paragraphs 2 and 25 of the Accountancy Disciplines to refer more broadly to "legitimate objectives." The regulatory goals referred to in Article VI.4(b) also should be expanded beyond "quality of the service."
- *"Scientific basis"/risk assessment.* The SPS innovation of requiring states to go through a process of risk assessment to validate their regulation should be considered for extension beyond the SPS area.

Although a "scientific" basis may not be the correct reference in the services field, a rational regulatory basis should be required. There are significant questions about the burdens implementing this type of requirement would impose on developing countries. If a "rational regulatory basis" requirement is imposed, a provisional "precautionary principle"–type authority also should be provided, along the lines of Article 5.7 of the SPS Agreement.

- *More narrow prudential carve-out.* The prudential carve-out in financial services seems too broad, although I recognize that it has been popular with member states. It could be improved by greater definition, which could be provided through dispute settlement. It is worth considering, however, why financial services regulation merits a prudential carve-out when the entire purpose of the SPS Agreement is to discipline health regulation. At some point nongovernmental organizations will begin to criticize this free ride for financial regulation compared with the substantial burdens placed, for example, on health regulation. This consideration could be improved by data regarding whether commitments have been undermined, or could be improved, by greater disciplines on nondiscriminatory regulation of financial services.

- *Equivalence/recognition requirement.* Article VI.4 should be used to provide for either horizontal or vertical equivalency requirements. For example, paragraph 19 of the Accountancy Disciplines requires some level of equivalency. States should not be required to recognize other states' regulation on a blanket basis, but equivalence anticipates a judicially supervised requirement to recognize foreign regulation where the foreign regulation achieves the regulatory goals.

- *Incentives for international standards.* Both the SPS Agreement and the TBT Agreement provide incentives for compliance with certain international standards. This also could be provided in services on a horizontal or vertical basis.

- *Relating unilateralism to multilateralism.* Economies like the United States will evaluate certain types of foreign service providers before allowing them access to U.S. markets. For example, the 1993 Foreign Bank Supervision Enhancement Act, responding to the BCCI crisis, serves as a basis for U.S. regulators to evaluate foreign

regulatory systems before they allow banks located in those systems to establish themselves in the United States. At the same time, the U.S. has referred to the Basel Banking Principles, and has "unilaterally multilateralized" its evaluation. The Accountancy Disciplines require that member states take account of internationally recognized standards of international organizations in determining conformity with technical standards.

Endnotes

1. For an extended taxonomy, see Marceau and Trachtman (2002).
2. We discuss below the extent to which this was actually changed under the SPS Agreement and the TBT Agreement.
3. Although the SPS Agreement may apply to a limited range of health, food- and drug-testing, and certification services, this chapter will not consider these services.
4. Article 915 of NAFTA defines the services covered by Chapter 9 to include only land transportation and telecommunications.
5. I recognize that WTO negotiators understand this as an "Article XVII" issue, separate from other disciplines on regulation. Without wishing to dispute that view, I find it necessary to discuss national treatment in order to provide an integrated framework for analysis.
6. For an analysis of several of these tests in comparison to cost-benefit analysis, and a critique of cost-benefit analysis in this context, see Trachtman 1998.
7. Note the inconsistency between this perspective and the economic theory of regulation, which assumes that the reason for regulatory intervention is that the health risks are not sufficiently reflected in the marketplace.
8. The *chapeau* requires that measures exempted under Article XX must not be applied in a manner that would constitute "a means of arbitrary or unjustifiable discrimination between countries where the same conditions prevail, or a disguised restriction on international trade."
9. The GATS distinguishes among four modes of delivery, allowing states to list different exceptions to liberalization under each mode. The advent of e-commerce is increasingly blurring the distinction between modes 1 and 2, and mode 4 can be seen as a variant on 3 for our purposes. The four modes are: (1) from the territory of one nation into the territory of another; (2) in the territory of one nation to a consumer in another nation; (3) by a service supplier of one nation through commercial presence in the territory of another nation; and (4) by a service supplier of one nation through presence of natural persons of a nation in the territory of another nation. This categorization is one of the keys to the evolutionary nature of the GATS: it achieves two seemingly contradictory purposes by casting the widest net possible for liberalization while allowing nations to carve out areas to exempt from liberalization even within subsectoral categories listed in their schedules.
10. Of course, with a multinational corporation such as a bank, especially one that operates through branches, it may be difficult to regulate the corporation without regulating extraterritorially.

11. This approach may be inconsistent with the line taken by the panel in *Canada—Certain Measures Affecting the Automotive Industry* (WTO Appellate Body Report 2000, para. 10.248) to the effect that "like service providers" are providers who provide the same service.

12. This approach may be inconsistent with that taken by the panel in *Canada—Certain Measures Affecting the Automotive Industry* (WTO Appellate Body Report 2000, para. 10.248) to the effect that "like service providers" are providers that provide the same service.

13. United States—Section 337 of the Tariff Act of 1930, 36 B.I.S.D. 345, 392, paras. 5.25–5.27 (1990) ("It was clear to the Panel that a contracting party cannot justify a measure inconsistent with another GATT provision as 'necessary' in terms of Article XX(d) if an alternative measure which it could reasonably be expected to employ and which is not inconsistent with other GATT provisions is available to it"); Thailand—Restrictions on Importation of and Internal Taxes on Cigarettes, 37 BISD 200, 223 (1991) (citing the Section 337 Panel Report).

14. The SPS Agreement specifically (although not unambiguously) adds a reasonableness qualification (see note 17 below). These provisions leave some ambiguity in light of Article 2.2 of the SPS Agreement, which provides a necessity test with regard to the application of sanitary and phytosanitary measures, but lacks a reasonableness qualifier.

15. TBT Agreement, Article 2.2 (emphasis added).

16. Indeed, Farber and Hudec (1994, pp. 1401, 1431) argue that both the Standards Agreement and the SPS Agreement "call for a balancing analysis similar to what one finds in the opinions of U.S. courts in [dormant Commerce Clause] cases." Moreover, in the recent *Asbestos* and *Korea-Beef* decisions, the Appellate Body seems to have found that the Article XX necessity test involves substantial balancing.

17. SPS Agreement, Article 5.6, footnote 3, states the following: "For purposes of paragraph 6 of Article 5, a measure is not more trade-restrictive than required unless there is another measure, reasonably available taking into account technical and economic feasibility, that achieves the appropriate level of sanitary or phytosanitary protection and is significantly less restrictive to trade." This is necessity testing subject to a "reasonably available" qualification. See also Article 2.2: "Members shall ensure that any sanitary or phytosanitary measure is applied only to the extent necessary to protect human, animal or plant life or health."

18. However, Article 5.4 of the SPS Agreement exhorts WTO Members, "when determining the appropriate level of sanitary or phytosanitary protection, [to] take into account the objective of minimizing negative trade effects."

19. Article VI.2 is not conditioned upon scheduling.

20. It is worth asking what is left out of this list of types of measures. Was this provision intended to exclude any particular type or method of regulation? One example might be "onerous visa procedures." See WTO Working Party on Domestic Regulation (2001).

21. Dispute Settlement Understanding, Article 3(8).

22. For a useful discussion, see WTO Working Party on Domestic Regulation (1999).

23. This is similar to Article 2.2 of the SPS Agreement and Article 2.2 of the TBT Agreement.

24. There is an interesting issue, beyond the scope of this chapter, regarding the legal status of this type of WTO "secondary legislation," both within the WTO and in member states.

25. This suggests that the EU jurisprudence can serve as a source of principles for articulation through nonjudicial means in other contexts.

26. Proportionality, in the strictest sense, examines whether the means are proportionate to the ends—whether the costs are excessive in relation to the benefits. A wider definition of proportionality developed in the EU context includes three tests: (a) proportionality stricto sensu, (b) a least trade-restrictive alternative test, and (c) a simple means-end rationality test.

27. See, for example, Case C-76/90, *Sager v. Dennemeyer*, 1991, ECR I-4221. This case held that a national regulatory measure is enforceable against a service provider only if the public interest at stake "is not protected by the rules to which the person providing the services is subject in the Member State in which he is established." This indicates a possibility of judicially required recognition based on a necessity test, although it is noteworthy that the definition of "public interest" is notoriously open-ended. *See also* the European Commission interpretative communication concerning the free movement of services across frontiers, O.J. No. C334, 9.12.1993, at 3.

28. "Members shall accept the sanitary or phytosanitary measures of other Members as equivalent, even if these measures differ from their own or from those used by other Members trading in the same product, if the exporting Member demonstrates to the importing Member that its measures achieve the importing Member's appropriate level of sanitary or phytosanitary protection."

29. "Members shall give positive consideration to accepting as equivalent technical regulations of other Members, even if these regulations differ from their own, provided they are satisfied that these regulations adequately fulfill the objectives of their own regulations."

30. In the *Hormones* decision, the Appellate Body rejected the panel's finding that "based on" and "conform to" have the same meaning (WTO Appellate Body Report 1998b, para. 165).

31. WTO Appellate Body Report (1998b), citing WTO Report of the Panel 1997, para. 8.65; FAO; see Victor 2000, pp. 885–95.

32. Codex standards are generally adopted by consensus. Although the Codex Rules of Procedure provide for voting, voting is generally not used. In the event of a vote, decision is by majority of states present at the particular session. Compliance with Codex standards is voluntary (electronic mail message from Ellen Y. Matten, staff officer, U.S. Codex Office, to Joel P. Trachtman, dated August 8, 2001). Furthermore, under the Statements of Principle Concerning the Role of Science in the Codex Decision-Making Process and the Extent to Which Other Factors Are Taken into Account, "When the situation arises that members of Codex agree on the necessary level of protection of public health but hold differing views about other considerations, members may abstain from acceptance of the relevant standard without necessarily preventing the decision by Codex."

33. Rule VI.2, Rules of Procedure of the Codex Alimentarius Commission (Procedural Manual, 11th Edition, FAO and WHO, 2000).

34. Accountancy Disciplines, para. 26. International standards are those produced by relevant international organizations "whose membership is open to the relevant bodies of at least all Members of the WTO" (Accountancy Disciplines, footnote 2).

35. In this context, the EU has made the following statement: "New disciplines negotiated under Article VI.4 should develop new levels of guarantee providing increased transparency, predictability and certainty for regulators and operators. Concepts, which are not open to clear application without the further evaluation of specifically relevant criteria, might prove more valuable as overall guidelines rather than adopted as general disciplines. It is the purpose of this work further to clarify Members' obligations and not to create an unpredictable mandate for dispute settlement procedures to do so " (WTO 2001, para. 6).

36. Of course, there are dangers of lost democratic accountability associated with some of these quasi-legislative mechanisms. See, for example, Porter (2001), Slaughter (2001), and Zaring (1998).

37. For a broader discussion, see Nicolaïdis and Trachtman (2000).

38. Similarly, the Annex on Telecommunications allows for limitations of access to include "measures necessary to ensure the security and confidentiality of messages," restrictions on resale or shared use, requirements to use specified technical interfaces for interconnection, requirements for the interoperability of telecommunication services, approval by type of terminals attached to the network, restrictions on interconnection of private leased or owned circuits, and, last but not least, notification, registration, and licensing of foreign service providers (para. 5).

39. For a more extensive analysis of the objections to balancing tests, see Trachtman (1998).

References

The word "processed" describes informally produced works that may not be available commonly through libraries.

Abbott, Kenneth W., and Duncan Snidal. 2001. "International 'Standards' and International Governance." *Journal of European Public Policy* 8: 345–70.

Barcelo, John T. 1994. "Product Standards to Protect the Local Environment—the GATT and the Uruguay Round Sanitary and Phytosanitary Agreement." *Cornell International Law Journal* 27: 755–76.

Emiliou, Nicholas. 1996. *The Principle of Proportionality in European Law: A Comparative Study.* The Hague: Kluwer Law International.

FAO (Food and Agriculture Organization of the United Nations. 2000. "The Procedures for the Elaboration of Codex Standards and Related Texts." Available at www.fao.org.

Farber, Daniel A., and Robert E. Hudec. 1994. "Free Trade and the Regulatory State: A GATT's-Eye View of the Dormant Commerce Clause." *Vanderbilt Law Review* 47: 1401–40.

GATT Working Party Report. 1970. "Border Tax Adjustments." GATT Basic Instruments and Selected Documents 18S/97, December 2.

Geistfeld, Mark. 2001. "Reconciling Cost-Benefit Analysis with the Principle That Safety Matters More Than Money." *New York University Law Review* 76: 114–89.

Howse, Robert. 2000. "Democracy, Science and Free Trade: Risk Regulation on Trial at the World Trade Organization" *Michigan Law Review* 98: 2329–57.

Howse, Robert, and Petros C. Mavroidis. 2000. "Europe's Evolving Regulatory Strategy for GMOs—The Issue of Consistency with WTO Law: of Kine and Brine." *Fordham International Law Journal* 24: 317–70.

Low, Patrick, and Aaditya Mattoo. 1999. "Is There a Better Way? Alternative Approaches to Liberalization under the GATS." In Pierre Sauvé and Robert M. Stern, eds., *GATS 2000: New Directions in Services Trade Liberalization.* Washington, D.C.: Brookings Institution Press.

Marceau, Gabrielle, and Joel P. Trachtman. 2002. "TBT, SPS, and GATT: A Map of the WTO Law of Domestic Regulation." Processed.

Mattoo, Aaditya. 1997. "National Treatment in the GATS: Corner-Stone or Pandora's Box?" *Journal of World Trade* 31: 107–35.

Nicolaïdis, Kalypso. 1996. "Mutual Recognition of Regulatory Regimes: Some Lessons and Prospects." In *Regulatory Reform and International Market Openness.* Paris: Organisation for Economic Co-operation and Development.

———. 1997. "Promising Approaches and Principal Obstacles to Mutual Recognition." In *International Trade in Professional Services: Advancing Liberalization through Regulatory Reform.* Paris: Organisation for Economic Co-operation and Development.

Nicolaïdis, Kalypso, and Joel P. Trachtman. 2000. "From Policed Regulation to Managed Recognition: Mapping the Boundary in GATS." In Pierre Sauvé and Robert M. Stern, eds., *GATS 2000: New Directions in Services Trade Liberalization.* Washington, D.C.: Brookings Institution Press.

Ontario Ministry of Agriculture, Food, and Rural Affairs. 2000. *CODEX Alimentarius and CODEX Commission.* <http://www.gov.on.ca/OMAFRA/english/food/inspection/codex.htm>.

Pauwelyn, Joost. 1999. "The WTO Agreement on Sanitary and Phytosanitary (SPS) Measures as Applied in the First Three SPS Disputes." *Journal of International Economic Law* 4: 641–64.

Porter, Tony. 2001. "The Democratic Deficit in the Institutional Arrangements Governing Global Finance." *Global Governance* 7: 427–39.

Roberts, Donna. 1998. "Preliminary Assessment of the Effects of the WTO Agreement on Sanitary and Phytosanitary Trade Regulations." *Journal of International Economic Law* 1: 337–405.

Self, Richard B. 1996. "General Agreement on Trade in Services." In Terrence P. Stewart, ed., *The World Trade Organization: Multilateral Trade Framework for the 21st Century and U.S. Implementing Legislation.* Washington, D.C.: American Bar Association.

Slaughter, Anne-Marie. 2001. "Global Government Networks, Global Information Agencies, and Disaggregated Democracy." Harvard Law School, Public Law Working Paper 018. Cambridge, Mass. <http://papers.ssrn.com/abstract=283976>.

Stewart, Terence P., and David S. Johanson. 1998. "The SPS Agreement of the World Trade Organization and International Organizations: The Roles of the Codex Alimentarius Commission, the International Plant Protection Convention, and the International Office of Epizootics." *Syracuse Journal of International Law and Commerce* 26: 27–53.

Thailand—Restrictions on Importation of and Internal Taxes on Cigarettes. 1990. DS10/R, GATT 37 BISD 200.

Trachtman, Joel P. 1998. "Trade and . . . Problems, Cost-Benefit Analysis and Subsidiarity." *European Journal of International Law* 9: 32–85.

———. 1999. "The Domain of WTO Dispute Resolution." *Harvard International Law Journal* 40: 333–77.

———. 2000. "Regulatory Competition and Regulatory Jurisdiction." *Journal of International Economic Law* 3: 331–48.

Victor, David G. 2000. "The Sanitary and Phytosanitary Agreement of the World Trade Organization: An Assessment after Five Years." *New York University Journal of International Law and Policy* 32: 865–937.

WTO (World Trade Organization). 1994a. Agreement on the Application of Sanitary and Phytosanitary Measures. Annex 1A, Results of the Uruguay Round of Multilateral Trade Negotiations: The Legal Texts. April 15.

———. 1994b. Agreement on Technical Barriers to Trade. Annex 1A, Results of the Uruguay Round of Multilateral Trade Negotiations: The Legal Texts. April 15

———. 1998. *Disciplines on Domestic Regulation in the Accountancy Sector.* S/L/64, December 17.

———. 2001. Communication from the European Communities and Their Member States: Domestic Regulation: Necessity and Transparency. S/WPDR/W/14, May 1.

WTO Appellate Body Report. 1997. *European Communities—Regime for the Import and Sale of Bananas.* WT/DS27/AB/R, AB 1997-3, September 9.

———. 1998a. *Australia—Measures Affecting Importation of Salmon.* WT/DS18/AB/R, November 6.

———. 1998b. *EC Measures Concerning Meat and Meat Products (Hormones).* WT/DS26/AB/R, WT/DS48/AB/R, January 16.

———. 1998c. *United States—Import Prohibition of Certain Shrimp and Shrimp Products.* WT/DS58/AB/R, November 6.

———. 1999. *Japan—Measures Affecting Agricultural Products.* WT/DS76/AB/R, March 19.

———. 2000. *Canada—Certain Measures Affecting the Automotive Industry.* WT/DS139, 142/R, June 19.

———. 2001a. *European Communities—Measures Affecting Asbestos and Asbestos-Containing Products.* WT/DS135/AB/R, April 5.

———. 2001b. *Korea—Measures Affecting Imports of Fresh, Chilled and Frozen Beef.* WT/DS/161,169/AB/R, January 10.

———. 1997. *EC Measures Concerning Meat and Meat Products (Hormones).* Complaint by the United States. WT/DS26/R/USA, August 18.

———. 1998. *Japan—Measures Affecting Consumer Photographic Film and Paper.* WT/DS44/R, April 22.

WTO Working Party on Domestic Regulation. 1995. Informal note by the Secretariat on Negotiating History of the Coverage of the Agreement on Technical Barriers to Trade with Regard to Labelling Requirements, Voluntary Standards, and Processes and Production Methods Unrelated to Product Characteristics. WT/CTE/W/10; G/TBT/W/11, August 29.

———. 1996. Informal note by the Secretariat on the Relevance of the Disciplines of the Agreements on Technical Barriers to Trade and on Import Licensing Procedures to Article VI.4 of the General Agreement on Trade in Services. S/WPPS/W/9, September 11.

———. 1999. "Application of the Necessity Test: Issues for Consideration." Informal Note by the Secretariat. Job 5929, October 8. <http://www.wto.org/english/tratop_e/serv_e/serv_reg_secretariatnot_e.htm>.

———. 2001. "Examples of Measures to Be Addressed by Disciplines under GATS Article VI.4." Informal Note by the Secretariat. Job (01)/62, May 10.

WTO Working Party on Professional Services. 1998. "Discussion of Matters Relating to Articles XVI and XVII of the GATS in Connection with the Disciplines on Domestic Regulation in the Accountancy Sector." Informal Note by the Chairman. Job 6496, November 25.

Zaring, David. 1998. "International Law by Other Means: The Twilight Existence of International Financial Regulatory Organizations." *Texas International Law Journal* 33: 281–330.

DOMESTIC REGULATION AND TRADE IN TELECOMMUNICATIONS SERVICES: EXPERIENCE AND PROSPECTS UNDER THE GATS

Daniel Roseman

Executive Summary

The General Agreement on Trade in Services (GATS) Annex on Telecommunications and the Reference Paper on procompetitive regulation, together with the GATS' most-favored-nation obligation, provide members of the World Trade Organization (WTO) with the basic elements of "best"/procompetitive regulatory practices in the telecommunications sector. The issues and principles addressed and codified in the annex and Reference Paper were identified in the course of telecommunications liberalization in the countries that were among the first to open their telecommunications markets to competition. The incorporation of these principles in a multilateral trade agreement has enabled other countries to learn and borrow from the experiences of these first countries, thus sparing them considerable trial-and-error and shortening their regulatory learning curves. The presence of a procompetitive regulatory framework increases security of access and predictability, thus attracting investment in new service providers and permitting consumers and users to reap the benefits of competition much earlier than if these countries were to start on their own at the very beginning of reform. An important and positive effect of liberalization is the growth of network externalities; where telecom penetration rates are lowest and rise quickly over time, the benefits would be greatest because of network externalities.

The implementation of GATS telecom obligations and regulatory disciplines generally has gone well, although some WTO members have been slow to implement their commitments. Everyone has had difficulties devising effective interconnection rules. Other problem areas in some countries have been licensing and the independence of the regulator. Formal WTO dispute settlement procedures have been invoked in only one instance to date. In purely domestic disputes WTO obligations are rarely invoked in regulatory and judicial processes. The principal reasons are that trade obligations usually are not directly binding in domestic law, and trade agreements leave considerable scope for each country to implement its obligations in the way it sees fit. Therefore, the applicable law and the context of domestic disputes is domestic law.

The disciplines of the annex and Reference Paper are primarily relevant in the context of the transition from monopoly to competitive markets. Technologies and markets are not static, and regulations—and trade rules governing domestic regulation—therefore should be revisited from time to time to ensure both their effectiveness and their continued relevance. The ongoing GATS negotiations afford the opportunity to reexamine issues that may have been inadequately addressed in the annex and Reference Paper and to address new challenges that were unanticipated or left unresolved during the previous negotiations. If these negotiations are to make a qualitative difference, at a minimum they will need to address the application of trade rules to nontraditional telecommunications networks and services (i.e., cable television and wireless), interconnection and unbundling, and licensing. Disciplines on government procurement of telecommunication services (and subsidies) could also yield benefits in terms of competitive neutrality and transparent, reasonable, and nondiscriminatory regulation, leading to enhanced competition and benefits to users.

The new negotiations also afford an opportunity to determine whether telecom-type trade disciplines can be negotiated for other service sectors. It would be advisable to undertake a sectoral testing exercise, by means of which the principles and disciplines elaborated in the Telecommunications Annex and Reference Paper would be examined for their relevance and adaptability to other service sectors. Consideration should also be given to employing a two-step approach in other sectors that deal with regulatory issues relating to access and use separately from the development of a regulatory framework for actual competition in the supply of specified services. However, one must be wary of "one-size-fits-all" approaches that fail to recognize the specificities of individual sectors.

Unlike the General Agreement on Tariffs and Trade (GATT), the General Agreement on Trade in Services (GATS) is not so much about barriers at the border as barriers inside the border. Regulatory reform is one step further still beyond the removal of internal quantitative restrictions on market access because it attempts to establish the economic, technical, social, environmental, and other terms and conditions under which market participants act. Although the GATS recognizes the "right to regulate," it also provides rudimentary regulatory requirements, as well as a basis for the negotiation of more detailed rules governing regulatory measures. This approach to trade liberalization was a result of lessons drawn in the countries that first opened their markets to competition. They learned that commitments to liberalize market entry and to

remove restrictions on foreign investment would not of themselves bring about competitive outcomes, especially in industries, such as telecommunications, where there are significant economies of scale and scope, network effects, and positive externalities. Rather, a regulatory environment that complements and supports the decision to permit competition would be needed.

Brief Background to the Negotiation of Existing GATS Obligations in Telecommunications

The GATS rules governing regulatory measures in the telecommunications sector were developed in two steps: (1) with the Annex on Telecommunications negotiated during the Uruguay Round, dealing access to and use of (essentially monopoly) public telecommunications transport networks and services; and (2) with the Reference Paper developed during the negotiations on basic telecommunications, which provides procompetitive principles to guide the development of regulations in the context of competition in the supply of telecom transport networks and services.

From the beginning of the Uruguay Round it was recognized that telecommunications would play a prominent role in the services negotiations, both as an important economic sector in its own right and as a key enabler of other economic activities. In the 1980s the pressure to liberalize telecommunications markets was coming from big users of public telecommunications networks and services, especially from transnational corporations such as banks, insurers, and manufacturers, but also from providers of value-added telecom services. Riding a wave of technological and market innovations (digitization, convergence of telecoms and computing, the rapid evolution of the telecommunications business "from POTS to PANS"[1]), and the increasing globalization of trade and investment, these users pushed for the right to exploit the possibilities made available by new technologies to provide seamless and efficient global intracorporate and value-added communications that would enable them to operate more effectively on a global basis and to exploit the "first-mover" advantages they had acquired in markets that had already opened to competition, particularly in the United States but also to some extent in Canada, Japan, and the United Kingdom.

The Uruguay Round offered these users an opportunity to achieve on a multilateral basis what Canada and the United States had done in their Free Trade Agreement (FTA) annex on computer services and telecommunications network-based enhanced services. However, although it was possible in the FTA to paper over the slim regulatory differences between Canada and the United States by leaving key definitional issues to "the regulator having jurisdiction," it was necessary to go further to ensure some convergence on common regulatory standards among the participants in the Uruguay Round. Thus the GATS Annex on Telecommunications would spell out in some considerable detail key definitions, as well as rights and obligations on access and use that impinge on domestic policymakers and regulators.

Basic telecommunications were essentially carved out of the Uruguay Round because of the reluctance of the United States to allow most-favored-nation (MFN) treatment to apply as long as most other markets were closed to competition in the provision of basic services. Notwithstanding U.S. protests, however, other industrial countries were eager to engage in a negotiation that would provide governments with a lever to advance an agenda of telecom liberalization in the face of resistance from domestic interests that found comfort in the old monopoly market structures. The process that worked out the deal to hold further negotiations on basic telecommunications made clear that regulatory issues would be an integral part of the efforts to ensure effective market access; that is, when specific commitments were given, they would not be nullified or impaired by the absence of the necessary supporting domestic regulatory disciplines.

Summary of GATS Disciplines on Telecom Regulation

The sections that follow describe the core elements of the package of GATS rules in telecommunications services negotiated during the Uruguay Round and the negotiations on basic telecommunications.

GATS Annex on Telecommunications

During the Uruguay Round negotiations that created the GATS, the consensus emerged fairly early that the eventual agreement would contain specific recognition of governments' continued "right to regulate" (i.e., the ability to maintain existing measures and to introduce new ones affecting covered services whenever they might deem it necessary). At the same time, however, parties to the agreement would undertake that such measures would be consistent with their trade obligations (e.g., there would be nondiscrimination, transparency, and reasonableness in the setting and implementation of rules, regulations, and standards).

Although few countries were prepared at that time to countenance competition in basic telecoms, the common understanding emerged that it would be desirable to put some telecom sector-specific rules in place on a multilateral basis that would recognize the need for flexibility by each country in the way it would respond to technological and market changes, while ensuring against the development of a patchwork of inconsistencies and discriminatory practices. The focus of the telecom negotiations therefore came to be the users' agenda; that is, the development of a set of principles and rules to govern access to and use of public telecommunications transport networks and services (PTTNS—i.e., the basic networks and services of common carriers, including voice and data transmission facilities and services) in order to facilitate intracorporate communications and the sale of services to third parties (not only value-added services, but all others covered in members' schedules).

The annex is all about regulatory issues. It was "designed to supplement and strengthen the disciplines" (Tuthill 1996: 91) of the GATS framework, in particular Article III on transparency, Article VI on domestic regulation, Article VIII on monopoly and exclusive suppliers, and Article XI on business practices, so as to deal more adequately with what negotiators called "the specificities of the telecommunications sector." The annex supplements and amplifies the framework disciplines in a manner that liberalizes markets beyond any specific commitments given in the telecommunications sector because the benefits of the Annex apply automatically to any sector in which a commitment is scheduled.[2]

The annex establishes minimum international standards of good regulatory behavior and sets out agreed terms and conditions for transparent, nondiscriminatory, and reasonable access to and use of PTTNS once market access is granted by a member to a supplier of scheduled services (enhanced telecom services, computer services, financial services, engineering, and so forth). The essence of the annex is the obligation to ensure that market access commitments are not frustrated by restrictions on access to and use of basic telecom networks and services. The annex created, in effect, additional commitments of a regulatory nature, but these commitments are common to all members of the World Trade Organization (WTO) and cannot be derogated from, except paragraph 5(g) for developing countries (compare below).

The following is a brief summary of key provisions:

- The footnote to Article 2(a) addresses the question of the extent to which the GATS imposes obligations affecting the behavior of privately owned telecom carriers, as well as governments and governmental bodies. The issue was a matter of equity and the symmetry of obligations among parties who were at different stages of liberalization of their telecommunications markets; it was a major sticking point between the European Commission (EC) and the United States. The EC, representing the interests of a large number of member states with state-run providers of telecommunications services, was at the time embarking on a process to liberalize telecoms in Europe; they wanted all parties to the negotiations fully accountable in the WTO for the actions of all their service providers, including private service providers operating in competitive markets (e.g., AT&T, MCI, and Sprint in the United States). For their part, the U.S. authorities were reluctant to allow trade rules to impinge on actions of the Federal Communications Commission (FCC) vis-à-vis private U.S. persons; they argued that the United States offered a fully competitive market for access and use where anyone having trouble obtaining the PTTNS they require from a service supplier needs merely to turn to a competitor for service or seek regulatory redress on the basis of U.S. domestic laws and regulations. The wording represents the extent to which the EC and the United States were able to reconcile their perspectives.

- Paragraph 2(b), at Canada's request, carved cable and broadcast distribution of radio and television programming out of the annex, in view of the development of dial-up video and so forth. This creates a vacuum in terms of trade disciplines governing the regulation of online audio and video content, as well as uncertainty about the application of the annex to cable companies and other nontraditional telecom service suppliers over whose networks scheduled services (e.g., online information services) may be delivered.

- Paragraph 3(b) defines "public telecommunications transport service" as "any telecommunications transport service required, explicitly or in effect, by a Member to be offered to the public generally. Such services . . . typically involv[e] the real-time transmission of customer-supplied information between two or more points without any end-to-end change in the form or content of the customer's information."

- Paragraph 3(c) defines "public telecommunications transport network" (PTTN) as "the public telecommunications infrastructure which permits telecommunications between and among defined network termination points." These definitions establish which services (i.e., PTTNS) are subject to the annex's requirements to afford access and use on transparent, reasonable, and nondiscriminatory terms and conditions.

- Article 4 builds on the GATS' transparency obligations and requires that "all relevant information . . . is publicly available." Its specifics are tailored to the circumstances of the annex. Article 4 enters into areas that would not be considered "measures" in some jurisdictions (e.g., specifications of technical interfaces), and it requires the creation of measures to govern such specifications where none would otherwise exist.

- Article 5 sets out the key obligations of the annex.

- Paragraph 5(a) requires access to and use of PTTNS on nondiscriminatory and reasonable terms and conditions, without the possibility of an MFN exemption or reservation for national treatment. The footnote clarifies that "non-discriminatory" means not only MFN and national treatment, but also "terms and conditions no less favorable than those accorded to any other user of like PTTNS under like circumstances"; that is, one may provide for different terms and conditions among different classes of users, but not within the same class, provided that such differential treatment (including, for example, the identification of different classes of users) is reasonable, not an arbitrary form of discrimination, nor a disguised or unnecessary restriction on trade. Thus paragraph 5(a) introduced into trade policy a third meaning for the term "nondiscrimination" that was commonly understood by regulators, but new in a trade agreement context.

- Paragraphs 5(b) to 5(g) set out the ways in which the obligations of 5(a) shall be implemented. Paragraphs 5(b) and 5(c) set out the rights of users, and paragraphs 5(d) to 5(g) set out the allowable exceptions.

- A paragraph calling, on a best-efforts basis, for "cost-oriented pricing" for access and use was in the text until December 1993 when it was removed at the behest of India. In the absence of this clause, it would still be possible to press a nonviolation case for pricing that was so far out of line that it effectively nullified or impaired the benefits reasonably expected to obtain under the GATS.

- Paragraph 5(b) establishes that the obligations of the annex apply to access to and use of PTTNS "offered within and across the border." Thus the annex satisfied the demands of user industries for both a "right of non-establishment" and a "right to connect," while taking into account the different modes of supply recognized in the GATS.

- Paragraph 5(b)(i) establishes the scope of terminal equipment that can be attached to the network, and paragraphs 5(b)(ii) and 5(b)(iii) establish the right to interconnect private networks of leased lines or owned facilities using proprietary protocols. Because the term "equipment which interfaces with the network" was more liberal than some participating governments had envisaged, its adoption added to the liberalizing effect of the annex. This was an effort to ensure that standards would not act as barriers to trade, but rather facilitate competition by ensuring maximum interconnectivity and interoperability. In this instance it was recognized that mandatory interface standards may at times be appropriate, but internal network standards should be of the suppliers' choice.

This is very important because it affects the ability of firms to provide their services and conduct intracorporate communications as best suits their own business strategies.

- Paragraph 5(c) elaborates on the rights to intracorporate communications and the movement of information "within and across borders," and paragraph 5(d) establishes that these rights shall be subject only to an exception for "security and confidentiality of messages" (old International Telecommunication Union [ITU] language). Those who had sought to prevent or impede cross-border data flows had lost. The EC's proposal for an exception for the protection of personal privacy, which would override the obligation to allow the movement of information across borders, found its place in the broader GATS Article XIV on general exceptions.

- Although recognizing that members may wish to attach conditions to the use of telecommunications by a service supplier, paragraph 5(e) permits such conditions to be imposed only to the extent necessary: to "safeguard the public service responsibilities" of the network operator, including its universal service obligations (5[e][i]); to "protect the technical integrity" of the network (5[e][ii]); and to prevent the user from supplying a service for which the member has not made any specific commitment (5[e][iii]). Decried by some user representatives as a "regulators' bill of rights," this section nonetheless tightly circumscribed those rights.

- Paragraph 5(f) sets out, for greater clarity, an illustrative list of the kinds of conditions that normally would be permitted if they meet the tests in 5(e), including restrictions on resale, mandatory standards, type approval of terminal equipment, restrictions on interconnection with the public network, and licensing conditions.

- Paragraph 5(g) recognizes that some developing countries may need to impose additional conditions on access to and use of their public networks. Any such special conditions, however, would have to be "consistent with their level of development" and "specified in the Member's schedule" (i.e., negotiated beforehand and bound). This provision was much less than the "special and differential treatment" that some developing countries initially sought; nonetheless, it has never been used.

Reference Paper on Procompetitive Regulatory Principles

As with the Uruguay Round negotiations on the Telecommunications Annex, during the WTO negotiations on basic telecommunications negotiators needed to take account of "the specificities of the telecommunications sector." Given the different focus of the negotiations (i.e., competition in the supply of basic networks and services rather than access to and use of the same), governments were confronted with a much more complex set of interests to balance. In particular, the interests of suppliers were ascendant (both offensive and defensive) compared with the interests of users, and labor unions were more vocal because of the greater threat of job losses as a result of competition. For their part, governments by and large were coming to recognize that state-owned monopoly service providers were an impediment to economic growth.

The Reference Paper is a tool for the negotiation of additional commitments (i.e., commitments beyond those on market access and national treatment) regarding regulatory measures concerning basic telecommunications. Unlike the Annex on Telecommunications, the Reference Paper attains legal status only to the extent that WTO members have incorporated it in their schedules of commitments under the GATS. Thus, when the basic telecom negotiations concluded in February 1997, of the 69 WTO members undertaking commitments, 63 members subscribed to the Reference Paper in whole or in part. A further 5 members gave "late" commitments that included the Reference Paper, and all countries acceding to the WTO since February 1997 have adopted the complete Reference Paper.

The objective of the Reference Paper was to ensure effective market access by means of additional commitments to put in place a procompetitive regulatory regime to protect against the nullification and impairment of the benefits that members could reasonably expect to flow from market access liberalization. Committing to the Reference Paper enhances the value of, and adds security to, specific commitments on market access and national treatment in basic telecommunications. This is important because the complex nature of telecommunications and the economies of scale and scope in the industry make it unrealis-

tic to leap from monopoly to open, unregulated markets and then to expect the full benefits of liberalization to be realized.

The Reference Paper sets out minimum standards for the measures that governments should take to ensure a procompetitive, transparent, reasonable, and nondiscriminatory regulatory environment. In this way the document helps ensure that former monopoly service providers do not subvert their governments' reforms. Like the Annex on Telecommunications, it "supplements and strengthens" the GATS framework disciplines on transparency, domestic regulation, monopolies and exclusive service suppliers, and restrictive business practices. The document is procompetitive, but it is neutral as to outcomes (i.e., it does not tip the balance in favor of new entrants or incumbents). Although it establishes minimums to be fulfilled, the Reference Paper leaves the details and the choice of means to each member to decide.

The following is a brief summary of key provisions:

- Under "Scope," the Reference Paper sets out "definitions and principles on the regulatory framework for the basic telecommunications services" (sic). It then sets out definitions of users, essential facilities, and major suppliers.

- Building on GATS Articles VIII (monopoly and exclusive suppliers) and IX (business practices), Section 1 establishes minimum "competitive safeguards." Members who subscribe to the obligations must maintain "appropriate measures" to prevent "suppliers who, alone or together, are a major supplier from engaging in or continuing anticompetitive practices" (e.g., anticompetitive cross-subsidization, misuse of information from competitors, and withholding necessary technical information). These competition safeguards were inspired by competition law, but the Reference Paper is sector specific in its prescriptions. WTO telecom trade negotiators understood that achieving effective market access would require establishing disciplines against anticompetitive behavior by private individuals. However, they needed to strike a careful balance. On one hand, telecom policymakers and regulators were increasingly receptive to the idea that a telecom trade agreement would need to include safeguards against anticompetitive behavior. On the other hand, some competition authorities were very concerned that the incorporation of competition policy principles in a trade agreement could lead to conflicting interpretations of these principles when made pursuant to different statutory authorities, and could compromise their own relative independence. Thus, the Reference Paper steps into the competition law area by seeking to deter private barriers to the development of efficient markets, in addition to governmental barriers to trade and investment. This constitutes an important contribution to the development of the interface between trade and competition policy.

- Recognizing that the right to interconnect is the most important competition safeguard in a network industry,[3] Section 2 creates a requirement for measures to permit interconnection of competing suppliers of public telecommunications transport networks and services "at any technically feasible point in the network" (subsection 2.2, *chapeau*), "under non-discriminatory terms [and] conditions" (subsection 2.2[a]), "in a timely fashion," and "on terms, conditions (including technical standards and specifications) and cost-oriented rates that are transparent, reasonable, having regard to economic feasibility, and sufficiently unbundled so that the supplier need not pay for network components or facilities that it does not require for the service to be provided" (subsection 2.2[b]), and "upon request, at points in addition to the network termination points offered to the majority of users, subject to charges that reflect the cost of construction of necessary additional facilities" (subsection 2.2[c]).
- Sections 2.3 and 2.4 set out transparency requirements regarding the public availability of interconnection procedures and agreements. Section 2.5 supplements the Article VI.2 requirement for local mechanisms to review and, if necessary, remedy administrative decisions regarding domestic measures by creating an obligation on members to maintain a body to resolve interconnection disputes among telecom service suppliers.
- Section 3 acknowledges "the right" of each member "to define the kind of universal service obligation it wishes to maintain," and it states that "[s]uch obligations will not be regarded as

anti-competitive per se." However, it qualifies this right with the proviso that universal service obligations be "administered in a transparent, non-discriminatory and competitively neutral manner and are not more burdensome than necessary for the kind of universal service defined by the Member." This provision balanced the concerns of Canada and the United States, which had achieved virtually universal service largely by means of private operators, with the scepticism of the Europeans and others regarding the ability to achieve universal service objectives without direct governmental interventions.

- Licensing was a highly controversial subject, pitting the United States, with the FCC's slow-moving and onerous ex ante licensing procedures against those who were partial to a light-handed regime that would deal with potentially anticompetitive behavior ex post market entry.[4] Section 4 creates additional transparency obligations by requiring the public availability of information regarding licensing criteria, processing periods, and terms and conditions, as well as the "reasons for denial of a licence." That is as far as negotiations were able to go in this sensitive area.
- Section 5 requires the establishment of an "Independent Regulator"—independent in the sense that the regulator must be "separate from, and not accountable to, any supplier of basic telecommunications services" and that its procedures and decisions (e.g., licensing, competition safeguards, approval of tariffs, operating agreements, and the settlement of disputes) "shall be impartial with respect to all market participants." Establishing an independent regulator is indirectly a liberalizing measure because it is effectively a precondition for greater transparency and nondiscrimination in regulatory decisionmaking processes and outcomes.
- Section 6 requires that information regarding and procedures for the "allocation and use of scarce resources" (e.g., frequencies, numbers, rights of way) must be transparent and nondiscriminatory. This is necessary to ensure that the incumbent, as the former sole user of such resources, does not retain any undue advantage in the marketplace by continuing to monopolize spectrum, rights of way, and so forth.

Impact of GATS Disciplines on Domestic Regulation

The negotiations themselves—during the Uruguay Round on the Telecommunications Annex and even more so subsequently on basic telecommunications—acted as catalysts for reform. Their high profile invigorated and helped channel domestic debates in the direction of liberalization and procompetitive regulation, raising the issue to the highest levels of government in a large number of countries.

In terms of impact on domestic regulation in the telecommunications sector, the first and most obvious impact of the GATS is that it provides the outlines of a regulatory framework for countries opening their telecom services markets, whether in whole or by degrees (e.g., moving along the spectrum from private line resale to liberalized terminal attachment, to resale of basic services and full facilities-based competition). Drawing on more than a decade of experience with telecom liberalization in a handful of industrial countries, negotiators from the Uruguay Round and the Group on Basic Telecommunications (GBT) created documents that represent a transfer of know-how to other countries, documents that offer the opportunity to avoid years of trial and error. These WTO/GATS agreements provide direction, as well as a degree of urgency, thanks to deadlines and the threat of binding dispute settlement. All operators in the market know that changes are coming and that they must respond in some way. Investors receive assurances of greater security and predictability in a rules-based environment. Users and consumers receive greater choice and, at least in long distance services, reduced prices.

Implementation of the GATS Annex on Telecommunications and the WTO Agreement on Basic Telecommunications (ABT) appears to have proceeded generally quite well. Fink, Mattoo, and Rathindran (2001: 13) noted that competitive markets have contributed substantially to increased service penetration rates, service quality, and labor productivity in Asia, but that "the creation of a separate regulator is a necessary rather than a sufficient condition for effective regulation." Roseman (2002: para. 90) noted that "the existence of independent and effective regulators that pursue procompetitive mandates is an important factor that helps to ensure that the benefits of liberalization are not frustrated by incumbent operators." Rose-man (2002: para. 100) also noted the positive "impact of liberalization [on] the growth of network externalities, which increase with higher telecom penetration rates and usage . . . ; that is, where telecom penetration rates are lowest and rise quickly over time, the benefits would be greatest, due to network externalities." The Republic of Korea is an excellent example of this phenomenon. Not only has it achieved industrial country penetration rates during the past decade of liberalization; it also leads the world in broadband usage.

PricewaterhouseCoopers (PwC) undertook a study for the Asian Pacific Economic Cooperation forum (APEC) that shows that some APEC economies have been slow to implement their ABT commitments. PwC (2000) identified the need to:

- Improve transparency in most economies
- Reduce the influence of incumbent operators in some cases
- Ensure the independence of the regulator from operators
- Improve the responsiveness of regulatory authorities and the timeliness of their decisions
- Enhance regulatory methods, reporting requirements, and information dissemination
- Ensure effective competition safeguards and enforcement
- Accelerate local loop competition
- Further relax foreign ownership restrictions in some cases.

This is happening to a large extent in the APEC region, and in other regions of the world, but these are tasks for the long term, particularly with respect to the least-developed countries.

These reforms are important for the development of both the telecommunications sector and the overall economy. But they are not cost free, and many developing countries lack the human and financial resources to implement them without external assistance. To this end PwC (2000) recommended the following for APEC economies:

- Greater assistance from multilateral agencies
- Adoption of best practices of other countries
- Exchanges of experts.

These recommendations apply in other regions as well, particularly for small developing countries that do not possess individually the wherewithal to staff and finance a national regulatory body.

Technical and financial assistance and cooperation are important for developing countries, in order to ensure that these countries have appropriate institutions and that their policymakers, regulators, and operators have the right mindsets and skillsets to ensure successful implementation of telecom reforms. Every effort should be made to provide a wide variety of training—for example, training to help key personnel understand the implications of different technologies and regulatory models when it comes to implementing WTO commitments, such as cost-oriented interconnection, which are key to the regulatory framework. Furthermore, developing countries would do well to consider pooling human and financial resources with their neighbors so as to reap the benefits of liberalization while amortizing the costs of a regulatory authority over a larger market. With the support of the World Bank, the member countries of the Organization of Eastern Caribbean States (OECS) are pooling resources into a new regional body, the Eastern Caribbean Telecommunications Authority (ECTEL), which will provide technical expertise, advice, and support for national regulations.[5] Another approach is illustrated by the ITU's Centres of Excellence, which provide technical assistance to developing countries on a regional basis without creating regional regulatory authorities. These two approaches are complementary.

To date there have not been a large number of complaints over implementation of the WTO/GATS Agreement on Basic Telecommunications. But complaints are inevitable in a competitive market, where incumbents, new entrants, and users have competing ambitions and conflicting views—particularly over interconnection, whether over unbundled local loop access or the pricing of international carriage of Internet services. The European Union and the United States have complained about high interconnection charges in Japan and have used the threat of WTO dispute settlement to reduce those rates somewhat. There were also U.S. complaints about interconnection arrangements and prices in Germany, which were eventually resolved by actions of the German regulator. A large number of countries from the Asian Pacific region, South America, and Africa have complained about the large outpayments their service providers make

to interconnect and exchange traffic with international Internet backbone service providers.[6] The only case in which WTO dispute settlement procedures have been invoked is an ongoing dispute between Mexico and the United States relating to U.S. complaints about a lack of effective disciplines on the former monopoly, Telmex; failure to ensure timely, cost-oriented interconnection; and failure to permit alternatives to the traditional method of international call settlement.[7] Formal consultations took place in Geneva, and the dispute was temporarily resolved after the Mexican regulator, Cofetel, made clear that it would enforce its regulations against anticompetitive behavior, and Mexican and U.S. carriers agreed on new settlement rates.[8] Subsequently, however, the United States requested a panel over unresolved issues (United States Trade Representative 2002). The EU has threatened recourse to a disputes panel over the alleged lack of an independent regulator in Japan, but it has not so far followed through. In addition, there have been a number of complaints over delays in the United States regarding the licensing of foreign entrants and authorizing foreign acquisitions.[9]

WTO/GATS obligations, however, work not only when there are high-profile trade disputes. Indeed, one could argue that trade disputes arise when the obligations are not working well enough, in the sense of providing clear rights and obligations. Although international pressures frequently provide governments with the impetus necessary to undertake telecom reforms, when a country sets out on the path of competition and reform, if they are implemented in a manner that is consistent with the disciplines of the GATS, there may be no further reference to international trade pressures or obligations. Rather, any change undertaken is done "for good domestic policy reasons."

Most domestic regulatory battles are fought without reference to international trade obligations when a country has implemented those obligations in its domestic legal and regulatory framework. The principal reasons for this are:

1. The high-level generality of the provisions relating to regulatory matters in trade agreements; these leave considerable scope for each country to implement its obligations in the way it sees fit.
2. The legal reality that trade obligations are not usually directly binding in domestic law.

An example of the first reason is the Reference Paper requirement for an independent regulator. This requirement is without prejudice as to whether the regulator should be separate from the ministry that makes telecom policy. Some countries tended to favor a regulator who is separate or at arm's length from the government in order to insulate regulatory decisions from political interference and to insulate government from pressures to make day-to-day interventions in the market based on political and economic pressures rather than in the context of broad public interest; transparent processes; economic, legal, and technical arguments; and specialized expertise. Canada, the United Kingdom, and the United States had regulators separate from their policy departments. Eventually, the continental European members of the Organisation for Economic Co-operation and Development (OECD) also adopted this approach, as did Mexico. Japan and Korea, however, continue to perform telecom regulatory functions from inside the policy ministry. In Korea's case, the Ministry of Information and Communications (MIC) is the major shareholder in Korea Telecom (KT) and, with the Ministry of Finance and Economy, MIC approves KT's tariffs for local services. In Japan's case, the Ministry of Public Management, Home Affairs, Posts, and Telecommunications (MPHPT) is regulator and policymaker and the Ministry of Finance holds the largest share in Nippon Telephone and Telegraph, the former monopoly domestic service supplier.

The requirement for an independent regulator is also without prejudice as to whether the independent regulator should be a sector-specific regulator of telecommunication services or a regulator operating under the general economic laws of competition policy. Because of sensitivities in some countries (notably New Zealand), the WTO did not impose any requirements to (re)introduce sector-specific regulation. There were also sensitivities in some countries (notably the United States) that a negotiation on telecommunication services should not upset the balance of power and jurisdiction (i.e., turf) between existing sector-specific and general economic regulators (i.e., the U.S. Federal Communications Commission, the Federal Trade Commission, and the Department of Justice).

As to the second reason why most domestic regulatory matters are resolved without reference to international obligations (i.e., trade obligations are not usually directly binding in domestic law), the people in the regulatory trenches (regulators, ministries, courts, and industry participants) argue their positions primarily on the basis of domestic laws, regulations, and precedents. Only *in extremis* will parties invoke international obligations to support their positions on domestic regulatory matters. One example in which a Canadian company invoked the WTO/GATS in front of the CRTC and the Canadian Federal Court of Appeal was the case of North American Gateway, a small reseller engaged in international switched hubbing against the wishes of Teleglobe, to whom the right to allow international switched hubbing effectively had been delegated by the Government of Canada and the CRTC. Canada had reserved in its schedule of commitments its restrictions on the routing of Canadian traffic, and Teleglobe sought to enforce its rights. In trade policy terms, however, the restrictions were fundamentally inconsistent with MFN and not capable of being covered by any scheduled reservation. Ultimately the CRTC ruled that it was in the public interest to eliminate the routing restrictions, without making specific reference to their incompatibility with Canada's trade obligations.[10]

Another Canadian example is Covad Canada, which used an interpretation of Canada's schedule of commitments and the Reference Paper to argue that the CRTC should change its policy on local competition so that non-facilities-based suppliers of digital subscriber line (DSL) services would be allowed interconnection, access to unbundled facilities, and co-location on the same terms and conditions as facilities-based suppliers.[11] Roseman (2000) did not share the interpretation of Canada's trade obligations provided by Covad's counsel and in a submission on behalf of an incumbent telephone company, Telus, argued that the CRTC's policy was consistent with the provisions of the GATS Annex on Telecommunications that permits the differentiation among different classes of users of PTTNS (in this case, between facilities-based and non-facilities-based suppliers of DSL services), where such differentiation can be justified in terms of the principles set out in GATS Article VI ("reasonable, objective and impartial" administration of measures affecting trade in services). However, the CRTC looked at the domestic market and the relatively slow development of DSL competition, and it decided—without making any reference to the question of WTO compatibility—that it was in the public interest to grant Covad's request (CRTC 2000). This decision was accepted by all interested parties without appeal.

A French example is the dispute over the financing of France Télécom's universal service obligations. The European Court of Justice found that France was in violation of EU directives on competition in the markets for telecommunications services and on interconnection with regard to ensuring universal service and interoperability through application of the principles of open network provision (European Court of Justice 2001). Nowhere in this decision does one find any reference to WTO/GATS obligations. It is unlikely that either of the parties to the dispute felt it necessary to invoke the provision in the Reference Paper, recognizing "the right" of each member "to define the kind of universal service obligation it wishes to maintain," on condition that "such obligations . . . are administered in a transparent, non-discriminatory and competitively neutral manner and are not more burdensome than necessary . . . ," for the EU's own directives are the applicable law and in this case they provided a sufficient (and more detailed) basis on which to resolve the dispute.

A third and ongoing Canadian example is the municipalities' fight against the CRTC's jurisdiction over municipal rights of way.[12] This dispute has worked its way up through questions of fees for pavement restoration and lost parking meter revenue to become an important constitutional issue that may ultimately be referred to the Supreme Court of Canada for resolution. So far, in the thousands of pages of written submissions there have been no references by industry participants or by federal, provincial, or municipal representatives to the Reference Paper, the relevant provision of which is broad but requires that "[a]ny procedures for the allocation and use of scarce resources, including . . . rights of way will be carried out in an objective, timely, transparent and non-discriminatory manner." Because sections 42–46 of Canada's Telecommunications Act set out in some detail the substantive law that the CRTC is to apply, the Reference

Paper would probably be too general to provide useful guidance in this dispute if it had direct effect in Canadian law. However, the Reference Paper can provide useful guidance to countries that have less developed systems of law than Canada (or the EU).[13]

Korea offers an example in which the government used the pressures of international telecom negotiations and the obligations that flowed from them to strengthen its hand vis-à-vis domestic interests to advance a program of liberalization and regulatory reform. Lee and Lie (2000: 2) noted that "deregulation . . . has succeeded in enhancing the overall performance in the market through the promotion of competition." The WTO agreement "facilitated contestability of the international service market by allowing voice resellers to enter," helped new mobile service providers to raise capital ("resulting in enhancing competition in the mobile sector"), and "accelerated the privatization of [Korea Telecom]" (Lee and Lie 2000, p. 18). From the perspective of industrial organization, Lee and Lie (2000. p. 19) noted that the Korean market is now characterized by "homogeneity of service, frictionless entry and exit, no universal service obligation enabling . . . cream-skimming, and price advantage of resellers over [facilities-based service providers]." They conceded that foreign investment came at a price: the *chaebols,* which had been national champions in the reconstruction of the country, had to cede "some rights of management" (Lee and Lie 2000, p. 27) in their mobile affiliates. However, the result was "not only [to] improve their corporate governance system[s], e.g. rational decision making on investment, but also [to make] the mobile services market [flourish]" (Lee and Lie 2000, p. 27). Foreign investment is now viewed less suspiciously in Korea: "relics of the [old] protectionism ha[ve] been replaced by the positive way of thinking that [foreign direct investment] could play a significant role in diluting [the] concentrated ownership of *chaebols* and securing a funding resource" (Lee and Lie 2000, p. 26). Korea has—in the face of international trade and financial pressures—adopted a regulatory framework that is decidedly procompetitive, whereas Japan has been dragging its feet to the detriment especially of wireline competition and consumers of wireline services[14] (excerpted from Roseman 2002).

Scope for Further Competition Safeguards and Regulatory Disciplines in Telecommunications Trade

The Annex on Telecommunications and the Reference Paper set out the rudiments of best (procompetitive) practices in the regulation of telecommunications. These documents are primarily relevant for countries as they make the transition from monopoly to competitive markets. However, the technologies and markets for telecommunications services continue to evolve rapidly and to raise new challenges and questions about whether and how to regulate in domestic markets. Few people imagined during the basic telecom negotiations that, on one hand, soon after the basic telecommunications negotiations would close, telephone companies would begin converting their public, circuit-switched voice networks to Internet protocol (IP) technologies. On the other hand, many expected the convergence of telecom and broadcasting technologies and services to occur much faster than they have done in practice.

The ongoing services negotiations provide governments, industries, and other interested parties an opportunity to review existing obligations in light of their experiences to date, with a view to updating them where necessary and anticipating changes in markets where possible. Although there appears to be little enthusiasm for a revisiting of telecom regulatory disciplines and competition safeguards in the WTO's new round—lest this cause the Reference Paper to unravel or become "contaminated" by extraneous issues—there are issues that will need to be addressed at some point, particularly because telecom markets are not static and electronic commerce is likely to drive the next stage of negotiations on telecom regulatory matters.

For these reasons, this section will assume that further work on procompetitive regulatory disciplines will be undertaken eventually during the new round to ensure the continued relevance and effectiveness of existing disciplines. In particular, this section will highlight a number of areas where it is for consideration whether the negotiations should aim to go beyond the existing GATS framework, the Telecoms Annex, and the Reference Paper in terms of the further development of a global regulatory framework for telecommunications, first where implementation has been problematic and second in areas that are not expressly covered by WTO/GATS trade rules, where such rules could enhance the value of existing or future specific commitments in the telecom sector.

Transparency

The Annex on Telecommunications and the Reference Paper have supplemented and strengthened the GATS framework disciplines of Article III on transparency more than any other provision of the agreement. However, a major transparency obligation that still does not apply in the telecommunications sector is that of prior consultation on draft laws and regulations, with reasonable notice and time for comments. Such a provision exists under the GATS for the accountancy sector, in regard to which the Working Party on Professional Services (now the Working Party on Domestic Regulation) developed the "Disciplines on Domestic Regulation in the Accountancy Sector" in 1998; these Disciplines apply to all members who have scheduled specific commitments on accountancy under the GATS.[15]

Properly, a right of prior consultation is relevant to all services sectors and therefore more a horizontal question than a sector-specific one. Indeed, a number of interested parties have called for the enhancement of GATS Article III with the inclusion of a provision on prior comment.[16] Because of the heterogeneous nature of services and their regulation, however, it may be more appropriate to deal with prior consultation on a sectoral basis, as has been done for accountancy. A determination as to the preferability of a sector-specific or horizontal solution should result as much from negotiations as from specific testing of how the obligation would play out in a number of sectors and scenarios.

Advocates of prior comment should take into account, and develop recommendations to deal with, the increased administrative workload that a prior consultation requirement would create, especially for developing countries.[17] A further consideration that the advocates of prior consultation must address is the concern of those WTO members whose constitutions, domestic laws, or both forbid prior consultation with foreign parties; such members need to be convinced that it would be in the broad public interest for the views of all interested parties to be heard before new laws and regulations are enacted.

Licensing

During the basic telecom negotiations, Roseman (1996) proposed the development of specific disciplines to govern licensing in telecommunications.[18] Although some of the problems addressed in that article have been ameliorated since the Agreement on Basic Telecommunications, there continue to be lengthy delays in licensing processes in some jurisdictions that are still wedded to *ex ante* licensing processes because these processes continue to be open-ended and regulators feel compelled to modify their licensing criteria frequently—for example, in response to extraneous (political) issues (see also Sidak 1997).

Xavier addressed this issue in calling for the streamlining of licensing procedures to deal with potential anticompetitive behavior. He noted that "many countries are demonstrating [that] the concerns can be addressed by appropriate regulatory safeguards and/or through regulation on the basis of competition law" (Xavier 1998, p. 491).

Fredebeul-Krein and Freytag (1999, pp. 630–31, 641) identified a need for provisions that limit discretion and prevent unduly onerous licensing conditions. They noted the lack of specific guidelines for the interpretation of a "reasonable period of time" for processing license applications. In their view, an upper limit for license fees would also be desirable.

It is possible that horizontal disciplines elaborated pursuant to GATS Article VI.4 could deal with these problems, but such efforts should not preclude a priori the possibility of negotiating sector-specific rules to deal with the issues listed there (namely, qualification requirements, qualification procedures, technical standards, licensing requirements, and licensing procedures) in the telecommunications context. The key challenge may be to amplify the principles of proportionality and necessity (i.e., that domestic measures be "not more burdensome [or more trade restrictive] than necessary to ensure the quality of the service").

Interconnection and Unbundling

There are many types of telecommunications networks and services, and to the extent that they are interconnected, the economic and social benefits of investment in these networks and services will be greater. The obligations of transparent, reasonable, and nondiscriminatory interconnection pursuant to the Annex on Telecommunications apply to the full array of public telecommunications transport networks and services: voice, data, video, wireline, wireless, terrestrial, satellite, local, long distance, or international communications, including Internet protocol-based communications, whereas the additional requirements of the Reference Paper (that is, cost-oriented interconnection at any technically feasible point, sufficiently unbundled) apply only to a subset of suppliers of PTTNS, namely "major suppliers" of "basic telecommunications services."

Clearly, with so many networks and services—not to mention interested parties—there are many complex aspects to this difficult and important issue, and the Reference Paper's few short lines may not provide the most effective guidelines to domestic regulators. Indeed, most jurisdictions have had and continue to have difficulties with interconnection pricing and the unbundling of network elements, albeit fewer difficulties with regard to implementing long distance voice competition than with providing competitive broadband data services in the local loop.[19]

For example, the Reference Paper requires that interconnection charges be "cost-oriented," given that these charges can significantly affect the development of a competitive market. As Intven (2000, pp. 3–23) remarked in his *Telecommunications Regulatory Handbook* for the World Bank:

The level and structure of interconnection charges are . . . major determinants of the viability of operators in a competitive telecommunications market.

The Yankee Group (2001a) also observed an impact on services-based and facilities-based competition:

The level of interconnection charges will . . . have major impacts on the development of wholesale or retail markets and on decisions to invest in infrastructure.

The pricing of interconnection takes into account three basic cost elements: one-time start-up costs, costs of network elements that incumbents make available to new entrants, and contributions to the funding of universal service. Placing too high a price on any of these elements, singly or in combination, can make it difficult or impossible for long-term sustainable competition to take root.

However, there may be considerable resistance to international convergence in costing/pricing approaches. For one, there is frequently considerable regulatory history behind a country's chosen costing methodology.[20] For another, there is no industry consensus on this issue.[21] Nevertheless, Intven (2000, p. 3-29) identified a set of "Principles for Efficient Interconnection Price Structures," which are not drafted in the language of international trade agreements or the Reference Paper but which could be used as a starting point for further discussions on cost-oriented interconnection.[22]

Consequently, it may be worthwhile to explore the possibility of reaching an international agreement on costing/pricing principles and/or methodologies for determining interconnection charges. Although this could be even more challenging for trade negotiators than the opening of market access during the basic telecom negotiations, it may be desirable to negotiate such principles and methodologies in the WTO—in parallel with work at the OECD and ITU—for the effort to agree on common principles could focus international and domestic debates and inspire changes in the right direction. As Bigham (1997, p. 269) observed:

> While costing information does not resolve policy debates over the appropriate pricing of telecom services as competitive market structures are promoted, such information does focus these debates on the size and direction of the required changes.

Another issue relates to interconnection arrangements, and specifically to the Reference Paper provisions on interconnection "at any technically feasible point in the network" and "sufficiently unbundled that the supplier need not pay for network components or facilities that it does not require for the service to be provided." The rationale behind unbundling is to kick-start competition by lowering the economic and technical costs for new entrants. A comparison of Canadian and U.S. approaches illustrates the differing practices and performances between two OECD/WTO members and raises the question whether these provisions should be reconsidered or further elaborated, too.

First, the Canadian Radio-television and Telecommunications Commission does not mandate interconnection "at any technically feasible point." Rather, it has taken an approach, based on network efficiency considerations, that considers both the technical and economic aspects of interconnection.[23] For example, regarding local competition, the CRTC (1997a, para. 31) has mandated the designation of a single point of interconnection (POI) in each exchange area as a gateway for the interchange of traffic among local exchange carriers (LECs), finding that this would "provide . . . greater network efficiency for all local exchange service providers." The commission then left the task of establishing the criteria for designation of gateway locations to negotiations among industry parties,[24] meeting in the context of the CRTC Interconnection Steering Committee (CISC) and its various subcommittees that deal with all forms of interconnection.

Second, the CRTC's (1997a, para. 74) definition of "essential" required that three criteria be satisfied:

1. The facility, function, or service in question must be monopoly controlled.
2. A competitive local exchange carrier (CLEC) requires it as an input to provide services.
3. A CLEC cannot duplicate it economically or technically.

Thus for facilities to be considered essential by the CRTC, they must be monopoly controlled. This is narrower than the Reference Paper concept of facilities that are "exclusively or predominantly provided by a single or limited number of suppliers."

Third, regarding the unbundling of essential facilities,[25] the CRTC in Telecom Decision 97-8 stated:

> . . . *either too narrow or too broad a definition of an essential facility may impair the development of competition.* If it is too narrow, competitors may not be able to enter the market because of an inability to obtain the necessary network components. If it is too broad, giving overly generous access to ILEC [incumbent local exchange carrier] inputs, CLECs [competitive local exchange carriers] may not have sufficient incentives to invest in their own facilities, and would enter and remain in the market primarily as resellers. The Commission is of the view that

efficient and effective competition will be best achieved through facilities-based competitive service providers; otherwise competition will only develop at the retail level, with the ILECs retaining monopoly control of wholesale level distribution [CRTC 1997a, para. 73, emphasis added].

The Commission is of the view that resale can promote the development of a competitive market while allowing competitors time to construct their own facilities. While resale competition can help promote the development of a competitive market, it is the Commission's view that the full benefits of competition can only be realized with facilities-based competition [CRTC 1997a, para. 237].

Accordingly, the CRTC has determined that only central office codes (NXX's), directory listings, and local loops in certain bands are essential and, therefore, subject to mandatory unbundling.[26]

It is interesting that although there have been disagreements in Canada over the implementation of interconnection, they have been contained within the CRTC's CISC process, except for the differential treatment accorded facilities-based and non-facilities-based suppliers (discussed above with respect to Covad Canada and the regulation of local competition), which the CRTC resolved under its own procedures for regulatory relief. Otherwise, the Commission's approach of providing for interconnection at any economically and technically feasible point seems to be accepted by interested parties.

In contrast, the U.S. Federal Communications Commission's approach to unbundling has engendered considerable controversy, while appearing to be fully consistent with the Reference Paper, relevant parts of which were inspired by the *Telecommunications Act of 1996*.[27] In its *First Report and Order on Implementation of the Local Competition Provisions* under the Act, the FCC (1996) set out a list of seven unbundled network elements (UNEs) that ILECs must offer, whether they are essential or not. This policy was challenged all the way to the Supreme Court, which directed the FCC to develop a new standard to determine to which network elements ILECs must offer unbundled access (U.S. Supreme Court 1999). The Court noted that the FCC had failed to show that provision of the UNEs

it had listed was "necessary" for competitors to enter the market. The Court also required that the FCC, in establishing a new list, address whether it would "impair" a competitor's ability to provide service absent access to those UNEs.[28] Subsequently, the FCC (1999a) reevaluated its standard, issued a revised policy framework, and removed one of the seven UNEs from its list. This modest concession was followed a few months later with a further decision by the FCC (1999b) not to require ILECs to unbundle DSL access multiplexers, and a nondecision by the FCC not to mandate nondiscriminatory third-party Internet service provider (ISP) access to cable networks. Rather than being motivated by the reasons set out in its reevaluation of the standard for the unbundling of network elements, these subsequent decisions were motivated by the FCC's hands-off attitude toward the Internet, a desire to let cable companies maximize revenue for reinvestment in their networks (to ensure they had adequate incentives to invest in upgrading existing infrastructures), and a view that cable networks are private rather than public networks (i.e., not PTTN/S).[29]

This discussion of interconnection and unbundling has focused on the different approaches of Canada and the United States, but there are differences around the world. According to the OECD (2001c, p. 15), Australia, Canada, Iceland, Japan, Norway, and the United States had all introduced local loop unbundling by October 2001, each in its own way, whereas the Czech Republic, Hungary, Korea, and Poland had made decisions to require unbundling, but unbundling had not yet begun to be offered. The European Union adopted a regulation requiring incumbents to offer unbundled local loop access as of January 2001, but implementation is inconsistent across the EU (OECD 2001c, p. 15). New Zealand may introduce unbundling after a review of telecommunications policies is concluded in 2003 (OECD 2001c, p. 15). Mexico and Turkey have to date adopted no policies or plans to introduce local loop unbundling (OECD 2001c, p. 15), and Switzerland has no plans to implement unbundling for at least five more years ("Swiss Regulator" 2001). Nevertheless, these countries have subscribed to the Reference Paper requirement of "sufficiently unbundled." It would seem that a number of governments feel that zero unbundling is "sufficiently unbundled."

The Yankee Group (2001b) has compared the Canadian and U.S. situations and reached the following conclusions:

> Unbundling has been a cornerstone of telecommunications policy in the United States, reinforced by the Telecommunications Act of 1996. This market represents one of the few in the world where we have the opportunity to identify some concrete outcomes of LLU [local loop unbundling]. Here, the jury may soon be in, with a negative verdict. Despite a long-standing Federal Communications Commission (FCC) commitment to unbundling, U.S. incumbents retain the lion's share of local access markets.

> On the flip side is the Canadian environment, where local competition has developed quickly to an impressive stage since LLU was mandated. Canada has taken an LLU path deliberately different from that of the United States, including distinguishing urban and rural local loops. Canada also requires incumbent cable carriers to allow access to their facilities for use by competitive providers of high-speed services. Mandating access to cable TV access lines in this way sets Canada apart from most nations, which have resisted this course to date.[30]

It is noteworthy that Korea enacted its statutory and regulatory requirements for incumbent facilities-based service suppliers to provide unbundled network elements to their competitors when the country was already well on its way to leading the world in broadband access penetration rates. The Telecom Business Act was enacted there in December 2000 and the Government finalized the regulation setting out the detailed requirements for unbundling, including pricing, only in December 2001.

The work of Bourreau and Dogan (2001, p. 182) lead them to favor a narrow conception of unbundling:

> Unlimited provision of unbundled elements may be inefficient and may destroy the incentives of entrants to develop their own access networks.

Given the range of actions undertaken by WTO members subscribing to the Reference Paper obligation on mandatory interconnection and unbundling, the WTO's credibility risks being undermined if there is no attempt to clarify and improve these provisions. Perhaps the solution is to borrow a page from the CRTC and to bring the obligation into line with the concept of economic and technical nonsubstitutability of facilities deemed essential, by amending the Reference Paper to read "at any *economically and technically* feasible point." The effectiveness of such an amendment would likely require agreement on costing/pricing principles, methodologies for determining interconnection charges, or both in order to prevent abuses and provide useful guidance to regulators and service providers.

Another cluster of issues looming on the horizon with regard to interconnection and unbundling relates to the transition from traditional, voice-centric wireline networks to a multinetwork (telecoms, cable, satellite, terrestrial wireless), multi-supplier, data-centric, IP-based environment. There is the idea that members' commitments under the GATS and their domestic regulations should be technologically neutral with regard to functionally equivalent services.[31] However, this is frequently not the case. It is not clear that the existing Reference Paper principles apply adequately to fixed-to-mobile interconnection, or whether new rules are needed. In any case, fixed-to-mobile interconnection is subject to different rules and rates than fixed-to-fixed interconnection in most countries.

Furthermore, in a multisupplier environment it is not clear whether there will still be major suppliers and essential facilities. It is possible that in such an environment the Reference Paper would impose more regulation than is necessary to ensure competitive markets, or that it would unduly restrict members' ability to choose the mix of services- and facilities-based competition policies best suited to their individual circumstances. Moreover, if some (industrial) countries were to push for a text providing for forbearance from regulation (and from the terms of the Reference Paper) by regulators when certain criteria are met as to the sustainability of competition in a particular market, this would raise the question of the symmetry of obligations between industrial and developing countries, for the latter are less likely to achieve in the near future a state of sustainable competition in their telecommunications markets.

Definitions of PTTNS and Basic Telecoms

It may be necessary to negotiate new definitions, or a new paper altogether, for the new data-centric, IP-based environment. For example, the access and use provisions of the Annex on Telecommunications apply to all public telecommunications transport networks and services (PTTNS). The key elements of the definitions of PTTNS are "public" ("required, explicitly or in effect, . . . to be offered to the public generally") and "real-time" (not defined in the annex). In many jurisdictions, this definition allows cable, terrestrial wireless, and satellite networks and services, as well as many new wireline service suppliers (e.g., Internet backbone providers), to escape the requirements of transparent, reasonable, and nondiscriminatory access and use. That leaves only traditional, former monopoly, wireline suppliers subject to the disciplines of the annex, and perhaps not even these if their networks are based on technologies (e.g., IP) that perform automatic caching and store-and-forward functions outside of certain engineering parameters that define "real-time" communications.[32] Similarly, the Reference Paper deals with basic telecommunications; if suppliers of Internet backbone networks and broadband Internet services are not deemed to be basic, then the provisions of the Reference Paper do not apply to them either. This issue is relevant, for example, to those people concerned about international charging arrangements for Internet services and the costs of interconnecting with Internet backbone providers, as well as those who see the Internet as a public good.

In the context of the U.S. debate over third-party access to broadband, Bar and others (2000, p. 498) argued that these services are real-time services:

. . . Broadband internet is much more than a faster version of the old narrowband internet. Rather, it enables real-time, bandwidth-intensive applications that would be impossible with dial-up narrowband access, such as near broadcast quality video streaming, IP-based videoconferencing, or effective connections to a remote LAN.

However, this would still not make broadband Internet networks and services "public telecommunications transport networks and services," in the parlance of the Telecoms Annex, for unless the FCC decides otherwise, they are not "required . . . to be offered to the public generally." The CRTC definition of "public" as "offered to third persons for compensation" would cause more service suppliers to fall within the concept of PTTNS; some may consider this a progressive development, others a regressive one.

Among those who view the Internet as a public good, Lessig (2001) argued:

The commons is under attack. Those who were threatened by its potential have sought to contain it. Changes in the network's physical infrastructure and in the legal environment within which the network exists threaten to destroy it. The physical infrastructure is transforming as cable companies, and soon telecommunications companies, persuade governments to free them of traditional common carrier responsibilities. As a result, companies can exercise more control over what runs along their wires and even decide which content flows at what speed—something called "policy routing."

Underlying sensitivities to the erosion of the traditional common carrier concept is the question of the appropriate balance between public and private interests. These definitional lacunae create real opportunities for discriminatory behavior in the marketplace, and they encourage service providers to configure their networks and services so that they will fall outside established definitions and obligations and thereby circumvent common carrier obligations. Policy routing will enable "exclusive content partnerships" and "walled gardens," leading to "you-can't-get-there-from-here" and the suboptimization of potential network externalities. Perhaps it is possible to devise a progressive and light-handed regulatory framework that aims to maximize network externalities as they are in the public interest.

Clearly the Internet and IP technologies will have a major impact on how telecommunications networks and markets function. If the GATS is to keep up to date and relevant in light of developments in key sectors like telecommunications, it will be necessary to revisit and update key definitions. Again, account should also be taken of the fact that developing countries may feel that in the new IP-based environment the existing obligations fall more heavily on them than on industrial countries; that is, the former will have less developed networks and less competition, but they must implement a regulatory burden of which the latter largely will have largely freed themselves.[33] Developing countries will need to be encouraged to bear that regulatory burden for it is ultimately in their own interest, and they will need to be given technical assistance to do so effectively. Financial assistance may also be necessary in light of the loss of international settlement inflows and the growth of Internet interconnection outpayments.

Independent Regulator

Given that governments in some jurisdictions retain ownership interests in former monopoly telecom service providers, and that some of these governments have not chosen to separate out the regulatory body from the ministry that makes telecommunications policy, it may be desirable to try to elaborate further rules to ensure the independence of the regulator from undue political influence. The United States Supreme Court (1999) has, for example, submitted that

> [a] truly effective regulator also must be protected from direct political influence from industry or other government entities.

However, a balancing act is clearly required. On one hand, the regulator must be open to interventions by interested parties (including former monopolies, new entrants, users, and consumers). The key is the transparency of these interventions so that no undue favors are given. On the other hand, mechanisms must be in place to ensure that the regulator is accountable and acts in conformity with the relevant legislation, regulations, and judicial precedents—and, in some cases, in conformity with the temper of the times for there are indeed circumstances in which it is appropriate for elected governments to give direction to or impose their views on regulatory bodies. Mechanisms for accountability include procedural requirements for internal reviews, as well as for judicial and ministe-

rial reviews. Governments also need to establish a clear and transparent interface between the regulator and other bodies whose responsibilities overlap to some extent with the regulation of telecommunications (e.g., the general competition authority, as well as consumer protection, privacy,[34] and copyright[35] authorities). Revisiting the Reference Paper provisions on independent regulators would provide an opportunity to spell out more clearly how the interfaces should be drawn.

As telecom markets are opened and competition becomes sustainable without the need for detailed regulatory interventions—in short, as telecommunications becomes a "normal industry"—the scope for oversight by a general competition authority increases. However, there are a number of problems with transitioning from sector-specific to general economic regulation under competition laws. The first is knowing when—and if—the transition to competition is complete and the sectoral regulator's job is done. It is not merely a matter of establishing sunset provisions for sectoral regulations and regulators. Regulatory forbearance in respect to particular aspects of the market is a step-by-step approach that varies from country to country and from market segment to market segment. The theoretical and empirical basis likely does not exist at this time for the negotiation of common rules to guide the evolution from sector-specific to general economic regulation. However, the development of such a basis would be appropriately addressed in forums such as the OECD. The second major problem with transitioning from sector-specific to general economic regulation is that a telecom regulator has detailed, in-depth sectoral knowledge and performs multifarious functions, which may include technical matters (e.g., spectrum allocation, number allocation, rights of way, interconnection, service quality, type approval, and standards setting), as well as economic matters (licensing, universal service, price regulation, and, again, interconnection and rights of way). A competition authority deals with a much narrower range of issues, chiefly anticompetitive behavior and mergers, and usually does not possess expertise in the nitty-gritty technical details. It is not impossible, however, to transplant such responsibilities and know-how to a single overarching authority. The third problem is that there are few cases of telecom liberalization without having a telecom regulator, and New Zealand's experience stands out as a particularly inauspicious one.

There is also the question of creating a broad communications regulator with a mandate spanning both telecommunications and broadcasting. As a result of convergence, certain cross-sectoral commonalities (in particular, a history of public service responsibilities and universal service obligations) and favorable experiences in such countries as Canada and the United States, an evolution toward a more unified regulatory approach for the communications industries is likely to be more common in the near future than an evolution toward regulation under a general competition authority.

Universal Service Obligations

As the last two years have made abundantly clear, investing in telecommunications infrastructure and services is not without risk. Investors will, for the foreseeable future, shy away from high-risk, low-return projects, particularly in underserved, low-density, low-income rural and remote areas. This in turn will put the political objective of universal service at risk. Many governments are concerned that the gap (the so-called digital divide) between haves and have-nots is growing both within their societies and between industrial and developing countries. Many countries also are considering means to ensure the universal availability of broadband Internet access within their territory. Governments can be expected to try new measures to ensure that companies have adequate incentives to invest in building, maintaining, and upgrading infrastructures.

As discussed above, the Reference Paper provides minimum disciplines to ensure the competitive neutrality of universal service obligation programs and mechanisms. An OECD secretariat paper asserts that the inclusion of a contribution deficit charge for purposes of funding universal service obligations would "make it impossible to achieve cost-oriented interconnection charges."[36] If this were so, then the inclusion of contribution deficit charges in interconnection fees would presumably violate the commitment given under the Agreement on Basic Telecommunications by many WTO members to ensure cost-oriented interconnection. To some extent, the concern that universal service obligations might be administered in a competitively biased manner can be mitigated by means to ensure transparency and nondiscrimination in the calculation and application of contribution rates. As Intven (2000, p. 30–31) advised:

> If [universal service obligation] or [access deficit contribution] charges are established, it is clearly a good practice to identify them as separate from interconnection charges. Blending the two charges removes transparency from the interconnection process.

Limiting themselves to telecom regulatory responses to trade distortions possibly arising in the course of implementing universal service policies, Fredebeul-Krein and Freytag (1999, p. 642) argued for a "more binding" agreement on regulatory principles, and they propose four further disciplines:

1. Criteria have to be developed to identify the maximum set of services for which costs may be taken into account of calculating any burden associated with universal service obligations.

   [This was addressed above in the context of the recommendation to develop costing/pricing methodologies and principles for calculating interconnection charges.]
2. Rules have to be elaborated for determining the universal service provider.

   [For example, would auctions for the right to bear the universal service obligations and to receive universal service funding be a solution where competition is not viable?]
3. Requirements for funding schemes have to be specified in order to guarantee that financing universal service obligations [are] objective and nondiscriminatory.

   [This would mean an amplification of the disciplines of GATS Article VI.1, which requires the "reasonable, objective and impartial" administration of measures, and of Article VI.4 on qualification requirements and procedures.]
4. Criteria have to be developed by which the costs of the universal service provision can be identified and measured.

   [Again, the issue of costing methodologies arises.]

There is a wide range of possible governmental actions in favor of universal service that would not fall under the disciplines of the Reference Paper, or of other GATS disciplines. Notably, governments have budgets to subsidize the rollout of desired telecommunications projects, and through their budgets they are also major buyers of telecommunications services. For example, British authorities are entering into public-private partnerships with British Telecom (BT) to increase demand for and accelerate the rollout of DSL services in the United Kingdom ("BT Offers ADSL" 2001). Government procurement and subsidies can shape the development of markets, however, and governments frequently face temptations to make special deals on behalf of local industries. International trade agreements can prevent undue distortions and help governments resist the pressures of special interests.

GATS Article XIII provides a basis for the negotiation of disciplines on government procurement, but for now there are no GATS rules on government procurement of telecommunications networks and/or services, and they are not likely to be negotiated in that forum. Rather, the Agreement on Government Procurement is more likely to be the venue in the WTO context to negotiate such disciplines, although its next step will likely fall short of that and be at most an agreement on transparency in government procurement. Nonetheless, it will be a step forward. As for subsidies, GATS Article XV provides the basis to negotiate disciplines on service subsidies, but in the interim the only disciplines relevant to telecommunication services subsidies are the Reference Paper provision on universal service and GATS Article XVII (national treatment) that requires that all measures, including subsidies, apply on a national treatment basis unless a member has reserved the right to discriminate in favor of locally owned or locally controlled service suppliers and services in the grant of subsidies. The GATS could usefully (but is unlikely to be used to) develop disciplines to ensure that universal service policies do not result in discriminatory conditions of market access or anticompetitive behavior by recipients of government procurement contracts or subsidies,[37] because unless disciplines on government procurement and subsidies are in place, the markets in industrial countries for telecommunication services (and other services subject to universal service obligations) will be less than fully contestable, even with the benefit of commitments on market access and national treatment.

Few developing countries can afford the luxury of subsidizing companies that bear universal service obligations, and the governmental sectors in these countries do not generally possess sufficiently large budgets to stimulate the rollout of telecom services and infrastructure with procurement contracts. Consequently, developing countries tend to rely on cross-subsidies from high-revenue to low-revenue routes, as well as privatization and licensing processes, to implement their universal service objectives. These countries have considerable flexibility under GATS Part III on specific commitments and under GATS Article VI.4 on licensing to limit their obligations to those that they can easily undertake. Some countries have subscribed to the Reference Paper *minus* cost-oriented terms and conditions of interconnection so that their cross-subsidy schemes do not fall afoul of the WTO, and some have maintained a monopoly in telecom services as a means to generate monopoly rents and as an incentive to the service provider to build out the network into low-profit areas. However, the competitive neutrality of universal service obligations, cost-oriented interconnection, competitive markets, and transparent, reasonable, and nondiscriminatory licensing procedures are very important instruments that support the development of efficient markets and benefits to users.

Relevance of GATS Telecom Regulatory Disciplines for the Regulation of Other Network Services

The GATS Annex on Telecommunications and the Reference Paper are successes, and these successes have created a "demonstration effect" for many governments and interested parties considering market access liberalization and regulatory reform in other sectors.[38] There is some speculation whether it would be possible to replicate those successes in other complex sectors, in particular in other network services (such as transportation, energy distribution, postal services,[39] and broadcasting) that trade negotiators have failed so far to liberalize and bring under detailed WTO disciplines. This would mean distilling from telecoms the essence of new provisions that would apply to specific sectors. Alternatively, others envisage adapting the telecom disciplines to all sectors. This would mean distilling the essence of the telecom disciplines into language that would apply to all sectors as new horizontal disciplines, by means of amendments to GATS articles or other generic means (e.g., additional commitments in members' headnotes to their schedules of commitments). These two approaches (sector-specific or cross-sectoral adaptations of the Annex on Telecommunications and Reference Paper) need not be mutually exclusive.

Feketekuty (1998) has, for example, proposed to strengthen Article VI on domestic regulation by introducing a generic version of the "competitive safeguards" contained in the annex and the Reference Paper:

> . . . a general restatement of the competitive safeguards built into the Telecommunications Annex of the GATS and the Agreement on Basic Telecommunications Services. Such a provision would help to ensure that monopoly providers of essential services would not abuse their position by charging unreasonable fees or by giving themselves preferential access to essential services in the competitive provision of downstream products. This provision could apply not only to "transport services" provided over electric conduits or pipelines but also to a variety of other monopoly inputs such as water.

This may be a good idea, particularly if it is broadened beyond competition safeguards alone, to deal with the other regulatory issues that the annex and the Reference Paper address.

Despite its successes, the telecom accords under the GATS are not perfect. Indeed, they are works in progress, as the discussion of new issues in the previous section demonstrates. Moreover, the further one delves into the specifics of the telecommunications sector, and the more detailed and invasive the obligations become, the less likely that they can be easily adapted to the circumstances of other services sectors, let alone the great generality of all commercially traded services.

In the absence of careful analysis and reflection by government officials, industry representatives, and other interested persons, the implications of the telecom model for other sectors are not obvious. For this purpose, a "sectoral testing exercise"[40] would be invaluable to show to what extent the reg-

ulatory principles of the annex and the Reference Paper are indeed relevant to other sectors and whether they can be aggregated at a higher level of generalization in amended GATS articles or in new cross-sectoral additional commitments, or whether it is necessary to tailor these principles to fit the needs of individual sectors. The key issues to be examined for their relevance and adaptability to other sectors are definitions, transparency, licensing, competition safeguards, interconnection and unbundling, independent regulator, and universal service obligations.

Among the lessons learned by negotiators during the Uruguay Round was that services are highly heterogeneous and "one size does not fit all," except at a high level of generalization. Another lesson was that the circumstances of individual countries vary markedly, and therefore it is necessary to allow flexibility in the assumption and implementation of obligations. Without testing against other sectors ideas for an amended Article VI, or other amendments to the GATS framework, or new cross-sectoral additional commitments, or whatever, it is not clear whether the Telecoms Annex and Reference Paper provide a useful model for market liberalization and regulatory reform in other sectors.

Conclusion

The GATS outcomes on telecommunications have been significant and substantive because they have facilitated the globalization of trade and investment in telecommunications and the enhanced role of telecommunications as a key enabler for other economic activities. The annex and the Reference Paper put pressure on governments to adopt best practices in terms of market liberalization and procompetitive regulations. They demonstrate that the development and adoption of international standards for (or disciplines on) regulations can encourage trade and investment. But they leave considerable scope for each country to decide how it will implement liberalization and regulatory reform.

The annex and the Reference Paper, however, are not the last word on telecom reform. Rather, they are products of their time: of what was negotiable, and of the state of telecommunication services and networks, at that time. They are primarily relevant during the transition from monopoly to competitive markets. However, technologies and markets are not static, and regulations and trade disciplines should be revisited and, if necessary, updated to continue to play a procompetitive role in the context of new technologies, networks, and services.

Other sectors might benefit from similar approaches. The two-step approach employed by telecom negotiators in dealing with regulatory issues relating to access and use separately from the matter of a regulatory framework for actual competition in the supply of telecom services may be a key lesson for those seeking to negotiate international regulatory disciplines for other services sectors. But one must be wary of "one-size-fits-all" approaches that fail to recognize the specifics of individual sectors. For this reason, it would be advisable to undertake sectoral testing exercises to determine whether the principles and disciplines developed for telecommunications under the GATS are relevant and adaptable to other sectors.

Endnotes

1. That is, from "plain old telephone services" to "pretty awesome new stuff," as some people quipped in those days.

2. Because of the structure of the WTO agreements, manufacturers and other producers of goods do not benefit de jure from the Telecoms Annex. De facto, however, goods producers as well as suppliers of unscheduled services also benefit because governments tend to liberalize the terms and conditions of access and use for the benefit of all persons, not merely for the benefit of suppliers of scheduled services. But only suppliers of scheduled services have the benefit of their government's recourse to WTO dispute settlement procedures.

3. For a theoretical regulatory discussion see Melody (1997a, p. 66): "Efficient interconnection is crucial to the effective implementation of virtually all public policies permitting competitive opportunities in telecom.... Pro-active regulation on interconnection is necessary for competitive markets to get established and to continue functioning effectively."

4. Compare Roseman (1996).

5. This author recommended such a pooling of resources among OECS member states in the context of a project in the Caribbean on behalf of the WTO and World Bank in 1997–98. Undoubtedly others similarly observed the feasibility of such a cooperative endeavour. For a summary of the rationale for ECTEL and its role, see World Bank (2002, pp. 83–84).

6. The issue of international charging arrangements for Internet services (ICAIS) is today's successor to the old accounting rate problems. Although ICAIS may be "new," it evokes many old issues—for example, definitions (of public networks, the Internet), access, interconnection, costing, anticompetitive behavior in third markets, as well as the digital divide and special and differential treatment, some of which will be discussed later in this writing.

7. Compare Intven (2000, p. I-23).

8. It is doubtful that the United States would have been able to pursue a dispute over settlement rates in the WTO, given the understanding of the Group on Basic Telecommunications that these "would not give rise to action by Members under dispute settlement under the WTO" at least until there had been a review of the matter and a positive decision to the contrary by the Services Council (S/GBT/4, para. 7).

9. Deutsche Telekom's takeover of VoiceStream Wireless and PowerTel was the most high-profile case, but among others were license applications by Telesat and Iridium North America.

10. Compare North American Gateway (1997), Call-Net Enterprises (1997), and CRTC (1997b).

11. Covad Canada Communications Inc. (2000); and Law Firm of Osler, Hoskin, and Harcourt to Johnathan Daniels, Covad Canada Communications Inc. May 5, 2002.

12. Compare CRTC (2001a).

13. A further, case-specific reason why the Reference Paper may not have been invoked in this dispute so far is that, with Canada's restrictive foreign ownership rules, there are no carriers under foreign control to argue that their trade rights are being denied by the municipalities.

14. Wireless interconnection charges in Japan remain notoriously elevated, and wireline interconnection charges have been reduced only modestly under severe pressure from the United States.

15. The provisions exist but the obligations have not yet entered into force.

16. See, for example, European Services Forum (2001, p. 4).

17. See the discussion in OECD (2001b).

18. Compare Roseman (1996).

19. In this observer's opinion, this is because the focus of the basic telecom negotiations was on voice services, and long distance at that; the Internet was still too new in 1994–97 to have been taken sufficiently into account so as to anticipate the issues that it would pose for telecommunications and trade rules.

20. For extensive discussions of U.S. and Canadian costing approaches, see Melody (1997b) and Bigham (1997).

21. For example, the Business Industry Advisory Council (BIAC) to the OECD has been unable to bridge conflicting interests in this area among its members, who include users and suppliers. Consequently BIAC addressed pricing for local loop access and access for value-added service providers, including Internet service providers, in the following terms: "Several pricing models are used, and one should not be the prescriptive guiding principle" (BIAC 2001).

22. For example, Intven went beyond the Reference Paper by calling for interconnection charges to be based on long-run average incremental costs, including cost of capital, plus a reasonable markup to cover forward-looking joint and common costs, fixed costs to be covered by fixed charges, and variable costs to be covered by variable charges.

23. Depending on the type of networks and services to be interconnected, the CRTC provides for line-side interconnection, trunk-side interconnection, direct connection from toll to local networks, tandem access connections, local access, cable access, co-location, and so forth, not to mention arrangements that companies may work out purely on the basis of commercial negotiations.

24. See CRTC (1997a, para. 34). One result of these negotiations is that there is one POI for all of Toronto.

25. Defined in the Reference Paper as "facilities of a public telecommunications transport network or service that (a) are exclusively or predominantly provided by a single or limited number of suppliers; and (b) cannot feasibly be economically or technically substituted in order to provide a service."

26. See CRTC (1997a, para. 84). The CRTC found that local loops situated in small urban and rural areas meet the criteria set out in its definition of an essential facility. Significantly, the Commission recognized that even within urban areas, local loops not meeting the definition of essential facilities cannot be quickly provided in significant numbers in the early stages of competition. The Commission therefore required that these loops be subject to mandatory unbundling and costed as essential facilities for a five-year term.

27. Indeed, with respect to interconnection, the words "at any technically feasible point in the network" appear in both the Reference Paper and Section 251 of the Act.

28. The FCC's methodology for determining cost-oriented interconnection and access is still being challenged in the courts (compare Pelofsky 2001).

29. The matter could be challenged still further in the U.S. courts. In the absence of a foreign-controlled ILEC or CLEC in the United States, however, a WTO challenge on the grounds that the FCC's requirements are more burdensome than necessary is not feasible. Similarly, in the absence of a major foreign-controlled ISP, a WTO challenge based on the denial of nondiscriminatory access to and use of cable networks is also not possible.

30. Some will feel that the Yankee Group's assessment of Canada is overly generous because new entrants in Canada's local telecom markets are weak and the cable companies are generally dragging their feet on implementing technologies that will permit third-party ISP access to their networks. But the point is that the CRTC's approach seems to work at least as well as that used by the FCC and prescribed by the Reference Paper.

31. Compare ITU (2001) at paragraph 4.22: "Functional equivalence is a regulatory concept used by various countries to link some or all of the above criteria in developing a policy as to whether some forms of IP telephony should be treated on the same basis as conventional switched telephony. The premise for this approach is that similar or equivalent services should be treated in a similar way. Other countries do not share this premise, and thus have chosen not to apply the same requirements to new services based on their view that this would hamper economic growth and the development of innovative services." Compare paragraph 4.24: "Technological neutrality is a principle that is invoked by some policy-makers and regulators when addressing IP telephony and other emerging communications technologies. This concept can be generally characterized as an effort to apply regulations in an even-handed manner to like services, regardless of the technology used to provide these services. Unless other policy imperatives take precedence, the purpose of this concept is to support competition policy by ensuring that one provider is not given more favorable regulatory treatment than another when providing equivalent services. There is, however, a range of interpretations of this concept and it has been implemented in different ways by various member States." And compare paragraph 4.26: "A different view is that policy-makers and regulators should not be indifferent to technology. Emerging technologies might benefit from a 'window,' that is, a

form of regulatory asymmetry during a transitional phase, which would allow them to develop and grow outside traditional obligations. This approach may enable small and medium-sized enterprises, offering new technologies and services, to provide competition for traditional industry operators and foster market-based results. If or when market failures arise, competition policy could be employed to reduce bottlenecks or curb abusive practices, without the need for sector-specific regulation or definitions and classifications that may quickly become outdated."

32. Compare ITU (2001, para. 4.20), which cross-references ITU-T Recommendations G114 and G131.

33. In the old voice-centric world where accounting rates were the norm, developing countries were the net recipients of international settlement payments. In the emerging IP-based environment, they are increasingly net payers. This change of circumstance raises questions of equity.

34. Perhaps more important than more competition rules for the development of efficient markets for, and the increasing uptake of, electronic commerce would be clear rules on consumer protection, privacy, and liability for illegal materials.

35. It may be necessary in the WTO context to address the trade implications of the WIPO Copyright Treaty and the WIPO Performances and Phonograms Treaty. There is considerable uncertainty about which players in the communications chain bear liability in the digital online environment. This has a chilling effect on ISPs and telecommunications carriers who have no control over the content that they carry. It is not obvious that it would be desirable from the point of view of the development of electronic commerce to transpose these provisions into the TRIPS, let alone make them subject to WTO dispute settlement.

36. Compare OECD (2001a, p. 21).

37. Subsidies to end users who would be free to choose their own supplier(s) of telecom and Internet services would be less likely to distort trade and investment flows than subsidies to service suppliers.

38. The financial services sector is, of course, covered by a number of annexes, protocols, and other special documents under the GATS. However, few would claim that these are models for other sectors. Indeed, some would like to undo the principal accomplishment of past financial services negotiations—the "prudential carve-out." This allows governments great freedom to take measures for prudential regulations, with little constraint by GATS disciplines; the great potential for abuse that the carve-out affords reduces predictability, security, and transparency. The Financial Leaders Working Group (FLWG) has undertaken an initiative inspired by the Reference Paper and the process of the telecom negotiations. See, for example, Cooke (2001), in particular Annex 1, "Launch of Pro-Competitive Regulatory Principles for Insurance." The FLWG has since completed its "model schedule" of commitments in insurance services, and Cooke made a presentation to the FLWG's WTO seminar in Geneva on October 11, 2001.

39. Postal services are perhaps closest to telecoms in terms of issues relating to cross-subsidization for purposes of universal service and traditional international settlement arrangements. It is more likely that these similarities are testimony to a legacy of similar policy objectives, industrial organizations, and regulations under common ministries and administrations of posts, telecommunications and telegraphs in much of the world than that similarities are inherent in the nature of the services.

40. Trade negotiators and services experts undertook such exercises at the OECD and in Geneva during the Uruguay Round in order to test whether the traditional trade principles embodied in the GATT "worked" in the context of services, whether these could be translated into a general agreement on trade in services, and whether additional disciplines would be necessary for specific service sectors. The result was the GATS Annex on Telecommunications, among other things.

References

The word "processed" describes informally produced works that may not be available commonly through libraries.

Bar, François, Stephen Cohen, Peter Cowhey, Brad DeLong, Michael Kleeman, and John Zysman. 2000. "Access and Innovation Policy for the Third-Generation Internet." *Telecommunications Policy* 24: 489–518.

BIAC (Business Industry Advisory Council to the OECD). 2001. "Comments Received from BIAC Members on Competition Issues in Telecommunications" *BIAC in Response* May 22.

Bigham, Fred. 1997. "Telecom Costing in Canada: The Story and the Lessons." In William H. Melody, ed., *Telecom Reform: Principles, Policies and Regulatory Practices*. Lyngby: Technical University of Denmark.

Bourreau, Marc, and Pinar Dogan. 2001. "Regulation and Innovation in the Telecommunications Industry." *Telecommunications Policy* 25: 167–84.

"BT Offers ADSL through Public-Private Partnership." 2001. *Total Telecom* December 11.

Call-Net Enterprises. 1997. Submission in the Matter of *Proceeding to Review and Consider Whether to Vary Teleglobe Canada Inc.—Resale and Sharing of International Private Line Services*. Telecom Decision CRTC 97-10, August 11.

Cooke, John. 2001. "Developments in Services." *Third Yearbook of the World Trade Law Association*. London: World Trade Law Association.

Covad Canada Communications Inc. 2000. Part VII Application in the Matter of *Bell Canada Tariff Notice No. 6475 as Modified by Tariff Notice No. 6475A*. May 5.

CRTC (Canadian Radio-television and Telecommunications Commission). 1997a. *Local Competition*. Telecom Decision 97-8, May 1.

———. 1997b. *Letter Decision* [in the Matter of *Teleglobe Canada Inc.—Resale and Sharing of International Private Line Services*. Telecom Decision CRTC 97-10], December 19.

———. 2000. *Digital Subscriber Line Service Providers' Access Approved for Unbundled Loops and Co-location*. Order 2000-983, October 27.

———. 2001a. *Ledcor/Vancouver—Construction, Operation and Maintenance of Transmission Lines in Vancouver*. Decision 2001-23, January 5.

European Court of Justice. 2001. Judgment in Case C-146/00, *Commission of the European Communities v. French Republic*. December 6.

European Services Forum. 2001. "Domestic Regulation: Preliminary Discussion Paper." June 5. Brussels.

FCC (Federal Communications Commission). 1996. *First Report and Order on Implementation of the Local Competition Provisions in the Telecommunications Act of 1996, and Interconnection between Local Exchange Carriers and Commercial Mobile Radio Services Providers*. August 8. Washington, D.C.

———. 1999a. *Third Report and Order and Fourth Further Notice of Proposed Rulemaking on Implementation of the Local Competition Provisions of the Telecommunications Act of 1996*. September 15. Washington, D.C.

———. 1999b. "FCC Promotes Local Telecommunications Competition." News Release. September 15. Washington, D.C.

Feketekuty, Geza. 1998. "Setting the Agenda for the Next Round of Negotiations on Trade in Services." <http://www.commercialdiplomacy.org/articles_news/trade_services.htm>.

Fink, Carsten, Aaditya Mattoo, and Randeep Rathindran. 2001. "Liberalizing Basic Telecommunications: The Asian Experience." World Bank, Development Research Group Paper prepared for the conference, "Trade, Investment, and Competition Policies in the Global Economy: The Case of the International Telecommunications Regime." Hamburg, Germany, January 18–19.

Fredebeul-Krein, Markus, and Andreas Freytag. 1999. "The Case for a More Binding WTO Agreement on Regulatory Principles in Telecommunication Markets." *Telecommunications Policy* 23: 625–44.

Intven, Hank, ed. 2000. *Telecommunications Regulatory Handbook*. Washington, D.C.: World Bank.

ITU (International Telecommunication Union). 2001. *Report of the Secretary General on IP Telephony*. World Telecommunications Policy Forum, Final Report. March 9. Geneva.

Lee, Nae-Chan, and Han-Young Lie. 2000. "Korea's Telecom Services Reform through Trade Negotiations" Research Paper. Seoul: Korea Information Society Development Institute.

Lessig, Lawrence. 2001. "The Internet's Undoing." *Financial Times*, November 29.

Melody, William H. 1997a. "Interconnection: Cornerstone of Competition." In William H. Melody, ed., *Telecom Reform: Principles, Policies and Regulatory Practices*. Lyngby: Technical University of Denmark.

———. 1997b. "Network Cost Analysis: Concepts and Methods." In William H. Melody, ed., *Telecom Reform: Principles, Policies and Regulatory Practices*. Lyngby: Technical University of Denmark.

North American Gateway. 1997. Reply in the matter of *Teleglobe Canada Inc.—Resale and Sharing of International Private Lines*. Telecom Public Notice CRTC 96-25, March 18.

OECD (Organisation for Economic Co-operation and Development). 2001a. "Interconnection and Local Competition." DSTI/ICCP/TISP(2000)3/final, February 7. Paris.

———. 2001b. "Transparency in Domestic Regulation: Practices and Possibilities." TD/TC/WP(2001)31, August 13. Paris.

———. 2001c. "The Development of Broadband Access in OECD Countries." DSTI/ICCP/TISP/2001)2/Final, October 29. Paris.

Pelofsky, Jeremy. 2001. "FCC, Bells Spar over Rates before Supreme Court." *Total Telecom* October 11.

PwC (PricewaterhouseCoopers). 2000. *Implementing the WTO Agreement on Basic Telecommunications in APEC Member Economies—Questionnaires Project*. APEC TEL02/99T, February. Washington, D.C.

Roseman, Daniel. 1996. "Licensing in the Context of International Telecommunications Liberalization." OECD/ICCP/TISP(96)4, August 12.

———. 2000. "CRTC Regulations Affecting the Supply of Digital Subscriber Line Telecommunication Services by Resellers and the General Agreement on Trade in Services—Analysis of the Arguments Presented by Osler, Hoskin, & Harcourt on Behalf of Covad Canada Communications Inc." Memorandum. June 5.

———. 2002. *Economic Impact of Trade and Investment Liberalization in the Telecommunications Sector: A Review of the Lit-*

erature for Selected Countries. Ottawa: Department of Foreign Affairs and International Trade.

Sidak, J. Gregory. 1997. *Foreign Investment in American Telecommunications.* Chicago: University of Chicago Press.

"Swiss Regulator Sees No Unbundling in Next Five Years." 2001. *Total Telecom* November 27.

Tuthill, Lee. 1996. "Users' Rights? The Multilateral Rights on Access to Telecommunications." *Telecommunications Policy* 20(2): 89–99.

United States Supreme Court. 1999. *AT&T Corp. et al. v. Iowa Utilities Board et al., certiorari to the U.S. Court of Appeals for the Eight Circuit* (119 S.Ct. 721, decided January 25, 1999).

United States Trade Representative. 2002. "U.S. Requests WTO Panel to Rule on Mexican Telecom Restrictions." Press Release 2002-19, February 13. Washington, D.C.

World Bank. 2002. *Global Economic Prospects and the Developing Countries.* Washington, D.C.

WTO (World Trade Organization). 1999. "Principles of Competitive Entry: Independent Telecommunications Regulation and Interconnection Principles." Communication by the United States of America, S/C/W/110/Add.1, June 15. Geneva.

Xavier, Patrick. 1998. "The Licensing of Telecommunication Suppliers: Beyond the EU's Directive." *Telecommunications Policy* 22(6): 483–92.

Yankee Group. 2001a. "What Are the Implications of Regulated Uniform Interconnection Pricing Arrangements for Incumbents and New Entrants?" One to One Analysis, Global Regulatory Strategies <http://www.yankeegroup.com>.

———. 2001b. "The Race to Win the Last Mile: Local Loop Unbundling around the Globe." *The Yankee Report* 1(4/August).

7

GATS REGULATORY DISCIPLINES MEET GLOBAL PUBLIC GOODS: THE CASE OF TRANSPORTATION SERVICES

Richard Janda

Executive Summary

The subject of multilateral disciplines on domestic transportation regulation raises important questions concerning the overall architecture of global governance. On the one hand, as this chapter documents, there are examples of domestic transportation regulation that serve to place a disproportionate burden on foreign service providers—thereby becoming barriers to trade. On the other hand, countries do pursue legitimate policy objectives designed to ensure the creation of and access to transportation infrastructure and, notably, to maintain confidence in and sustainability of that infrastructure through safety, security, and environmental standards. Such domestic regulatory activity is marked by the supply of public goods necessary to provide market services. The lighthouse is a classic example of a public good, an entity to which nonrivalrous and nonexcludable access was an indispensable condition of flourishing maritime trade.[1] Yesterday's lighthouse is today's satellite-based maritime or aviation naviga-

tion system. And for such increasingly complex systems to work, they must be buttressed by rigorous safety standards and recommended practices regarding the manufacture and maintenance of means of transport (airworthiness, seaworthiness); registration of craft (aircraft and vessels); training and certification of crew; provision of emergency facilities (aerodrome and seaport); accident investigation and prevention; and transport of hazardous materials. Indeed, one can reasonably assert that maintaining open access to airspace and sea-lanes is a primary global public good that rests on international coordination of domestic safety, security, and environmental regulation.[2] Such international coordination for air and maritime transport has been left to the International Civil Aviation Organization (ICAO) and to the International Maritime Organization (IMO), respectively, with the United Nations Conference on Trade and Development (UNCTAD) playing a complementary facilitation role. Regional intergovernmental organizations and a variety of

I am grateful to Ruwantissa Abeyratne, Audrey Beguira, Adelle Blackett, Stuart Hyndman, Aisatou Jallow-Sey, Nicholas Kasirer, Pierre Larouche, Rod Macdonald, Armand de Mestral, John Weale, Joseph Wilson, and Robert Wolfe for their comments and assistance with this research and the review of this chapter.

influential industry and nongovernmental organizations round out the *dramatis personae* on the world stage. Thus when the World Trade Organization (WTO) enters to take up a role in disciplining regulatory barriers, the audience is entitled to expect that all of the actors, including the newcomer, are performing in the same play. And the audience does not expect that, from the moment the WTO appears, the remainder of the production is to be a soliloquy. It will only be good theatre if the actors develop the plot together. In considering how a horizontal framework of regulatory disciplines might apply to air, maritime, and multimodal transport, this chapter seeks to develop some hypotheses concerning possible mechanisms for coordination among the WTO and other relevant actors, notably ICAO and IMO.

In considering how a horizontal framework of regulatory disciplines might apply to air, maritime, and multimodal transport, this chapter outlines a number of hypotheses concerning possible mechanisms for coordination among the WTO and other relevant actors, notably ICAO and IMO. Institutional rivalries and turf battles must give way not only to the search for complementarities, but also to the acknowledgment of limited institutional capacity on both sides. Whereas ICAO and IMO are not well placed by themselves to advance the integration of trade in services in their domains, so too the WTO lacks the capacity and the legitimacy to develop regulatory standards, which are a necessary part of the equation if meaningful annexes on maritime and air transport services are ever to be developed. In short, the problem of regulatory disciplines presents in microcosm the question of how today's loose network of international institutions can be bound more tightly together so as to bolster legitimate and salutary governance regimes.

The first part of the chapter sketches the limited extent to which air and maritime transport have been incorporated into the General Agreement on Trade in Services (GATS). This discussion points out that for transportation services there are no regulatory disciplines that can reinforce substantial market access commitments, as exist in the fields of telecommunications and financial services. A preliminary question is therefore whether it makes sense to apply Article VI.4 regulatory disciplines or disciplines analogous to those of the telecom Reference Paper on Regulatory Principles to sectors that have eluded

significant incorporation into the GATS. In coming to a provisional affirmative conclusion, I argue that regulatory disciplines would have merit independent of substantive market access commitments and indeed that they can help create a context that is propitious to future market integration.

The second part of the chapter attempts to classify the kinds of regulatory measures that can give rise to market barriers in transportation. Two distinctions are pertinent in considering the implications of domestic regulation for trade: (1) private goods (market) failure vs. public goods regulation, and (2) under-enforcement barriers vs. over-enforcement barriers.

The third part of the chapter considers what sorts of cross-sectoral horizontal disciplines could apply to this set of regulatory issues, canvassing comparisons with existing regulatory disciplines. Whereas one could imagine a set of disciplines that would tilt analysis entirely toward market-opening outcomes, the objective must be to achieve disciplines that also reinforce the provision of global public goods. The main institutional implication of this is the need to find ways to integrate ICAO and IMO into the quest for balanced regulatory disciplines. This entails much more than the pro forma agreement between the World Intellectual Property Organisation (WIPO) and the WTO for technical cooperation respecting Trade-related Aspects of Intellectual Property Rights (TRIPs),[3] and more in the nature of the agreements with the Codex Alimentarius Commission, the International Office of Epizootics, and the International Plant Protection Commission under the auspices of the WTO Agreement on the Application of Sanitary and Phytosanitary Measures (SPS Agreement).

Transportation and the GATS

A striking feature of maritime and air transport services is the limited extent to which both sectors are subject to GATS rules and market opening commitments. This begs the question as to whether a rationale can nonetheless be found to apply GATS regulatory principles in both sectors.

The Negotiations to Date

In addressing the above question, the chapter's opening section briefly recalls the generally unhappy negotiating history of GATS in maritime and air transport sectors.

Maritime Transport Services Both transportation in general and maritime transport in particular have been underachievers in GATS negotiations. Whereas the Uruguay Round did attract maritime transport commitments from 32 countries, the United States was not among them, and many of the commitments that were made—for example, by the European Union—excluded international shipping and port services and included only auxiliary services (e.g., storage and warehouse services other than in ports; freight transport agency/freight forwarding services; preshipment inspection) and miscellaneous other services (e.g., lease of vessels with crew).[4] Given the limited results that were achieved up to the conclusion of the GATS, an Annex on Negotiations on Maritime Transport Services was included to provide a mandate for further negotiations, like those bearing on financial services and telecommunications, with a deadline of June 30, 1996. Unlike the other sectoral negotiating groups that received a post-1994 mandate, however, the Negotiating Group on Maritime Transport Services came up empty-handed. The United States refused to make any formal offer until it saw significant offers from the other 33 participants in the negotiations. Although 24 countries did submit a package of draft offers, from the U.S. standpoint those offers remained inadequate and generally failed to address commercial presence in the field of multimodal transport.[5] Ultimately the Negotiating Group agreed to suspend the negotiations and resume them with the next round of comprehensive services negotiations.[6] Pending the conclusion of those negotiations, GATS Article II will not take effect regarding international shipping, auxiliary services, and access to and use of port facilities. Negotiations will resume on the basis of existing or improved offers. Finally, a "peace clause" was agreed on, and pending the completion of future negotiations, it provides that countries take no measures affecting maritime trade that are designed to improve their negotiating position, except in response to measures taken by other countries.

In the run-up to new negotiations, the European Union (EU), Hong Kong (China), Japan, the Republic of Korea, Norway, and Singapore issued a joint statement stressing the need to build on the proposals that had been made prior to the 1996 suspension of negotiations.[7] In a separate negotiating proposal, Korea highlighted the need to include maritime multimodal transportation services and to address (a) limitations on equity holdings by foreign companies; (b) restrictions on the establishment of branch offices by foreign carriers; (c) the grant of exclusive cargo carriage to vessels bearing national flags; (d) restrictions on the use of shipping agents, discriminatory taxation measures, and port dues; and (e) discrimination against foreign carriers in the use of port services.[8] In its negotiating proposal, Colombia did not single out maritime multimodal services but has targeted liner conferences, suggesting that "the effective liberalization of [maritime] service should result in the elimination of cartels that fix prices and frequencies."[9] Australia issued the most ambitious negotiating proposal to date, suggesting not only that multimodal transport be added as a fourth pillar to maritime transport, auxiliary services, and port services, but also that a competition policy framework be elaborated for the maritime sector and incorporated as a special annex.[10] Australia included a list of trade restrictions subject to negotiation that is similar to Korea's list but added (a) requirements for joint venture arrangements and other legislative and regulatory restrictions on foreign presence in the maritime transport industry; (b) preferential treatment of shipping service providers from specific economies on the basis of international agreements or for other reasons; and (c) restrictions on carrying government cargo to vessels bearing national flags (other than defence and other national security-related cargoes). Of particular relevance to this chapter, Australia proposed the discussion of nontariff regulatory measures and anticompetitive business practices, including "unreasonable environmental and safety standards, burdensome vessel and cargo examination procedures, and lengthy and cumbersome port access and clearance procedures," and acknowledged the need to safeguard "legitimate safety, national security and environmental requirements pertaining to the industry."

More recently, on March 3, 2003, a diverse group of 38 members, including Australia, Canada, Chile, China, the EU, Japan, Mexico, and Nigeria, issued a Joint Statement on the Negotiations of Maritime Transport Services, calling for "binding substantive liberalization of the maritime transport service sector" that was "consistent with sustainable development, security and safety" (WTO Council for Trade in Services 2003).

Air Transport Services In the Uruguay Round, air transport services fared little better than maritime services.[11] Although an Annex on Air Transport Services was part of the GATS, its coverage does not extend to traffic rights or to services related to the exercise of traffic rights—so-called "hard rights." The annex makes explicit reference only to aircraft repair and maintenance, the selling and marketing of air transport services, and computer reservation services. Even given the modest scope of the annex, only 40 countries have made commitments under it.[12]

At the time the Air Transport Annex was being negotiated, it was argued that most-favored-nation (MFN) and national treatment disciplines were not appropriate to the reciprocal relationships that characterize the exchange of traffic rights, that the system of bilateral air transport agreements dealt appropriately with differential levels of developments and varying policy objectives, and that ICAO was the body that ought to oversee trade liberalization in this sector.[13] The broad annex carve-out nevertheless is subject to review by the Council for Trade in Services, which to date has not arrived at any concrete proposals for expanding the annex.[14] In preparation for new services negotiations, Colombia and New Zealand have formulated proposals that tend to reflect the cautious approach taken by countries during the Council for Trade in Services review. Colombia took quite a conservative view, reiterating its faith in ICAO and the Chicago Convention framework and proposing that hard rights continue to be excluded. It suggested that negotiations focus on expanding the set of ancillary services covered by the annex, in particular those related to ground handling services, rental and leasing services, catering services, and other supporting services, notably cleaning and disinfecting services.[15] New Zealand took a somewhat more expansive view and proposed including auxiliary services (including cargo handling and storage and warehouse services), as well as airport management services, air traffic control services, general aviation services, domestic air services, and other supporting services for air transport.[16] What is important for the purposes of this article is that New Zealand

explicitly addressed the interplay between GATS commitments on air transport services and existing regulatory measures (p. 3):

New Zealand recognizes that there are certain sensitivities in relation to the impact of improved specific commitments on the regulatory frameworks contained in existing bilateral and multilateral air services agreements, but believes that the GATS framework provides a flexible mechanism capable of accommodating the regulatory challenges across the full range of services sectors. After all, the GATS is not all-encompassing. Many areas currently regulated by governments or by intergovernmental agreement (e.g., aviation safety and security) would not be affected. It should also be noted that many other regulatory concerns traditionally addressed in existing bilateral and multilateral air services agreements (e.g., remittance of earnings) find close parallels in existing GATS provisions or other elements of the multilateral trading system (e.g., the GATT [General Agreement on Tariffs and Trade]) and should not constitute obstacles to more meaningful specific commitments in the air transport services sector.

ICAO members have for their part recently given consideration to expanding the scope of the GATS Air Transport Annex. Among the conclusions to the Fifth Worldwide Air Transport Conference held at ICAO from March 24 to 29, 2003, was the following:

[A]pplying the basic GATS principle of most favoured nation (MFN) treatment to traffic rights remains a complex and difficult issue. While there is some support to extend the GATS Annex on Air Transport Services to include so-called "soft rights" as well as some aspects of "hard rights," there is no global consensus on whether or how this would be pursued. It is also inconclusive at this stage as to whether the GATS is an effective option for air transport liberalization.[17]

Regulatory Disciplines for Skeletal Commitments

Only the bravest of pundits would predict that commitments to market opening for transportation services will be up for major expansion in this negotiating round. Certainly the Organisation for Economic Co-operation and Development (OECD 2001) has done its part to encourage a hard look at the creaky system of liner conferences, and the World Bank (2002, pp. 97–127) has weighed in on the side of an ambitious market-opening negotiating agenda for air and maritime transport. One might hold out residual hope for developments leading to a bandwagon effect in favour of a considerably bolstered package of commitments. Although they have left an unfortunate degree of ambiguity concerning the ultimate negotiating competency of the European Commission, recently issued decisions of the European Court of Justice have made clear that the traditional national ownership and control clauses included in bilateral air transport agreements violate European law.[18] One has reason to hope that this development might spark a sweeping EU–US bilateral negotiation. An Open Skies or Trans-Atlantic Common Aviation Area agreement between the European Union and the United States would have significant repercussions for aviation services in the rest of the world and could become the catalyst for a multilateral framework. However, if one takes the work of the Council for Trade in Services and current formal negotiation proposals at face value, the fairest expectation is for a much more modest outcome.

Where might regulatory disciplines fit against such a backdrop? Drawing inspiration from the Telecom Reference Paper on Regulatory Principles, the World Bank (2002, p. 95) went so far as to suggest that putting regulatory disciplines in place within the skeletal regime of existing commitments could become a driver for future liberalization of transportation services:

> Such disciplines could unleash a deeper exchange of liberalization commitments, as countries would be more confident that market access concessions are not reversed by regulatory barriers and that the gains from more liberal policies are not captured by private parties.

Before turning in the next section to the range of regulatory barriers to which future regulatory disciplines might appropriately apply, it is important to explore the premise that such disciplines could apply even in the absence of significant market access commitments. One can put this premise into sharp relief by considering a traditional regulatory barrier in the transportation sector: the protection of domestic flag carriers. If, at one extreme, the prevailing regulatory environment purposely excluded foreign carriers to benefit domestic ones, one could scarcely imagine meaningful regulatory disciplines being developed under Article VI.4. It is true that the Article VI obligation to minimize trade-restrictive elements of domestic regulation is a general obligation, but if foreign carriers are simply excluded, Article VI could only require their transparent exclusion! In the maritime sector, although such flag-preferring barriers are of sharply decreasing significance, they still play out partly through unilateral cargo reservations in a number of countries and partly through bilateral cargo-sharing arrangements—for example, under the all-but-obsolete UNCTAD Liner Conference Code of Conduct,[19] and often through restrictions on cabotage service (service between domestic ports by foreign carriers), as in the Jones Act of the United States.[20] In air transport, the cabotage prohibition is all but universal and foreign carriers can operate on international routes only on the basis of bilateral air services agreements. Such agreements frequently restrict the number of foreign carriers that can be designated, the destinations they can serve, and even the tariffs that can be charged or the capacity and frequencies of service, sometimes envisaging formal pooling arrangements between the foreign and domestic carrier. So one must return to these questions: because measures protecting flag carriers are not subject to GATS trade disciplines, can one really envisage the application of liberalizing regulatory disciplines to transportation? Would that not amount to the regulatory discipline tail wagging the dog of substantive market access commitments?

This may be obvious: even in the absence of WTO commitments, countries can create and have created regulatory environments tending toward open trade and competition. The WTO Secretariat's assessment of maritime transport services is eloquent. Reviewing the results of its survey of domestic regulation, the Secretariat concluded, "The overall picture resulting . . . is of a very liberalised sector as compared to many other services sectors and in particular to other transport sectors."[21] This is particularly true of bulk traffic through tramp shipping, which responds to spot demand and accounts for some 68 percent of the overall volume of traffic by tonnage. Even the 32 percent of traffic volume (but considerably higher proportion of traffic value) accounted for by containerized traffic through liner shipping, which operates on scheduled services, has witnessed declined influence of the price-fixing system of liner conferences. For example, although the 1998 U.S. Ocean Shipping Reform Act did not do away with the antitrust immunity afforded to liner conferences, it did abolish the "me-too" requirement under which the same published contract terms had to be offered to all similarly situated shippers, which tended to fix prices.[22] The 1998 Act also expanded the scope for nonconference shipping.

Whereas the liberalization picture for air transport is somewhat less resplendent, the tendency is the same. In its recent analysis of the overall state of bilateral air transport agreements, the WTO Secretariat noted the spread of liberal "open skies" bilateral agreements as well as the conclusion of some market-opening plurilateral and regional agreements, with the concomitant decline in the use of International Air Transport Association (IATA) tariff conference price fixing, and concludes that the trend line is toward "a gradual narrowing of existing regulatory discrepancies."[23] It can be added that even countries such as India that heretofore have been adamant in their resistance to open skies policies are often in the midst of internal procompetitive regulatory reforms that are expected to pave the way for improved future market access for foreign carriers.[24]

Thus even if regulatory disciplines were not part of a package of substantive commitments to reduce flag carrier preferences, they would nevertheless be implemented in a context that is increasingly propitious to those carriers. As a result, foreign transportation carriers are increasingly involved in domestic markets and thus can be significantly affected by domestic regulatory measures. The next part of the chapter seeks to classify the kinds of regulatory measures that can give rise to market barriers in transportation.

Classification of Regulatory Barriers to Trade in Transportation

In classifying regulatory barriers to trade, it is useful to sketch out a typology of rationales for regula-

tion. Through the heyday of U.S. deregulation in the late 1970s and the 1980s, it was commonly believed that regulation existed to correct market failures.[25] The argument for deregulation was usually based on a demonstration that putative market failures—natural monopoly, imperfect information, externalities—either did not exist or in fact could be addressed through market devices accompanied by antitrust law. Depending on the commentator's (intellectual) proximity to (the University of) Chicago, antitrust law was itself given a deregulatory reading in all but the area of hardcore cartels because, almost tautologically, markets were best placed to determine whether markets were behaving as markets should (see Posner 1976).

At the same time that the term "regulation" was understood in North America to mean "illegitimate intervention in markets," in Europe the ambitious regulatory enterprise of the European Commission sought to build a single market in the place of a patchwork of domestic impediments.[26] From a European perspective, the notion that regulation could be designed to enable and to ensure the existence of a market rather than to impede its natural operation presented no conceptual difficulty.

At root, the difference between market intervention and market-ensuring perspectives on regulation derives from whether one focuses on using regulation to produce private or public goods. *Pure private goods,* exemplified by commodities in the market, are backed by regulatory regimes that allow them to retain the following characteristics. They are:

- In private possession
- Under absolute control
- Obtained through rivalry
- Enjoyed exclusively by the owners
- Assessed by their exchange value
- Alienable
- Perishable through use.

Pure public goods, exemplified by common resources such as air, are backed by regulatory regimes that allow them to retain the following characteristics. They are:

- In collective possession
- Openly accessible
- Obtained through cooperation

- Enjoyed in common
- Assessed by the degree of confidence invested in them
- Inalienable
- Imperishable through use.[27]

Given that common and private uses are interdependent, no actual good is purely private or purely public. Private goods entail ancillary public goods that enable access to them and public goods entail ancillary private goods that enable their individual enjoyment. Thus a perfect market and the consumer welfare benefit it provides are a public good that allows access to private goods. This reveals that the term "market failure" contains an ambiguity because it could refer to the failure of supply of the public good, which is open access to the market, or to failure of supply of the private goods to which market access is given. For that reason it is helpful to distinguish between private and public goods failures.

Private goods failures arise when, were it not for regulatory intervention, the characteristics necessary for enjoying the goods could not be properly established. This occurs when the following problems become generalized in a market:

- Title is contested.
- Capacity to control is lost.
- Rivalry gives way to dominant position.
- Use creates spillovers.
- Information to assess value is asymmetrically available.
- Persistent excess capacity prevents alienability.
- Sunk cost investments cannot be consumed.

The regulatory measures that typically are designed to address these private goods failures are:

- Title registration
- Licensing
- Prevention of abuse of dominance
- Internalization of spillovers
- Disclosure rules
- Capacity controls
- Price allocation of sunk costs.

Public goods failures arise when, in the absence of regulatory intervention, the characteristics necessary for enjoying the goods cannot be properly

established. That occurs when the following problems occur in securing access to the good:

- There are barriers to entry.
- Control is captured.
- There is defection from cooperation in use of the good.
- There is free riding on sustaining investments.
- There is loss of confidence in quality of provision.
- There is under-capacity to provide the good.
- The good is depleted.

The regulatory measures that typically are designed to address these public goods failures are:

- Removal of entry barriers
- Guarantees of agency independence
- Standard setting
- Administration of taxes and user charges
- Certification and audit
- Universal service obligations
- Sustainable scarce resource allocation.

The foregoing classification is summarized in table 7.1.

Each kind of regulatory measure designed to address private or public goods failures, whether appropriately framed or implemented on the basis of a misdiagnosis or mismatch of instruments, can also give rise to discriminatory and disproportionate burdens for trading partners. Differential or arbitrary regulatory enforcement—often an index of regulatory capture—is in a sense contrary to the idea of regulation itself, which in the words of GATS Article VI must be "reasonable, objective and impartial." The trade issue to which this gives rise is the failure of a member to maintain a competent and independent regulatory framework. It can be seen as a matter of institutional organization and process rather than of substantive regulatory policy.[28] In addition, substantive regulatory policy can give rise to trade issues in circumstances of systematic over-enforcement or under-enforcement of measures. For our purposes here, what is meant by "over-enforcement" is the systematic governmental restriction of private choices that are consistent with the goals of the regulatory policy. Over-enforcement can arise as a trade issue when it is in fact pursued as a disguised trade restriction in favour of domestic service providers

TABLE 7.1   Private vs. Public Goods

Private Goods			Public Goods		
Characteristic	**Failure**	**Regulation**	**Characteristic**	**Failure**	**Regulation**
Private possession	Contested title	Title registration	Collective possession	Entry barrier	Removal of barriers
Control	Loss of control	Licensing	Open access	Capture	Agency independence
Rivalry	Dominant position	Competition safeguards	Cooperation	Defection	Standard setting
Exclusive enjoyment	Spillovers	Internalization of spillovers	Collective enjoyment	Free riding	Taxes and user charges
Exchange value	Asymmetrical information	Disclosure	Trust value	Loss of confidence	Certification and audit
Alienability	Excess capacity	Capacity controls	Inalienability	Under-capacity	Universal service
Perishability	Sunk costs	Recovery of sunk costs	Imperishability	Depletion	Sustainable allocation

who can meet the unnecessarily high standard at lower cost than can foreign competitors. What is meant by "under-enforcement" is the systematic absence of governmental restriction of private choices that are inconsistent with the goals of the regulatory policy. Under-enforcement can arise as a trade issue when a strategy of relaxed regulatory oversight produces social dumping in third countries.[29] Although one can imagine examples of over- and under-enforcement for each kind of regulatory measure, table 7.2 summarizes the typical potential regulatory burden of relevance for trade disciplines.[30]

The characteristic public goods failure addressed by the WTO scheme is the removal of entry barriers to the market. Regulatory measures addressing other private and public goods failures can constitute barriers to entry and thus present inherent tradeoffs against the trade regime. When one applies this rubric to maritime and air transport, one generates the specific regulatory burdens described in tables 7.3 and 7.4. These tables are included here to help identify the issues that may prompt the need for regulatory disciplines, and they form the background to the assessment presented in the next section.

TABLE 7.2   Typical Trade-Distorting Burdens Imposed on Domestic Regulatory Measures

Private Goods Failure		Public Goods Failure	
Regulatory measure	**Potential burden**	**Regulatory measure**	**Potential burden**
Title registration	Under-enforcement	Removal of entry barriers	Under-enforcement
Licensing	Over-enforcement	Guarantees of agency independence	Under-enforcement
Competition safeguards	Under-enforcement	Standard setting	Over- and under-enforcement
Internalization of spillovers	Over- and under-enforcement	Administration of taxes and user charges	Over-enforcement
Disclosure rules	Over- and under-enforcement	Certification and audit	Over- and under-enforcement
Capacity controls	Over-enforcement	Universal service obligations	Over-enforcement
Recovery of sunk costs	Over-enforcement	Sustainable allocation	Over-enforcement

TABLE 7.3   Trade-Distorting Burdens in Maritime Transport

Private Goods Failure		Public Goods Failure	
Regulatory measure	Potential burden	Regulatory measure	Potential burden
Title registration	Flags of convenience	Removal of entry barriers	Flag-based preference; access to port facilities; access to land leg
Licensing	Freight agency and terminal operator licenses	Guarantees of agency independence	Arbitrary agency action
Prevention of abuse of dominance	Liner conference antitrust immunity; Port monopolies	Standard-setting	Safety, security, hazardous material and environmental standards; port labor standards
Internalization of spillovers	Polluter pays	Administration of taxes and user charges	Tonnage tax; service tariffs; customs liability claims
Disclosure rules	Documentation requirements; Confidentiality of contract terms	Certification and audit	Seafarer certification; vessel inspection
Capacity controls	Restrictions on branch offices; Transhipment prohibitions	Universal service obligations	—
Allocation of sunk costs	—	Sustainable scarce resource allocation	—

Note: — denotes not applicable
Source: Assembled from Secretariat Background Note on Maritime Services, http://www.wto.org/english/tratop_e/serv_e/transport_e/transport_maritime_urneg_e.htm, and World Bank (2002).

Balancing Private Market Access against the Provision of Public Goods

We turn now to a consideration of the types of cross-sectoral horizontal disciplines that could be made to apply in the transportation sector in the light of the regulatory challenges identified in the previous section of this chapter.

The Fiendish Difficulty

Pierre Sauvé and Arvind Subramanian (2001) correctly have warned that finding the right trade-off between protecting legitimate public policy objectives and restricting measures that are unduly burdensome for trading partners is "fiendishly difficult." This is basically because the goods that various regulatory measures seek to promote, considered in isolation, appear to be incommensurable. If the task is somehow to measure, for example, the advantages of greater cabin safety against the advantages of increased trade in aviation services, we are involved in a "mug's game" that can

deteriorate into a fight over who gets to determine which default regime will be used to judge the other. If the trade regime wins out, all regulation will be judged according to whether it tends to restrict market access. If another public goods regime wins out—perhaps the transportation safety regime—then all regulation will be judged according to whether it tends to diminish the safety of service. At one extreme any safety requirement can be understood to diminish market access because it deprives consumers of choice about the level of safety they wish to purchase given their own risk aversion. At the other extreme, any pro-competitive access rule can be understood to diminish safety because it tends to place service providers in a context where their investments in safety will be limited by market-driven returns.[31]

It is fortunate that the goods that regulatory policies seek to enable are not elaborated in isolation from each other and are best understood as mutually dependent and complementary rather than as obliging tragic choices. For example, aviation safety regulation cannot be elaborated in isolation from

TABLE 7.4   Trade-Distorting Burdens in Air Transport

Private Goods Failure		Public Goods Failure	
Regulatory measure	Potential burden	Regulatory measure	Potential burden
Title registration	Registration of leased aircraft	Removal of entry barriers	Flag-based preference
	Fractional ownership rules		Access to airport and ground handling facilities
	Bankruptcy rules		Access to land leg
			Freedoms of the air, including cabotage
Licensing	Designation—substantial ownership and effective control	Guarantees of agency independence	Arbitrary agency action
	Charter licensing		
	Combination vs. cargo licensing		
Prevention of abuse of dominance	Alliance antitrust immunity	Standard setting	Safety, security, noise, hazardous material, and environmental standards
	Code-sharing		
	Airport, navigation services and ground handling monopolies		Cabin crew flight time rules
	Virtual travel agencies and multi-airline portals review		
	Predatory pricing		
Internalization of spillovers	Noise abatement and air pollution charges	Administration of taxes and user charges	Airport charges
			Air navigation charges
Disclosure rules	Documentation requirements	Certification and audit	ICAO safety/security audits
	Computer Reservation Systems (CRS) Codes of Conduct		Extraterritorial domestic audits
	Cargo tariff disclosure		Airman certification
Capacity controls	Pooling arrangements	Universal service obligations	Remote service obligations
	Change of gauge restrictions		
	Charter carriage of cargo restrictions		
Allocation of sunk costs	Tariff setting	Sustainable scarce resource allocation	Slot allocation

Source: Assembled from "Air Transport Services," Background Note by the Secretariat for the Council for Trade in Services, S/C/W/59, November 5, 1998, together with subsequent Secretariat Notes titled "Developments in the Air Transport Sector Since the Conclusion of the Uruguay Round" S/C/W/163 and Addenda 1 to 6; and World Bank (2002).

the effort to establish an aviation market. Standards and policies adopted are premised on an evaluation of risk reflecting the movement of passengers on commercial terms.[32] Regarding market access, the acknowledgment in the GATS preamble that changing domestic regulatory policies are part of the envi-

ronment in which trade is conducted is more than just the toleration of a necessary evil. For example, the Reference Paper positively mandates the creation of an independent domestic body at minimum to settle interconnection disputes. This is not to say that complementary and interdependent trade and other regulatory policies obviate the need for difficult tradeoffs. It is simply to say that the search for such tradeoffs is inherent in each of the regimes before one seeks to align them through formal regulatory disciplines.

Indeed, there is an important sense in which other regulatory policies can be strengthened through the GATS, especially if dispute settlement leads to the kind of nuanced treatment both of domestic regulation and of the framework of international law outside the WTO (Appellate Body Report 1998) that was displayed by the Appellate Body in *United States-Shrimp*[33] In particular, both ICAO standards and IMO standards—which are addressed by the terms of Articles VI.5 and VII.5 for the purposes of mutual recognition of authorization, certification, and licensing—could flesh out GATS principles and be given greater influence in domestic standard setting. As the WTO Secretariat noted with respect to ICAO standards on airport charges, in a conclusion that could apply equally to other ICAO and IMO standards:[34]

> In total, it appears clearly that the airport charging system is based on principles in essence similar to those of GATS, although much more sophisticated and detailed. In spite of this degree of detail and of its ability to take into account, through periodical redrafting, the new economic and regulatory developments, the system seems to lack the necessary enforcement and dispute settlement mechanisms to produce its full effects. In that respect it is in a situation similar to the WIPO intellectual property conventions before the creation of the TRIPS Agreement or of interconnection rules in telecommunication before the creation of the reference paper.

If regulatory disciplines are structured not simply to provide a way to strike down domestic measures but also to reinforce global standards, the appropriate balance will have been struck and the fiendish difficulty fended off. How might this be done?

The Twisted Interpretation?

Addressing the form and content of possible transportation regulatory disciplines requires attention to a preliminary matter of interpretation as to the scope of what can be devised under Article VI.4. A

number of the regulatory measures giving rise to trade-distorting burdens relate to policy frameworks that give preferential treatment for domestic flag carriers. It has been concluded (incorrectly, in my view) that such measures can be subject to disciplines only through scheduled commitments under Articles XVI and XVII, not under Article VI.[35] This conclusion was drawn by the Working Party on Professional Services (WPPS), apparently with the support of the Secretariat, and is the operating premise for the Working Party on Domestic Regulation. The reasoning behind this conclusion was explained by the Secretariat as follows (see WTO Working Party on Professional Services 1996, p. 3):

> In the discussions it was noted that there was a fundamental legal distinction in the GATS between those provisions: while Articles XVI and XVII belonged to Part III of the Agreement on Specific Commitments, Article VI belonged to Part II on General Obligations and Disciplines. As a consequence the elimination of restrictions on market access and national treatment is subject to the negotiation of specific commitments, whereas the obligation to minimise the trade-restrictive elements of domestic regulation is a general obligation which would be subject to the disciplines to be developed under Article VI:4. The legal status of these measures also naturally differs. Measures restricting market access and national treatment are prohibited, unless scheduled, in sectors where specific commitments have been undertaken, whereas they can be maintained in sectors which are not committed. The right to maintain domestic regulatory measures is however specifically recognized and will be subject to the disciplines to be developed under Article VI:4 with the aim of minimizing their negative impact on trade. These measures cannot be entered as limitations in a Member's schedule. The WPPS came to the conclusion that, in order to ensure legal certainty and the conformity of the disciplines with the structure of the GATS, there should not be any overlap between Articles XVI and XVII on the one hand and Article VI on the other hand.

Nevertheless, the notion that the measures covered by Article VI.4 are in a watertight compartment separate from Articles XVI and XVII has proved difficult to maintain. Indeed the Secretariat explained to the members of the Working Party on Domestic Regulation that it had difficulty preparing a paper listing examples of regulatory measures covered under Article VI.4, in part because "the dividing line between measures covered under Article VI:4 and those covered under Articles XVI and XVII was not always easy to draw."[36] It is not easy to draw this dividing line because, although the analyses conducted under the two sets of provisions are different in kind, the separate analyses actually can apply to the same regulatory measures. One can ask, for example, whether licensing standards are consistent with national treatment and market access, and ask separately whether they are administered reasonably, objectively, transparently, and so as to create only those trade burdens that are necessary. The latter questions can be asked even if no market access or national treatment commitments have been made. On the other hand, sometimes the failure to apply licensing standards objectively or transparently can itself have implications for market access or national treatment. Indeed, it is striking that the telecom Reference Paper, which is incorporated into commitments under Articles XVI and XVII, creates a number of regulatory disciplines that clearly would fall under Article VI.4. These disciplines include (a) transparent and reasonable technical standards governing interconnection; (b) transparent universal services obligations (often license conditions) that are not more burdensome than necessary; and (c) publicly available licensing criteria and terms and conditions of license. One could argue that all of the remaining Reference Paper disciplines also fall under the terms of Article VI.4 both because they all "relate" to qualification requirements and procedures, technical standards, and licensing requirements and procedures, and because the list of disciplines that could apply to such measures under Article VI.4 is not exhaustive.[37] Thus if regulatory disciplines under Articles XVI and XVII need not respect the watertight compartment of Article VI.4, why is Article VI.4 disabled in the other direction?

It is also important to note that Article XVIII allows the negotiation of commitments with respect to measures affecting trade in services not subject to scheduling under Articles XVI or XVII, including those regarding qualifications, standards, or licensing matters. This means that the Reference Paper can be explained by the combination of all three Articles: XVI, XVII, and XVIII. However, Article VIII also demonstrates that the legal architecture of the GATS does not place disciplines regarding trade-restrictive domestic regulatory measures only under the roof of Part II. The real issue is whether members wish to elaborate a Part III "patchwork" framework of disciplines applicable only through specific commitments or a Part II general framework of disciplines applicable to all members. Because the text of the GATS is at best ambiguous, it seems sensible to leave to members the choice of framework best suited to any particular problem. In any event, whatever the members agree to under Article VI.4 will have to be interpreted as a coherent part of the GATS, and will certainly not be viewed as creating market access or national treatment commitments through the back door.

In light of the foregoing discussion, I offer the conclusion that Article VI.4 could be used to craft regulatory disciplines for transportation covering the full range of regulatory measures that may be more burdensome on trade than necessary. Whether such disciplines are desirable or whether they are feasible are entirely separate questions. Most recently, the members of the Working Party on Domestic Regulation have agreed to ask themselves the following questions when considering if a regulatory measure ought to come within the ambit of Article VI.4:

(a) Is the measure already covered by Articles XVI and/or XVII?

(b) If not, is it addressed by any other provisions of the Agreement (e.g., Articles II, III, VIII, IX)?

(c) If not, does it fall clearly within the scope of Article VI, in particular VI.4 (licensing requirements, qualification requirements, technical standards, licensing procedures, and qualification procedures)?

(d) If so, is the measure adequately addressed by the relevant provisions of the Accountancy Disciplines, or are modifications required?

This methodology will indeed tend to keep Article VI.4 as a residual provision (WTO Working Party on Domestic Regulation 2003, p. 2).

The next section of this chapter addresses the questions of what disciplines to include, and both whether and to what degree those disciplines should be part of a horizontal or sector-specific set of disciplines. Although a reality check may suggest that none of what is discussed below is feasible in the short term, the purpose of the discussion is to contribute to a principled assessment of what sorts of disciplines ought to be elaborated.

The Enlightening Comparisons

Four sets of existing disciplines offer enlightening comparisons for the disciplines that might apply to transportation regulation: the Reference Paper on Regulatory Principles, the Disciplines on Domestic Regulation in the Accountancy Sector, the Technical Barriers to Trade (TBT) Agreement, and the Sanitary and Phytosanitary (SPS) Agreement.[38]

The Reference Paper on Regulatory Principles
Could the form and content of the telecom Reference Paper be a model for transportation disciplines?[39] As to form, the Reference Paper may be less than ideal for transportation services for reasons that were just discussed. If the mechanism adopted for implementing regulatory disciplines pursues the GATS Part III model of inscription through separate country commitments, the disciplines would be linked to the success of negotiations on adding to the substantive content of transportation annexes (which have not been promising). Furthermore, even if such an approach could bear fruit, countries would be free to modify the terms of the disciplines, as a number of countries, including India, did in their telecom Reference Paper commitments.[40] This may seem to maximize flexibility in line with the overall GATS acknowledgment of the need for regulatory diversity, but it also detracts from the effort to build stable and reliable disciplines within which regulatory diversity can flourish. In short, disciplines are ideally worked out through Article VI.4 and applied equally to all. The Reference Paper's departure from this logic can be forgiven because it did, after all, represent the first effort to devise the GATS regulatory disciplines and was drafted before any disciplines had been worked on under Article VI.4.[41]

As to content, on the other hand, the Reference Paper is remarkably adaptable to transportation services. Of the topics it addresses—competitive safeguards, interconnection, universal service, public availability of licensing criteria, independent regulators, and allocation of scarce resources—all except the second have obvious relevance. Although the interconnection problem does seem specific to telecommunications, one can interpret the issue to be one of access to essential facilities. Such an interpretation would allow the concepts in the Reference Paper to be applied horizontally rather than in a sector-specific way. The parallel problem for transportation is nondiscriminatory access to port and airport facilities based on cost-oriented charges. Because the Reference Paper does not prescribe a regulatory code but rather ensures the transparent, nondiscriminatory, competitively neutral, and proportionate application of domestic regulation, it could all but apply equally to parallel domestic transportation issues. Obvious missing elements are the health, safety, security, and environmental dimensions of regulation, which are far less prominent in telecommunications than in transportation and are unlikely to arise as trade barriers in that field.[42] Furthermore, the necessity test in the Reference Paper falls short of what would be needed for a horizontal discipline because it is formulated to apply only to a subset of the measures covered in the Reference Paper, that is, universal service as defined by the member. Taking the Reference Paper as a whole, however, one can conclude that it provides a core of concepts around which more ample horizontal regulatory disciplines could be built.

Disciplines on Domestic Regulations in the Accountancy Sector Although the Accountancy Disciplines, formulated under Article VI.4, are sectoral rather than horizontal, they contain a number of elements that could be horizontal and of relevance to transportation.[43] The General Provisions contain a necessity test that could be rendered horizontal: "Members shall ensure that such measures are not more trade-restrictive than necessary to fulfil a legitimate objective." The legitimate objectives, on the other hand, would seem to be best defined sectorally. The legitimate objectives listed for the Accountancy Sector—protection of the public and consumers generally, quality of service, professional competence, and professional integrity—could apply to other professions but are not a perfect fit for transportation. One could add the following objectives, consistent with Articles XIV and XIV*bis* and thereby produce a more complete list appropriate to transportation: public safety; public security; public health; and air, water, land, and noise pollution abatement. One could add fair distribution and preservation of scarce resources; competition safeguards; and universal service to the complement of objectives, but those objectives might better be addressed through separate disciplines.

The transparency provisions add the useful general principle that competent authorities subject to the obligation can include nongovernmental agencies. In the case of transportation this could include the IATA, which still has a residual tariff-setting function recognized in some bilateral air transport agreements. In the Accountancy Disciplines, transparency obligations are specifically enumerated to apply to activities and professional titles regulated by the profession and to the list of individuals and firms entitled to practice. The transportation parallel would be to the categories and licensing arrangements governing pilots; captains; instructors; traffic controllers; crew; specialized ground, security, and dock personnel; and working conditions (e.g., flight time rules).

The licensing procedures provision of the Accountancy Disciplines contains only general principles that elaborate on Article VI and could be applied horizontally. The licensing requirements discipline builds on the general transparency and objectivity criteria but specifies their application to requirements governing firm name, residency requirements, and requirements for membership in a professional organization as well as to indemnity insurance and regulatory fees. Insurance requirements and fees or charges are measures that exist in the transportation sector. Additional transportation licensing requirements pertain to citizenship, financial capacity, and air- or seaworthiness.

The accountancy qualification requirements are tailored to specifics of the accounting profession and would have to be adapted to transportation, particularly with regard to permitted requirements that are formulated as an exhaustive list. For example, medical requirements, applicable to pilots, are not included; nor are specialized training requirements, such as those applicable to specific classes of craft.[44] The Accountancy Disciplines contain the concept of equivalence, which also finds its way into Article 2.7 of the TBT Agreement and Article

4.11 of the SPS Agreement. With regard to transportation, it would be useful for equivalency to extend not only to qualification requirements but also to licensing and to technical standards so as to formalize mutual recognition.

Finally, the provisions governing qualification procedures and technical standards are formulated very generally and could be applied horizontally. One would expect to find greater specificity in disciplines governing technical standards for transportation. In particular, as is discussed below, the roles of ICAO and IMO ideally should be specified in a way that resembles the framework governing intergovernmental organizations under the SPS Agreement. The Accountancy Disciplines simply reiterate the Article VI.5(b) requirement "that account shall be taken of internationally recognized standards of relevant international organizations." The relevant organizations are not even listed.

Taken as a whole, the Accountancy Disciplines demonstrate that horizontal disciplines could coexist with a sectoral elaboration of them. That would streamline the horizontal disciplines and avoid the difficulty of choosing from a broad menu those disciplines relevant to individual sectors. But any sector-specific approach depends on the continued stability of the sectoral definitions. In that regard it is interesting to note that the Accountancy Disciplines are silent about multidisciplinary practice and intra-firm conflicts of interest, stating merely that the "disciplines are to be applicable to Members who have entered specific commitments in accountancy in their schedules."[45]

The TBT and SPS Agreements   In contrast to the Reference Paper and to the Accountancy Disciplines, the TBT Agreement and the SPS Agreement build on what was already a relatively mature GATT framework. They are two complementary agreements that incorporate each other by reference and are far more elaborate than their GATS cousins. More than the Reference Paper and the Accounting Disciplines, they are the models for what the GATS horizontal regulatory disciplines should resemble.

The TBT Agreement can be understood as the horizontal disciplines for the GATT; the SPS Agreement is the "sectoral" supplement that applies to regulatory measures necessary to protect human, animal, or plant life and health. For present purposes only the following subset of relevant features of these agreements require specific mention:

- The necessity tests elaborated under both agreements explicitly address risk assessment according to scientific and technical (engineering) criteria.
- Emergency safeguard provisions save inconsistent measures.
- Legitimate objectives are formulated through a nonexhaustive list.
- There is a presumption in favour of the validity of measures that are in accord with international standards. Although it has been argued that this might not always be appropriate in the case of services, it bears emphasizing that the presumption can be rebutted when justified.[46]
- Transparency guarantees include notice and comment requirements.
- Both the SPS and the TBT Agreements give rise to their own institutional monitoring framework within the WTO.

Each of the foregoing features could be incorporated into a horizontal set of regulatory disciplines for services.

The most remarkable and impressive feature of the SPS Agreement is the way in which it manages relationships with the WTO's sister intergovernmental organizations active in the field of sanitary and phytosanitary standards. Not only does Article 12 encourage the use of international standards; it also establishes a framework for seeking the advice of the Codex Alimentarius Commission (CAC), the International Office of Epizootics (IOE), and the international and regional organizations operating within the framework of the International Plant Protection Convention (IPPC). Article 3 announces the objective of achieving harmonization of international standards and provides that "Members shall play a full part, within the limits of their resources, in the [CAC, IOE, and IPPC]." The SPS Agreement oversight committee, the Committee on Sanitary and Phytosanitary Measures, has observer members from the CAC, IOE, and IPPC and has the mandate to monitor harmonization and to coordinate with sister agencies. In cases that go to dispute settlement, "a panel may, when it deems it appropriate, establish an advisory technical experts group, or consult the relevant international organizations, at the request of either party to the dispute or on its own initiative." The relationship between the GATT and the CAC, IOE, and IPPC is the kind of relationship that should be created with ICAO and IMO regarding regulatory measures in fields where ICAO and IMO have developed standards.[47]

Conclusion

A robust ICAO-IMO-WTO linkage mechanism, patterned on the SPS Agreement, should be built into a schedule of specific transportation disciplines that would complement new horizontal Article VI.4 disciplines. ICAO, with 187 members, and IMO, with 161 members, are mature and broadly representative intergovernmental institutions with sophisticated procedures in place to review and revise their standards. If the WTO can buttress its standard-setting function through access to binding dispute settlement, ICAO and IMO can help buttress the legitimacy of the WTO by orienting the trade framework toward enabling and ensuring global public goods of safety, security, and environmental protection in the field of transportation.

ICAO has developed an elaborate series of Standards and Recommended Practices in the fields of personnel licensing, rules of the air, aeronautical meteorology, aeronautical charts, units of measurement, operation of aircraft, nationality and registration marks, airworthiness, aeronautical telecommunications, air traffic services, search and rescue, aircraft accident investigation, aerodromes, aeronautical information services, aircraft noise and engine emissions, security and the safe transport of dangerous goods. Beyond the Chicago Convention, ICAO administers a series of conventions including five instruments dealing with aviation security. Since 1996 ICAO has implemented a system of safety audits of its members. It now initiates those audits of its own, seeking the agreement of members, and in February 2002 staged a conference that led to a new mandate to develop a security audit function as well. The organization's capacity to reinforce confidence in global aviation markets was tested recently when Lloyd's of London re-insurers cancelled war risk insurance after the September 11 terrorist attacks in the United States. ICAO has been leading an initiative to establish new global self-insurance pooling arrangements for the world's carriers and has intervened with member states to ensure that governments temporarily provide backstop insurance coverage.

IMO oversees a series of conventions, Memoranda of Understanding (MOUs), and standards that address the safe operation of ships, safety of life at sea, safety of navigation, safety management, tanker safety, carriage of hazardous materials, pollution from ships, marine pollution, oil pollution preparedness, maritime security, training and certification of seafarers, ship number identification, port control and facilitation, piracy and armed robbery, stowaways, and illegal migrants. The 1995 amendments to IMO-sponsored International Convention on Standards of Training, Certification and Watchkeeping for Seafarers entrusted IMO with powers to audit its members in their performance of those convention obligations. IMO has Facilitation, Maritime Safety, and Marine Environment Committees that coordinate its standard-setting and oversight activities.

These brief accounts serve to show that ICAO and IMO are playing critical roles as trustees for global public goods in transportation markets. A necessity test for transportation services could draw on their standards to help assess whether domestic measures fulfil legitimate objectives and are not more trade restrictive than necessary. Such a test should be accompanied by an obligation for WTO members to participate fully in implementing ICAO and IMO standards. The two organizations could be asked to provide advice to Dispute Settlement Understanding (DSU) panels as they interpret transportation disciplines. Such an advisory activity would help ensure that panels consider safety, security, and environmental goals to be global public goods with their own inherent value and not simply consider their value to be ancillary to trade.

An example may serve to drive this final point home. The Gambia recently has concluded an Open Skies bilateral air transport agreement with the United States.[48] As part of the negotiations, the United States insisted that The Gambia's carrier and the airport at Banjul meet U.S. safety and security standards. The Gambia sought an ICAO audit and assistance in meeting ICAO standards. Partly on the strength of ICAO advice, its government sought to sever the carrier assessment from the airport assessment, having concluded that it could more quickly meet airport standards. In short, The Gambia was prepared to negotiate access to its airport solely for

foreign carriers so as to improve market access of its citizens to the United States. Ultimately the U.S. Federal Aviation Administration (FAA) conducted its own audit of Banjul airport and concluded that more stringent standards than those of ICAO would have to be met if The Gambia wanted Open Skies. Assisted by the FAA, The Gambia soon succeeded in complying with U.S. standards.

How would one assess whether the United States met a necessity test in imposing its regulatory standards on The Gambia in exchange for market access? If a DSU panel were simply to ask whether the United States unilaterally imposed standards more stringent than international standards, the United States would lose. But if the panel could analyse whether the higher U.S. safety and security standards were (a) rationally connected to the goals that underlie international standards, (b) not in violation of positive international obligations, and (c) implemented in a manner proportionate to a legitimate domestic objective, the United States might win. The latter analysis, however, would draw precisely on the expertise and oversight of ICAO. That organization should serve as the WTO's advocate general in such matters. It should not be assumed that ICAO views its own standards as creating ceilings on domestic regulatory measures. In the example of The Gambia, ICAO fully understood that it was helping to bring that country up to par in preparing for FAA review. ICAO and the FAA have a pattern of close cooperation and, in fact, ICAO has audited the FAA!

Afterword

In 2001 Joel Trachtman agonized about what he takes to be a looming legitimacy crisis for the WTO (see Porter and others [2001], p. 357):

> [W]e have a conundrum: we cannot strengthen the WTO's legislative capacity without greater legitimacy, but the WTO's legitimacy is challenged by its reliance on dispute resolution to respond to most of the important issues it faces. . . . This conundrum has no easy solution: until the social reality of benefits from WTO activities justifies an assignment of greater legislative capacity, we should not enhance its legislative capacity.

The problem of regulatory disciplines is situated at the heart of this conundrum. In assessing domestic policies through dispute resolution, the WTO lacks a deliberative norm-making function that can articulate public goods and promote the social benefits that flow from them. A small start in addressing this conundrum can be made by linking the WTO more closely to intergovernmental institutions that through their assemblies already have a deliberative norm-making capacity that achieves a form of global consensus.

I agree with Robert Howse and Kalypso Nicolaidis that constitutionalizing the WTO in response to its looming legitimacy crisis is a step too far.[49] But a contemporary return to the "embedded liberalism bargain," as they suggested, must take account of the greater institutional capacity the WTO has achieved through dispute settlement. Through institutional linkages like the one proposed by this chapter for ICAO and IMO, the WTO's capacity can be used to expand the set of goods enabled and ensured through other institutions of global governance. In this way legitimacy can be augmented at least in some issue areas through a double movement that reinforces deliberative settings outside the WTO and adds to the range of goods promoted within the WTO. This amounts to embedding the WTO more firmly within the wider network of intergovernmental institutions, and placing the onus on those institutions to root themselves more firmly in national democratic consensus.

Endnotes

1. Ronald Coase (1974) has famously challenged the notion that the public good must be publicly supplied.
2. On global public goods generally, see Kaul, Grunberg, and Stern (1999). Noting that global public goods are "outcomes" for a global public rather than things supplied to individuals, they divided the global "public" into three groups—countries, socioeconomic groups, and generations—and suggested (pp. 10–11) that a global public good should

    1. Cover more than one group of countries—that is, as distinguished from a regional public good or a club good, the benefits of which are excludable (arguably free trade is a club good!).
    2. Benefit not only a broad spectrum of countries but also a broad spectrum of the global population, divided in terms of rich and poor; access to knowledge, information, and technology; ethnicity, gender, religion, and political affiliations; and so forth.

3. Meet the needs of the present generation without jeopardizing those of future generations.

    Noting that few pure global public goods would meet these criteria, the authors suggested a definition of impure global public good: whereas, "[a] pure global public good is marked by universality—that is, it benefits all countries, people and generations—an impure global public good would tend towards universality in that it would benefit more than one group of countries, and would not discriminate against any population segment or set of generations" (p. 11).

3. WTO-WIPO Cooperation Agreement, made at Geneva on December 22, 1995. Available at http://www.wto.org/english/tratop_e/trips_e/wtowip_e.htm (consulted February 7, 2002).
4. For a thorough review, see "Maritime Transport Services," Background Note by the Secretariat for the Council for Trade in Services, S/C/W/62 November 16, 1998. See also "Uruguay Round and Post-Uruguay Round Negotiations in Maritime Transport Services." Available at http://www.wto.org/English/tratop_e/serv_e/transport_e/transport_maritime_urneg_e.htm (consulted February 7, 2002). After the Uruguay Round was completed, five more countries added maritime transport commitments.
5. See Negotiating Group on Maritime Transport Services, Minutes of June 4, 1996, S/NGMTS/13.
6. Decision on Maritime Transport Services, S/L/24, July 3, 1996.
7. See Joint Statement from the European Communities and Their Member States; Hong Kong, China; Japan; Republic of Korea; Norway and Singapore, S/CSS/W/8, October 6, 2000.
8. See WTO Council for Trade in Services, Special Session: Communication from the Republic of Korea—Negotiating Proposal for Maritime Transport Services, S/CSS/W/87, May 11, 2001.
9. See WTO Council for Trade in Services, Special Session: Communication from Colombia—Maritime Transport Services, S/CSS/W/123, November 27, 2001.
10. See WTO Council for Trade in Services, Special Session: Communication from Australia—Negotiating Proposal for Maritime Transport Services, S/CSS/W/111, October 1, 2001.
11. For helpful overviews, see Hubner and Sauvé (2001) and Abeyratne (2001). See also "Air Transport Services," Background Note by the Secretariat for the Council for Trade in Services, S/C/W/59, November 5, 1998, and subsequent Secretariat Notes titled "Developments in the Air Transport Sector Since the Conclusion of the Uruguay Round," S/C/W/163 and Addenda 1 to 6.
12. In a communication, Costa Rica urged members to make more substantial commitments and to strengthen existing commitments regarding aircraft repair and maintenance services (S/CSS/W/138, March 19, 2002).
13. For an account of these views—and a dissent from them—see Janda (1994). It should be borne in mind that the 1944 Convention on Civil Aviation (Chicago Convention), administered by ICAO, in essence affirms domestic sovereignty over airspace and does not establish a formal framework for the exchange of traffic rights. This is left to bilateral negotiations by individual states.
14. Hubner and Sauvé (2001, p. 981) presented a helpful summary of the communications from Australia, the European

Union, Japan, New Zealand, and Norway made in the context of the Council for Trade in Services review.

15. See WTO Council for Trade in Services, Special Session: Communication from Colombia—Air Transport Services, S/CSS/W/124, November 27, 2001.

16. See WTO Council for Trade in Services, Special Session: Communication from New Zealand—Negotiating Proposal for Air Transport Services, S/CSS/W/92, June 26, 2001.

17. Commission of the European Communities v. Austria, Belgium, Denmark, Finland, Germany, Luxembourg, Sweden, and the United Kingdom, case numbers, respectively, C-475/98, C-471/98, C-467/98, C-469/98, C-476/98, C-472/98, C-468/98, C-466/98. See also "Communication from the Commission Concerning the Consequences of the Court Judgments of 5 November 2002 for European Air Transport Policy," COM (2002), 649 final, November 19, 2002; and Janda and Wilson (2003, pp. 46–50).

18. See ICAO Secretariat (2003, p. 7). What ICAO calls "inclusive," Australia, Chile, and New Zealand have urged should be "properly and thoroughly explored." See WTO Council for Trade in Services (2002).

19. UNCTAD Liner Conference Code of Conduct, 1974 (entry into force 1983). The Code reserves cargo according to the following formula: 40 percent ships of the exporting country; 40 percent ships of the importing country; 20 percent other ships. The WTO Secretariat (note 4, p. 3) noted the diminishing significance of this regime that had only applied effectively to Western Europe–West Africa trade, which accounts for less than 3 percent of world liner trade and was dealt a death blow when the EU dissolved the conferences on the grounds of competition concerns.

20. United States Code Annotated, Title 46 Appendix. Shipping, Chapter 24, Merchant Marine Act, 1920 §866. For a review of recent U.S. developments, see Onley (2001). As Onley puts it, the Jones Act "reserves (with some exceptions) the coastwise, inter-coastal and non-contiguous domestic maritime trades to U.S. built, U.S. owned and U.S. crewed vessels" (p. 104).

21. See note 4.

22. Ocean Shipping Reform Act ("OSRA"), 46 U.S.C. Pub. L. No. 105-258, 112 Stat. 1902.

23. "Developments in the Air Transport Sector Since the Conclusion of the Uruguay Round—Part IV." Background Note by the Secretariat. S/C/W/163/Add. 3 at 31, August 13, 2001. See also "Air Transport Services: The Positive Agenda for Developing Countries." Report of the UNCTAD Secretariat TD/B/COM.1/EM.9/2, p. 5–14, April 16, 1999.

24. See Ministry of Civil Aviation, India, Draft Civil Aviation Policy, August 2000 (http://civilaviation.nic.in/moca/civ_pol.html> (consulted February 7, 2002).

25. A *locus classicus* of the period is Breyer (1982).

26. For a fascinating critique of the notion of regulation as intervention, see Macdonald (1985).

27. This typology, which adds to the standard characterization of public goods as nonrivalrous and nonexcludable, is drawn from a larger work in progress.

28. I nevertheless characterize the provision of an independent regulatory framework as the regulatory measure designed to ensure open access to the public good at issue, for example, transportation safety. A strategy of not providing an independent regulatory framework can itself be seen as a problem of under-enforcement, as described below.

29. On social dumping generally, see Bean and others (2001).

30. This list does go beyond the scope of GATS Article VI.4, but for the purposes of the chapter it is assumed that regulatory disciplines could be elaborated for each of these measures. The Working Party on Domestic Regulation is operating on the premise that regulatory disciplines would be confined to the kinds of measures enumerated by Article VI.4 and thus extend to qualification requirements and procedures, technical standards, and licensing requirements and procedures. See Minutes of October 5, 2001, S/WPDR/M/10.

31. Thus, for example, Paul Stephen Dempsey (1990) has criticized airline deregulation as inherently jeopardizing the protection of aviation safety.

32. For example, under the U.S. Aviation Act the policy standards developed by the secretary of transportation "shall consider the needs for effectiveness and safety in transportation systems" (49 USC 302).

33. For an excellent discussion of that decision, see Blackett (2003).

34. "Developments in the Air Transport Sector Since the Conclusion of the Uruguay Round—Part II." Background Note by the Secretariat, S/C/W/163/Add. 1 at 58, October 25, 2000.

35. WTO Council for Trade in Services, Article VI.4 of the GATS: Disciplines on Domestic Regulation Applicable to All Services, Note by the Secretariat, S/C/W/96, March 1, 1999, p. 3.

36. WTO Working Party on Domestic Regulation, Report on the Meeting Held on 20 March 2001, Note by the Secretariat, S/WPDR/M/10, May 10, 2001.

37. See the WTO Working Party on Professional Services (1996). The Secretariat has given the following broad definition of the five kinds of measures covered in Article VI.4: "qualification requirements, that is to say substantive requirements which a professional service supplier is required to fulfil in order to obtain certification or a licence; qualification procedures, administrative or procedural rules relating to the administration of qualification requirements; licensing requirements, comprising substantive requirements other than qualification requirements, which a service supplier is required to comply with in order to obtain a formal permission to supply a service; licensing procedures, administrative procedures relating to the submission and processing of an application for a licence; and technical standards, requirements which may apply both to the characteristics or definition of the service and to the manner in which it is performed."

38. These are addressed in far greater detail in other chapters in this book. The focus here is their relevance to aviation and maritime services.

39. The Reference Paper was suggested as a model for regulatory disciplines in aviation in the 1999 UNCTAD Report of the Expert Meeting on Aviation Services: TD/B/COM.1/25, TD/B/COM.1/EM.9/3, p. 5, August 23, 1999.

40. For an excellent overview, see Bronckers and Larouche (forthcoming). India's schedule of telecom commitments is GATS/SC/42/Suppl.3.

41. The Reference Paper was issued by the Negotiating Group on Basic Telecommunications on April 24, 1996. The first meeting of the Working Party on Domestic Regulation was held on May 17, 1999.

42. Note, however, the emerging research concerning the health effects of electromagnetic radiation emanating from cell phones (WHO 2002).

43. Disciplines on Regulations in the Accountancy Sector, S/L/64, December 17, 1998.
44. For an example of the detail into which transportation qualification requirements can go, see 14 CFR §§1-199.
45. Disciplines on Regulations in the Accountancy Sector, S/L/63, December 15, 1998.
46. Communication from European Union and Their Member States—Domestic Regulation: Necessity and Transparency, S/WPDR/W/14, May 1, 2001.
47. For a helpful assessment of the shortcomings of institutional linkages in the global economy, see Stein (2001).
48. I am indebted to Aisatou Jallow-Sey for this example.
49. See Howse and Nicolaidis (2001, p. 227), who argued for a need to return to the embedded liberalism bargain, which allows states to elaborate differential regulatory policies within the trading system based on justified assessments of superior public policy objectives. For another account of embedded liberalism, see Wolfe (1997) and, more recently, "See You in Geneva: Democracy, the Rule of Law and the WTO," draft available at http://qsilver.queensu.ca/~wolfer/Papers/ISAruleof%20law.pdf.

References

Abeyratne, Ruwantissa. 2001. "Trade in Air Transport Services: Emerging Trends." *Journal of World Trade* 35: 1133–68.

Bean, Charles, Samuel Bentolita, Giuseppe Bertola, and Juan Dolado, eds. 2001. *Social Europe: One for All?* London: Centre for Economic Policy Research.

Blackett, Adelle. 2003. "Defining the Contemporary Role of the State: WTO Treaty Interpretation, Unilateralism, and Linkages." In Chi Carmody and others, eds., *Trilateral Perspectives on International Legal Issues: Conflict and Coherence.* Washington, D.C.: American Society of International Law.

Breyer, Stephen. 1982. *Regulation and Its Reform.* Cambridge, Mass.: Harvard University Press.

Bronckers, Marco, and Pierre Larouche. Forthcoming. "The WTO Regime for Telecommunications Services." In Arthur Appleton and Patrick Macrory, eds., *The Kluwer Companion to the WTO.* London: Kluwer.

Coase, Ronald. 1974. "The Lighthouse in Economics." *Journal of Law and Economics* 17: 457–76.

Dempsey, Paul Stephen. 1990. *Flying Blind: The Failure of Airline Deregulation.* Washington, D.C.: Economic Policy Institute.

Hubner, Wolfgang, and Pierre Sauvé. 2001. "Liberalization Scenarios for International Air Transport." *Journal of World Trade* 35: 973–87.

International Civil Aviation Organization (ICAO) Secretariat. 2003. Consolidated Conclusions, Model Clauses, Recommendations and Declaration, ATConf/5, Montreal, March 31 <www.icao.org>.

Janda, Richard. 1994. "Passing the Torch: Why ICAO Should Leave Economic Regulation to the WTO." *Annals of Air and Space Law* 19(1): 409–32.

Janda, Richard, and Joseph Wilson. 2003. "Has Europe Kickstarted the Global Liberalization of Airline Ownership and Control?" In World Markets Research Centre, *Aviation Strategies: Challenges and Opportunities of Liberalization.* London.

Kaul, Inge, Isabelle Grunberg, and Marc Stern, eds. 1999. *Global Public Goods.* Oxford, U.K.: Oxford University Press.

Macdonald, Roderick. 1985. "Regulation by Regulations." In Ivan Bernier and Andree Lajoie, eds., *Regulations, Crown Corporations and Administrative Tribunals.* Toronto: University of Toronto Press.

OECD (Organisation for Economic Co-operation and Development). 2001. "Liner Shipping and Competition Policy Report," November 6. Paris.

Onley, Austin. 2000. "A Report from the Marine Regulatory Front: Partly Cloudy with a Chance of Thunder Storms." *University of San Francisco Maritime Law Journal* 13: 91–123.

Porter, Roger, Pierre Sauvé, Arvind Subramanian, and Americo Beviglia-Zampetti, eds. 2001. *Efficiency, Equity, Legitimacy: The Multilateral Trading System at the Millennium.* Washington, D.C.: Brookings Institution Press.

Posner, Richard A. 1976. *Antitrust Law: An Economic Perspective.* Chicago: University of Chicago Press.

Sauvé, Pierre, and Arvind Subramanian. 2001. "Dark Clouds over Geneva? The Troubled Prospects of the International Trading System." In Roger Porter, Pierre Sauvé, Arvind Subramanian, and Americo Beviglia-Zampetti, eds., *Efficiency, Equity, Legitimacy: The Multilateral Trading System at the Millennium.* Washington, D.C.: Brookings Institution Press.

Stein, Eric. 2001. "International Integration and Democracy: No Love at First Sight." *American Journal of International Law* 95: 489–534.

WHO (World Health Organization). 2000. "Electromagnetic Fields and Public Health: Mobile Telephones." Fact Sheet 193, June. <http://www. who.int/inf-fs/en/fact193.html> (consulted February 7, 2002).

Wolfe, Robert. 1997. "Embedded Liberalism as a Transformation Curve: Comment." In Thomas J. Courchene, ed., *The Nation State in a Global/Information Era: Policy Challenges.* Kingston, Ont.: John Deutsch Institute for the Study of Economic Policy.

World Bank. 2002. *Global Economic Prospects and the Developing Countries, 2002.* Washington, D.C.

WTO (World Trade Organization) Appellate Body Report. 1998. *United States—Import Prohibition of Certain Shrimp and Shrimp Products.* WT/DS58/AB/R, 38 I.L.M. 118, October 12.

WTO Council for Trade in Services. 2002. Special Session: Communication from Australia, Chile, and New Zealand—Review of the GATS Annex on Air Transport Service, S/C/W/206, March 18.

WTO Council for Trade in Services. 2003. Special Session: Communication from Australia, Canada, Chile, the People's Republic of China, Croatia, Cyprus, Czech Republic, Dominican Republic, Estonia, the European Communities and their Member States, Gambia, Georgia, Guatemala, Hong Kong, China, Iceland, India, Japan, the Republic of Korea, Kyrgyz Republic, Latvia, Lithuania, Malaysia, Malta, Mexico, New Zealand, Nigeria, Norway, Pakistan, Panama, Papua New Guinea, Peru, Poland, Romania, Singapore, Slovenia, Switzerland, and the Separate Customs Territory of Taiwan, Penghu, Kinmen and Matsu, TN/S/W/11, March 3.

WTO Working Party on Domestic Regulation. 2003. "Report of the Meeting Held on 4 December 2002." Note by the Secretariat. S/WPDR/M/19, January 20.

WTO Working Party on Professional Services. 1996. "The Relevance of the Disciplines of the Agreement on Technical Barriers to Trade (TBT) and on Import Licensing Procedures to Article VI:4 of the General Agreement on Trade in Services." Note by the Secretariat. S/WPPS/W/9, September 11.

8

REGULATORY REFORM AND TRADE LIBERALIZATION IN FINANCIAL SERVICES

Stijn Claessens

Executive Summary

Fostered by globalization and technological advances, including the emergence of electronic finance, financial services industries around the world are undergoing rapid changes: they are becoming less special and making prudential regulation less necessary while competition policy becomes both more feasible and necessary. Because financial services heavily depend on networks for their production and distribution, competition policy for financial services will need to resemble that used in other network industries. With globalization accelerating, competition policy will also need to be global, supported by greater cross-border institutional collaboration and the disciplines of the World Trade Organization (WTO) process. More than in the past, a horizontal approach to the General Agreement on Trade in Services (GATS) negotiations will be required as financial services today increasingly interface with many other industries and rely heavily on electronic networks. A horizontal approach also will help deal with the political economy issues that are so prevalent in the financial sector. Developing countries have some special conditions when liberalizing and internationalizing their financial systems. There is much evidence that, as in other countries and provided a minimum degree of oversight is in place, both regulatory reform and trade liberalization support the development of an efficient and stable financial system that offers wide access to high-quality financial services at low cost. The WTO, however, can be of more value to developing countries because it provides a binding, procompetition framework that has proven more difficult to establish in any other way.

Perhaps even more than before, the current round of WTO negotiations in the services area has highlighted the link between trade liberalization and domestic regulatory reform. The effectiveness of liberalization and the potential gains from it increasingly depend on the degree to which and the manner in which the domestic sectors are being regulated. The increased importance of the link

This article was presented at the joint OECD–World Bank Conference on Regulatory Reform and Trade Liberalization in Services held March 4–5, 2002, in Paris. The author would like to thank the commentators, José F. Poblano and Sebastian Saez, and the conference participants for useful comments.

129

between trade liberalization and domestic regulation is also true for financial services. More than any other sectors, financial services are heavily regulated. This implies that a variety of domestic regulations and the way they are implemented can exert anticompetitive effects. At the same time, financial services are easily traded across borders, which makes the degree of trade liberalization an important determinant of the overall competitive landscape of a country's financial sector. The experience with financial integration within the European Union (EU), for example, has shown how critical to ensuring effective competition is harmonizing regulation and supervision in conjunction with the removal of barriers between markets. Not only do the competitive effects of trade liberalization depend on the degree and form of domestic regulatory reform, but the gains from financial services liberalization also can depend significantly on the quality of domestic regulation and supervision. It has been argued in the case of East Asia, for example, that financial services deregulation proceeded too fast, undermined the stability of the domestic financial system, and may have contributed to the 1997 financial crisis.

Thus arises the question, what modalities are best suited to ensure that financial services liberalization and domestic regulatory reforms are supportive processes? To answer that question we need to consider how the financial services industries might evolve. Around the world those industries have been undergoing rapid changes fostered by globalization and technological advances, including electronic finance. Banking systems are consolidating in many markets and banks are extending their presence across borders. New financial service providers are emerging, including online-only banks and brokerages, and companies that enable consumers to compare more easily the price and quality of various financial services. Nonfinancial entities, including telecommunication and utility companies, also are entering financial markets. The impact of various forms of e-finance on incumbent financial institutions are particularly large. In securities markets, trading systems for equities, fixed income, and foreign exchange are consolidating globally and moving toward electronic platforms. The effects are not limited to industrial countries and the advanced emerging markets, but have also started to affect many developing countries.

Those changes should affect what constitutes the appropriate future regulatory framework for the financial sector. The design of the framework should also depend on the objective of financial sector regulation and supervision. Many people would agree that an efficient and stable financial system that offers wide access to high-quality financial services at low cost is a laudable goal. The degree to which and the forms in which this goal requires public policy interventions have been hotly debated issues, especially in environments such as those of many developing countries in which market and government failures have been large. In most countries the trend in public policy has been domestic deregulation of many aspects of financial services, particularly the removal of product, price, and market restrictions. And there has been a trend toward tighter imposition of some prudential standards, such as capital adequacy requirements, and increased emphasis on supervision. Nevertheless, banking crises with large fiscal costs, particularly in developing countries, have been increasing. To some extent, these crises have resulted from a combination of inconsistent policies, in terms of type and speed of domestic regulatory reforms and capital account liberalization, and weak supervisory capacity. They also have reflected the continued desire to treat financial services as somewhat special (see box 1), including the provision of fiscal support to weak financial institutions that is often motivated more by political economy factors than by clear economic needs.

The rapid changes in the industry, especially the gains made by e-finance, require further changes in public policies toward financial services. An improved enabling regulatory environment will be needed in such critical areas as the telecommunications framework, the information infrastructure, and consumer and investor protection. For the full gains to consumers and firms to come about, the competitive framework must be adequate. The same changes will allow regulators to treat financial markets more like other markets in the matter of competition policy. Because of the financial sector's influence on economywide performance, competition policy has not been applied actively to financial services. The changes currently under way are making financial services less special, and thus are making regulation imposed for prudential reasons less necessary. Financial services are now more

BOX 1   Why Have Banks Been Considered to Be Special?

Banks have traditionally been considered special for two reasons. First, they provide credit to other firms and manage the flow of payments throughout the economy. Disruptions in the credit supply and a breakdown in the payments system could have large spillover effects for the rest of the economy in terms of reduced real output. Bank failures or losses in capital can lead to contractions in aggregate bank credit, with large social costs to bank borrowers outside the banking system. Second, banks are inherently fragile and susceptible to contagious runs owing to the combination of information asymmetries, intertemporal contracting, demandable par-value debt, and high leverage (Diamond and Dybvig 1983). Even small shocks to solvency may lead to costly systemic runs when depositors overreact to information and force the closure of even solvent institutions. Historically, clearinghouses and other private monitors have dealt with some of those concerns by limiting the risktaking of financial institutions. More recently, governments have responded to the special nature of banks by providing a safety net.

It also has been argued that banks are special because only banks can provide some essential forms of credit to corporations, especially forms

of short-term liquidity. Kashyap, Rajan, and Stein (1999) have argued that banks can provide short-term liquidity more cheaply than other institutions because they combine committed lending (such as lines of credit) with deposit-taking services. The authors contend that banks are more cost-efficient in providing liquidity because deposits act like loan commitments that can be withdrawn at any time. As a result banks need a buffer stock of liquid assets to support their provision of demand deposits, just as they need a buffer stock to support their loan commitments. Because banks offer lending and deposit-taking services together, they can economize on the quantity of cash and safe securities they hold and thereby maintain a smaller buffer than would be required by two financial intermediaries offering these services separately. Those savings allow banks to provide liquidity to their customers at a lower cost than could other financial institutions. Diamond and Rajan (1998) argued further that the somewhat fragile capital structure of banks, which subjects them to runs, disciplines them to monitor corporations properly.

Finally, banks historically have played a dominant role in providing payment services because those services often were linked with the extension of credit and the exchange of bank claims.

widely available and the role of banks is less crucial in the production of those services. Technological advances have shrunk the economies of scale in the production of many financial services, particularly among services that easily can be unbundled and commoditized. Such developments may well lessen the overall relevance of systemic concerns.

Although applying competition policy to financial services has become more feasible, it will not be easy to implement. In the past, calculating concentration indexes in a market or testing for market power were good starting points, but today product definitions, which are critical to any competition tests, have become more complex. As cross-border delivery of financial services has become much easier, defining markets has become more difficult. Network effects—in payment services, trading systems, and exchanges—which can hamper competition, have increased in importance. Furthermore, sunk costs—such as reputation—and high fixed costs in the production of financial services—such

as information technology (IT) investments— make competition policy challenging. Network externalities, particularly prevalent in payment and trading services, can present further barriers to entry. Competition policy in the financial sector will thus be more feasible and desirable, but not necessarily easier to implement.

To investigate the various links among domestic regulatory reform, trade liberalization, competition, and the quality of the regulation and supervision, this article addresses the following issues. How might the financial sector evolve in the coming five years? What will be the key regulatory issues facing the sector in the medium term? What is the current approach for enhancing regulation and supervision, especially in developing countries? How should one think of competition policy in general in the financial sector? When are financial sector regulations themselves a barrier to trade and effective competition? What are the specific issues facing developing countries? Is it possible to define the regulatory conditions that need to be fulfilled prior to liberalization, especially in developing countries? What is the role of the GATS in the process of strengthening domestic regulation? Is the prudential carve-out useful for developing countries or is it possibly too broad in scope? How can the GATS rules more generally be improved in light of ongoing changes in the global financial services industries?

The article argues that competition policy in the financial sector has become more important and that moving to a global competition policy will be necessary. The features of the desired global competition policy for financial services will need to be similar to those policy features applied to other network industries. It will also require harmonization of rules, global information sharing, and common definition of and sanctions for violations. In that context, the GATS process can be an important driving force for procompetitive reform, as has been the case in the telecommunications sector.

Changes in the Financial Services Industries

Globalization and Regulatory Reform

Financial services are being reshaped by the globalization of financial markets and by technological and structural changes, including the lowering of regulatory barriers. The globalization of financial services has involved greater financial integration, increased mergers and acquisitions of financial institutions, and lower barriers between markets. Cross-border capital flows have been the most important form of increased financial integration. But as the costs of establishing a physical presence have declined, cross-border entry of financial institutions has increased. This increase has also been spurred by governments that have removed entry barriers. Bank consolidations and mergers and acquisitions among financial institutions, both within and across borders, have increased. The dismantling of regulatory barriers separating banking, insurance, and securities activities is also driving consolidation. Boundaries between different financial intermediaries are being blurred and universal (or integrated) banking is becoming the norm, as shown most clearly by the recent repeal of the Glass–Steagall Act in the United States. An impor-

tant market incentive for the reduction in barriers has been the disintermediation of bank assets and liabilities by capital market transactions. Those forces pressure banks to expand their financial services to cater to all customer needs and preferences.

Technological Advances

Although there has been a recent retrenchment, new developments in IT, particularly the Internet, are an important force in reshaping the financial services industries (see Allen, McAndrews, and Strahan 2002; Claessens, Klingebiel, and Glaessner 2002). Given its information intensity, financial services greatly benefit from developments in technology that enable providers to conduct business more cheaply and efficiently. There are direct as well as indirect cost reductions. The Internet, for example, eliminates many processing steps and allows "straight-through processing"—the complete processing of transactions electronically—at every segment of the transaction chain, thus avoiding costly duplication of human interventions and minimizing possible errors. The Internet also functions as a new, low-cost distribution channel. Furthermore, it facilitates personalized pricing structures and more cost-effective customer stratification.

Technological advances also are lowering the costs of entry into new markets. Many new types of specialized financial service providers have entered the marketplace. Aggregators enable consumers to comparison shop and obtain access to all their financial accounts in one place. Online brokers make retail investing easy and e-payment providers permit financial transactions over the Internet. Financial portals expose the customer to a whole range of financial services providers and enable them to compare prices and quality. For example, LendingTree in the United States allows consumers easy comparison of mortgage products. Many of the entrants have been nonbanks, such as telecommunication companies and utilities, and ties between financial and nonfinancial institutions have become more extensive. Several banks, for example, have entered alliances with retail chains to sell financial services through their networks of stores. Those links have been motivated by desires to consolidate around recognized brand names and by financial services providers seeking access to the wide distribution networks of telecommunication operations, portals, and other merchants. In the securities markets, developments are rapid as well. Exchanges are demutualizing and many new trading systems have been started. Through enhanced communications capability, trading remotely has become much easier and trading services are no longer restricted to any physical exchange, thereby reducing the need for local markets.

Changing Industry Structures

The new industrial structure emerging is becoming more partitioned in the production and distribution of financial services, and in the process is redefining the nature of banks, other financial institutions, and financial markets. The functions of production and distribution of financial services formerly tended to be vertically integrated in banks, financial conglomerates, or exchanges.[1] Now some of those functions are being separated vertically. On the production side, electronic enablers and other third parties provide software and hardware support to financial service providers. Many financial services themselves are being produced in distinct markets where financial and other institutions participate, and at the same time commoditize their characteristics. Commercial loans, for example, may be generated by banks but are then quickly sold off in markets where other banks and institutional investors participate. Besides traditional banking products, such as checking accounts, mortgages, brokerage services, insurance, and credit cards, the range of financial services now includes e-wallets, electronic bill presentment and payment, and many electronic business services. In securities markets, listing, trading, clearing, and settlement services are becoming separately provided services.

Financial institutions are becoming either entities that specialize in the production of certain services or diversified entities that add value by tailoring and combining financial products for their clients without necessarily producing all the input financial services themselves. Aggregators help distribute the final services, provide price comparisons, and may undertake such functions as preprocessing of loan applications. In addition, there are companies functioning mainly as distribution channels, or portals.

The means of accessing financial services themselves today include not only the brick-and-mortar banks, but also telephones, kiosks, wireless devices, personal computers with modems, and private networks. Advances in information and communication technology further assist in the delivery of a broad array of financial services through a provider that need not be a financial service supplier itself. From a technological point of view, there is no reason why a telecommunications company cannot be the first contact for many customers seeking financial services.

Those trends have varied by the type of financial service and, in turn, have depended on the existence of entry barriers and the ease and degree of commoditization. Entry has been particularly strong in financial services that could be unbundled and commoditized easily and that offered attractive initial margins. These include many nonbanking financial services, such as brokerage, trading systems, some retail banking, and such new offerings as bill presentment or payment gateways for business-to-business e-commerce. Because these services also are subject to less regulation, new entrants can innovate easily with new technology. Services involving sunk costs and low commoditization, such as corporate advisory services or mergers and acquisitions within investment banking, have seen much less new entry. Instead, the trend has been toward global consolidation among investment banks to reap the advantages of reputation, brand name, and economies of scale. Although deposit-taking and many traditional payment services exhibit large potential for commoditization—through online banks, payment services using "smart" cards, and other technologies—entry has been limited, in part because of regulatory barriers. From a production point of view, however, these services can easily be commoditized. There are few technological barriers, for example, to allowing telecommunications companies to provide small payments services using the balances many mobile phone users carry on the prepaid calling card in their phone.

Trends—in terms of the degree of consolidation and entry, the types of services subject to commoditization trends, and the rate of introduction of e-finance—have also varied by market. In some countries, as a result of market potential or regulatory barriers, new entry has been more limited or specialized in some financial services. In the Republic of Korea, for example, online brokerage firms have captured the lion's share of brokerage business, but because the country is overbanked, banking services remain with existing banks and through traditional distribution channels. And in developing countries, which tend to have concentrated financial systems that are also dominated by banks, the degree of commoditization of financial services has been slight because incumbents have mounted barriers and have faced less incentive to innovate in their own operations. There is, however, evidence of convergence in e-finance across countries. Despite institutional disadvantages (such as weaker telecommunications infrastructure) and more adverse demand and supply factors, Internet-based services are sometimes as popular in emerging markets as in industrial countries. In Brazil, for example, online banking is more prevalent than in most developed countries.

Changing Competitive Structures

Removal of barriers between markets and products and the technological gains have generally led to more competition. The financial service industry has become much more competitive in many segments, both through new entrants and from already existing entities operating more efficiently. Barriers to entry in many areas have been lowered. It has become much less expensive, for example, to launch a new bank as electronic delivery modes reduce the need to depend on a bank branch network. Or a new market can be accessed at low cost using the Internet. Financial products can be purchased more easily off the shelf. Many subservices can more easily be outsourced. Information about borrowers is cheaper and easier to obtain.

Those advances are leading to benefits for consumers and firms, with lower costs and better quality services. On the retail side, brokerage fees have fallen in many markets from more than $50 per trade to virtually zero. Internet-only banks have put pressure on margins of incumbent banks with higher deposit rates and more competition for loans. With better two-way communication channels, customers have more information and better transparency about financial services and the process they are engaged in. The speed of service has also improved dramatically—for example, in online loan applications. Institutional customers

have benefited as well because transaction costs on securities are lower, as are search and monitoring costs for tracking corporate information and behavior.

Implications for Regulation and Competition Policy

The changes in the financial services industries are in part a response to domestic regulatory reform efforts. At the same time, the changes—especially those resulting from technological advances—call for an evaluation of the current regulatory approach. The current, internationally driven approach has become increasingly standards based and aimed at achieving financial sector stability. Changes in public policy focus increasingly on consumer and investor protection and a need to approach regulation more globally. Most important, changes call for a more active competition policy. Current policy approaches, however, do not yet reflect such changes.

The Standards-based Approach

The approach to financial services regulation is increasingly based on the compliance of domestic financial systems with internationally formulated norms, the most important being the Basel Core 25 Principles for Effective Bank Supervision. Many other standards are being applied to financial markets, including standards on systemically important payments systems, securities markets, insurance, and so forth. In some sense the financial sector perhaps more than other sectors has recently been subject to harmonization through a number of globally formulated standards. As noted by Trachtman (chapter 5), these standards have the status of "soft laws" in that they are rules that are not formally binding, but many still have substantial binding force.[2] The standards are being used increasingly, for example, by international bodies to assess financial sector stability and efficiency, as in the IMF/World Bank Financial Sector Assessment Program. Such assessments and monitoring have raised the standing and effectiveness or at least the force of these standards, with publication of compliance with many of these standards on the IMF Report on Standards and Codes Web site.

Revisiting the Approaches

The "standards" approach is beneficial in getting countries to enhance their regulation and supervision frameworks, especially in developing countries where weaknesses in those areas have contributed to financial crises. There are some general questions, however, about the approach as well as some specific issues in the context of domestic regulatory reform efforts and trade liberalization of financial services. The general questions are not the focus here,[3] but an explicit consideration of competition policy issues is missing in the context of domestic reform and trade liberalization policies. Although some standards, including the capital adequacy requirements of the Basel I and II accords, were motivated in part by the desire to level the playing field among countries, little attention has been paid to the broader issues of effective competition. Although the further adoption of global standards will help equalize competitive opportunities among financial institutions in many respects. However, there will likely remain a lack of harmonization in many dimensions among markets and countries and many anticompetitive regulations and non-entry-type barriers may still arise. At the same time, the standards approach can create its own barriers against effective competition.

The most important implicit barrier is that the standards approach is based on the notion of a national financial system that is largely bank-dominated. That notion starts from the concept of a national supervisory authority for the banking system, a central bank that conducts monetary policy and may provide liquidity support to banks, and a national legal and regulatory system supporting it all. Together with the prudential carve-out rule in the GATS, such a framework encourages policy-makers to continue to treat financial services as special. Going forward, however, banks will be less unique in providing financial services so prudential regulation and supervision may become less necessary. The implications of recent changes in the financial services industries call for more emphasis on consumer and investor protection—which has been relatively ignored so far—and attention to global implications. Let us consider these public policy implications before addressing the consequences for competition policy.

Special Nature of Banks

Changes in the financial services industry and advances in technology are eroding the special nature of banks. This necessitates taking another look at the need for a safety net to protect banks. Traditionally, banks have had access to a publicly provided safety net for times of liquidity problems. The motivation for public provision arose from the so-called special nature of banks, which held that a bank's illiquidity and its consequences for system stability could cause real sector consequences (box 1). Prudential regulation and supervision to prevent moral hazard have accompanied the safety net provision.

The emergence of many substitutes for bank deposit and loan products and the fact that the proprietary information that the banks had on their borrowers is now cheaper and more widely available, however, are altering the role of banks. Because banks as deposit-taking and lending institutions have become less important to financial intermediation and stability, there may be less of a need for a public safety net and associated prudential regulation and supervision.[4] Although "banks" may continue to be important in financial intermediation, their importance may no longer be related to providing liquidity or to overcoming information asymmetries. Rather, they may be important as large financial conglomerates that combine deposit-taking functions with insurance, investment banking, asset and pension fund management, and other financial intermediation functions.

Consumer and Investor Protection

As banks and other financial products become less special, consumer and investor protection and education will become more important. Increasingly, regulators will not be able to monitor the quality of all financial services being delivered and, as is the case with nonfinancial products, consumers and investors will have to be aware of the risks of financial services. Extending this responsibility to consumers and investors requires standards in areas such as fraud, privacy, and transparency. Nontraditional financial service providers further complicate the application of investor protection mechanisms that are based on current institutional frameworks.[5] Who, for example, should regulate an Internet-based intermediary with no obvious physical presence that provides investment advice and directs potential customers to (affiliated) brokers? And, because everything operates on a global scale, harmonizing standards and practices for consumer and investor protection becomes more urgent. As cross-border products and services expand, questions about the judicial entity that enforces standards need to be answered. What entity, for example, has regulatory authority over the sale by a Brazilian investor of an equity share in a Thai company listed on a German exchange to a Belgium national? Although regulators worldwide will have to consider these and other enforcement issues, improved disclosure and consumer education will often be the only solution.

Global Public Policy Changes

With globalization and especially with the advent of e-finance, capital account restrictions limiting capital flows and restrictions on the cross-border provision of financial services become much more difficult to enforce. Increased economic integration could also carry with it new or increased global risks. More commoditization of financial products could lead to less risk sharing by institutions, which could lead to more asset price volatility. Different national markets could become more susceptible to herding, contagion, and spurious currency attacks. With more delivery of offshore financial services, the costs of exit from providing financial services in a country could be reduced significantly. An increase in the number of creditors may complicate coordinating actions prior to or during a financial crisis. Changes in the international financial architecture to address these issues thus become more urgent.

Prudential Regulation and Competition Policy

The changes in financial services and technology also make competition policy more feasible and more important. Competition will be important in helping all segments of society secure greater access to financial services. Ensuring effective competition in the provision of financial services is complex for a variety of reasons, not least of which is the fact that competition policy as it applies to financial services is still in its early days of development. The limited development of such policy for this industry arises from the so-called special character of the financial sector and the associated argued need for a safety net and prudential regulation. The domination of prudential regulation and supervision over competition in the policy agenda in most countries leads authorities, for example, to restrict entry so as to preserve franchise value for incumbents. Or the payments system may not be open to all types of financial and nonfinancial institutions. In many countries small banks are often effectively excluded from efficiently providing payments services because they face high access costs to the payment system. The link between competition and prudential regulation can be institutionalized—for example, when competition policy is explicitly delegated to the supervisory agency, as was the case in Brazil. Or it can involve the ministry of finance or a supervisory agency lobbying or interfering with the competition authority, as happened recently in South Africa. More generally, entry to and exit from the financial sector has often been influenced by political economy factors argued for, in part, by the systemic aspects of banking.

A revision of the prevailing paradigm for financial sector regulation and supervision is thus a key condition necessary to allow competition policy to be applied more effectively to financial services. Even with such a revision, however, it will not be easy to implement competition policy in the financial sector and a mixture of institutional, functional, and production approaches will likely be most productive. In the following section we consider institutional and functional approaches, which have been the traditional approaches, and then turn to the complications in implementing them, arguing that the production approach may be necessary as well.

Institutional Approach to Competition Policy

The institutional approach to competition means that the entry and exit regime for different types of financial institutions should be procompetitive, or at least as contestable as possible given stability issues. Evidence suggests that more contestable systems have better performance, are more efficient, have better quality financial services available, and can lead to a wider extension of and greater access to financial services.[6] More competitive systems also can be more stable, provided entry involves a diversified set of institutions. Among other activities, the institutional approach involves merger review, investigation of the issues of market power and dominance of institutions, and review of market entry barriers at the countrywide, regional, or global level. There are some conceptual issues regarding, for instance, the exact need to balance competition with preserving a certain franchise value for some types of financial institutions while preserving their incentives for stable conduct of business or to invest in information acquisition). In addition, there are many implementation problems (e.g., how to balance free cross-border provision with adequate enforcement and consumer protection).

Functional Approach to Competition Policy

The functional approach uses the same concept of contestable markets but it applies the concept to the services rather than to the institutions. There is general supportive evidence that it is the functions of finance rather than the exact institutional form through which they are delivered (e.g., banks versus stock markets) that matter most for access, growth, and stability (see Demirgüç-Kunt and Levine 2001). The functional approach implies a leveling of the playing field across providers for each financial service and across similar types of financial services. It means a proper entry and exit regime for each financial service and minimum differences in the regulatory treatments of similar services. Even when tried in earnest, however, the principle of a level playing field across functions is difficult to put into practice. One reason is that substitutability among specific financial services may be high in many dimensions but may involve subtle differences in some dimensions—for example, credit risks, access to the safety net, and so forth. Whether remaining differences are distortionary will often be difficult to ascertain. Furthermore, historical differences can be difficult to correct. For example, differences in the tax treatments of pension savings and other savings may be significant although the savings vehicles may be equivalent in many ways.

Even when attempts are made to level the playing field by each financial service provider and across each financial service, regulatory and other differences that create barriers to full competition may continue to exist. Standards may conflict, as in the need to require capital for local branches of foreign banks. Information requirements may differ by product—securities products may require more information disclosure than do pension products although the products are otherwise similar. One possibly useful development in this respect is the trend toward single supervisory agencies (e.g., the U.K. Financial Services Authority model), which may help reduce unnecessary differences in the regulatory treatment of similar types of financial services.

Even when distortions in treatment across products have been minimized, however, it will be difficult to assess whether markets for specific financial products are fully competitive. Financial institutions typically bundle services and often cross-subsidize them. They may do so because they derive their comparative advantage from the bundling of services rather than from any specific individual service. Or they may do so because the financial institution has regulatory or other advantages that allow it to provide the bundle of services in a way that is more advantageous for them than for a single-service provider. Differences in access to the safety net or different supervisory approaches, for example, may lead to differences in net regulatory burdens in one service that are then spread over other services to reduce the burdens. Open entry in one market segment consequently may not guarantee a competitive market for that specific product. Or perhaps predatory cross-subsidization in the presence of natural entry barriers gives existing institutions an unfair advantage. More generally, it is difficult to ascertain that no anticompetitive barriers remain.

Beyond the Institutional and Functional Approaches

Even when accepted, it will be difficult to put the principle of contestable markets for financial institutions and financial services fully into practice using the institutional and functional approaches. It may therefore be necessary to go beyond those approaches. There are three specific reasons to seek another approach. First, it is quite difficult to apply competition policy to financial services. Sunk costs, the reputation value of existing brand names, stickiness of consumers, and other factors can present effective barriers to entry that are difficult to regulate. Second, financial services use many production, provision, and distribution networks. Examples are trading systems, payment and clearing systems, automatic teller machine systems, and information systems. Any of those networks may not be openly available or may have pricing policies that easily create entry barriers or otherwise involve restrictive practices. Some of the networks will be private and explicitly closed by their owners; others will be public in nature but the regulator may be selective in providing access to them. Third, many financial services are subject to network properties—that is, use by one enhances the value of the service to another. Such financial services traditionally have included stock market trading services and payments services, but as more and more financial services are being commoditized, those properties arise now on a larger scale. For all of these reasons we may need to complement the institutional and functional approaches with a more production-based approach.

Production Approach to Competition Policy

With the production approach the various inputs, including network services, that are required to produce and distribute financial services must be available to anyone who is interested in using them, fairly priced, and provided efficiently. No part of a specific financial services production and distribution chain should have any barriers to entry or exit or any unfair pricing rules. For most inputs (labor, services, and so on), that simply requires competitive supply markets. But because the production and distribution of financial services rely heavily on a common infrastructure with network properties, this approach requires more. Specifically, it requires an "efficient" market infrastructure, which itself is not an easily defined concept partly because many elements of financial infrastructure have been subject to recent changes. In the next section we consider the analytical elements as well as the recent changes triggered by a number of developments, and then analyze their possible impact on competition.

Dimensions of Market Infrastructure and Recent Changes

Dimensions of market infrastructure center around ownership—public versus private ownership—and the forms of control, oversight, and corporate governance. The commonly shared infrastructure of (retail or large-value) payments systems, for example, can be run by central banks, by banks themselves, or by third parties. Choices further vary between for-profit and not-for-profit organizations, and between related mutual or demutualized structures. As another example, stock exchanges can be set up as mutual, not-for-profit organizations or as for-profit corporations. Or the trading system may be a completely new, private sector initiative. The design and balance of various oversight structures—self-regulatory, government, or purely private arrangements—correspondingly can and should vary by setup because the participants' incentives for self-regulation will vary.

The trend recently has been toward separating and privatizing various parts of the financial market infrastructure, for example, the demutualization of stock exchanges, and the separation and privatization of central counterpart, clearing, and settlement functions. Parallel to this trend, oversight functions tend to be placed more with government agencies.[7] Technology, especially the Internet, has also led to changes because it has redefined the elements of a marketplace and the infrastructure supporting financial services provision. The Internet is not only a marketplace itself; it also allows for the rapid construction of electronic-based infrastructures, either closed or open, including front-end trading systems and back-end settlement systems. With the Internet has come its own set of governance issues, including who controls the granting of access to some private marketplace. Who, for example, should monitor the access policies of the newly emerging trading systems for foreign exchange (e.g., FXall and Currenex)? For many of the new systems, there is no obvious regulatory authority besides possibly a competition policy agency) with jurisdiction over potential restrictive or anticompetitive practices.

The dimensions according to which one can evaluate the various arrangements for the provision of market infrastructure services, and the recent changes, are numerous, of course, with competition being only one of them. Efficiency in providing relevant (supportive) services, risk dimensions, integrity, incentives to innovate and upgrade, and so forth are relevant as well. The general assessment is that the trend toward demutualization and privatization of stock markets, for example, has led to efficiency gains in the delivery of these services, without necessarily compromising (and often even enhancing) the objectives of proper risk management, integrity, and stability. But whether they are also always procompetitive is not yet clear.[8]

Competition Effects

Conceptually, the nature of infrastructure services can give rise to many competition issues. Most infrastructure services are subject to large economies of scale and many services display network properties. A private provider of essential services, such as clearing and settlement, can act as a natural monopolist. Correspondingly, changes in the delivery mechanisms, such as moving away from a publicly provided system to a private natural monopoly, as has happened for many stock exchanges, can be anticompetitive. A change in ownership of one input element of the production chain is, however, only a special and simple case. Many financial services are produced and distributed in a vertically integrated way. Banks provide, for example, retail payment services through their own branches while they also process the transaction and link up to the payments system. Many stock exchanges deliver not only front-end trading services but also clearing and settlement services through their own systems. Although the commoditization of financial services, helped by policy interventions and technological changes such as the advent of the Internet, has led to the unbundling of many elements of financial services, such a process is still far from complete. As a result, it is difficult to evaluate the impact of changes in the competitive structure of any input on a particular production chain.[9]

Another aspect is that how infrastructure services are provided can affect the allocation of profits among activities and can support cross-subsidization. Specifically, parts of the infrastructure may be mutually owned (including on a not-for-profit basis) by agents who derive profit not directly from the arrangement but by generating profits elsewhere in the system. As an example, pay-ments services may be not be profitable, but the arrangement may support a larger than necessary float in the system, which then benefits the operators of the payments system. As another example, it has been argued that members of the New York Stock Exchange oppose demutualization because they benefit by receiving free research funded by commissions charged by brokers. The competitive effects of any change to or regulation affecting parts of these vertically integrated production chains or cross-subsidies have to be evaluated with respect to the whole system.

The Telecommunications Model for Competition Policy

Given the considerations enumerated above, it should be clear that encouraging effective competition can be difficult in financial services. It will be hard to generalize where it is most important to intervene from a competition point of view (and evaluated against the dimensions of efficiency, quality of services, and risk management). The competition model appropriate for financial services may have to go beyond the institutional and functional approach, and develop in a similar manner to the model for telecommunications regulation. Concepts used in applying competition policy to the telecommunications industry are right of access, fair pricing rules, limits on interconnection charges, requirements on interoperability and other standards, and separation of the ownership (or control) of the network from the services delivered over it. Many of those concepts may be applicable to the network aspects of financial services. Academic work is being done for some financial services markets, such as payment cards, but that is still a relatively new area of research. It is clear, however, that in many aspects the competition policy paradigm needed for financial services is neither one based on the "specialness" of financial services nor the paradigm traditionally used for manufacturing services.

Developing Country Considerations

In many ways financial services industries in all markets have been subject to similar trends. Despite differences among countries—including such factors as the state of the financial system, the readiness of the telecommunications infrastructure, and the quality of the regulatory framework—there is commonality and convergence in the way financial services industries are being reshaped (Claessens, Klingebiel, and Glaessner 2002). In securities markets global trading is becoming the norm. Increased connectivity has accelerated the migration of securities trading and capital raising from emerging markets to a few global financial centers (Claessens, Klingebiel, and Schmukler 2002). In banking, consolidation is proceeding in many markets and with the United States and other countries abolishing restrictions, integrated financial service provision has become the norm. Following their extensive entry into the more advanced emerging markets, such as those in Central Europe, Argentina, Brazil, Mexico, and to a lesser degree East Asia, financial institutions have extended cross-border entry to low-income countries (Claessens and Lee 2001). In terms of e-finance, the penetration in banking has been more varied across countries. Spurred by the entry from outside the financial sector, however, many financial services providers are now offering e-finance services, with major banks in emerging markets adopting state-of-the-art technology. And most emerging markets have seen the entrance of specialized financial service providers, such as portals and aggregators.

Despite the similarities in the evolution of financial services industries around the world, there remain large differences among countries in terms of their overall development, the stages of financial sector development, and the quality of their regulatory and supervisory frameworks. These disparities raise the question whether there is a need to approach the issues of trade liberalization, domestic regulatory reform, and competition policy differently according to a country's level of development. Three broad categories of differences among countries are relevant: the country's stage of financial liberalization, the quality of its domestic regulation and supervision framework, and the general development of its financial sector.

Stages of Financial Liberalization

The stage at which the country is in terms of liberalization can be analyzed along three dimensions: capital account liberalization, financial services liberalization, and domestic regulatory reform. Generally, as countries develop they liberalize along all three dimensions, albeit at different speeds and intensities. These three forms of financial liberalization all support financial sector development, economic growth, improved financial sector stability, and greater access to financing.[10] In particular, increased competition has produced benefits, including creating pressures for financial institutions to reduce costs, to improve quality of and access to services, and to move downscale. In South Africa, for example, the large domestic banks only felt pressure to extend their services to the lower segments of the market following the removal of capital account controls and liberalization of entry. Foreign entry has been an important part of this, both directly and indirectly. Foreign banks in Argentina, for example, have been found to provide financing to small and medium-sized enterprises on an equal or better basis than do local banks (Clarke and others 2000). In general, foreign bank penetration seems to improve financing conditions for enterprises of all sizes, although large firms benefit relatively more (Clarke and others 2000).

There are, however, issues of consistency and coherence among the three forms of liberalization. Financial services liberalization may require some degree of capital account liberalization. Domestic regulatory reform and capital account liberalization may involve the removal of lending restrictions, which must be done in a consistent fashion across the two forms. Inconsistencies can arise as they did in the Republic of Korea when firms were allowed freely to access certain forms of international capital but were restricted in their domestic borrowing. This led to the buildup of vulnerabilities. The three forms can also interact in beneficial ways. For example, entry by foreign financial institutions may improve the stability of the domestic financial system by having greater loan loss provisions and by ensuring greater access to foreign capital during periods of crisis.[11] And capital account liberalization can complement domestic reform efforts when it puts greater competitive pressures on domestic financial institutions to offer efficient services to consumers and firms.

Required Supervision and Other Constraints

Reaping the full benefits of the three forms of liberalization can require a certain minimum level of financial sector regulation and supervision. For a variety of reasons, countries are at different levels of development of their regulatory and supervisory capacity, quality of legal and judicial systems, and other institutional dimensions. Many developing countries' deficiencies can be identified in an assessment of their compliance with international standards (see the previous section). Potential deficiencies include not only the quality of regulation and supervision but also accounting standards and practices, disclosure requirements, and the general culture of transparency. The standards extend to all financial markets and capital markets, including pension management, insurance, and payments systems, and they concern enhancing the quality of the legal system and the usefulness of financial information, which will typically be poorer in developing countries. The deficiencies in each of these areas are expected to be addressed over time in the follow-up from such assessments and through general pressures associated with that process (such as through disclosure of deficiencies and pressures from peers and investors).

Although it will be important to continue to upgrade standards and to invest in supervisory capacity in developing countries, partly because deficiencies have contributed to financial crises, one has to acknowledge that important constraints will remain. One such constraint will be the often-insufficient pay of supervisors in developing countries. Those low wages may result in poor-quality supervisors, and may create greater incentives for corruption. There also will often be deeper reasons why failures in regulation and supervision do not allow developing countries to reap the full benefits of liberalization efforts. In particular, a country's failure to take appropriate regulatory actions when liberalizing is often prompted by political economy, which leads to moral hazard and excessive levels of deposit insurance. In the end, those political economy reasons are more often the cause behind banking system crises than information asymmetries or the pure lack of regulatory capacity.

In an empirical analysis of the effects of regulatory and supervisory practices on banking sector development and fragility in 107 countries, Barth, Caprio, and Levine (2001) concluded that reform strategies that place excessive reliance on an extensive checklist of regulatory and supervisory practices involving direct government oversight of and restrictions on banks are more likely to support political constituencies than to help correct market failures. In particular, they found that regulatory barriers to entry, restrictions on banking activities, greater supervisory power, and greater government ownership of banks were associated with more government corruption. And for most countries, greater supervisory powers without checks and balances correlate with worse outcomes for financial sector development.

Such findings do not mean one should not invest in supervisory capacity, but they do suggest that one must be selective and careful in reinforcing the independence of supervisors when there are no checks and balances in the system. They also have implications for how successful one can expect regulation and supervision to be without changes to the general political economy in a country and to the ownership structure of the corporate and financial sectors in particular. Most of those changes, including achieving greater political openness, will be gradual processes, but one should consider how reforms could help overcome some of those political economy constraints. In addition to bringing foreign enterprise into a country, entry by foreign financial institutions can also lead to reduced political pressures on the supervisory system. Similarly, broadening the scope of institutions that are able to provide payments services may reduce the political influence of incumbent banks.

Promotion of Financial Stability   Beyond the need for a consistent approach to market opening and the need to deal with political economy factors, arguments can be made that there are no fixed preconditions imposed on the quality of regulation and supervision that allow effective internationalization of financial services. Countries with weak and strong regulation and supervision both can do well when there is extensive foreign entry. In the first case, foreign entry brings with it improved regulation and supervision, which enhances the quality of the overall domestic financial sector; in the second case, strong domestic regulation and supervision ensures that new entry is not disruptive. It may be that the intermediate cases (i.e., countries with regulatory and supervisory systems that are neither particularly weak nor particularly strong) present greater risks because foreign financial institutions may compete away the franchise value of incumbents and thus create incentives for imprudent behavior, and because domestic and foreign investors may misjudge the stability of the system. In such cases, good closure rules for weak financial institutions and quantitative restrictions on financial exposures may be the most appropriate responses while liberalizing.

It is also the case that the nature of crises continues to change. Contagion and volatility may have taken on more relevance today as causes of financial crises than have pure fundamental weaknesses. In the fall of 1998, for example, financial markets in countries with very well developed and regulated financial sectors, such as the United States, were adversely affected by the global financial crisis when asset prices behaved irregularly. At that time the optimal regulatory response for reducing the turmoil was not obvious to many people. The causes (or at least the proximate causes) of financial crises seem to keep changing so it is hard to develop firm preconditions for regulation and supervision that will ensure effective domestic regulatory reform, capital account liberalization, and internationalization of financial services. Countries are likely to continue to experience some financial crises despite efforts to enhance regulation and supervision. A balanced multipillar approach should be sought—one that is tailor-made to each country's circumstances and includes regulation and supervision, bank owners' incentives, and market discipline.

Developing Countries and Competition Policy

Country conditions do have relevance for the way in which competition policy is conducted, including the disciplines associated with the GATS/WTO. Despite reforms, many developing countries' financial sectors are still characterized by a lack of "effective" competition. They may have a very concentrated market structure, extensive links among financial institutions and between financial institutions and corporations, and high ultimate ownership concentration of the financial sector. Although entry by foreign financial institutions may be open in principle, such entry may be limited to some niche areas, in part because of foreign institutions' perceptions of the risks in a specific

country. It is important to realize that links among various types of financial institutions and telecommunication companies may be hindering effective competition and that incumbent financial institutions may have a lock on networks that are essential for financial services provision. Incumbents are more likely to block new initiatives and to do so by a variety of means. The net results will be less pressure to reduce costs, to improve the quality of financial services, and to move down the credit scale into lower-income retail and small-enterprise lending.

Although again it is difficult once more to generalize about how competition policy should be differentiated by level of development, it will be even more important in developing countries to include competition issues when designing reform efforts, including payments systems, credit information arrangements, and telecommunications regulatory and legal frameworks. Specifically, one must be careful in the design of networks, whether they involve payments systems or are related to telecommunications (e.g., as in the case of cellular providers), because these networks can become important barriers to entry. In the area of retail payments, for example, the use of a third-party provider (not a consortium of banks) for the provision of different forms of retail payment services could be a more appropriate plan from a competition point of view for many developing countries.

An effective competition authority is critical, but it will require adequate support, jurisdiction, and backing vis-à-vis other supervisory agencies. In many developing countries, the overall efficiency and independence of competition authorities need to be enhanced and proper enforcement tools must be provided. Support often will be lacking and conflicts may exist between the competition policy agency and the agency that deals with prudential regulation. In such cases more support for the competition policy agency would be called for. Also, a case for more restrictions on cross-holdings can be made, particularly in smaller developing countries. Limits on groups and on bank commerce, including telecommunications links, may be necessary to ensure effective competition. In some countries there also may be a need to hold banks to tighter group-lending exposures because such lending will be an indirect way to support groups.

The Role of the GATS and the WTO

The GATS is an important force for a more procompetitive policy in financial services. The past financial services negotiations, however, have been arduous and extended. Final success arguably has been relatively limited because many countries have made commitments that bind less than the regulatory status quo. In others words, most developing countries have not used the WTO process to bind themselves to an (accelerated) process of liberalization. In part this outcome has arisen because the approach for financial services thus far has been sector specific and carried out largely outside the normal GATS negotiating framework (see Sauvé and Steinfatt 2002).

Going forward, a horizontal approach similar to that for other services may be preferable for financial services (Mattoo 1999). Such an approach is to be preferred because of the increased inputs from other sectors in the production and distribution of financial services, including those from such network industries as telecommunications. Liberalizing financial services industries alone may not lead to the fullest possible gains. A horizontal approach is also more feasible today because financial services have become less "special" and the horizontal approach is thus less likely to lead to conflicts with prudential concerns. A key argument for a horizontal approach, however, is that the political economy factors that are so prevalent in financial services have been dominating the negotiation outcome when there was no ability to trade off interests. With financial services increasingly being recognized as essential inputs in overall economic production, the support from other sectors for efficient financial services provision, and consequently for liberalization, has increased, making a horizontal approach more attractive.

Applying a horizontal approach to financial services liberalization may require revisiting the prudential carve-out of the GATS. The carve-out has already been used as an argument to keep financial services out of the Uruguay Round negotiations. There are some issues in interpreting the scope of the carve-out (see chapter 5). Under some interpretations, the carve-out cannot be used to evade other GATS commitments and must be aimed primarily at prudential regulation. Even with that strict interpretation, however, the issue remains what constitutes justifiable prudential regulation? On one hand, a more common view on prudential regulation has developed through the promulgation of international banking and other standards, thus reducing the likelihood of differences in frameworks across countries leading to nontrade barriers. At the same time, as argued above, there is a need to rethink prudential regulation in the first place in the financial sector, given changes in financial services industries globally. The heavy emphasis on standards today as part of the new international financial architecture implies that there are legitimate fears that the approach will overshoot in matters of safety, soundness, and stability at the expense of concerns over free trade in financial services.

The potential anticompetitive way in which the prudential carve-out can be applied does not imply that it needs to be removed fully. For one thing, it is likely to be used sparingly in any case. Countries realize the reputation costs of invoking the carve-out and applying prudential regulation in an anticompetitive way. Particularly in the context of developing countries, investors will look for signs of credibility, and invoking the carve-out will send the opposite signal. Furthermore, invoking the prudential carve-out when in a financial crisis might be taken as a negative sign by investors. It is also unclear what types of regulations can reduce the risk of financial contagion and volatility, arguably the more likely causes of crises going forward. Useful regulations will include some prudential regulations (e.g., requiring certain loan-loss provisioning) but they also could be more macroeconomic in nature (e.g., limiting exposures to certain sectors) or be aimed specifically at some balance-of-payments objectives (e.g., restrictions or taxes imposed on short-term capital flows). Whether such regulations fall (or ought to fall) under the prudential carve-out is unclear. Nevertheless, there might be circumstances when some degree of carve-out will be useful. As such, a form of a prudential carve-out will be necessary although it can be more circumscribed than is currently the case.

In addition to assessing the scope of the prudential carve-out, it will be useful to complement the forthcoming round of market access commitments in the GATS with a set of procompetitive principles of sound regulation.[12] Proposals in that respect have been made by many participants in the financial services industry, especially the insurance industry. They center around commitments on improved transparency and domestic regulatory reform, including transparent domestic rules and administrative procedures (see European Services Network 1999 and 2001 for discussions of the general approach). The proposal from the insurance industry (Financial Leaders Group 2001b), for example, involves greater specificity on further commitments on trade (modes 1 and 2) and investment (modes 3 and 4) and suggestions for best practices in insurance regulation and supervision.[13] That approach would be consistent with the single-market approach pursued in the EU and with the general need highlighted in this article for trade liberalization to be complemented with a more active competition policy.

Conclusion

Changes in financial services industries globally are making a more active competition policy in financial services both feasible and necessary, prompting a need for a tighter link between domestic regulatory reform efforts and trade liberalization. Financial services have become less special. This implies that they need to be less subject to prudential objectives and that increases the importance of competition policy. Competition policy for financial services will need to involve elements of the traditional contestability approach and to include dimensions that are both institution and function oriented. In an international context, the "necessity" approach to evaluating any remaining domestic barriers in financial services can be used. Given the many network aspects of financial services provision, however, competition policy for financial services should also include features of approaches used for other network industries.

A different approach to competition policy in financial services will be neither easy nor necessarily sufficient to achieve the desired outcomes of efficient and stable financial systems that offer a wide access to high-quality financial services at low cost. There remains a need to go deeper to reap all the potential gains of global financial integration. That will require some minimum harmonization in

some aspects. It will take time, and many differences in regulation and supervision potentially amounting to discriminatory barriers are likely to remain in the short run. Therefore it will also be important to aim quickly for some minimal acceptable standards and to introduce procompetitive principles of sound regulation, including possibly mutual recognition, as additional competitive forces.

Although developing countries can benefit the most from the GATS because it helps bind their domestic regulatory regimes and can enhance the credibility of their reform efforts, the gap between commitments under the GATS and existing practices is the largest for these countries. It will remain important to acknowledge the different views from developing countries on financial services negotiations. As importers, rather than exporters, they are understandably less enthusiastic about opening up. They have concerns about financial instability, although the evidence suggests that greater internationalization of financial services supports more, not less, stability. And they have greater difficulty in establishing sound regulation and supervision, although here internationalization can also help. In the end, the greater reluctance to bind is best attributed to political economy constraints, which point out the need to match the opening up of financial services to gains somewhere else in the negotiations—and that makes another argument for horizontal negotiations.

Endnotes

1. Even within a single financial institution, product lines were often vertically integrated, with few links among products. For that reason, customer relationship management has taken on more importance recently as financial institutions have realized the need to provide consumers with a complete package of financial services tailored to their situations, without necessarily producing the individual services themselves.

2. Formally, the standards are recommended minimums; for many countries, they have become the desired levels.

3. Some general questions are the following: Are the standards being formulated by a broad enough representation of countries to have global legitimacy? Is a standards-based approach sufficiently flexible to deal with the inevitable global changes? Can similar standards be expected to apply to all or many countries? Are the standards' evaluators sufficiently consistent, independent, and subject to some review themselves? and Will standards not distract from the deeper causes of financial crises? A less developed aspect of

the standards approach has been the degree of mutual recognition; except for the EU, few countries allow free entry on the basis of a recognized home supervisor (see Corcoran and Hart 2001 for extensive description of the EU approaches). More generally, there are few formal rewards for compliance with standards.

4. Another reason to revisit the safety net is that the entry of nonfinancial services providers is blurring the lines between financial and nonfinancial institutions. This may result in a de facto extension of the public safety net to various forms of nonfinancial institutions in times of financial distress. That is especially important in emerging markets because there has been a tendency to define the safety net too widely. More generally, developments make it more difficult for supervisors to monitor financial services providers and increase the potential for leakage of the safety net to activities not related to deposit taking.

5. One example is that of portals. Many portals provide investment advice on their sites, but they may have exclusivity agreements with a small number of financial services providers. Who has jurisdiction over portals? Do they fall under the umbrella of the securities regulator or under a consumer protection agency?

6. Specifically, see World Bank (2001) for general evidence and Claessens and Jansen (2000) for the international dimension.

7. Although it is hard to generalize in this area as many countries, especially emerging markets, coming from more centralized models are still in the opposite process of giving greater responsibility to the private sector.

8. In the assessment of some people, public policy concerns related to delivery of trading, clearing, and settlement services are no longer about quality of services or risk, but about the industrial organization of an industry with mostly private agents. See, for example, Steil (2002). See also the public discussion around the recent purchase by Deutsche Borse of its remaining stake in Clearstream, which makes for a fully vertically integrated stock exchange.

9. Cruickshank, who headed a competition policy review commission in the United Kingdom (Review of Banking Services in the United Kingdom, available at the Her Majesty's Treasury Web site, www.hm.treasury.gov.uk), stated in his press release: "There are real problems with the way banks control networks which allow money to flow around the economy, whether it be cheques, credit and debt cards, or electronic transfers, big and small."

10. See World Bank (2001) for review. Reports by commissions like Cruickshank in the United Kingdom also stress the beneficial effects of competition on financial services provision to retail consumers and to small and medium-size enterprises.

11. Kono and Schuknecht (2000) found evidence that entry by foreign financial institutions leads to less volatility in capital flows. Demirgüç-Kunt, Levine, and Min (1998) reported that foreign presence reduces the risks of financial crises.

12. Details on such proposals can be found on the Web sites of the U.S. Coalition of Service Industries (www.uscsi.org) and of the European Services Forum (www.esf.be).

13. The form in which these additional commitments and strengthened disciplines on procompetitive regulation could be made might be as a reference paper or appendix to the Financial Services Agreement or the Understanding.

References

The word "processed" describes informally produced works that may not be available commonly through libraries.

Allen, Franklin, Jaime McAndrews, and Philip Strahan. 2002. "E-Finance: An Introduction." *Journal of Financial Services Research* 22(1/2): 1–26.

Barth, James R., Gerard Caprio, and Ross Levine. 2001. "Bank Regulation and Supervisions: What Works Best?" Working Paper 2725. World Bank, Washington, D.C.

Claessens, Stijn, and Marion Jansen, eds. 2000. *The Internationalization of Financial Services: Issues and Lessons for Developing Countries.* The Hague: Kluwer Law International.

Claessens, Stijn, and Jong-Kun Lee. 2001. "Foreign Banks in Low-Income Countries: Recent Developments and Impacts." In James Hanson, Patrick Honohan, and Giovanni Majnoni, eds., *Globalization and National Financial Systems.* Washington, D.C.: World Bank.

Claessens, Stijn, Daniela Klingebiel, and Thomas Glaessner. 2002. "E-Finance: A New Approach to Financial Sector Development?" *Financial Markets, Institutions and Instruments.* Vol. 11. Boston: Blackwell Publishing

Claessens, Stijn, Daniela Klingebiel, and Sergio Schmukler. 2002. "The Future of Stock Exchanges in Emerging Markets." In Robert E. Litan and Richard Herring, eds., *Brookings-Wharton Papers on Financial Services 2002.* Washington, D.C.: Brookings Institution Press.

Clarke, George, Robert Cull, and Maria Soledad Martinez Peria. 2001. "Does Foreign Bank Penetration Reduce Access to Credit in Developing Countries? Evidence from Asking Borrowers." Working Paper 2716. World Bank, Development Economics Research Group, Washington, D.C.

Clarke, George, Robert Cull, Laura D'Amato, and Andrea Molinari. 2000. "On the Kindness of Strangers? The Impact of Foreign Entry on Domestic Banks in Argentina." In Stijn Claessens and Marion Jansen, eds., *The Internationalization of Financial Services: Issues and Lessons for Developing Countries.* The Hague: Kluwer Law International.

Corcoran, Andrea M., and Terry L. Hart. 2001. "The Regulation of Cross-Border Financial Services in the EU Internal Market: A Primer for Third Countries." Working Paper. Commodity Futures Trading Commission, Washington, D.C.

Demirgüç-Kunt, Asli, and Ross Levine, eds. 2001. *Financial Structure and Economic Growth: A Cross-Country Comparison of Banks, Markets, and Development.* Cambridge, Mass.: MIT Press.

Demirgüç-Kunt, Asli, Ross Levine, and Hong-Ghi Min. 1998. "Opening to Foreign Banks: Issues of Stability, Efficiency, and Growth." In *Proceedings of the Bank of Korea Conference on the Implications of Globalization of World Financial Markets.* Seoul: Bank of Korea.

Diamond, Douglas, and Philip H. Dybvig. 1983. "Bank Runs, Deposit Insurance and Liquidity." *Journal of Political Economy* 91(June): 401–19.

Diamond, Douglas, and Raghuram Rajan. 1998. "Liquidity Risk, Liquidity Creation and Financial Fragility: A Theory of Banking." Working Paper 476. University of Chicago, Center for Research in Security Prices.

European Services Network. 1999. "ESN Position Paper on GATS Horizontal Issues: GATS Principles for Domestic Regulation and the Development of Pro-Competitive Regulation Principles." Brussels. Processed.

———. 2001. "Domestic Regulation." Preliminary Discussion Paper, Brussels. Processed.

Financial Leaders Group. 2001a. "Commentary on Proposals for Liberalisation in Financial Services." Washington, D.C. Processed.

———. 2001b. "Insurance: Proposed Model Schedule and Best Practices." Washington, D.C. Processed.

Kashyap, Anil K., Raghuram Rajan, and Jeremy Stein. 1999. "Banks as Liquidity Providers: An Explanation for the Co-Existence of Lending and Deposit-Taking." University of Chicago. Processed.

Key, Sydney. 2001. "GATS 2000: Issues for the Financial Services Negotiations." *American Enterprise Institute Series of Sectoral Studies on Trade in Services*. Washington, D.C.: American Enterprise Institute.

Kono, Masamichi, and Ludger Schuknecht. 2000. "How Does Financial Services Trade Affect Capital Flows and Financial Stability?" In Stijn Claessens and Marion Jansen, eds., *The Internationalization of Financial Services: Issues and Lessons for Developing Countries*. The Hague: Kluwer Law International.

Matoo, Aaditya. 1999. "Developing Countries in a New Round of GATS Negotiations: From a Defensive to a Pro-Active Role." Paper prepared for the WTO/World Bank Conference on Developing Countries in a Millennium Round.

Sauvé, Pierre, and Kartsen Steinfatt. 2002. "Financial Services and the WTO: What Next?" In Robert E. Litan, Paul Masson, and Michael Pomerleano, eds., *Open Doors: Foreign Participation in Financial Systems in Developing Countries*. Washington, D.C.: Brookings Institution Press.

Steil, Benn. 2002. "Changes in the Ownership and Governance of Securities Exchanges: Causes and Consequences." In Robert E. Litan and Richard Herring, eds., *Brookings-Wharton Papers on Financial Services 2002*. Washington, D.C.: Brookings Institution Press.

World Bank 2001. *Finance and Growth: Policies in a Volatile World*. Washington, D.C.

9

REGULATORY REFORM AND TRADE LIBERALIZATION IN ACCOUNTANCY SERVICES

Claude Trolliet
John Hegarty

Executive Summary

Once upon a time, everything was quiet in the orderly world of accountancy sector regulation. Like a Zen garden, everything was in its place—however, the rationale for that placement was only understood by the "insiders."

In 1957, some passionate researchers had a vision; they planned an experiment in Europe that would catalyze the advent of a single market in the accountancy sector (as in most other sectors). Almost fifty years later that goal has still not been realized. The Treaty of Rome key did not open the magic door of domestic regulation in the accountancy sector after all.

In the meantime, the industry organized itself to operate in a global economy and to respond to clients' needs (despite the absence of liberalizing reform in the sector). Networks were the solution: independent local firms agreed by contract to exploit a single brand and to submit themselves to a common set of rules.

In 1995, the World Trade Organization (WTO) was born. Some assumed the WTO would finally crack open the regulation of the sector and mark a new era where accountancy services and professionals could flow across borders freely. This paper explains how these expectations, for the most part, were not fulfilled: On standards, recognition of credentials, and principles of domestic regulation, the Working Party on Professional Services—especially created for the purpose of furthering work in the accountancy sector—mainly treaded water. On standards, it encouraged the work of institutions, but did not delegate any power, and made no commitment to results. On recognition, it made an inventory of elements to be considered when negotiating a recognition agreement, but failed to provide any guidance for the conduct of the process. Finally, on domestic regulation, it produced weak disciplines that would not lead to any change in the regulation of the sector, and it hardly simplified the task of the Dispute Settlement Body should any

---

The views expressed are personal and should not be attributed to the World Trade Organization or the World Bank.

national regulation be challenged in front of the WTO.

It is in this context of missed opportunities that the Enron scandal engulfed the small world of accountancy regulation, and created a storm in the quiet and orderly garden.

Like all tales, this one concludes with a moral:

Developments to date in the accountancy sector have been unable to overcome the antagonism between *regulation* and *liberalization*. Liberalization is not possible unless governments gain confidence in other countries' regulatory regimes. Regulation should concentrate on what needs to be regulated, and do so in the most appropriate way. Even if the uniformity of regulation is not the solution, it nevertheless raises the issue of what the appropriate regulatory framework is for the sector. Work of IFAC and IASB on the development and implementation of standards, of IOSCO on the recognition of such standards, and last but not least, of the World Bank on the observance of standards and codes (ROSC), still leaves many questions unanswered for the moment. The role of the WTO and the impact of current services negotiations in this context remain far from clear.

The Accountancy Sector

Accountancy is a critical component of the infrastructure for a market economy. No economically sound activity would be possible without it. Beyond the information it provides on the financial position and profitability of operations, it is the foundation of countries' fiscal systems and it plays a key role in corporate governance. Accountancy is relied on when enforcing prudential requirements for banks, insurance companies, securities dealers, and other market participants. As a result, the accountancy sector is among the most regulated in the world's advanced economies.

Although precise statistical data remain scarce[1] (an endemic problem in the field of services), all of the information available on the evolution of the sector points to significant growth of trade in accountancy services over the last decade. It reflects the increasing internationalization of the economy and the demands of corporate clients doing business across borders. This economic dynamism of the sector, however, has not been matched by a

comparable evolution of its regulation, so that it cynically could be suggested that the sector's development was achieved in spite of, rather than thanks to, countries' laws and regulations governing the sector.

Some would even argue that the approach adopted for regulating the sector is completely at odds with the logic of trade liberalization. Regulators have had as their main objectives the protection of the public and the promotion of the quality of the service, which have been pursued through increasingly detailed regulations or standards on most aspects of the accountancy profession and its practice. Today, most of these regulations and standards remain purely national and differ significantly among countries. This variability does not create a context favorable to greater mobility of services and professionals across borders.

As is true in many other sectors, the globalization of the world economy has brought new challenges to accountancy regulators that can no longer be addressed in a purely national context. Financial scandals regularly bring this issue to the fore and put pressure on regulators to reform the regulation of the sector, but it is not always easy to distinguish their causes between those attributable to weaknesses in the design of the national regulatory framework and those resulting from failures to operate that framework as designed. When any regulatory reform is considered for the sector, it is therefore necessary to seek better protection of the public while trying to remove the barriers that unnecessarily restrict trade in accountancy services. This is a daunting task. The authors hope this chapter will contribute modestly to the reflection on these issues and they favor the emergence of a regulatory framework better suited to the needs of the sector as well as of the economy and society at large.

The first section of the chapter takes stock of the work done to date in the World Trade Organization on trade liberalization in the accountancy sector, whether during or after the Uruguay Round. The second section considers various other experiences of regulatory reform and trade liberalization in the European Union or at international level. The third section considers the broader picture in which accountancy regulation is entangled and finally discusses the prospects for further regulatory reform in the sector.

Accountancy and the World Trade Organization: Progress to Date

Uruguay Round Outcomes

The Uruguay Round was the first attempt at a multilateral level to liberalize trade in services in general, and trade in accountancy services in particular. Few doubts were expressed by WTO members[2] about including the accountancy sector under the scope of the General Agreement on Trade in Services (GATS). There was little support for the contention that the special nature of statutory audit made it eligible for exception under Article I.3(b) and (c) for services supplied in the exercise of governmental authority. As a result, trade in accountancy services is governed by the general obligations and disciplines of the GATS, in particular as far as most-favored-nation (MFN) treatment (Article II), transparency (Article III), increased participation of developing countries (Article IV), domestic regulation (Article VI), and recognition (Article VII) are concerned.

In the course of the negotiations, accountancy services received significant attention and served as a useful case study on how liberalizing trade in services requires attention to "behind-the-border" issues in that the main barriers to trade derive from provisions of domestic regulation governing the sector. To a certain extent these matters were addressed in Articles VI (Domestic Regulation) and VII (Recognition) of the GATS, but those provisions did not, in and of themselves, remove any impediments to international trade. Furthermore, restrictions on market access and national treatment fell to be dealt with in accordance with Articles XVI (Market Access) and XVII (National Treatment).

This structure of the GATS meant that measures that are subject to scheduling under Articles XVI and XVII would not be eliminated as a result of the general obligations of members. In other words, where a specific domestic regulation has the effect of denying market access or national treatment, the regulation could only be modified when a specific commitment has been negotiated under the request-offer procedure and scheduled; it could not be negated automatically as a result of the entry into force of the agreement. This came as a disappointment to those who had hoped to see at least some behind-the-border issues dealt with by way of

general rules having general application, rather than by permitting countries to retain significant impediments to international trade in accountancy services until such time as they make specific commitments with respect to the sector and decide, through negotiations, to remove the barriers. The negotiating guidelines and procedures[3] for the current services negotiations, adopted in March 2001, confirm this approach.

At the end of the Uruguay Round, 47 members (counting the 12 member states of the European Community [EC] as 1) had undertaken specific commitments in the accountancy sector.[4] Subsequent accessions to the WTO have now brought that total up to 69 members.[5] Most refer to the United Nations Central Product Classification (CPC) nomenclature[6] in their description of the sector. A large majority still maintains some form of market access limitations, national treatment limitations, or both for one or more of the four modes of supply.[7] In the accountancy sector, or for professional services in general, 7 members have kept MFN exemptions,[8] all requiring reciprocal treatment for the exercise of the profession. At best, specific commitments have bound the status quo ante in the countries that have undertaken them. The main positive outcome of the Uruguay Round in the accountancy sector is therefore considered to be increased legal certainty with respect to access to the markets of those countries that have covered the sector in their schedules of commitments. Although the Uruguay Round had led to a deeper understanding of the impact of domestic regulation on international trade in accountancy services, it was difficult to point to any meaningful liberalization that came about as a result of the negotiations.

Article VI.4, however, did foresee a future, post-Round work program to explore how the liberalizing potential of Articles VI and VII could be enhanced. Just prior to the conclusion of the Uruguay Round negotiations on December 15, 1993, members also adopted a Decision on Professional Services.[9] The objective was to ensure continuation of work on the liberalization of professional services,[10] and of accountancy services in particular. The decision was also perceived as an attempt to minimize the frustration generated by the limited results of the Uruguay Round described above. The decision foresaw creation of a Working Party on Professional Services (WPPS) and defined its mandate. The primary focus of that mandate related to domestic regulation. As a matter of priority the WPPS was requested to make recommendations for multilateral disciplines in the accountancy sector so as to give operational effect to specific commitments.

In making its recommendations, the WPPS was instructed to concentrate on the following:

- Developing multilateral disciplines relating to market access so as to ensure that domestic regulatory requirements are based on objective and transparent criteria, such as competence and the ability to supply the service, and are not more burdensome than necessary to ensure the quality of the service, thereby facilitating the effective liberalization of accountancy services
- Using international standards and, in doing so, encouraging cooperation with the relevant international organizations as defined under paragraph 5(b) of Article VI, so as to give full effect to paragraph 5 of Article VII
- Facilitating the effective application of paragraph 6 of Article VI of the GATS by establishing guidelines for recognizing qualifications.

In elaborating these disciplines, the WPPS was requested to take account of the importance of the governmental and nongovernmental bodies regulating professional services.

Developments Since the Creation of the WTO

The Working Party on Professional Services In March 1995, following the entry into force of the GATS and the creation of the WTO, the Council for Trade in Services (CTS) established the WPPS to develop the disciplines necessary to ensure that measures relating to qualification requirements and procedures, technical standards and licensing requirements, and procedures in the field of professional service do not constitute unnecessary barriers to trade.

The WPPS devoted limited attention to the issue of technical standards. It organized two symposia with the international standard-setting bodies for the accountancy sector[11] during its first year of operation, and was briefed in particular on the work program of the International Organization of Securities Commissions (IOSCO)[12] and the International Accounting Standards Committee (IASC) on the possible endorsement of a core set of international accounting standards (IAS). The WPPS also considered the possibility of transposing in the accountancy sector some of the rules already in force for trade in goods and contained in the agreement on technical barriers to trade,[13] such as the presumption of necessity in favor of measures that comply with international standards, but members' national regulators, who should have led the work, blocked any progress in that direction. The only outcome was the inclusion of the following sentence in the Singapore Ministerial Declaration in December 1996: "We encourage the successful completion of international standards in the accountancy sector by IFAC [International Federation of Accountants], IASC and IOSCO."[14] The statement had no apparent effect.

In May 1997 the CTS endorsed the Guidelines for Mutual Recognition Agreements or Arrangements in the Accountancy Sector,[15] which had been developed by the WPPS. The most common means to achieve recognition had been through bilateral agreements, and Article VII recognizes that means as permissible by not subjecting such agreements to MFN obligations. Bilateral negotiations enable those involved to focus on the key issues and differences of their two environments. When a bilateral agreement has been achieved, however, members have an obligation to afford adequate opportunity for other interested members to negotiate their accession to that agreement.[16] Ultimately, this obligation would extend mutual recognition more broadly. There is evidence to suggest that the number of mutual recognition agreements worldwide is increasing, but they remain primarily between pairs of industrial countries with relatively similar arrangements for the certification and accreditation of accountants. The Guidelines acknowledge that there are differences in education and examination standards, experience requirements, regulatory influence, and various other matters, all of which make implementing recognition of foreign professional qualifications and licenses on a multilateral basis very difficult. The second sentence of the introduction to the Guidelines reads: "These guidelines are non-binding and are intended to be used by Members on a voluntary basis, and cannot modify the rights or obligations of the Members of the WTO."

There is no consensus on the actual value added by the Guidelines to the provisions of Article VII. Some believe they provide practical guidance for governments, negotiating entities, or other entities entering into mutual recognition negotiations on the authorization, licensing, or certification of accountancy services providers. Supporters believe the Guidelines' nonbinding nature facilitates rather than mandates liberalization. The objective is to make it easier for parties to negotiate recognition agreements and for third parties to negotiate their accession to such agreements or to negotiate comparable ones. The critics of the Guidelines, on the other hand, argue that they constitute a rather weak document that fell hostage to the diverging practices already in existence in various regions of the world.[17] No member could ever have conceded that its own approach to recognition was not the ideal one. As a result, despite the very different recognition regimes currently in place around the world in the accountancy sector, all regimes comply with the Guidelines. What made this compliance possible in the Guidelines was the mere inventory of all the issues that negotiators might wish to address when discussing recognition of foreign accountancy qualifications, rather than any particular guidance on how to proceed and in which order. Adopting a nonbinding approach to the subject did not allow sharpening of the Guidelines content. To support the views of the critics, there is no evidence that the Guidelines have been used since their adoption: no member has notified the CTS under GATS Article VII.4 of the opening or conclusion of negotiations on the recognition of foreign accountancy qualifications.[18]

The Disciplines on Domestic Regulation in the Accountancy Sector were adopted in December 1998[19] by a decision of the CTS.[20] The work benefited from a significant number of contributions on the regulation of the sector and on regulatory reform in various parts of the world.[21] The purpose of the Disciplines is to facilitate trade in accountancy services by ensuring that domestic regulations affecting such trade meet the requirements of Article VI.4, so that measures relating to licensing requirements and procedures, technical standards,[22] and qualification requirements and procedures are not prepared, adopted, or applied with a view to, or with the effect of, creating unnecessary barriers to trade in accountancy services.

As indicated above, in GATS terminology "domestic regulation" constitutes a subset of what is covered by the regulation of the sector in most countries. The WPPS confirmed that limitations to market access covered by Article XVI[23] and to national treatment covered by Article XVII were excluded from the scope of the Disciplines, even if they related to qualification, standards, or licensing. According to the provisions of Articles XVI and XVII, such measures had to be eliminated through negotiation unless inscribed in the member's schedule of specific commitments. Having been adopted only by a decision of the CTS, the Disciplines do not have the same legal standing as the GATS, which is part of an international treaty ratified by each member. Paragraph 2 of the decision adopting the Disciplines indicates that the intention is to integrate them into the GATS no later than the conclusion of the services negotiations now under way. According to paragraph 3 of the decision, until this integration occurs, members will not take measures that would be inconsistent with the Disciplines. It should also be noted that the first paragraph of the decision limits the application of the Disciplines to members who have entered specific commitments on accountancy in their schedule. This last limitation could not have been anticipated from the mandate of Article VI.4, but might have found its origin in the formulation adopted in paragraph 2 of the decision on professional services, which reads: "As a matter of priority, the Working Party shall make recommendations for the elaboration of multilateral disciplines in the accountancy sector, *so as to give operational effect to specific commitments*" (emphasis added). The consequence of this was to make the undertaking of specific commitments in the accountancy sector more onerous for members in the future.

The Disciplines contain detailed provisions with respect to:

- Transparency
- Licensing requirements
- Licensing procedures
- Qualification requirements
- Qualification procedures
- Technical standards.

On the Disciplines' capability to further trade liberalization in the accountancy sector, opinions diverge along almost the same lines as in the Guidelines. For the optimists, the Disciplines have potentially far-reaching consequences for those aspects of domestic regulation that influence international trade. They represent an important step forward in defining rules on domestic regulation under the GATS because they contain a binding necessity test. Members are required to "ensure that measures not subject to scheduling under Articles XVI or XVII of the GATS, relating to licensing requirements and procedures, technical standards and qualification requirements and procedures are not prepared, adopted or applied with a view to or with the effect of creating unnecessary barriers to trade in accountancy services. For this purpose, Members shall ensure that such measures are not more trade-restrictive than necessary to fulfill a legitimate objective. Legitimate objectives are, *inter alia*, the protection of consumers (which includes all users of accounting services and the public generally), the quality of the service, professional competence, and the integrity of the profession."

If the skeptics accept that the necessity test contained in paragraph 2 is without doubt the most substantial provision in the Disciplines, they consider that the rest of the text adds little to existing GATS articles. They argue that the necessity test was already mentioned in the mandate of Article VI.4, which means that nothing less was expected in the Disciplines. It is true, however, that they spell out what domestic regulation ought to be necessary for: to fulfill a legitimate objective, such as the protection of consumers, the quality of the service, professional competence, and the integrity of the profession. That is somewhat narrower than the formulation in paragraph (b) of Article VI.4. Beyond this small legal precision, the Disciplines limit themselves to an illustration of what would normally be expected of members in terms of transparency, licensing, qualification, and standards, or they specify the application of the necessity test to types of measures. In some key cases, however, the specific rules contain language weaker than that in the necessity test.

For example, the provision on residency requirements states that members "shall consider" whether less trade-restrictive means could be used to achieve the same policy objective, and the provision on qualification requirements states that "a Member shall ensure that its competent authorities *take account* of qualifications acquired in the territory of another Member, on the basis of equivalency of education, experience and/or examination requirements" (emphasis added). The formulation adopted in many parts of the text is frequently nonprescriptive, and the extensive use of "shall" is counterbalanced by qualifications such as "in principle," "wherever possible," and the like. A proposal to create a presumption in favor of a test of competence as the least trade-restrictive measure received little support. The Disciplines also fail to deal with the cumulative effect of requirements, each of which would be individually considered necessary but would be unnecessarily duplicative in many respects. The end result is a nicely balanced political compromise with limited legal clout that does not really challenge the regulation of the sector in most respects. We are not aware of any regulatory change that would have occurred in the sector as a result of the adoption of the Disciplines. The CTS has received no notification under Article III.3 of any regulatory change introduced as a consequence of the adoption of the Disciplines.[24]

Some final observations should be added as a conclusion on the work of the WPPS on the accountancy sector. With the exception of the sentence included in the Singapore Ministerial Declaration in which the organizations named and the process referred to are specific to that sector, the other outputs of the WPPS are nonspecific. The Guidelines and the Disciplines could apply almost as such to any other professional service sector. This is not necessarily a drawback in the context of the GATS, but the lack of specificity is revealing about the limited capability of the WTO to adopt an approach to liberalization that would really be tailored to the particulars of one subsector. If the discussions in the WPPS lead to a better understanding of the interaction between Article VI.4 measures and market access or national treatment restrictions covered by Articles XVI and XVII, this legal debate seems to be constrained by the formal framework and internal structure of the GATS rather than to lead to greater liberalization in the sector.

Following its adoption of the Disciplines, and despite the fact that the WPPS responded only to the first part of its mandate to deal specifically with the accountancy sector, in April 1999 the CTS decided to replace the WPPS with a Working Party on Domestic Regulation (WPDR). The WPDR was charged with expanding the Article VI.4 work program to services in general, including an assessment of the extent to which the accountancy Disciplines might be applied to other professions.[25] The WPDR was asked to report back with recommendations no later than the conclusion of the current negotiations. No definitive conclusions have yet emerged from its work, which will continue in parallel with the sectoral negotiations on specific commitments and the work on the development of further rules for emergency safeguard measures,[26] government procurement,[27] and subsidies[28] in the area of services.

New Services Negotiations As the market access bargaining phase of the services negotiations begins,[29] it is an opportune moment to take stock and to look forward to what might be achieved during the current round of negotiations, bearing in mind more general developments that could have an influence on talks taking place within the WTO context. Everything depends, however, on the enthusiasm of interested parties to take advantage of the opportunities being offered.

To begin, it is useful to recall some of the more significant barriers that still impede international trade in accountancy services.[30] In addition to those that apply to services generally, some having specific relevance to accountancy include:

- Nationality and citizenship requirements
- Residence and establishment requirements
- Professional certification and entry requirements
- Restrictions on the mobility of professional personnel
- Scope of practice limitations
- Restrictions on advertising, solicitation, and fee setting
- Quantitative restrictions on the provision of services
- Restrictions on the business structures that can be used to provide services
- Restrictions on international relationships (including foreign ownership) and the use of firm names
- Restrictions on international information flows, including the electronic transmission of reports and accounting documents
- Differences in accounting, auditing, and other standards.

These barriers relate to all four modes of delivery listed in the GATS. Many of the obstacles are interrelated or derive from related aspects of domestic regulation. They illustrate the inextricable links between the provisions of GATS Article VI.4 and Articles XVI and XVII, because certain aspects of the same measure might be covered by the former and other aspects by the latter. Compounded by the complexity of the regulation inherent in the accountancy sector, the even higher level of sophistication of the internal architecture of the GATS constitutes one additional hurdle that will have to be overcome to produce meaningful liberalization. An arduous exegesis is frequently necessary to assess the liberalization potential of any additional commitment that would be undertaken in the WTO, whether as part of the Disciplines of Article VI.4 or of a member's schedule of specific commitments. This leaves ample room for diverging legal interpretations among specialists and is a further challenge for those trying to increase liberalization. The legal certainty that was supposed to result from the GATS still has its limitations.

To date, only two members have submitted a negotiating proposal for the accountancy sector: the United States[31] and Australia.[32] In addition, the European Union,[33] Canada,[34] Switzerland,[35] and Colombia[36] presented proposals relating to professional services in general. The United States proposed that members who have not yet done so undertake commitments in the accountancy sector. In making that proposal the United States suggested that those members address a number of obstacles to trade liberalization that are listed in the proposal and that cover, with a different formulation, most of the obstacles mentioned in the previous paragraph. "Some items in the list may be market access restrictions, or national treatment limitations, or both. In addition, some obstacles, although not limitations on market access or national treatment *per se*, may result from regulatory provisions or other measures which make it difficult for foreign suppliers to market their services."[37] To that effect, the United States is suggesting that, according to Article XVIII, members make additional commitments relating to the regulation of the sector, along the lines of the Disciplines. That would replicate the approach already adopted during the extended telecommunication negotiations with the inclusion by certain members of a Reference Paper on regulatory principles in their schedule of specific commitments. This way of incorporating the Disciplines into the GATS, as required by the decision adopting the Disciplines, might be one of the most practical solutions available, but it has its limitations. It further links the provisions of Article VI.4 to scheduled commitments and leaves it up to each member to integrate the regulatory principles, as a whole or in part, into its schedule of specific commitments. From a systemic point of view, that would have the additional disadvantage of abandoning any chance of adopting the Disciplines as a set of regulatory principles integrated into the GATS general obligations.

Australia adopted a slightly different approach. After also listing those impediments to further liberalization in the sector it considered most significant, it proposed to extend the reach of revised Disciplines to measures subject to scheduling under Articles XVI and XVII. That extension would blur further the distinction painstakingly established between the remit of these two articles on the one hand and Article VI.4 on the other.

Those members who made proposals for professional services in general have addressed some specific market access or national treatment limitations like residency/establishment or nationality/citizenship requirements, calling for their removal. They all recognize the particular importance of Mode 4 and suggest improvements to existing commitments and work on the recognition of qualifications and licenses. Canada and Switzerland also proposed extending the scope of the Disciplines to cover other sectors (either horizontally or sectorally), and the European Union (EU) suggested removing existing MFN exemptions covering professional services because they are covered by Article VII.

Taking into consideration the substantial work already done on the main barriers to liberalization listed above or in members' various proposals, as well as the complexity of the existing GATS legal architecture, it seems that the movement of natural persons and foreign ownership could be among the issues of most relevance to the accountancy sector and could most usefully be addressed during the negotiations on specific commitments currently under way in the WTO. Most interested parties are still reflecting on this, however, and might come to different conclusions at a later stage in the process.

- *Movement of Persons.* Mode 4 is an important means of accountancy services provision, not only in its own right but also in association with Mode 3 (Commercial Presence), where the temporary movement of skilled or managerial personnel or both may be necessary. This is of interest to industrial-country providers in terms of access to other industrial countries,[38] as well as to developing countries.[39] It also is of interest to certain developing countries with strong accountancy services sectors, such as India, seeking access to industrial and developing country markets alike. Progress depends to a large extent on the separate discussions on Mode 4 generally, but for accountancy services it is also strongly linked to questions of licensing and accreditation. Improvements in communications technologies, however, also may have an influence, to the extent that the possibilities for "off-shoring" certain accountancy work may enable the work to be brought to the accountants rather than the other way around, thereby switching from Mode 4 to Modes 1 and 2. Of interest, for example, are mutual recognition negotiations currently under way between Italy and India, which would enable Indian professionals to acquire the Italian certification necessary to allow them to carry out in India on behalf of Italian clients certain activities regulated in Italy, using communications technology.

- *Foreign Ownership.* Although few countries have adopted measures having as their stated objective the prohibition/restriction of foreign ownership of domestic accountancy services firms, this is nonetheless the consequence of rules that require local firms to be owned (by majority or in full) by locally licensed professionals, and whereby access to the local license requires compliance with citizenship, nationality, residence, establishment, or burdensome recertification procedures. Although many such rules were adopted at a time when foreign ownership was simply not thought to be a possibility, continuing such requirements (which are prevalent in both industrial and developing countries) is a severe impediment to the international integration of accountancy firms. That can have negative consequences with respect to the transfer of know-how and methodologies, but it also complicates the governance of international firm networks in a manner by weakening their ability to enforce uniform quality standards across the network. The East Asian financial crisis highlighted a number of cases in which the level of assurance conveyed by well-known international firms differed significantly from one network member firm to another, and in which the absence of mechanisms normally associated with ownership and control prevented the uniform enforcement of standards to which the network had agreed. International ownership of integrated international firms by all of their partners worldwide rather than the continuation of separate, locally owned firms linked only by network agreements could enhance the quality and availability of accountancy services internationally and in individual countries. Any changes to national regulations to permit foreign professionals to participate in the ownership of local firms should still ensure that such firms remain subject to domestic requirements and domestic jurisdiction.[40] One key issue to be resolved is how to ensure that professional firms remain under professional control if a local license is no longer required of its owners, or where it is considered excessively burdensome to require that foreign professionals with no desire to practice in the country acquire the local qualification. Within the EU a distinction has been suggested between the license necessary to provide accountancy services in a country (which continues to be the local designation) and the license necessary to be considered acceptable to participate in the ownership of a domestic firm (which could be a designation from any EU member state).[41] This raises issues of mutual recognition for purposes of acquiring ownership rather than practice rights, and further work is required to develop modalities that would enable this to be done in a multilateral context. Some people may speak against foreign ownership because of a desire to protect local firms from competition (infant-industry policy), but the efficacy of the policy more generally is open to question, given the risks of permanent infancy. Many of the countries of continental Europe made it difficult for foreign accountancy firms to have access to their markets until the

1970s or 1980s, but the common view is that all firms—domestic and foreign—benefited when such access was facilitated.

The debate in these two domains is therefore much wider than the sectoral context of accountancy services. Progress on either front will depend on the capacity of members to find solutions to the systemic questions that underlie the debate on the temporary movement of natural persons and the articulation between the provisions of Articles VI.4, XVI, and XVII. If the stakes are high, the odds are low!

Experiences of Regulatory Reform and Trade Liberalization in the Accountancy Sector

Although the GATS is the first attempt ever made at a multilateral level to liberalize trade in services, to a large extent the design of the GATS, specific commitments undertaken by members, and the way the WTO was able to deal with the liberalization of the accountancy sector have been shaped by preexisting factors. The fundamental principles enshrined in the GATS (MFN treatment, market access, national treatment, and so forth) have been inherited from the GATT legal tradition, and countries' laws and regulations in the accountancy sector have conditioned their specific commitments and the outcome of the work of the WPPS. The first section of this chapter analyzed the limited expectations one may have for the current WTO services negotiations. It would be useful at this stage to identify other sources of inspiration to feed our reflection on regulatory reform and trade liberalization. We will examine successively the EU experiment, the efforts at standardizing accountancy deployed at the international level, and the approach adopted by big audit networks to develop their business at the global level in spite of the many barriers to any form of worldwide practice.

European Union Accountancy Framework

Harmonization and mutual recognition are different but complementary techniques. Mutual recognition is not possible in practice without a minimum level of prior harmonization. Conversely, mutual recognition can act as a lever to augment the results already obtained through harmonization. In the accountancy sector, these two approaches have been used at different levels (bilateral, regional, international) with varying outcomes, dependent mainly on the legal framework within which they applied.

The most favorable framework is undoubtedly that of the EU Single Market created by the Treaty of Rome and subsequent acts since 1957. Within a group of countries that are relatively homogenous in terms of economic development and sophistication, a common set of rules governs the free movement of services, professionals, and capital (to cite only those legal elements of most relevance to the accountancy sector) under the management and control of a single set of institutions. Both harmonization and mutual recognition have been applied to the EU accountancy sector.

On the harmonization front, various directives have been adopted on the preparation of accounts[42] and on the qualification of statutory auditors.[43] More recently, the EU institutions have interested themselves in questions of the independence of the statutory auditor and the assurance of the quality of statutory audit services. On the mutual recognition side, the general system of mutual recognition of diplomas[44] applies to accountants and auditors in the EU and gives them the right to obtain the local professional title of the host member state after passing only an aptitude test.[45] Financial statements produced in one member state according to laws and regulations that comply with the various accountancy directives are recognized in the other EU member states without restatement.

The European Court of Justice undoubtedly has contributed to the legal construction of the Single Market. One of the most significant contributions is certainly its jurisprudence on necessity and proportionality that also applies to the provision of services, and hence to the provision of accountancy services within the EU. This jurisprudence has been codified for the free movement of services across borders in a communication of the European Commission[46] adopted on December 6, 1993. The jurisprudence of the Court has established that a restriction to the free movement of services can be maintained by member states only if three conditions are cumulatively met: the restriction has to be justified by reasons linked with the protection of the general interest; this interest should not already be protected by the rules of the member state where the supplier is established; and the same result should not be capable of achievement through less demanding rules. Each of these three conditions has been progressively defined and applied by the Court, initially to trade in goods and then to trade in services. The formula that defines proportionality and each of its components is supported by a significant body of case law. By comparison with the text in paragraph 4 of GATS Article VI of the GATS and with the current absence of jurisprudence on it in the WTO, this seems more precise. The most interesting aspects of the EU jurisprudence on proportionality from the point of view of regulatory reform are the way it addresses the cumulative effect of regulations in the home and host member state as well as in the host member state alone, and the obligation to let less demanding provisions capable of achieving the same result prevail. A requirement can be justified only if no already existing provision, in either the home or the host member state, can achieve the same objective. Contrary to the text of the GATS or of the Disciplines, which remain silent in this regard, the Court imposes that the least demanding measure always be favored. Finally it should be noted that the rule of proportionality actually has been applied to the accountancy sector in one case[47]: the Court ruled that, if the requirement to have a professional establishment in the host member state where regulated audit services were provided was proportionate in the sense of the Treaty of Rome, the compliance with the requirement actually could be obtained through less demanding measures, such as the existence of temporary links with a locally established professional.

However, when one looks to results rather than to the various legal measures and decisions adopted to implement the mandate of the Treaty of Rome so as to create a single market in the EU accountancy sector, one can only conclude that this objective remains as distant as ever. Very few accountancy professionals have taken advantage of the general system of mutual recognition of diplomas; cross-border provision of regulated accountancy services remains impossible for the most part; and there are no firms jointly owned by accountants from different member states that would be recognized as an accountancy firm in any of the member states concerned (the rule is still majority ownership at least by locally licensed accountants). Trade in regulated accountancy services, with or without establishment in the member state of the client, remains minimal within the EU. This situation pales in comparison with what has been achieved for lawyers, for example.

Given the favorable institutional, political, legal, and economic context of the EU, it is disappointing to note the extent to which the accountancy sector has not been subject to regulatory reforms that would have led to more significant intra-EU trade, greater mobility of professionals, or a form of EU-level consolidation of some of the larger national firms in the sector. Nowhere in the world are the conditions better. If progress has not proved possible in the EU until now, one can only wonder about the prospects elsewhere in the world, to say nothing of prospects at the international level.

Standardization Efforts at the International Level

The accountancy profession itself took the initiative early in the 1970s and successively created two international bodies that had as one of their main functions the production of international standards in the domains of relevance to the practice of the accountancy profession. IFAC has produced a significant body of standards on various subjects, including the International Standards on Auditing (ISA) and the Code of Ethics for Professional Accountants. IASC was created to develop International Accounting Standards (IAS). Both bodies also have worked on the interpretation of their standards. Until now the use of the standards produced by either institution has been purely voluntary, even for the national professional bodies that are their members. That voluntary nature has been one of the main weaknesses of the standardization process in the sector, and one of the major concerns of IFAC and IASB, which have worked to remedy it. To that effect, IASC recently underwent a very significant reorganization that transformed it into the International Accounting Standards Board (IASB) and made it much more independent from the accountancy profession through the involvement of all other parties interested in the production and

use of financial statements. IFAC is currently reflecting on a reorganization of its own that, among other things, would raise the profile and recognition of the standards it produces.

Another significant obstacle to wider use of ISA and IAS has been the absence of reliable verification of the conformity of practice with the standards. Neither IFAC nor IASB has the means of checking that the professional bodies, the professionals (individuals or firms), or the companies that claim to abide by their standards do indeed comply with them. Numerous surveys have been performed on the conformity of national rules with ISA or IAS, or on the use of IAS in companies' financial statements, but little has been done to check whether the companies claiming to comply with IAS actually live up to that objective. In July 2001 David Cairns (Secretary General of IASC from 1985 to 1994) released his second survey on an assessment of the use of IAS in the financial statements of listed companies around the world.[48] Quite tellingly the survey identifies a number of examples in which the conformity of the financial statements with IAS is not what it should have been, and that in turn raises questions about the absence of appropriate qualifications in the audit opinions expressed on these accounts.

Since the current services negotiations began in the WTO, two developments of particular note have taken place in relation to international standards. In May 2000 IOSCO endorsed a core set of International Accounting Standards for financial statements used in all cross-border offerings and foreign listings. Although not binding for its members, the decision of IOSCO is a very significant step toward the international acceptance of IAS. In June 2000 the European Commission announced its intention to propose legislation to make the use of IAS mandatory for all listed companies in the EU by 2005 at latest. The draft regulation has since been published and was endorsed by EU heads of state and of government at their Stockholm Summit in March 2001 as part of their support for a package of proposals to strengthen the integration and regulation of the EU's capital and financial markets. That endorsement should dispel the hesitations with respect to IAS that may have existed during the Uruguay Round. However, the previous IOSCO endorsement of ISA has since been withdrawn, and the EU has not yet decided whether to mandate the use of ISA for the audit of financial statements prepared in accordance with IAS. Neither IOSCO nor the EU has endorsed the recently revised IFAC Code of Ethics.

Audit Networks: An Industry Response to Its Regulatory Environment

Of particular note has been the lack of greater pressure from the international accountancy firm networks for the removal of trade barriers that complicate the specific governance and regulatory arrangements applicable (or not applicable, as the case may be) to them. Despite the impression that some may gain from the use of a common name across jurisdictions, the international networks are not single entities operating under common ownership, management, and control, nor are the networks themselves licensed to perform any regulated activities. In most countries the license to perform statutory or legally required audits may only be granted to a separate, locally established entity, and only locally accredited professionals may have majority ownership (at least), management, and control of that entity. The activities of the entity are subject to local regulation. The international networks therefore consist of multiple member firms linked by contract, and the ability to enforce networkwide standards of performance is contingent on the degree of willingness by the parties to these contracts to agree to such standards, which in turn depends on their perceptions of the relative costs and benefits of network membership. Entry to and exit from network membership is relatively frequent (especially at the level of smaller networks), and there has been a steady trend toward greater concentration in the sector. Many network member firms existed prior to joining the network, rather than being new entities created with the assistance of the network, which can complicate the process of coming into compliance with agreed network requirements. Different networks have different internal dynamics, and it is understood that the degree of enforceability of networkwide standards varies significantly from network to network. Recent cases also call into question the robustness of firms' internal procedures for enforcing compliance with regulatory requirements even in the context of single jurisdictions, which may give rise to concerns about the mechanisms for enforcing network requirements across multiple jurisdictions. In addition, because the networks themselves are not regulated in any jurisdiction, agreement on the standards of performance that should be applied across the networks is itself a voluntary matter, as opposed to those standards that local regulations impose on locally licensed network-member firms. Particular tensions may arise when networkwide standards are more demanding than, or in conflict with, local requirements.

The use of a common name by network member firms gives rise to an expectation of "One Name–One Standard," and it is a significant commercial benefit of network membership that users operate under this impression, not least in those jurisdictions where confidence in the local regulatory regime for auditors is lacking. In reality, however, the substance of the assurance given by network membership is nonobservable by users, and in the case of disputes, users have only the local regulatory arrangements to rely on to seek redress. The separate legal personalities of the network and its individual member firms make it difficult to take legal action other than against the member firm directly involved, in its home jurisdiction, and the standard against which performance is measured when resolving disputes is the local rather than the network standard.

This gives rise to special problems when the work of one member firm is being relied on in another jurisdiction, where users may have expectations with respect to the level of performance—implicitly warranted by the use of the network name—based on knowledge of the regulatory framework and performance of the network member firm in the jurisdiction of the user or elsewhere.

The absence of an appropriate regulatory framework suggests that at least part of the solution to these difficulties might lie in the application of the caveat emptor principle, but this can only work if the users have adequate information on which to base their decisions—and that would require sufficient transparency about the internal arrangements of the various networks whose member firms use a common name across jurisdictions. However, networks have not made explicit the nature of the performance standard assertion implicit in the use of the network name. The internal procedures to ensure compliance with this performance standard are not disclosed to users. No independent external assurance is provided that these network procedures are adequate and operate as intended. There is no transparency for the network-internal sanctions that exist for cases of noncompliance (e.g., expulsion from the network or withdrawal of the right to use the network name). Users have no recourse against the network as a whole in cases of unsatisfactory performance by an individual member firm or failure of the network to properly control one of its member firms. Member firms of some networks may use differential standards (e.g., one standard for "local work" and another for "transnational work") and it is difficult to see how this can be reconciled with the One Name–One Standard expectation. One mechanism to assist transparency in such cases would be to use different brands to signal the differences in performance standards, but networks are reluctant to surrender the marketing advantage that comes from the One Name–One Standard expectation. And where networks become aware of member firms' failure to comply with local requirements, there are no specific obligations for reporting the noncompliance to local regulatory authorities.

The commitment of accountancy firms to significant regulatory reform of the sector, which would be necessary to accompany and facilitate liberalization, is therefore uncertain.

Regulatory Reform: What Are the Prospects?

At the multilateral level, domestic regulation has been defined in GATS Article VI.4 as qualification requirements and procedures, technical standards, and licensing requirements and procedures to the extent they do not constitute a limitation to market access or national treatment in the sense of Articles XVI and XVII. Article VI confirms the competence of national regulators in this domain, but requires that the resulting domestic regulation does not unnecessarily restrict trade. Previous sections of this chapter have considered the possible effect of these rules in the accountancy sector. The current absence of consensus among the main parties is a major impediment to further progress. This state of affairs in the sector is not fatal, however, and there is merit in studying possible developments that could help achieve convergence among some of the more divergent views on the regulation of the sector.

Understanding the Regulation of the Sector

There are several reasons why countries were reluctant to commit to liberalizing these areas during the Uruguay Round.[49] In the absence of comprehensive and reliable statistics, the potential benefits of liberalization were difficult to quantify. Linkages with other reform initiatives were poorly understood. Domestic and international constituencies that stood to benefit from liberalization were not as vocal as those that feared they might lose from change. To a significant extent, there was also a lack of involvement and commitment on the part of those ministries and agencies responsible for the domestic regulatory regimes governing accountancy; they were not convinced of the need to make changes in response to trade policy considerations. Most systems of national regulation have evolved to address national concerns to protect the interests of national users and providers of accountancy services, and the need to take the international dimension into account was not sufficiently widely recognized to enable positive progress during the Uruguay Round. To the extent that accountancy regulators did wish to address international issues, they chose other forums for doing so, and were reluctant to have such matters covered as part of trade talks. Specifically, there was hesitation to submit to a process that could result in binding commitments to reform, given a strong preference for voluntary and unilateral (albeit coordinated) changes in this field. This was the case with regard to accounting standards, for example, where negotiations between IASC and IOSCO had not yet reached the stage where IOSCO felt able to endorse IAS. There may also have been unreasonable expectations as to the extent to which countries could negotiate equivalent opportunities for their domestic accountancy services providers abroad at the same time they were opening their local markets.

Since the Uruguay Round a stronger understanding has emerged of the contribution of accountancy services to creating a sound investment climate. Business services such as accountancy and legal services are important in reducing transaction costs and are essential for creating and enforcing contracts. Improving the availability and quality of accountancy services is supportive of, and is supported by, simultaneous reforms in related fields such as corporate governance, securities market regulation, and financial services (e.g., banking and insurance) regulation. Enhancing confidence in the regulation and operation of domestic markets helps attract foreign direct and portfolio investment, often to the extent that domestic issuers no longer need to list abroad to attract foreign capital but can attract foreign investors to buy their securities on the domestic market. As in most sectors of the economy, liberalizing trade in accountancy services can be positive in two ways: by enabling foreign accountants and firms to provide services that are not other-wise available locally, and by encouraging local providers to improve the availability and quality of their services by exposing them to foreign competition.

There is also increased recognition of the international and systemic externalities of weaknesses in domestic regimes for the regulation of accountancy. Poor standards of governance, accountability, and transparency contributed to the East Asian financial crisis in 1997, the repercussions of which were felt in countries around the world. Shortcomings in the quality of accounting and audit were among the causes. This has led to several international initiatives to improve global financial stability and the global financial architecture, and accounting and auditing are included in the areas identified for strengthening. The World Bank, for example, has supported moves to improve the functioning of the relevant international standard setters, IASB and IFAC, and the quality of the standards they produce. As part of the joint International Monetary Fund (IMF)/World Bank Reports on Observance of Standards and Codes (ROSC)[50] initiative, the Bank is working with some of its member countries to benchmark national accounting and auditing requirements against the international standards and to assess the quality of compliance with those requirements. Enhanced convergence on international standards and the putting in place of robust enforcement mechanisms to ensure compliance are among the outcomes that will flow from these assessments, building on the recognition that significant weaknesses in a country will weaken its attractiveness to increasingly prudent international investors. The major international accounting firms, whose audit reports on financial statements are relied on by

investors when allocating funds among companies and countries, are conscious of the need to ensure greater consistency of the services provided by their affiliates around the world. The expectations to which they must now respond are international, not national, but differences in national regulatory systems can make attaining that consistency difficult. The Enron collapse has served to underline the fact that concerns about the quality of accounting and auditing are not confined to emerging markets.

These developments highlight the important network effects that influence accountancy regulation. Countries wish to be integrated into the global financial system to have access to capital, and they recognize that their national regulatory regimes must facilitate that integration rather than impede it. At the same time, national systems of accountancy regulation must recognize that the users of accountancy services are no longer defined in national terms and that countries must have access to services, and adopt standards, that meet international needs. These reforms need not necessarily apply to all domestic enterprises and accountancy services providers because many will continue to operate in purely domestic markets or to engage in transactions for which international standards may not be fully appropriate, but it is difficult to imagine countries for which the international dimension is of no relevance.

Dealing with These Issues at the WTO— What Are the Chances of Success?

Given that much of the progress in accountancy-related fields is taking place outside the context of the WTO, two questions present themselves: why should the current negotiations address trade in accountancy services rather than leave it to other organizations and forums, and what is the likelihood of significant progress?

Responding to the first question, those who would have the topic dealt with as part of the negotiations provide several justifications. First, when domestic reforms are anchored in binding commitments under the GATS, there is legal certainty and enhanced external confidence in the durability and irreversibility of the changes. Second, given that the negotiations touch on many related regulatory issues, such as the rules governing financial services, coverage of accountancy services enables negotiators to ensure consistency of approach and to avoid unintended conflicts. Third, the WTO recognizes the mandates of other organizations and forums, and provides a useful platform for discussing enhanced cooperation among countries on regulatory issues and for ensuring that the trade dimension is taken appropriately into account when national reforms are being considered. Fourth, although trade negotiations are not a zero-sum game, coverage of accountancy does open the possibility of receiving credit for liberalizing measures in this field in the context of the negotiations as a whole. Fifth, the necessity test is now available as a powerful tool to assist in identifying those domestic regulations that create unnecessary barriers to trade in accountancy services. Based on these responses, advocates would predict the high likelihood of a successful outcome.

Those of a less optimistic disposition would challenge each of those justifications. They believe that the legal complexity of the GATS, and in particular the somewhat nonoperational distinction between Article VI.4 measures and market access and national treatment restrictions to be scheduled, is confusing and does not provide the desired legal certainty. They conclude from the WPPS experience with the production of the Disciplines that the WTO is not best suited to the discussion of regulatory issues. They would further argue that the necessity test has not yet entered into force, does not provide positive guidance for the design of an appropriate regulatory regime, and is an inadequate basis for enabling members to decide on which regulatory reforms are suited to fostering trade liberalization while maintaining prudential safeguards. The lessons learned from the East Asian crisis of 1997 and more recently from the Enron collapse in the United States demonstrate the need for robust regulation of financial reporting and auditing. Members can be expected to be very cautious about any reforms that are perceived to weaken rather than strengthen domestic regimes. They also are unlikely to place on other members' regimes the greater reliance that is necessary to lower existing barriers to trade (e.g., accepting foreign licenses as a sufficient basis for ownership of local firms) unless they can be assured that those

other regimes are designed in accordance with internationally accepted benchmark standards and codes and that those standards and codes are complied with in practice.

Some people also believe that the recognition of the role of international standards in Article VI of the GATS suggests that designating and adopting such standards and codes would simultaneously satisfy the twin objectives of trade liberalization and regulatory strengthening. For them, the chances of a positive outcome therefore depend on the extent to which there is in place a sufficient body of accepted international standards that together form a comprehensive framework for regulating accountancy services. It is unfortunate that the experience gained from the ROSC accounting and auditing assessments suggests that there are major gaps in that framework, and those gaps suggest that even strengthened GATS rules will be insufficient to achieve significant incremental liberalization without further progress in developing an international regulatory framework in the sector.

Determining a Need for an International Regulatory Framework

As demonstrated by the results of the World Bank/IMF Financial Sector Assessment Program (FSAP)/ROSC assessments, when compared with the regulatory principles adopted by IOSCO (for securities regulation), the Basel Committee (for banking supervision), and the International Association of Insurance Advisors (IAIS) (for the insurance sector), IAS and ISA cannot be considered principles of regulation. Rather, they are methodological rules for preparing and auditing financial statements, and are silent on many key aspects of regulation where differences of approach among countries give rise to the more substantial barriers to trade in accountancy services. Both the accounting and auditing ROSC assessments and other empirical research have shown that adopting international standards, by itself, does little to enhance the quality of financial reporting unless accompanied by measures to ensure the enforcement of those standards, and it is in the area of enforcement that the current framework of standards and codes is most deficient.

The November 2001 cross-sectoral comparison among the regulatory principles adopted by IOSCO, the Basel Committee, and the IAIS[51] reveals a high degree of commonality of coverage of the following issues:

Attributes of supervisory systems
- Operational independence and adequate resources
- Enforcement powers and capabilities
- Clarity and transparency of the supervisory process
- External participation in the supervisory process

The supervised entity
- Licensing, qualifications, ownership transfer, and corporate control
- Corporate governance

Ongoing supervision
- Groupwide supervision
- Monitoring and on-site inspection
- Reporting to supervisors
- Cooperation and information sharing
- Confidentiality

Prudential standards
- Risk management
- Internal controls
- Risk concentration
- Capital requirements
- Accounting policies and practices

Markets and customers
- Markets
  - Market integrity
  - Financial crime
- Customer protection
- Information, disclosure, and transparency
- Issuers

Although not all of the above considerations are relevant to accountancy services,[52] they nonetheless highlight features of any regulatory system that would need to be addressed before any body of standards could have the desired effects in terms of protection of the public and increased trade liberalization. It is evident that IAS and ISA alone fall far short of that benchmark, and the gap to be filled is considerable.

International standards in the accountancy field fail to provide a comprehensive framework of regulatory principles in themselves and they neglect to address the interlinkages among accountancy regulation and other domains of market regulation and corporate governance. The study *Enforcement Mechanisms in Europe* (published by the Fédération des Experts Comptables Européens in 2001) draws attention to six different levels of enforcement of accounting and auditing standards and emphasizes how each depends on the other for full effectiveness:

1. Preparation of financial statements
2. Statutory audit of financial statements
3. Approval of financial statements
4. Institutional oversight systems
5. Judicial mechanisms for dealing with complaints and imposing sanctions
6. Monitoring by the press and the public.

Only the first and the second levels are addressed (and then only in part) by international standards of accounting and auditing, whereas others fall within the scope of market regulation and corporate governance. *The Relationship between Banking Supervisors and Banks' External Auditors* (prepared jointly by the Basel Committee and the International Federation of Accountants in 2001) is a positive first step in addressing these regulatory interlinkages, but it is descriptive rather than prescriptive, it refrains from indicating expected best practice, and it does not consider banking supervisors' enforcement role with respect to general purpose financial statements made available to the market (as opposed to financial information submitted to supervisors for prudential purposes).

Serious though the above gaps are, perhaps the major omission from the current international standards is any consideration of the appropriate relationships among the state, the institutions of the accountancy profession, and providers of accountancy services (whether firms or individuals). In fact, many of the non–standard-setting pronouncements of IFAC suggest a fundamental misunderstanding on its part of what this relationship should entail. References made to the profession's self-regulatory role imply that the profession is the source of its own regulatory mandate. IFAC does not appear to recognize that self-regulatory authority is delegated by the state, and that a professional body performing self-regulatory functions does so as agent of the state rather than as representative of its members. A better conception of the nature and role of self-regulatory organizations is set out in the IOSCO principles. IFAC's misconception of the possibility of the profession regulating itself without proper external accountability and supervision is mirrored in the difficulties being experienced in establishing an international public oversight board, a forum of firms, and an international peer review system. This idealized (if misplaced) view of the profession as master of its own affairs has disappeared in the EU[53] and will disappear definitively in the United States as a consequence of the regulatory reforms announced following the Enron collapse.

Because the framework of necessary regulatory principles variously affects different actors with a direct interest in the quality of accountancy services, it does not fall to any one body to develop those principles. A collaborative effort is required, but it is not obvious that an appropriate forum exists where that cooperation could take place. Following criticisms of the profession in the context of the East Asian crisis, the International Forum on Accountancy Development (IFAD) was established to bring together the major organizations in the field (including IFAC, the major international accountancy firm networks, IASB, the World Bank, the IMF, the European Commission, the Organisation for Economic Co-operation and Development, UNCTAD, IOSCO, the Basel Committee, the IAIS, and others), but efforts to agree on substantive issues have not yet proved successful. The World Bank is currently taking the lead in attempts to renew the IFAD initiative, but the outcome cannot be predicted with confidence.

Conclusion

As far as trade in accountancy services is concerned, the WTO has served primarily as a forum for capturing the current situation rather than as a force for achieving significant liberalization. There are no concrete indications that the new negotiations on services, which began on January 1, 2000, will lead to a different outcome. If progress is to be made, its impetus will have to come from elsewhere. Consensus must be built on a comprehensive set of principles to govern the regulation of accounting and auditing—principles that facilitate trade liberalization while they maintain and

enhance the protections available to the public. In the absence of this consensus, there will be an unwillingness to undertake domestic reforms and significant impediments to the confidence in other countries' regulatory regimes that is needed to underpin mutual recognition and acceptance. The GATS and the Disciplines on Domestic Regulation indicate what form regulations should *not* take, but they do not constitute a positive agenda for reform. If and when consensus is reached on an appropriate framework of regulatory principles, the GATS can serve as the means to anchor it in legal certainty, but this implies that the GATS will be the beneficiary rather than the cause of progress in other forums. Whether this progress can be achieved within a time frame consistent with the duration of the current negotiations remains to be seen.

Annex: Definition of Accountancy Services

There is no universally accepted definition of accountancy services, nor is there a strict correspondence between accountancy services and the activities of the accounting profession (European Commission 1997), because the skills deployed to produce, process, analyze, or audit financial information can also be used for other purposes.[54] Considering accountancy services to be the services provided by accountants leads to a definition that varies among countries because the scope of practice of accountants is far from consistent around the world.[55] In the context of the sectoral services negotiations held during the Uruguay Round, a large majority of negotiating parties used the Services Sectoral Classification List[56] prepared by what was then the GATT Secretariat on the basis of the provisional United Nations Central Product Classification. Accountancy services formed a subsector of professional services and were subdivided into accounting, auditing, and bookkeeping services, corresponding to section 862 of the provisional UN CPC:

862   Accounting, auditing, and bookkeeping services

Accounting and auditing services

86211   Financial auditing services

Examination services of the accounting records and other supporting evidence of an organization for the purpose of expressing an opinion as to whether financial statements of the organization present fairly its position as at a given date and the results of its operations for the period ended on that date in accordance with generally accepted accounting principles.

86212 Accounting review services

Reviewing services of annual and interim financial statements and other accounting information. The scope of a review is less than that of an audit and therefore the level of assurance provided is lower.

86213 Compilation of financial statements services

Compilation services of financial statements from information provided by the client. No assurances regarding the accuracy of the resulting statements are provided. Preparation services of business tax returns, when provided as a bundle with the preparation of financial statements for a single fee, are classified here.

Exclusion: Business tax preparation services, when provided as separate services, are classified in subclass 86302 (Business tax preparation and review services).

86219 Other accounting services

Other accounting services such as attestations, valuations, preparation services of *pro forma* statements, etc.

86220 Bookkeeping services, except tax returns

Bookkeeping services consisting in classifying and recording business transactions in terms of money or some unit of measurement in the books of account.

Exclusion: Bookkeeping services related to tax returns are classified in subclass 86302 (Business tax preparation and review services).

Endnotes

1. See paragraph 15 in WTO (1998c).
2. At the time of the Uruguay Round, WTO members were called GATT (General Agreement on Tariffs and Trade) contracting parties. For the sake of simplicity, this chapter will always refer to them as "WTO members" or "members," irrespective of whether the events discussed took place before or after the entry into force of the WTO agreement on January 1, 1995.
3. S/L/93 adopted on March 28, 2001.

4. The 47 members were Antigua and Barbuda, Argentina, Australia, Austria, Brazil, Brunei Darussalam, Canada, Chile, Colombia, Cuba, Cyprus, Czech Republic, Dominican Republic, El Salvador, European Communities, Finland, Guyana, Hong Kong (China), Hungary, Iceland, Israel, Jamaica, Japan, the Republic of Korea, Lesotho, Liechtenstein, Malawi, Malaysia, Maldives, Mexico, Morocco, Netherlands Antilles, New Zealand, Norway, Peru, Poland, Sierra Leone, Singapore, Slovak Republic, South Africa, Sweden, Switzerland, Thailand, Turkey, United States, República Bolivariana de Venezuela, and Zambia.
5. Twenty-two new members have undertaken specific commitments in the accountancy sector: Albania, Bulgaria, China, Chinese Taipei, Croatia, Ecuador, Estonia, The Gambia, Georgia, Jordan, Kyrgyz Republic, Latvia, Lithuania, Moldova, Mongolia, Oman, Panama, Papua New Guinea, Qatar, Slovenia, Solomon Islands, and the United Arab Emirates.
6. See the annex to this chapter.
7. For a detailed analysis of the specific commitments undertaken in the accountancy sector, please refer to paragraphs 37 to 42 in WTO (1998c). That analysis, however, was made at the level of the whole sector. A further distinction between statutory audit and the rest of the sector might have shown interesting results.
8. The seven members are Costa Rica, Dominican Republic, Honduras, Panama, Thailand, Turkey, and República Bolivariana de Venezuela.
9. WTO (1995e), dated April 4, 1995.
10. Professional services include legal services; accounting, auditing, and bookkeeping services; taxation services; architectural services; engineering services; integrated engineering services; urban planning and landscape architectural services; medical and dental services; veterinary services; and services provided by midwives, nurses, physiotherapists, and paramedical personnel.
11. The International Federation of Accountants produces the International Standards on Auditing and the International Code of Ethics. The International Accounting Standards Committee (now the International Accounting Standards Board [IASB]) produces the International Accounting Standards. See http://www.ifac.org/ and http://www.iasc.org.uk/cmt/0001.asp for further details.
12. IOSCO is the international organization regrouping stock exchange regulators. See http://www.iosco.org/iosco.html for further details.
13. See WTO (1996e), particularly paragraphs 20–26 on the use of international standards.
14. See WTO (1996b), paragraph 17.
15. S/L/38, May 28, 1997.
16. Article VII.2 of the GATS.
17. See WTO (1995b) and WTO (1996c).
18. The U.S. professional regulatory bodies (the American Institute of Certified Public Accountants [AICPA] and the National Association of State Boards of Accountancy [NASBA]) recently negotiated mutual recognition agreements with the Australian Chartered Accountants and Certified Public Accountants, and with the three U.K. chartered accountants bodies (although final agreement is being blocked by the British government). Both AICPA and NASBA have been negotiating with the Mexican professional body (and those negotiations are now concluded). The authors believe, however, that the Guidelines have had

no noticeable influence on the negotiations, and that the recognition agreement previously concluded with the Canadian Chartered Accountants within the North American Free Trade Agreement framework was the main guiding light in this process. The methodology followed was very similar and involved a detailed evaluation of each component of the foreign qualification by the U.S. International Qualifications Appraisal Board.

19. WTO 1998b.

20. WTO 1998a.

21. The results of several surveys on the regulation of the accountancy sector were presented to the WPPS by IFAC (July 1, 1995), the Organisation for Economic Co-operation and Development (OECD) (WTO 1995c), and the United Nations Conference on Trade and Development (WTO 1995d and 1996a). The WPPS also conducted its own survey (WTO 1996d) to which 29 members responded. The results are presented in WTO (1997b). Finally, between September 1994 and February 1997 the OECD organized three workshops—Liberalization of Trade in Professional Services, International Trade in Professional Services (assessing barriers and encouraging reform), and Advancing Liberalization through Regulatory Reform—that involved numerous WTO member delegates. The proceedings of those workshops were presented to the WPPS (see http://www.oecd.org/oecd/pages/home/displaygeneral/0,3380,EN-document-0-nondirectorate-no-9-16887-0,FF,html).

22. Technical standards also include codes of ethics.

23. See, in particular, the list of measures in paragraph 2 of Article XVI.

24. This might result, however, from the absence of legal obligation on members for the moment. Assuming that the approval of the Disciplines by consensus meant that members agreed that this was the correct way to regulate the sector, there is nevertheless no objective reason why they would have to wait until the Disciplines enter into force to adjust their domestic regulation.

25. This hypothesis is being tested by the WPDR. To date, all the responses to that question received from members confirm that no significant modification to the text of the Disciplines would be necessary to extend their applicability to other professional service sectors, and that confirms the views expressed in the previous paragraph. See WTO (2000a, c, d, e, 2001b, e, f, g, i).

26. Article X of the GATS.

27. Article XIII of the GATS.

28. Article XV of the GATS.

29. The last sentence of paragraph 15 of the Ministerial Declaration (WTO 2001j), adopted at the end of the third WTO Ministerial Conference held in Doha, Qatar, in November 2001, reads: "Participants shall submit initial requests for specific commitments by 30 June 2002 and initial offers by 31 March 2003."

30. On the most significant barriers to international trade in accountancy services, see also WTO (1995a), paragraphs 79 to 81, and the work of the OECD on liberalizing trade in professional services (in particular, for the workshop held September 26–27, 1994).

31. WTO 2000f.

32. WTO 2001a.

33. WTO 2000b.

34. WTO 2001c.

35. WTO 2001h.

36. WTO 2001d.

37. WTO 2000f, paragraph 6.

38. Most intracorporate temporary movement at present takes place between Organisation for Economic Co-operation and Development countries, and would be at much higher levels if visa, work permit, and other restrictions were eased.

39. Negotiations on the movement of natural persons are wrongly considered by many members of WTO to be a purely North–South issue. As shown in this chapter, that perception is too narrow.

40. On this issue, see the proceedings of the Organisation for Economic Co-operation and Development's third workshop on the liberalization of professional services, held February 20–21, 1997, particularly the chapter on Restrictions on Ownership and Investment and Alternative Approaches.

41. Trolliet 1995.

42. Fourth and seventh company law directives, bank accounts directive, insurance accounts directive, and so forth.

43. Eighth company law directive.

44. Directives 89/48 and 92/51.

45. This corresponds to the option chosen by member states when implementing the general system of mutual recognition of diplomas in the accountancy sector, not the provisions of the directives. For a detailed analysis of the system and its various options, see Trolliet (1995), paragraphs 401 to 643.

46. 93/C 334/03.

47. C-106/91 (Ramrath). For a detailed analysis of the case, see Trolliet (1995), paragraphs 754 to 827.

48. Cairns 2000.

49. Because the reservations with respect to the movement of persons are well known, they are not dealt with in this chapter.

50. ROSC forms part of the joint IMF/World Bank Financial Sector Assessment Program (FSAP).

51. This cross-sectoral comparison was carried out by the Joint Forum of the three organizations.

52. Given objective differences with the securities, banking, and insurance sectors.

53. The United Kingdom was the last member state to follow that route. The external Accountancy Foundation is now assuming responsibility for the regulatory tasks previously performed by the professional bodies.

54. WTO (1998c), paragraph 2.

55. For information about various possible ways of analyzing the scope of practice of accountants, see WTO (1995a), paragraphs 12–17.

56. WTO 1991.

References

Cairns, D. 2000. "International Accounting Standards Survey 2000." <www.cairns.co.uk>

European Commission. 1997. "Panorama of the EU Industry, Accountancy Services, NACE 836." Brussels.

Trolliet C. 1994. "L'exercice de la profession comptable dans la CEE." Editions Comptables Malesherbes. (Available in French only.)

―――. 1995. "Etude critique du processus de libéralisation de la profession comptable dans l'Union Européenne." Université de La Rochelle (France). Unpublished doctoral thesis. (Available in French only.)

WTO (World Trade Organization). 1991. "Services Sectoral Classification List: Note by the Secretariat." MTN.GNS/W/120, July 10.

———. 1995a. "The Accountancy Sector: Note by the Secretariat." S/WPPS/W/2, June 27.

———. 1995b. "Communication from the European Communities and Their Member States: Current Community System on the Recognition of Professional Qualifications Held by Members of the Accountancy Profession, Who Are Nationals of EC Member States." S/WPPS/W/3, October 17.

———. 1995c. "Communication from the OECD: Work in the Area of Professional Services." S/WPPS/W/4, with Addenda 1 and 2, November 14.

———. 1995d. "Communication from UNCTAD: Work of ISAR in the Area of Accountancy Services." S/WPPS/W/5, November 14.

———. 1995e. "Decision on Professional Services, Adopted by the Council for Trade in Services on 1 March 1995." S/L/3, April 4.

———. 1996a. "Communication from UNCTAD: Regulation of the Accountancy Profession in Developing Countries and Countries in Transition." S/WPPS/W/8, August 12.

———. 1996b. "Ministerial Declaration." WT/MIN(96)/DEC, December 18.

———. 1996c. "Mutual Recognition Agreements in the Accountancy Sector: Note by the Secretariat." S/WPPS/W/10, September 13.

———. 1996d. "Questionnaire on the Accountancy Sector: Note by the Secretariat." S/WPPS/W/7, with 29 Addenda, April 3.

———. 1996e. "The Relevance of the Disciplines of the Agreements on Technical Barriers to Trade (TBT) and on Import Licensing Procedures to Article VI.4 of the General Agreement on Trade in Services: Note by the Secretariat." S/WPPS/W/9, September 11.

———. 1997a. "Guidelines for Mutual Recognition Agreements or Arrangements in the Accountancy Sector." S/L/38, May 28.

———. 1997b. "Synthesis of the Responses to the Questionnaire on the Accountancy Sector: Note by the Secretariat." S/WPPS/W/11, May 5.

———. 1998a. "Decision on Disciplines Relating to the Accountancy Sector, Adopted by the Council for Trade in Services on 14 December 1998." S/L/63, December 15.

———. 1998b. "Disciplines on Domestic Regulation in the Accountancy Sector, Adopted by the Council for Trade in Services on 14 December 1998." S/L/64, December 17.

———. 1998c. "Accountancy Services: Background Note by the Secretariat." S/C/W/73, December 4.

———. 2000a. "Communication from the European Communities and Their Member States: Applicability of the Disciplines on Domestic Regulation in the Accountancy Sector to Other Professional Services." S/WPDR/W/5, May 19.

———. 2000b. "Communication from the European Communities and Their Member States: GATS 2000: Professional Services." S/CSS/W/33, December 22.

———. 2000c. "Communication from Hong Kong, China: Disciplines on Domestic Regulation for Professional Services; Result of Consultation with Professional Sectors." S/WPDR/W/3, April 28.

———. 2000d. "Communication from Poland: Disciplines on Domestic Regulation for Professional Services; Result of Consultation with Professional Sectors." S/WPDR/W/7, May 23.

———. 2000e. "Communication from the Republic of Korea: Disciplines on Domestic Regulation for Professional Services; Results of Consultation with Professional Sectors." S/WPDR/W/10, October 2.

———. 2000f. "Communication from the United States: Accounting Services." S/CSS/W/20, December 18.

———. 2001a. "Communication from Australia: Negotiating Proposal for Accountancy Services." S/CSS/W/62, March 28.

———. 2001b. "Communication from Canada: Disciplines on Domestic Regulation for Professional Services; Results of Consultations with Professional Sectors." S/WPDR/W/13, March 16.

———. 2001c. "Communication from Canada: Initial Negotiating Proposal on Professional Services." S/CSS/W/52, March 14.

———. 2001d. "Communication from Colombia: Professional Services." S/CSS/W/98, July 9.

———. 2001e. "Communication from Japan: Report of the Results of Research on Professional Services." S/WPDR/W/6, May 19.

———. 2001f. "Communication from Mexico: Disciplines on Domestic Regulation for Professional Services; Progress Regarding Consultations with Professional Sectors." S/WPDR/W/12, March 9.

———. 2001g. "Communication from Switzerland: Applicability of the Disciplines on Domestic Regulation in the Accountancy Sector to Other Professional Services." S/WPDR/W/16, September 4.

———. 2001h. "Communication from Switzerland: GATS 2000: Professional Services." S/CSS/W/75, May 4.

———. 2001i. "Communication from Thailand: Results of Consultation on the Applicability of Accountancy Disciplines to Other Professions." S/WPDR/W/18, September 28.

———. 2001j. "Ministerial Declaration: Adopted on 14 November 2001." WT/MIN(01)DEC/1, November 20.

10

STRENGTHENING WTO MEMBER COMMITMENTS IN ENERGY SERVICES: PROBLEMS AND PROSPECTS

Peter C. Evans

Executive Summary

Energy services have become a growing part of international trade but are not well represented in global trade agreements. A core group of World Trade Organization (WTO) members have recently begun the process of bringing energy services more fully under the General Agreement on Trade in Services (GATS) disciplines as part of a commitment to continue services trade liberalization negotiations following the Uruguay Round. In most countries, domestic regulations unnecessarily impede the gains that can arise from open and nondiscriminatory trade in energy-related services, with detrimental effects for economic growth, innovation, and the supply of cleaner and more efficient energy. This chapter examines the issues and prospects for deepening trade commitments in energy services in the WTO. It reviews the types of barriers that confront firms engaged in international energy trade and investment and explores how those barriers can be addressed through new or strengthened regulatory disciplines and market access commitments

under the GATS while responding to the specificities of the energy sector.

Energy services have become a growing part of international trade but are not well represented in global trade agreements. Unlike telecommunications or financial services, energy services were not taken up by World Trade Organization (WTO) members and negotiated as a separate sector during the Uruguay Round. At the time, a small number of countries made commitments in energy services; however, those commitments were limited and largely restricted to oil field services and mining. Few, if any, commitments were made in services related to electricity or natural gas, even though they constitute a substantial part of the energy sector. This has meant that most energy services are only subject to the general obligations of the WTO's GATS and not to its market access and national treatment provisions. They are also not subject to additional measures that countries could negotiate to enhance trade and competition, such as third-party access to essential facilities and independent regulation.

Portions of this chapter draw on work published (2002) in *Liberalizing Global Trade in Energy Services*. Washington, D.C.: The American Enterprise Institute Press. Reproduced with special thanks and acknowledgment to the series editor, Claude Barfield, and the AEI Press.

A core group of WTO members began the process of bringing energy services more fully under the GATS disciplines as part of a commitment to continue services trade liberalization negotiations following the Uruguay Round.[1] These talks were folded into the Doha Development Agenda launched in November 2001, which set forth the objectives for new global trade negotiations. Although the negotiations on energy are still in the preliminary stages, the priority now accorded to the sector suggests that countries are beginning to focus more seriously on how multilateral disciplines can remove restrictions on market access and enhance the conditions for competition in the supply of energy services. In most countries, domestic regulations unnecessarily impede the gains that can arise from open and nondiscriminatory trade in energy-related services, with detrimental effects for economic growth, innovation, and the supply of cleaner and more efficient energy.

This chapter examines the issues and prospects for deepening trade commitments in energy services in the WTO. It reviews the types of barriers that confront firms engaged in international energy trade and investment and explores how those barriers can be addressed through WTO disciplines. Far-reaching changes have taken place in the last 15 years as a result of the shift from government planning for and control of energy toward greater competition and private sector ownership and investment. Although these developments have helped expand international trade in energy services, domestic regulations continue to create unnecessary and costly impediments to the supply of energy services on a competitive, nondiscriminatory basis. The GATS provides a framework for countries to dismantle these barriers, but the framework is not ready-made or sufficiently tailored to the specific characteristics of energy markets for this task. As the trade community has begun to realize, measures are needed to clarify the existing GATS classification system and develop additional commitments relevant to the energy sector, including disciplines for third-party access to essential facilities, regulatory transparency, competition safeguards, and independent regulation. Also discussed are a number of additional issues associated with deepening energy services trade commitments, including the right of governments to pursue environmental protection, energy efficiency,

energy security, and other public policy objectives, and what, if any, special provisions may be needed regarding developing countries, emergency safeguards, and government procurement.

Energy Market Liberalization

The regulatory regime governing energy markets in both industrial and developing countries has experienced significant change since the mid-1980s. Regulatory frameworks that seek to encourage competition and private sector ownership and investment have increasingly replaced heavy market controls and government ownership. Among industrial countries, these changes were motivated by a fundamental shift in government attitudes toward regulation stemming from the poor performance of state-owned energy companies, growing subsidy burdens, and regulatory incentive structures that stimulated costly over-investment (Jaccard 1995). In the developing world, many of these factors were also present but were compounded by the pressures created by the debt crisis and severe capital shortages. Adjusting regulatory frameworks for energy has been widely embraced as a way to attract greater private sector investment, improve efficiency, and boost overall economic performance.

One of the most pervasive changes has taken place in ownership patterns. Major privatizations have occurred across energy sectors (oil, gas, power) and have involved firms in industrial as well as developing countries. Canada, Finland, France, Italy, and the United Kingdom were among the first to privatize their state oil companies. Gas distribution companies have also been opened to the private sector not only in Europe and North America but also among developing countries. Between 1990 and 1997, 26 developing countries introduced private participation in the transmission and distribution of natural gas (Izaguirre 1999). In the case of electric power, privatizations through public share issues, management or employee buyouts, franchise concessions, and direct sales of an equity stake in a state-owned enterprise to private investors have taken place throughout the world, including Africa, Asia, Europe, Latin America, and North America (Pollitt 1997).

In addition to shifting ownership patterns, the regulatory regime for energy has experienced a major reduction in price controls and import restrictions. The oil industry was among the first to benefit. With fewer price controls and other trading restrictions, both buyers and sellers found that they could gain by shopping around for the best deals on upstream supply. Spot markets grew in scope until they eventually established crude oil as a global commodity with trading centers emerging in Antwerp-Rotterdam-Amsterdam, London, New York, and Singapore (Horsnell and Mabro 1993). Active spot and futures trading markets spawned the development of derivatives and other financial vehicles that helped eliminate price differentials among regions, improve price transparency, and reduce price volatility and risk for different types of crude oil and downstream products, such as naphtha, heating oil, and gasoline. More recently trading has become prevalent in the natural gas and electric power industries.

Approaches to regulating gas and power markets also have undergone reform. In many countries opportunities have been introduced for domestic and foreign firms to sell power to state or private utility monopolies, which act as a "single buyer" (monopsony) purchaser of electricity for resale to end-use customers. Encouraging new capacity additions through competitive bidding mechanisms represented a way to ensure that power was procured at the lowest cost. These reforms led to a surge in power projects developed and financed by independent power producers (IPPs). Under these arrangements IPPs generally sell their output through long-term power purchase agreements that include take-or-pay conditions or fixed capacity charges to protect investors from market risk. Since the mid-1990s a growing number of countries have taken further steps to introduce competition by opening up opportunities for direct retail sales of gas and electricity, particularly in the industrial sector, and by creating the institutional and regulatory environment for competitive pools and direct bilateral contracting.[2] One result of these reforms is that much new power plant capacity has been built and is owned by IPPs rather than by traditional state-run utilities.

International trade in energy services has the potential to accelerate as underlying growth in world energy demand increases over the next decade. For example, demand for field services will expand in the coming years with rising oil demand.

The International Energy Agency (IEA) expects total world oil demand to grow by more than 25 percent over the current decade, rising from 76 million barrels a day in 2000 to 97 million barrels per day in 2010. Most of this new drilling activity will take place in Africa, the Caspian region, Latin America, and Russia.[3] Similar expansion could occur in services associated with the gas and power sectors.[4] More open gas and electricity markets will increase the need for a variety of services, including intermediaries such as brokers and marketers who can facilitate transactions between buyers and sellers of gas and electricity. Other energy services such as those associated with transportation and transmission and pipeline networks are likely to increase.

Barriers to Energy Trade and Investment

The degree to which trade in energy services grows hinges significantly on progress in eliminating restrictions on market access and other domestic regulatory barriers. Expanding international trade in energy services has the potential to yield significant economic benefits in lower prices, greater innovation, and cleaner and more efficient energy supply. However, barriers continue to hamper energy service providers in most countries. Several examples will illustrate the range of barriers that can be found among the different ways in which energy services are provided.

One set of barriers hinders the ability of companies to provide services across borders. For example, French companies have relatively unimpeded access to the German and British gas and electricity markets, but access in the other direction is not so open. A similar situation arises in the electricity markets between the Canada and the United States. Canadian energy companies have significant cross-border supply access to most states in the United States, but U.S. power providers face market access restrictions in British Columbia, Quebec, and other provinces. Another form of cross-border restriction concerns the entry of equipment and tools needed for production or maintenance services. This affects a variety of energy service providers, but has been particularly harmful to oil field service providers who depend on the ability to move seismic testing equipment, oil rigs, and other specialized equipment from one country to another.

In many cases establishing a local presence in a foreign country is the most efficient and effective way to supply energy services. However, companies often face a variety of establishment restrictions that can render these efforts noncompetitive or completely disallowed. A common form of restriction is associated with foreign ownership. Firms seeking to retain full ownership of their operations may be barred from establishing a local presence unless they join with a local joint-venture partner. Mergers and acquisitions may be restricted by rules that only allow minority foreign ownership. Certain segments of the market may be closed to foreign firms. These trade barriers and discriminatory practices affect all segments of the energy industry including oil, gas and power, mining, and construction.

The ability of energy companies to dispatch executives, technicians, and other specialists to foreign countries is essential to delivering energy services. However, countries often restrict the temporary entry of skilled people and managers. This is typically achieved by imposing unclear or discriminatory rules for multiple-entry visas and the period that managers and other professionals may stay in the country. In some cases temporary entry depends on a person passing local examinations or other tests before being recognized as a professional or specialist. In other cases services provided by self-employed people are not permitted.

The regulatory process in a host country may also hinder foreign participation in energy markets on equal terms. Opaque or discriminatory administrative decisionmaking can create barriers that unfairly disadvantage foreign suppliers, particularly because many energy projects and associated services require extensive licensing or permitting. A few countries have administrative rules that require regulatory agencies to consider input about regulatory measures from all affected parties, including foreign parties. However, many do not. Energy companies regularly face situations in which countries fail to promptly disclose new or revised regulations and exclude affected foreign parties from regulatory deliberations. Although these conditions are a fact of life that most companies operating internationally have come to accept as a part of the business environment, regulatory uncertainty and lack of transparency ultimately undermine compe-

tition and raise the cost of international trade in energy services.

Another potentially discriminatory measure that is gaining attention is associated with renewable portfolio standards. An increasing number of countries have introduced or plan to create incentives for inducing levels of renewable energy technologies that are higher than those supplied in a purely competitive context. Establishing certain mandatory portfolio requirements (numerical quotas) obliges electricity suppliers to produce a certain percentage of electricity generated from renewable energy. Governments may also issue certificates for the amount of renewable electricity generated, which can be traded in secondary markets. Producers who do not meet the minimum standard or hold a sufficient number of certificates face penalties (Espey 2001). Mandatory portfolio standards can impede trade if they tend to favor local products from specific regions and states and de facto exclude imports from eligibility.

By far the largest barrier facing international trade in energy services arises from the lack of structural reforms. This is particularly salient in the case of the network-based industries of gas and electricity. Energy service providers need both nondiscriminatory access to transmission and distribution systems and the right to sell to eligible customers. In the case of natural gas, brokers negotiate with transmission companies for transportation based on their ability to switch their gas from pipeline to pipeline through market hubs to destination. They can only provide this service if third-party access is guaranteed and consumer choice has been established. The right to sell to eligible customers has little meaning without access to essential facilities. Likewise, the right to access essential facilities will not foster competition without a clear right to sell to eligible customers.

There continues to be broad variation across countries regarding these market access terms and conditions. For example, in Europe there is significant variation in the degree of market opening among countries despite ongoing efforts to establish a unified market for gas and power (see table 10.1). In the case of electric power, a few countries have granted full choice to retail customers (Finland, Germany, Norway, Sweden, and the United Kingdom) and others have followed only the minimum requirements of the European Union direc-

TABLE 10.1   Gas and Power Liberalization among European Countries

| Country | Electric Power Reform Measures | | Market Opening in 2000 | |
	Transmission Grid Access Model	Type of Vertical Unbundling	Gas (%)	Power (%)
Austria	Regulated TPA + SB	Management	50	32
Belgium	Regulated TPA	Legal	47	35
Denmark	Regulated TPA	Legal	30	90
Finland	Regulated TPA + Pool	Ownership	90	100
France	Regulated TPA	Management	20	30
Germany	Negotiated TPA	Management	100	100
Greece	Negotiated TPA	—	—	30
Ireland	Regulated TPA	Management	75	30
Italy	Regulated TPA + SB	Legal	65	35
Luxembourg	Regulated TPA	Management	51	40
Netherlands	Regulated TPA	Legal	45	33
Norway	Regulated TPA + Pool	Ownership	—	100
Portugal	Regulated TPA + SB	Legal	—	30
Spain	Regulated TPA + Pool	Ownership	72	54
Sweden	Regulated TPA + Pool	Ownership	47	100
United Kingdom	Regulated TPA + Pool	Ownership	100	100

— Not available.
Note: TPA = Third Party Access, SB = Single Buyer.
Sources: Commission of European Communities 2001; IEA/OECD 2000.

tive. A similar pattern has emerged in the case of gas. The gas directive established progressive market opening beginning with a minimum of 20 percent in 2000 growing to 28 percent in 2003. Although most countries have exceeded these requirements, several—most notably France—have only met the bare minimum of the directive. Similar variation exists in the approach to transmission access and type of vertical unbundling. In practice this has meant that some markets in Europe are far more open and competitive than others (Stern 1998, Percebois 1999).

The competitive bottleneck created by monopoly control of Japan's 23 liquefied natural gas (LNG) terminals provides another example of how the structural features of markets can restrict trade and investment. Japan's vertically integrated power and gas utility monopolies built, own, and operate the terminals, tanks, and regasification equipment associated with these facilities, which receive nearly all of the country's gas supplies. A handful of companies control over 96 percent of the gas available in Japan (only 3 percent is produced domestically), and the ability to block competitors from accessing these facilities. Given the advantages of gas as a fuel

and its importance in power generation, the inability to gain access to Japan's LNG terminals has severely hampered new entry in both the gas and electricity sectors and has become a point of contention in bilateral trade talks.[5]

The cost of barriers to trade and discriminatory practices in energy services is difficult to determine. No economic studies have attempted to estimate the economic costs of barriers to trade in energy services in any comprehensive manner. Available data on trade in energy services are limited. Statistical reporting among domestic and international energy and trade bodies reflects the legacy of the vertically integrated energy industry and an emphasis on physical flows. Because services were generally bundled within integrated firms—and continue to be so in many countries—there has been little price transparency along the energy value chain. Still, the theoretical case for liberalizing is strong; where it exists, the empirical evidence suggests that much can be gained by opening markets to greater competition. The large size of the global business turnover of energy products worth approximately US$2.4 trillion[6] in 2000 alone suggests that even small improvements may offer significant welfare gains for both industrial and developing countries.

Energy Services and the GATS

The GATS provides a framework through which WTO member countries can work toward removing these and other barriers to international trade and investment in energy services. The framework agreement identifies different "modes" of supply through which countries are encouraged to make commitments in addition to various general obligations to which all GATS members must subscribe. It also identifies areas in which countries can make specific commitments, most notably on market access and national treatment. The significance and relevance of these provisions to energy services are discussed below. However, the existing GATS framework is not without limitations. Among other issues, there is a need to clarify the ambiguity surrounding the existing classification system and definitional issues, particularly regarding electricity.

GATS Modes of Supply Relevant to Energy

Three of the four modes of supply defined by the GATS are relevant to energy. Mode 1 covers services that are supplied cross-border but do not require the physical movement of the supplier or consumer. The category would include cross-border transit or interconnection rights associated with oil and gas pipelines and electric power transmission. Mode 2 has less relevance to energy services. It covers consumption abroad, as with a consumer traveling to the supplying country for services such as tourism and education and consumers traveling to a supply, as well as work such as the repair of aircraft or ships outside of an owner's home country. Mode 3 is highly relevant to energy. It covers services that require establishment of a local presence. This covers a wide range of energy services, such as seismic surveying, energy efficiency auditing, energy marketing, or any number of other activities that can only be reasonably supplied through physical, commercial presence in a foreign country. Mode 4 is also relevant to energy in that it covers the temporary entry and stay of those providing services. This category concerns visa terms and conditions, examination requirements, and other

regulations that can affect the ability of managers, consultants, or technicians with specialized skills to move in and out of a country in the course of normal business.

The four modes were developed when the GATS was developed as a way for countries to organize and schedule their market access and national treatment commitments. Liberalization is more likely achieved when countries make commitments across all the relevant modes; however, they are under no obligation to do so. The GATS provides countries the freedom to choose the modes in which they will make commitments. They may make commitments in energy services across all of the relevant modes or selectively choose among them. A country might choose to make commitments on cross-border supply (mode 1) and temporary movement of natural persons (mode 4), but not commit to the right of establishment (mode 3).

GATS General Obligations

The GATS contains more than a dozen general obligations. Two of the most important are most-favored-nation (MFN) treatment and transparency. GATS members must meet those general obligations, with certain caveats and exceptions. The general MFN obligation (Article II) seeks to avoid discrimination among trading partners by requiring that commitments apply equally to services and service providers from all other member countries. Countries can make exemptions but those are subject to negotiations and should last no longer than 10 years.[7] Thereafter, countries must seek a waiver, which must be approved by three-quarters of WTO members.

The second general obligation is transparency (Article III). No exemptions are permitted; the obligation, however, largely concerns post hoc notification. Governments must publish all laws, regulations, and administrative guidelines relevant to services trade, and countries must respond to requests from other member governments to provide regulatory information applicable to the operation of the GATS. Members notify the WTO on an annual basis of new laws, regulations, and administrative guidelines affecting sectors in which member countries have specific commitments. In practice, however, the content of those notifications has varied greatly from country to country, with some being quite specific and others very general (Thompson and Iida 2001). In its current form the GATS imposes no obligation on countries to consider input from affected parties, including foreign parties, about regulatory measures. It also does not constrain countries from disclosing new or revised regulations at the last minute or excluding affected foreign parties from regulatory deliberations. Creating an across-the-board, or horizontal, discipline and improving transparency through prior notification has been proposed; however, it remains unclear whether WTO members will agree to incorporate such a measure into the GATS in the near future (Iida and Nielson 2001).

Two additional general obligations concern domestic regulation and monopoly service providers. In regard to domestic regulation, Article VI states that "each Member shall ensure that all measures of general application affecting trade in services are administered in a reasonable, objective and impartial manner." Members must have judicial or administrative bodies and procedures that provide timely review and appropriate remedies for government decisions affecting trade in services. The article stops short of calling for independent regulation, but states simply that WTO members "shall ensure that the procedures in fact provide for an objective and impartial review." All provisions regarding domestic regulation apply only to those sectors for which specific commitments have been made.

Another, if limited, set of obligations concerns monopoly and exclusive suppliers. The GATS permits countries to maintain and even create new monopoly service providers, but seeks to ensure that they do not abuse their market power or compete unfairly by operating beyond the scope of their exclusive rights, and thus possibly undermine specific commitments (Article VIII). In addition, Article IX recognizes that certain business practices may restrain competition and consequently restrict trade. To address this concern, the GATS requires members to consult with one another to eliminate such restrictive practices. No obligations concern the scope and enforcement of policy rules about competition. Equally significant for the energy industry, no general provisions address third-party access to networks or other essential facilities (Melly 2001).

GATS Specific Commitments: Market Access and National Treatment

In addition to the general obligations that apply to WTO members in all service sectors, the GATS includes provisions for specific commitments. The basic GATS framework lists two: market access (Article XVI) and national treatment (Article XVII). Those disciplines come into effect only when they are explicitly listed in a country's schedule of specific commitments, a document appended to the GATS for each WTO member with the member's specific and additional commitments made during or after the Uruguay Round negotiations. The process reflects the so-called positive list approach at the core of the GATS goal of creating more open service markets. Articles XVI and XVII do not apply unless a country has positively affirmed that the sector will be bound by those disciplines.

Energy service providers operating internationally value commitments to market access because they clarify the rights of foreign firms and provide legal standing in a trade dispute. Article XVI lists measures commonly used to restrict market access and asks countries to eliminate these practices. By making a commitment, countries indicate that they will refrain from market access restrictions that impose limits on (a) the number of service suppliers permitted, (b) the value of transactions or assets, (c) total service output, (d) the number of business persons or specialists that may be employed, (e) measures that restrict or require specific types of legal entity or joint venture through which a service supplier may supply a service, and (f) limitations on the use of foreign capital, such as limits on foreign share–holding or the total value of foreign investment.

Another specific commitment concerns the principle of national treatment defined as treatment no less favorable than that accorded to similar domestic services and service providers. The commitment is valuable in trade terms because it would impose an obligation on countries to refrain from maintaining or imposing discriminatory practices that disadvantage foreign service providers. It also establishes a means of recourse to foreign energy service providers if they are denied equal treatment in the licensing process, taxation, and other regulatory matters.

Few countries made energy-related market access or national treatment commitments through the GATS during the Uruguay Round.[8] Only three countries—Australia, Hungary, and New Zealand—made commitments in pipeline transportation of fuels (a subsector of transport services). Eight countries made specific commitments covering services incidental to energy distribution, but a number of them defined this narrowly to mean consultancy services. Only two (Australia and the United States) of the eight making commitments in that area were Organisation for Economic Co-operation and Development (OECD) countries. More countries made commitments in services incidental to mining, that is, services supplied on a fee or contract basis in oil and gas fields, including drilling, derrick construction, repair and dismantling services, and casing services. Thirty-three members made commitments in that area but 11 of those limited their commitments to advisory or consulting services. With its access to the WTO, China recently made limited commitments in this area, but foreign providers can engage in onshore oil field services only in cooperation with China National Petroleum Corp. and only in designated areas approved by the Chinese government.

Other commitments associated with energy were made largely in construction and retail trade. Forty-six countries made commitments regarding general construction for civil engineering. This area covers long-distance pipelines, communications and power transmission lines, local pipelines, and cables. Thirty countries included energy in their wholesale and retail trade services. In wholesale trade this included solid, liquid, and gaseous fuels and related products; in retail trade, fuel oil, bottled gas, coal, and wood.

Expanding the limited number of specific commitments made during the Uruguay Round would considerably deepen coverage in energy services. The GATS, however, provides members with significant latitude to make exceptions and limitations on specific commitments. Presumably, Articles XVI and XVII would apply to a sector added to the schedule, but countries may make exceptions if they are clearly spelled out in their schedule (i.e., not simply listing a law or measure that contains provisions inconsistent with its trade commitments but indicating the specific provisions that are inconsistent). The process of taking exceptions is sometimes referred to as negative listing. Opportunities to limit actual commitments abound within the GATS framework. Nevertheless, the obligations to list exceptions clearly can contribute toward removing trade restrictions by forcing countries to publish discriminatory measures for all to see.

Ambiguity of Energy Classifications and Definitions

The WTO services sector classification list (W/120) was developed to help GATS signatories schedule commitments. The classification system, however, does not clearly represent energy services. Energy services were not identified as a separate division when the classification system was devised. At the time, state-owned monopolies operating within national or regional markets dominated the energy sector, and oil and gas companies and electric power utilities—whether public or private—internally supplied the breadth of energy services activities that emerged since market liberalization. The limitations in the descriptions of energy services found in the United Nation's provisional central product classification (UNCPC) mirror the limitations of the W/120. The limitations are problematic because the UNCPC is supposed to provide the corresponding central product classification (CPC) number that WTO members are to use to indicate an offer or commitment in each sector or subsector (WTO 2001a).

The ambiguity of the classification system impedes negotiations about energy services. In the three cases in which energy services appear in the W/120, they are listed as part of other generic service entries. Pipeline transportation of fuels is covered as a subsector, "transport services." Technical testing and analysis, mining services, maintenance and repair of equipment, and energy distribution services are found under "other business services." When energy services are not explicitly mentioned, where they should fall in the classification system is either uncertain or a matter of dispute.

Recognizing that the energy services negotiations are unlikely to produce meaningful results until the classification system is clarified, Canada, Chile, the European Union, Japan, Norway, the United States, and the República Bolivariana de Venezuela began meeting in October 2001 to rectify the problem. Despite some progress at periodic meetings, the group has yet to resolve several outstanding issues. The task is not simple, given the complexity of the energy industry and its logical overlap with many other sectors. The stakes are also high because the way energy services are classified can influence the terms and content of the subsequent negotiation process. As a result countries have used the clarification exercise as a way to secure their favored negotiation outcome.

At least four issues must be addressed. One issue concerns the organization of the W/120. The United States originally proposed creating a separate division within the W/120, with new categories for energy not clearly identified within the CPC. The three existing categories would be moved in their entirety to the new heading. The proposal aimed to create clearer and more commercially relevant listings and to place previously unlisted energy services categories under the new heading. Substantially changing the existing W/120, however, has met with resistance from other member countries. Canada has expressed concern that changes could affect existing commitments. Others have pointed to the additional time and confusion that could be involved in gaining the acceptance of the large number of WTO members who have not yet begun to focus on the energy services sector. Still others have argued that even if not specifically identified, energy services are already included because the CPC covers all products and services. Consequently the group's attention has shifted to clarifying where energy service activities may be found within the existing classification structure even though that placement is a less elegant and user-friendly solution.

Another issue is how broadly to define the scope of energy services. Determining the boundaries of the industry is difficult because energy services are often bundled with other activities, such as environmental, financial, transportation, legal, engineering, construction, safety, and research and development. One potential solution is to create core and noncore designations or what is sometimes referred to as a core-and-cluster approach.[9] This approach would list energy in terms of direct energy services (e.g., exploration and extraction) coupled with their associated services (e.g., engineering services, environmental services, and so forth). The method has the advantage of being highly inclusive with less risk that certain types of

services would not be covered by the GATS. Conversely the approach could complicate the classification system and create duplicate entries. Countries discussing classification issues are leaning toward creating a checklist of core and related energy services.

A related issue concerns what sectors are identified as important and relevant to negotiations on energy services. A pertinent example is energy-related shipping services. Given the importance and size of energy-related shipping, some countries (such as Norway) are likely to press for their inclusion in the scope of talks on energy services. The United States is likely to resist such moves and argue that maritime transport is not relevant to the energy services negotiations and, if taken up at all, should be part of separate maritime talks. This position reflects strong domestic political pressure to maintain cabotage restrictions, which prohibit the use of non–national flag vessels to transport cargo within the national jurisdiction. The Jones Act restricts waterborne shipments of goods between U.S. ports to ships that are built, owned, and crewed by Americans and therefore prevents foreign flag vessels from carrying oil and oil products between U.S. ports but also from serving as transport for offshore oil platforms developed by U.S. companies.

A third issue concerns how detailed to make the classifications. All countries agree that greater detail is necessary to make the classification system more commercially relevant. But countries differ on the level of disaggregation. Japan has proposed general categories whereas Venezuela has been pressing for a high degree of disaggregation, particularly in the area of upstream oil and gas field services. In general an aggregated list tends to promote liberalization because it encourages broad commitments, whereas a disaggregated list makes it easier for countries to omit sectors or list detailed reservations while giving the appearance of committing to many activities.

The last and perhaps most challenging classification issue concerns electricity. At least two issues are at stake. One concerns the need to clarify the confusion that arises from the term *incidental* in the entry "services incidental to energy distribution." It is not clear if commitments based on that entry include electric power generators, brokers, and marketers, or only distributors. The original intent of this entry seems to have been those services, such as management, operation and repair of the network, and meter reading, necessary for transmitting and distributing electricity on a fee or contract basis.[10] At the time the classification was made, transmission and distribution of electricity were rarely undertaken on a fee or contract basis.

The best option may be simply to revise the entry so that it unequivocally includes the actual transmission and distribution of energy, which are now regularly carried out on a fee or contract basis. Because only eight countries made commitments in the area during the Uruguay Round, changing the entry may not be too disruptive. Those countries should be permitted to make revisions without penalty if the change expands any country's commitment. Correcting this ambiguity would make future country commitments in this area clearer and reduce the chance that the GATS would not recognize important energy services. The time and effort associated with such a clarification seems justified given the size and importance of the downstream electricity services.

The other issue arises from ambiguity over the definition of electricity. Electricity has the characteristics of both a good and a service. It may be considered a good in the sense that it is manufactured through the process of materially transforming fuels into electrons. It is a service in the sense that it cannot be stored and must be produced as it is consumed. The ambiguity may explain the different way in which electricity has been treated over time. During the first General Agreement on Tariffs and Trade (GATT) discussions in the late 1940s, negotiators concluded that electricity should not be classified as a commodity. Several countries later took out tariff bindings on electricity, however, suggesting that they considered electricity to be a good. In a further complication, the WTO Secretariat has noted that the World Custom Organization (WCO) harmonized commodity description and coding system has made electricity an optional heading so that countries are not required to classify it as a commodity for tariff purposes (WTO 1991).

A major issue at stake for the GATS negotiations on energy services is how WTO rules will treat the electric power generation sector. The liberalization of power markets has spawned an international IPP industry, responsible for building an increasing share of new electric power plant capacity additions worldwide. Which WTO rules apply to most segments of the electric power chain is reasonable. Fuels such as coal and oil are considered goods and are therefore subject to GATT rules. With the caveats noted above, activities downstream of generation, including transmission and distribution, are services subject to the GATS. But because of ambiguity, electricity produced by IPPs could be subject to GATT rules if electricity is considered a good, which implies that it is manufactured. GATT rules do not apply to enterprises but only to goods. IPPs could be excluded from market access and national treatment disciplines, which are only granted under the GATS. It could also limit coverage access to essential facilities if WTO members agree to establish such additional commitments.

The implications are considerable given the significance of the generation sector, which is the largest segment in the electricity supply chain, making up close to a half of all revenues in the applicable U.S. market. Aside from fuel, generation is the segment of the industry with the greatest potential for competition and has been the most subject to liberalization in recent years. In competitive markets IPPs perform both generation and trading/marketing activities. An IPP could establish two legal entities, one covering the generation business and the other covering its marketing-trading operations. In practice, however, the two activities are integrally linked. Without the generation function the marketing-trading function cannot be performed, and vice versa. Trade rules should conform to commercial practices. Business should not be forced to establish legal entities to conform to trade rules, particularly where the rules make little commercial sense.

An odd and less than ideal outcome would result if the structure of a particular power market determined which WTO rules applied to IPPs. Power plants built to serve a single customer—be they captive inside-the-fence plants or build-own-transfer projects with a single utility buyer—would fall under GATT rules. An IPP that sought to enter a competitive market where there are opportunities to sell output to multiple parties would be considered a trader and therefore subject to the GATS. An IPP developer would gain establishment rights (mode 3) and any additional protections such as third-party access rights that WTO members may agree on as part of the GATS negotiations on energy services. An IPP restricted to a single buyer, however, would not have those rights because no investment or network access provisions are associated with GATT rules. Without comprehensive protection for multilateral investment, bringing IPPs under the scope of GATS rules to the extent possible would be preferable to such treatment. Those rules are more encompassing and therefore could give IPPs a greater range of legal protections.

Clarifying classification issues is an important precondition to a successful GATS agreement on energy services. But other issues will also shape the outcome of the negotiations. As governments found with telecommunications, the general obligations and specific commitments contained in the basic GATS framework are not sufficient to reduce trade barriers associated with domestic regulation. To ensure a procompetitive, transparent, reasonable and nondiscriminatory regulatory environment requires that WTO members consider developing commitments specific to the energy sector, amended to country schedules as permitted by the GATS. The next section takes up the nature of these commitments and what they should cover.

Is an Energy Services Reference Paper Justified?

The most effective strategy for using the GATS to achieve liberalization in services is the subject of debate. The agreements on telecommunications and financial services arose from sector-specific negotiations that had generic elements but also established rules applicable only to those sectors. Some trade negotiators are concerned about relying on that approach in GATS negotiations. Fearing the potentially heavy transaction costs associated with a sector-by-sector approach and creating a confusing patchwork of commitments and obligations, they advocate greater reliance on disciplines that can be applied horizontally to all service sectors. Because the economic case for regulation in all service sectors springs from common underlying market failures (natural monopoly, asymmetric information, and various externalities), generic principles should be available to address those and thereby apply to all service sectors. Proponents of a horizontal approach

argue that it can reduce the cost and time associated with international negotiations, can avoid the tendency to focus on politically important sectors at the expenses of more encompassing agreements, and can lessen the likelihood that special interests will capture sector-specific negotiations (Mattoo 2000b).

A horizontal approach, however, may yield less, not more, liberalization. Facing uncertainty, governments rationally act conservatively when making commitments to principles that apply across the board to all service sectors. As a result governments may agree only to horizontal disciplines that are too broad to have much meaning or bite for a specific sector. General principles such as MFN, market access, and national treatment can be powerful tools in the cause of liberalization, but they should be buttressed, where necessary, by rules that reflect the characteristics of a specific sector. The development of specific rules is also more likely to elicit the concentrated effort among regulators, the industry, and other stakeholders necessary to move negotiations forward. Finally a horizontal approach assumes that all service sectors are equally important for economic growth and ripe for negotiation. Both assumptions are questionable. Given energy's fundamental role in driving modern economies, WTO members act reasonably when prioritizing sectors, with energy services high on the list.

GATS Article XVIII provides a means for countries to negotiate additional commitments not covered by the basic GATS framework. The provision grew from the recognition that MFN, market access, and national treatment disciplines were not necessarily sufficient to ensure the full benefits of trade liberalization. In the case of telecoms, the need for additional commitments resulted in a separate telecommunications reference paper that set forth additional obligations for WTO members. Creating meaningful disciplines for energy services requires a similar reference paper and/or annex for energy.

The provisions in the telecoms reference paper provide a basis for consideration but do not directly apply to energy. Four core areas are important to securing procompetitive regulatory reform, some going beyond the principles established for telecoms. The areas are third-party access to essential facilities, market transparency, competition safeguards, and independent regulation.

Third-Party Access to Essential Facilities

The right to interconnect is widely viewed as one of the most important competition safeguards in a network industry. The basic telecommunications agreement would have been far less meaningful without the provisions guaranteeing suppliers access to public telecommunications transport networks or services under nondiscriminatory terms. Establishing the right to interconnect will be no less important for the energy services agreement. But parallels between telecoms and energy are imperfect. The term *interconnection* and principles developed to support it in the telecoms reference paper are likely to be too restrictive for energy services. The set of principles for energy services must severely limit the ability of a major supplier to refuse access not only to electric power transmission and natural gas pipelines but also to other essential energy infrastructure. Depending on specific circumstances, essential energy infrastructure may include gas storage facilities, liquefied natural gas terminals, oil pipelines, and oil storage facilities.

In developing the appropriate language. trade negotiators may look to the "essential facility doctrine" as it has developed in the context of competition policy in the United States and more recently in Europe. For example, the facility must be shown to have monopoly characteristics that make it truly essential. It is not enough that suppliers seeking access be inconvenienced or bear some degree of economic loss as a result of refusal of access; it must be reasonably clear that an alternative to the facility is not feasible.[12] Because oil pipelines and oil storage facilities are more readily constructed by a competitor than is infrastructure like electric power transmission systems, it is reasonable to believe that they will less likely be affected by an essential facility provision. There may be reasonable business justifications for denying access, but the criteria that are established for this exception should be circumscribed to avoid creating a major loophole in the rules. Where access is provided it should be granted in a timely fashion at reasonable fees that reflect the cost of these facilities.

Establishing the basic legal right of third-party access to networks—whether on mandatory or on negotiated terms—is but the first step in ensuring competitive access. A variety of subsequent issues determine the cost, timing, and fairness of actually connecting to the network. One problem that has arisen in the United States is the gaming that takes place among developers to secure the most advantageous place in the interconnection "queue." The place in the queue is important because it can determine who bears the costs of systemwide upgrades, which can range from as little as US$100,000 to several million dollars. Another problem is associated with who conducts the interconnection study. In the best case the study should be undertaken by an independent party with no stake in the outcome. This often is not the case, particularly in markets where there is no independent system operator or other disinterested party with sufficient knowledge and expertise regarding network conditions. Another access issue concerns how interconnection prices are determined and then allocated. At present, there is little consensus across countries on the proper costing methods that should be used to determine these charges, even though pricing of interconnection can significantly affect the development of a competitive market. Although the GATS is not the place to resolve all of these issues, it can encourage governments to establish standardized interconnection policies.

Transparency

GATS-related transparency provisions set forth in Article III are largely procedural. They require the prompt publication of relevant measures; notification to the WTO of significant changes in laws, regulations or administrative guidelines; and establishment of channels of commitment for timely responses to information requests from other WTO members. Although these provisions are valuable, they are not sufficient. The transparency disciplines found in the telecoms annex and reference paper provide a starting point. WTO members should consider adopting a right of prior consultation on draft laws and regulations, with reasonable notice and time for comments.[13] Given the importance of licensing in the energy industry, similar standards should apply to ensure an efficient and fair system for siting, permitting, and constructing new (or retiring old or inefficient) power plants, pipelines, and other energy-related infrastructure.

But governments should not limit additional commitments to regulatory transparency. In addition to those measures, trade negotiators should consider developing language that would focus attention on the need for market transparency. In a competitive context, withholding, delaying, or demanding excessive fees for basic market information can distort competition as readily as physical constraints. All market participants need access to timely information on prices, transmission capacity, congestion, scheduled volumes, and other data relevant to efficient and fair business transactions. An energy services reference paper would be well served to include provisions that encourage governments to take proactive measures to ensure the free flow of timely information and establish industrywide technical standards.

Provisions to promote market transparency alongside regulatory transparency will have several benefits. The combination would contribute to the goal of improving market efficiency by reducing transaction costs and market distortions. It could also reduce the types of questionable energy trading practices that have precipitated regulatory investigations in the United States. And it could reduce the incentives that feed corruption in the energy sector (Salbu 1999). Creating official and transparent channels for providing information to market actors can be a major help in reducing the existing incentives to bribe officials to gain the information needed in the normal course of business.

Competition Safeguards

The process of liberalization has drawn attention to two forms of market power. One form is the potential for anticompetitive behavior associated with vertical integration. The incumbent may take advantage of its control over the network (be it pipelines or transmission grid) to favor more costly in-house supply with costs (plus a healthy margin) that can be recovered through the regulated business. One approach attempts to control undue market power by policing better the activities of dominant providers. But imperfect information and regulators' lack of political independence often compromise that approach. Another approach to controlling market power is through vertical unbundling. The structural solution is generally considered more effective because it removes many incentives and abilities of incumbent utilities to engage in anticompetitive behavior.

The telecoms reference paper offers an avenue for addressing potential abuse by dominant providers. These provisions emerged from the recognized need to prevent telecom suppliers from engaging in anticompetitive practices, either alone or with others. Specific examples identified in the agreement include (a) engaging in anticompetitive cross-subsidization, (b) use of information obtained from competitors through interconnection negotiations or other means with anticompetitive results, and (c) failure to make available technical information about essential facilities or other commercially relevant information for new entrants to provide their services in a timely fashion.

The provisions directly parallel competition in network-based segments of the energy industry and would greatly strengthen the legal foundation for trade in energy services. The telecoms reference paper, however, does not speak directly to cases in which a generator or marketer may use its market dominance to control prices. Market share among generators in many power markets remains highly concentrated despite liberalization (see figure 10.1). So-called horizontal market power has been an issue in a number of energy markets. Even without evidence of collusion, studies have shown that market players may be able to manipulate prices through their bidding behavior when competitive pools have been established. Studies of the British electricity spot market in the early 1990s, when just three generators controlled much of the market, found that generators were charging prices significantly higher than their observed marginal costs (Wolfram 1999). The giant price spikes experienced in 2000 and 2001 in the wholesale markets, particularly in California, have also raised the issue of price manipulation by generators and traders.

Perhaps language borrowed from the telecoms reference paper could address such anticompetitive outcomes by requiring countries to maintain "appropriate measures" to prevent major suppliers from engaging in anticompetitive practices. The combination of the vagueness of appropriate measures and specific issues raised by network access, however, weakens this provision so that it is ineffective in addressing the undue exercise of market power by market actors other than the network operator. Negotiations on energy services must consider whether additional disciplines are needed to address these concerns about competition.

FIGURE 10.1   Market Share Remains Concentrated in Many Markets

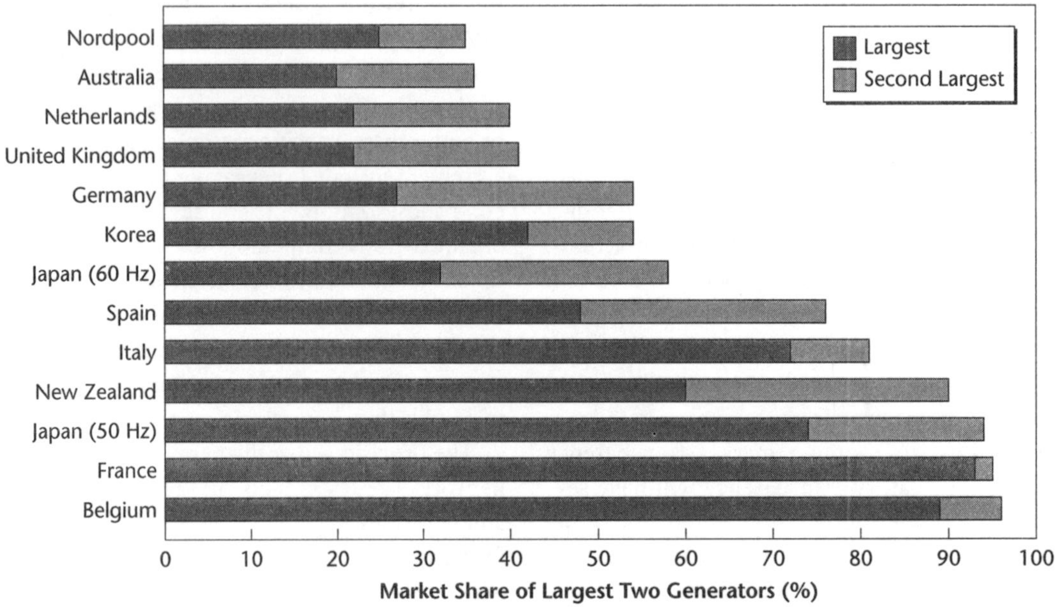

Note: The United States and Canada are not included because each is made up of various markets. The share in New Zealand was reduced to 53 percent in 1999. The share in the United Kingdom (England and Wales) was reduced to approximately 28 percent in 1999.
Source: IEA/OECD (2001a, p. 49).

Uncertainty over classifying complicates the issue. If electricity generation is not a service, then the GATS may not be the most effective place to seek a remedy.

Independent Regulation

The institutional structures that governments establish to regulate the energy sector vary widely from country to country (see table 10.2). In the 1990s privatization and the introduction of competition spurred a general trend toward the independent regulatory agency as the preferred model. Both the European Union (EU) electricity and gas directives require member states to establish an independent authority responsible for resolving disputes (Article 20). The developments have also encouraged the establishment of independent regulatory authorities in Argentina, Australia, Belgium, Brazil, Canada, Finland, France, Hungary, Ireland, the Netherlands, Norway, Poland, Portugal, Spain, Sweden, and the United Kingdom.

Certain characteristics of the energy industry make it particularly susceptible to rent seeking and

political interference. A great proportion of assets is sunk, technology exhibits important economies of scale, and customers generally fall into the same groups as voting populations. As a result, end-user energy pricing has long attracted the interest of politicians. The political sensitivity of prices and the inability of companies to move easily increase the risk of administrative expropriation: regulators, following public pressure or political expediency, may take actions that push prices below long-run average costs. The energy industry is full of examples of the struggle between regulatory attempts to extract those quasi-rents and industry attempts to fend them off (Spiller 1997).

Independent regulation is widely viewed as a way to reduce the problems raised by undue political interference. The OECD and the World Bank advise that policy functions and regulatory functions be separated and that procedures for transparency be enhanced (see World Bank 2001). Decisions removed from covert pressures are more likely to be made on the basis of the facts at hand rather than the influence of government, companies, or other parties. Experience suggests that reg-

TABLE 10.2 Institutions for Gas and Power Regulation in Selected Countries

Institutional Approach	Countries
Ministry and Independent Regulatory Agency and/or Dispute Resolution Agency	Argentina, Australia, Belgium, Brazil, Canada, Denmark, Finland, France, Greece, Hungary, Ireland, Mexico, Netherlands, Norway, Philippines, Poland, Portugal, Spain, Sweden, United Kingdom, United States
Energy or Industry Ministry	Austria, China, Czech Republic, Germany, Indonesia, Japan, New Zealand, Nigeria, Switzerland, Turkey, South Africa

Source: IEA/OECD (2001a, p. 32); and World Bank (2001).

ulatory decisionmaking can be improved if all communications and evidence submitted to the regulator are made public and if public hearings are conducted in a fair and impartial manner.

Negotiations on energy services offer an opportunity to reaffirm and codify the importance of independent regulation and transparency in the energy sector. In the case of telecoms, WTO members made independent regulators a requirement but did so without prejudice as to whether the regulator was separate from the ministry making telecom policy. That arrangement should be a minimum requirement in any agreement on energy services.

Additional Issues

The process of strengthening GATS disciplines for energy services raises additional issues that negotiators must address. The first concerns developing countries and their special circumstances. Among the questions raised is whether provisions for special treatment and developmental objectives are warranted. A second issue concerns the nature and scope of market restrictions that countries may impose in the pursuit of public policy objectives. A third issue deals with the scope of reservations that countries may take on scheduling commitments. Another issue concerns the advantages and disadvantages of emergency safeguards as part of an agreement on energy services (the GATS does not include safeguard instruments like those in the GATT for goods). Last is the issue of government procurement and whether GATS-specific disciplines should be added in this area.

Considerations of Developing Countries

Developing countries will play a critical role in the outcome of the energy services negotiations. The bulk of the projected increase in world energy demand will take place in developing regions, accounting for approximately two-thirds of the growth in world energy demand between 1997 and 2020 (see figure 10.2). Developing regions will become increasingly important buyers of energy services and are likely to increase their role as sellers of services, particularly in the area of oil field services. As a result, the scope and benefits of a GATS agreement on energy services will hinge to a great degree on the number of developing countries that agree to make commitments and on the nature of those commitments.

Developing countries present a specific set of issues that WTO members will need to confront. What, if any, special treatment should developing countries be accorded? The GATT established a precedent for granting such countries special transitional arrangements in meeting trade commitments and for applying differential treatment for countries at different levels of development. The GATS architecture already offers countries a high degree of flexibility.[14] Any country may impose restrictions on market access as long as it lists them in its schedule of commitments and is bound to provide national treatment only if it explicitly makes such a commitment. The actual need for special treatment should be weighed carefully, particularly for middle-income developing countries where special treatment might be less warranted, particularly if emergency safeguards are incorporated in an agreement on energy services.

FIGURE 10.2   World Energy Demand, 1997 and 2020

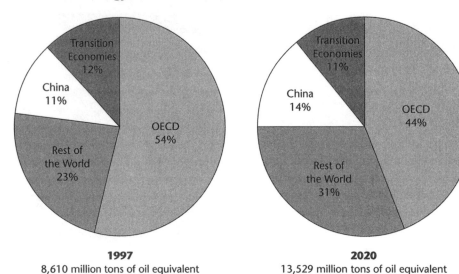

1997
8,610 million tons of oil equivalent

2020
13,529 million tons of oil equivalent

Source: IEA/OECD (2000, p. 52).

A second issue concerns what are broadly called developmental objectives. Developing countries can benefit from establishing linkage programs, which aim to increase domestic sourcing by foreign affiliates and to harness foreign direct investment for the purpose of upgrading the technology and managerial capability of local firms (United Nations Conference on Trade and Investment 2001). What role should the government have in this process? When do developmental objectives justify imposing FDI and trade restrictions on a discriminatory basis?

Developing countries have sought to preserve the right to place conditions on the market openings they choose to make in the name of developmental goals. Venezuela's delegation has asserted that "the negotiations should respect the developing countries' space to implement policies aimed at domestic capacity-building, in particular the capacity of their small and medium sized energy service suppliers" (WTO 2001b, p. 15). Performance requirements derive from the view that conditions on trade and investment of multinational enterprises can be used to increase local production, exports, or technology transfer for the host country. To the extent that those requirements impose conditions that are not market driven, however, performance requirements can distort investment decisions and international trade. The WTO Agreement on Trade-related Investment Measures (TRIMs) reached during the

Uruguay Round represented an effort to phase out local content, domestic sales requirements, local hiring targets, and other performance requirements for goods. Developing countries have resisted efforts to extend the reach of the controversial agreement: they often view performance requirements as an important element of their development strategy (Bora, Lloyd, and Pangestu 2000). The contending views and interests surrounding performance requirements are not easily reconciled and could pose a stumbling block to reaching a GATS agreement on energy services.

A third issue involves the domestic regulatory capacity of developing countries to oversee and regulate competitive energy markets effectively. Although the GATS may serve to promote and consolidate domestic energy regulatory reform efforts, multilateral trade rules cannot guarantee sound regulatory institutions. Multilateral trade rules are designed primarily to ensure market access and are not directly intended to promote security, environment, or social welfare goals. Building credible and independent regulatory institutions requires a parallel effort. The World Bank and other institutions long have supported regulatory capacity building along those lines. Such efforts must continue but must incorporate a greater trade element. Considerable work remains to be done to build compatibility between domestic regulation and multilateral trade disciplines for energy.

Finally, there is a need to encourage greater developing country participation in the GATS negotiations. Domination by OECD countries in negotiations on energy services would be a mistake, as would a view of the negotiations in North-South terms. The substantial trade in energy that takes place between developing countries is a trend that will grow. Developing countries stand to benefit not only from establishing stronger multilateral trade disciplines with industrial countries but also from establishing stronger trade rules between themselves.

Public Service Obligations

Previous GATS agreements explicitly acknowledge the right of governments to pursue legitimate public policy objectives. The agreement on financial services concluded in 1997 permits countries to impose prudential measures to protect the consumers of financial services and to ensure the overall integrity and stability of the nation's financial system. Maintaining universal service was an important priority for countries making commitments regarding telecoms. The basic telecoms agreement and supporting reference paper recognize the right of countries to impose special obligations about universal service.

The nature and scope of prudential measures will likely loom large in the negotiations on energy services. Many policy objectives associated with a country's energy policy have significant social and economic consequences. In addition to considerations of universal service similar to those that arise with telecoms, there are health, safety, rural electrification, pollution abatement, energy efficiency, and security goals. Governments have invoked all of these policy objectives at one time or another to justify quotas, subsidies, and other policy instruments in ways that discriminate against foreign-owned firms. Governments have justified market intervention and the contrivance of competition on the basis of immediate as well as long-term considerations regarding energy security. Immediate security considerations include market interventions taken to ensure the reliability of power systems. Long-term considerations about energy security include market interventions aimed at minimizing the country's dependence on a particular fuel or on a particular country or region.

As noneconomic obligations, environment, security, and other public policy objectives always present the nagging problem of how they should be met and paid for. Traditionally governments have funded public service obligations by permitting utilities to earn monopolistic rents and practice cross-subsidization. That solution has not been the most efficient one. Market liberalization has sought to improve efficiency but has reopened the question of allocating the burden of public service obligations while treating market incumbents and market entrants fairly.

It is often argued that although certain market interventions may be legitimate, regulators should strive for symmetry among market players in the application of those interventions. As Gregory Sidak and Daniel Spulber put it: "[Regulators] should scrupulously design rules that create no advantage for the entrant over the incumbent, or vice versa, but instead place all competitors on an even regulatory footing" (Sidak and Spulber 1998, p. 146). In practice achieving symmetry is not an easy matter. Liberalization often generates strong resistance by incumbent providers because they fear that new entrants will cherrypick the market and leave the incumbents saddled with the costs of meeting various social objectives. In the context of the GATS negotiations, those concerns help explain why some incumbent utilities have already expressed reservations about establishing procompetitive trade rules for energy services (see, for example, Takao 2001).

For those reasons, the process of introducing competition while ensuring symmetry among market players often requires new institutional arrangements and cost allocation mechanisms. One example is renewables portfolio standards for electric power generation to create incentives for inducing higher levels of renewable energy technologies than supplied in a purely competitive context. Establishing certain mandatory portfolio requirements (numerical quotas) obliges electricity suppliers to produce a certain percentage of electricity generated from renewable energy. Governments may also issue certificates for the amount of renewable electricity generated that can be traded in secondary markets. Producers who do not meet the minimum standard or who do not hold a sufficient number of certificates may face penalties. If applied fairly and reasonably, the approach can achieve the public goal of promoting certain energy sources in an efficient and least-cost manner. As noted above, however, mandatory portfolio standards can impede trade and create suboptimal outcomes if they unduly favor local suppliers at the expense of foreign suppliers. This may happen (intentionally or unintentionally) through the definition of renewable resources that is chosen. A case in point is the renewable energy portfolio legislation in New Jersey, which effectively excludes Canadian hydropower (Horlick, Schuchhardt, and Mann 2001). It does this by excluding electricity generated by hydropower (Class I renewable resources), only permitting hydropower generated from facilities that are of 30 megawatts or less (Class II renewable resources). The bulk of Canadian hydropower is generated in facilities much larger than 30 megawatts.

Thus the issue for trade negotiators is not whether governments have a right to pursue legitimate public policy objectives, but how these goals are achieved. Multilateral rules should ideally make it difficult for governments to rely on trade restrictions as a way of achieving public policy objectives. In most cases these objectives are better achieved through other nondiscriminatory means (Mattoo 2000b).

Emergency Safeguards

GATS Article X calls for negotiations on emergency safeguards, but the current agreement does not include such provisions. Some analysts have argued that the economic case for safeguard measures in services is weak. Bernard Hoekman and Michel Kostecki (2001, p. 270) have suggested that "GATT-type emergency protection is difficult to rationalize in the services context because in many cases it will require taking action against foreign firms that have established a commercial presence." They question why a government would take such action when it would harm the investment environment and negatively affect the national employees of the targeted foreign-owned firms. But government actions belie that logic, at least in the case of energy. U.K. regulators showed little concern for the effect on foreign firms when they placed a moratorium on the construction of new gas-fired power plants in 1997.

A precedent for safeguard measures already exists for energy in the context of EU energy inte-

gration. For example, article 24 of the EU gas directive states that member states may "temporarily take the necessary safeguard measures" in the event of a sudden crisis in the energy market in which the system's integrity is threatened.[15] Because those measures came into effect after the U.K. moratorium on gas-fired power plants, whether that action could have been justified as a safeguard measure is unclear. The inclusion of the safeguard instrument within the directive, however, indicates the special economic and security sensitivities associated with energy.

Incorporating safeguard-type measures within a GATS set of disciplines on energy services may also be useful in securing deeper commitments from countries. Previous service negotiations show that countries sometimes make binding commitments below their existing levels of liberalization.[16] Governments face considerable uncertainty with respect to liberalization. They can never fully predict the future demand for more protection at home. Governments respond to the uncertainty by seeking flexibility (Rosendorff and Milner 2001). Although problematic from the perspective of liberalization, such behavior can be perfectly rational. Governments may compensate for the lack of flexibility by undercommitting.

Given those considerations, governments may find the inclusion of emergency safeguard instruments in the negotiations on energy services worthwhile. That inclusion, however, should be temporary and apply only to the extent needed to prevent or remedy serious injury. Provided that they are framed to minimize abuse, emergency safeguards may elicit more meaningful commitments from governments than otherwise can be expected.

Government Procurement

Government procurement, a final area that trade negotiators must consider, can serve a catalytic role in stimulating competition. By opening procurement to all competitors, policies on government procurement can help establish new standards for entry and more competitive market conditions. More often, however, government policies restrict competition to preferred—generally domestic—suppliers. The policies may be legislated, as in the case of the U.S. Buy-America policies, which discriminate against foreign suppliers. Or policies—often those dealing with procurement of oil field services—may be determined on an administrative or political basis with little transparency and few "challenge procedures" that give firms an opportunity to object before the final procurement decision is made.

The significance of discriminatory procurement practices depends on several factors. One factor is the size of government procurement relative to the market. In some cases governments may play a minor role in service markets but a very large role in other markets, particularly if a government body holds a monopoly position as do many power and gas utilities. Another factor is how tradable the product is. Government procurement policies are unlikely to have major effects on the price of products traded in world markets, such as oil. Many services and locally produced products, such as electricity, however, are less likely to be traded. A third factor relates to the contestability of the market. Discriminatory practices are less likely to affect markets primarily supplied by private firms backed by strong procompetition policies.

The GATS does not now cover services supplied in the "exercise of governmental authority." The lack of coverage has not convinced everyone that standalone disciplines on government procurement are needed. Simon Evenett and Bernard Hoekman (2000) argued that there is no compelling reason to treat the procurement of goods and services differently and therefore that countries should focus on developing broad horizontal disciplines instead. They also suggested that as market access and national treatment commitments expand under the GATS, there will be less need for multilateral rules on procurement. Their suggested focus is on removing market access barriers, such as the right of establishment, and on cross-cutting transparency disciplines. But governments and other stakeholders do need to determine whether government procurement of energy is sufficiently great and market distorting to warrant developing specific rules for energy services.

Can the GATS Prevent Rollback?

Experience in previous service negotiations suggests that countries tend to make negotiating offers that reflect their existing levels of domestic liberal-ization. This finding has generated skepticism about the ability of the GATS to drive regulatory reform. But even those who are less sanguine about the GATS serving as a force for domestic regulatory reform point to the advantages that international trade disciplines provide in binding the status quo (Drake and Noam 1997). Although less relevant from the standpoint of expanding market access, standstill agreements have value in preventing slippage and in creating a firmer foundation for future rounds of liberalization.

Regulatory reversals and backsliding are not issues of idle concern for the energy industry. In recent years there have been major cases of governments pulling back from previously announced liberalization measures. One recent case is the decision by the California Public Utilities Commission to suspend retail competition. Another was the British government's decision in 1997 to place a moratorium on the construction of gas-fired power plants. Because foreign and domestic energy service providers were adversely affected in both cases, it is worth exploring what, if any, GATS disciplines might apply.

California's Suspension of Retail Competition

On September 20, 2001, the California Public Utilities Commission suspended retail competition. This decision revoked the right of consumers to choose their preferred electricity supplier—a right previously granted as part of the state's electricity liberalization program. The action was motivated by the need to complete a $13.4 billion bond offering that arose from the heavy fiscal obligations from California's power crisis in 2000/2001 (Cambridge Energy Research Associates 2001a). The crisis began in May 2000 when tight supplies and rising natural gas prices sparked a surge in wholesale electricity prices. The state took a number of actions in response but did not agree to tariff increases or to allowing the utilities to sign medium-term contracts intended to moderate rising wholesale prices. Instead, retail prices were capped. Those actions placed the utility companies in the untenable position of buying high in the wholesale markets and selling low in the retail markets. Eventually, as the utilities sank deeper into debt (or filed for bankruptcy in the case of Pacific Gas & Electric), the state stepped into the role of purchasing energy on behalf of retail customers.[17] With $11.5 billion rapidly spent to purchase power through the tax-supported general fund, additional revenue sources were needed. The bond offering was sought for this purpose. Because the state of California's credibility with investors was badly shaken by its handling of the crisis, however, the state had to pursue extraordinary measures to reassure investors that customers could not avoid paying for the bonds. This was accomplished, in effect, by blocking customers' ability to purchase electricity from alternative energy suppliers.

Closing off retail access was not the only solution available to California. One alternative would have been to apply a charge applicable to all customers that could not be bypassed. This would have allowed the state to recover the cost of bonds and contracts incurred by electricity purchases, but in a way that preserved market openness. Another possibility would have been to retain direct access. That approach assumes the bond issue would not have been undermined by customer switching and that retaining the option would have the added benefit of creating needed discipline to ensure that the state made prudent energy purchases. Only if the state's electricity contracts were too expensive would customers seek out lower direct-access prices.[18]

One way that California could have run afoul of the GATS was by violating market access commitments because the decision on retail access effectively limited the number of service providers to one—the state. Given the political and fiscal pressures created by the power crisis, a pure market solution may not have been realistic. By some estimates, prices would have spiked to 29 cents per kilowatt hour during the worst period of shortage but then would have fallen to around 11 cents per kilowatt hour, assuming that additional power plant capacity was brought online. Instead, the state's action effectively locked in prices at an average of 16 cents per kilowatt hour, which prevented a politically volatile price spike but effectively locked the state into higher prices for a much longer period of time (Leamer 2001). Had the GATS market access commitments been in place, they may have provided disciplines necessary to achieve a more efficient outcome. The GATS market access commitment might have provided

enough additional discipline to prompt the state to choose a more efficient response to the "protection" necessary to float the bonds while preserving market openness.

The U.K. Moratorium on Gas-Fired Power Plants

Liberalizing the U.K. power market unleashed a surge in new gas-fired power plant capacity additions during the 1990s. The so-called "dash for gas" led to a total of 9,500 megawatts of gas-fired capacity being built from 1990 to 1996. In December 1997 Britain's energy minister announced that his department was deferring decisions on outstanding applications to build gas-fired power plants (Godsmark and Bevins 1997). That action, which put proposals for 27 plants in limbo, was justified by a concern over the country's long-term security of supply fuel diversity and to reduce excessive dependence on one fuel. But employment considerations also loomed large. The government's action appeared to many analysts to be a stop-gap measure to stem the inevitable demise of Britain's coal industry.[19] In particular, the remaining high-priced, long-term coal supply contracts with power generators were set to expire the following spring. Anticipating that these contracts would be abandoned or renegotiated at a much lower price and on shorter terms, the main mining company threatened to lay off 5,000 workers if favorable long-term contracts were not renewed.

It is not clear if the United Kingdom's freeze on gas-fired plants could have been actionable under the GATS. That would depend on what binding commitments the government had made and how electricity is eventually defined. The ban, which lasted until 2000, was made public before the EU Gas and Power Directives were put into effect and so neither directive came into play. In a narrow sense the action was nondiscriminatory in that it applied to British firms as well as to foreign firms seeking to build gas-fired generating plants. If the United Kingdom had made relevant commitments, however, the action could have violated provisions against trade-distorting subsidies. The moratorium on gas created an anticompetitive subsidy by favoring some energy service suppliers over others. Protections granted to coal had a negative effect on electricity marketers and energy service companies that were attempting to build a portfolio of assets to compete in the increasingly competitive British market. It also negatively affected integrated engineering and project management service providers who were denied business and firms involved in servicing new natural gas fields (Wighton 1998). It is therefore questionable if a blunt instrument like an outright ban was the least trade-restrictive means available to protect the domestic coal industry. This case supports the need within the context of WTO rulemaking to ensure that protectionist policies enacted by governments cause no greater loss of economic welfare than is necessary (Sykes 2001).

Conclusion

Energy markets are undergoing major change throughout the world as a result of privatization and market liberalization. The era of vertically integrated monopolies with clearly defined service territories and locked-in customer bases is giving way to more flexible and competitive market arrangements. This is true even for those countries that have chosen to retain public ownership of their oil, gas, or electric utility companies. These changes are creating pressures not only to adjust domestic regulatory frameworks but also to establish international trade rules that harness the gains achieved through competitive markets. The interest shown by governments in negotiating GATS energy service disciplines as a part of the Doha Development Agenda reflects this new reality.

The GATS provides a framework for countries to expand their commitments to market access and national treatment significantly in the area of energy services. It also provides a way for countries to make additional commitments in important areas such as third-party access to essential facilities, competition, and independent regulation. Achieving those goals requires clarifying the existing classification system and making it more relevant to the way in which energy is produced and delivered. It will also require that countries not only make binding commitments but also follow through by putting in place the regulatory structures and procedures necessary to meet their obligations and specific commitments according to the negotiated deadlines.

Endnotes

1. By the end of 2001, initial negotiating papers had been submitted by Canada, Chile, the European Union, Japan, Norway, the United States, and the República Bolivariana de Venezuela.
2. For a discussion of these reforms see Newbery (1999).
3. The International Energy Agency projects that during the 1997–2020 period total oil supply will decline by an average annual rate of 1.4 percent among countries in the Organisation for Economic Co-operation and Development, but will increase by 1.1 percent in Russia, 3.9 percent in the Organization of Petroleum-Exporting Countries (OPEC) Middle East, 5.3 percent in the Caspian Sea region, and 5.7 percent in Latin America (see IEA/OECD 2000).
4. IPP developers could build as much as 430 GW (gigawatts) of the 771 GW of new capacity additions that are projected to be made between 2000 and 2010, which represents more than half of the capacity additions worldwide (Cambridge Energy Research Associates 2001b).
5. As part of its annual trade review with Japan the U.S. government has raised the issue of establishing access for all market participants, but has stopped short of demanding mandatory access with regulated tariffs for competing suppliers (see U.S. Trade Representative 2001, Annex 11-15).
6. Calculated from data reported in the *BP Statistical Review of World Energy*, June 2001 and Energy Information Administration, *International Energy Outlook 2001*.
7. In 1994 more than 60 WTO member countries submitted most-favored-nation exemptions, largely concentrated in three sectors: audiovisual, financial services, and transportation (road, air, and maritime).
8. For an extended discussion of these commitments see WTO (1998, pp. 19–35).
9. For a more complete description of how this approach might look see Thompson (2000).
10. Personal communication, United States Trade Representative staff, April 11, 2002.
11. For a discussion of why the right to block access is justified see Nagahara (2001).
12. Useful criteria for determining the reasonableness of a refusal to deal are spelled out in various U.S. court cases. See, in particular, *MCI Communications Corp. v. American Tel. & Tel.*, 708 F.2d 1081 (7th Cir.), 1983.
13. For more on how prior consultation might work see Iida and Nielson (2001, pp. 115–35).
14. Some argue that the GATS, as currently framed, is too flexible and that is one reason it has been a relatively weak instrument in advancing liberalization (see Low and Mattoo 2000).
15. Directive 98/30/EC of the European Parliament and of the Council of 22 June 1998, Concerning Common Rules for the Internal Market in Natural Gas, *Official Journal* L 204, July 21, 1998, pp. 1–12.
16. One example is the level of foreign equity participation permitted in commercial banks. The Philippine government made a binding commitment of only 51 percent even though domestic law allows 60 percent (see Mattoo 2000a, p. 371).
17. The California state legislature removed the state's investor-owned utilities from the role of purchasing energy on behalf of retail customers and gave that function to a government agency—the California Department of Water Resources (CDWR). CDWR subsequently signed a series of

contracts, some extending 20 years, at what turned out to be the peak of market prices, in the first and second quarters of 2001.

18. This approach was advocated by two commissioners who dissented from the majority California Public Utilities Commission ruling. See California Public Utilities Commission, Decision No. 01-09-060, Application 98-07-003 et al., September 20, 2001.

19. Over the 10-year period from 1984 to 1994 employment in the British coal industry fell from nearly 250,000 miners to only 7,000 (see Newbery and Pollitt 1997).

References

Bacon, R. W. 1995. "Privatization and Reform in the Global Electricity Supply Industry." *Annual Review of Energy and Environment* 20: 119–43.

Bora, Bijit, Peter J. Lloyd, and Mari Pangestu. 2000. "Industrial Policy and the WTO." *World Economy* 23(4): 554–55.

British Petroleum. 2001. "BP Statistical Review of World Energy" (June). <http://www.bp.com/centres/energy/index/asp.>

Cambridge Energy Research Associates. 2001a. *Beyond California's Power Crisis: Impact, Solutions, and Lessons.* Special Report. Cambridge, Mass.

———. 2001b. *Global Power Horizons: Strategic and Regional Outlooks.* Cambridge, Mass.

Commission of European Communities. 2001. "Completing the Internal Energy Market." Staff Working Paper. SEC 438. December 3. Brussels.

Drake, William J., and Eli M. Noam. 1997. "The WTO Deal on Basic Telecommunications: Big Bang or Little Whimper?" *Telecommunications Policy* 21(9): 799–818.

DRI-WEFA. Report to the European Commission Directorate General for Transport and Energy to Determine Changes after Opening of the Gas Market in August 2000, Volume 1: European Overview, July 2001.

Espey, Simone. 2001. "Renewables Portfolio Standards: A Means for Trade with Electricity from Renewable Energy Sources?" *Energy Policy* (29): 557–66.

Evenett, Simon J., and Bernard M. Hoekman. 2000. "Government Procurement of Services and Multilateral Disciplines." In Pierre Sauvé and Robert Stern, eds., *GATS 2000: New Directions in Services Trade Liberalization.* Washington D.C.: Brookings Institution Press.

Godsmark, Chris, and Anthony Bevins. 1997. "Blair Calls Halt to Gas-Fired Power Stations as Coal Crisis Mounts." *The Independent*, December 4.

Hoekman, Bernard, and Michel Kostecki. 2001. *The Political Economy of the Multilateral Trading System*, 2nd ed. London: Oxford University Press.

Horlick, Gary, Christiane Schuchhardt, and Howard Mann. 2001. *NAFTA Provisions and the Electricity Sector.* Background paper. Commission for Environmental Cooperation, Montréal, Canada, November 8.

Horsnell, Paul, and Robert Mabro. 1993. *Oil Markets and Prices: The Brent Market and the Formation of World Oil Prices.* New York: Oxford University Press.

IEA/OECD (International Energy Agency/Organisation for Economic Co-operation and Development). 1999. *Japan 1999 Review: Energy Policies of IEA Countries.* Paris.

———. 2000. *World Energy Outlook 2000.* Paris.

———. 2001a. *Competition in Electricity Markets.* Paris.

———. 2001b. *Regulatory Institutions in Liberalized Electricity Markets.* Paris.

Iida, Keiya, and Julia Nielson. 2001. "Transparency in Domestic Regulation: Prior Consultation." In OECD, *Trade in Services: Negotiating Issues and Approaches.* Paris.

Izaguirre, Ada Karina. 1999. "Private Participation in the Transmission and Distribution of Natural Gas—Recent Trends." *Public Policy for the Private Sector.* Note 176, April. Washington, D.C.: World Bank.

Jaccard, Mark. 1995. "Oscillating Currents: The Changing Rationale for Government Intervention in the Electricity Industry." *Energy Policy* 23(7): 579–92.

Leamer, Edward. 2001. "Short Circuit: Will the California Energy Crisis Derail the State's Economy?" The UCLA Anderson Forecast for the Nation and California, The Anderson School at UCLA, June.

Low, Patrick, and Aaditya Mattoo. 2000. "Is There a Better Way? Alternative Approaches to Liberalization under the GATS." In Pierre Sauvé and Robert Stern, eds., *GATS 2000: New Directions in Services Trade Liberalization.* Washington D.C.: Brookings Institution Press.

Mattoo, Aaditya. 2000a. "Financial Services and the WTO: Liberalization Commitments of the Developing and Transition Economies." *World Economy* 23(3): 351–86.

———. 2000b. "Shaping Future GATS Rules for Trade in Services." Development Research Group, World Bank, Washington, D.C., June.

Melly, Christopher. 2001. "Power Market Reform and International Trade in Services." Paper presented at the United Nations Conference on Trade and Development, Experts Meeting on Energy Services in International Trade: Development Implications, Geneva, July 23–25.

Nagahara, Hisashi. 2001. "The Antimonopoly Implications of the Deregulation of the Japanese Gas Utility Industry." Paper presented at a program on U.S.–Japan relations, Harvard University, Cambridge, Mass., April.

Newbery, David M. 1999. *Privatization, Restructuring, and Regulation of Network Utilities.* Cambridge, Mass.: MIT Press.

Newbery, David M., and Michael G. Pollitt. 1997. "The Restructuring and Privatization of the U.K. Electricity Supply—Was It Worth It?" *Public Policy for the Private Sector.* Note 124, September. Washington, D.C.: World Bank.

Percebois, Jacques. 1999. "The Gas Deregulation Process in Europe: Economic and Political Approach." *Energy Policy* 27: 9–15.

Pollitt, M. 1997. "The Impact of Liberalization on the Performance of the Electricity Supply Industry." *Journal of Energy Literature* 3: 3–31.

Rosendorff, B. Peter, and Helen V. Milner. 2001. "The Optimal Design of International Trade Institutions: Uncertainty and Escape." *International Organization* 55(4): 829–57.

Salbu, Steven R. 1999. "Battling Global Corruption in the New Millennium." *Law and Policy in International Business* 31(1): 47–78.

Sidak, J. Gregory, and Daniel F. Spulber. 1998. "Deregulation and Managed Competition in Network Industries." *Yale Journal on Regulation* 15(1): 117–48.

Spiller, Pablo T. 1997. "Regulatory Commitment and Utilities' Privatization: Implications for Future Comparative Research." In Jeffrey S. Banks and Eric A. Hanushek, eds., *Modern Political Economy: Old Topics, New Directions.* New York: Cambridge University Press.

Stern, Jonathan P. 1998. *Competition and Liberalization in European Gas Markets.* Washington, D.C.: Brookings Institution Press.

Sykes, Alan O. 2001. "'Efficient Protection' through WTO Rulemaking." In Porter, Roger, Pierre Sauvé, Arvind Subramanian, and Americo Beviglia-Zampetti, eds., *Efficiency, Equity, Legitimacy: The Multilateral Trading System at the Millennium.* Washington, D.C.: Brookings Institution Press.

Takao, Tomoyuki. 2001. "TEPCO's Position on WTO Energy Services Trade Negotiations." Corporate Planning Department, Tokyo Electric Power Company, September.

Thompson, Rachel. 2000. "Integrating Energy Services into the World Trading System." Washington, D.C.: Energy Services Coalition.

Thompson, Rachel, and Keiya Iida. 2001. "Strengthening Regulatory Transparency: Insights for the GATS from the Regulatory Reform Country Reviews." In OECD, *Trade in Services: Negotiating Issues and Approaches.* Paris.

United Nations Conference on Trade and Investment. 2001. *World Investment Report 2001: Promoting Linkages.* Geneva.

U.S. Department of Energy, Energy Information Administration. 2001. *International Energy Outlook 2001.* Washington, D.C.: Government Printing Office.

U.S. International Trade Commission. 2000. "Electric Power Services: Recent Reforms in Selected Foreign Markets." Investigation No. 332-441, Publication 3370. Washington, D.C.

U.S. Trade Representative. 2001. "Annual Reform Recommendations from the Government of the United States to the Government of Japan under the U.S.–Japan Regulatory Reform and Competition Policy Initiative." October 14. Washington, D.C.

Wighton, David. 1998. "Ban on Gas-Fired Stations Set to Proceed." *Financial Times*, September 14, p. 8.

Wolfram, Catherine D. 1999. "Measuring Duopoly in the British Electricity Spot Market." *American Economic Review* 89(4): 821.

World Bank. 2001. *Power and Gas Regulation—Issues and International Experience.* Draft Working Paper, Washington, D.C.

WTO (World Trade Organization). 1991. "Services Sectoral Classification List: Note by the Secretariat." MTN.GNS/W/120, July 10.

———. 1998. "Energy Services: Background Note by the Secretariat." Council for Trade in Services, S/C/W/52, September 9.

———. 2001a. "Guidelines for the Scheduling of Specific Commitments under the General Agreement on Trade in Services (GATS)." S/L/92, March 28.

———. 2001b. "Negotiating Proposal on Energy Services." Council for Trade in Services, Special Session, Communication from the República Bolivariana de Venezuela, S/CSS/W/69, March 29.

11

REGULATION OF HEALTH SERVICES AND INTERNATIONAL TRADE LAW

David Luff

Executive Summary

The object of this chapter is to compare regulation in the health services sector with the application of current World Trade Organization (WTO) rules. The first section offers a brief summary of the most important regulatory issues arising in the health sector, drawing primarily from the European experience.

The chapter's second section delineates the margin of discretion left to domestic regulators by WTO rules. The analysis concludes that the General Agreement on Trade in Services (GATS) is the relevant WTO agreement and that it is characterized by its total flexibility. Obligations imposed on governments pursuant to the GATS mostly depend on individual commitments made. Such commitments must however be crafted appropriately. Furthermore, the absence of specific limitations in commitments generates legal uncertainty on several aspects of the domestic regulation of health services. The chapter identifies those key GATS issues most in need of interpretation in the health sector. Although questions concerning the applicability of the GATS to ser-

vices supplied by the government do not deserve the greatest attention, the concepts of the "quality of a service" or the "necessity of a measure" need further clarification.

The third part of the chapter assesses the adequacy of GATS rules in relation to the current priorities of national health policies. Where relevant, supplementary international rules are suggested. In this context, to take the GATS to its limits, the chapter assumes that full commitments are made by WTO members, even if this is currently not the case. The adequacy of an agreement such as the GATS should not be tested against the capacity of members individually to limit the applicability of its provisions. On the contrary, one should assume that all of its provisions are fully applicable and should check to what extent the provisions can be adjusted to domestic regulatory concerns. The Preamble to the GATS explicitly recognizes the right of members to regulate the supply of services in order to meet national policy objectives, even after commitments are negotiated. Therefore, the last section of the chapter will be prospective in nature and is intended to highlight possible shortcomings of

The author is grateful to Aaditya Mattoo, Rudolph Adlung, Julia Nielson, Pierre Sauvé, Jolita Butkeviciene, Malcom McKinon, Johannes Bernabe, and Debra Lipson for their useful comments and advice on a first draft of this study.

horizontal provisions in GATS in relation to the regulation of health services.

A final objective of the chapter is to determine whether horizontal regulation under the GATS could be sufficient or if the sector concerned would require specific international regulation to be included in the scope of the WTO. The chapter makes no assumption as to the desirability of increasing trade in the health services sector.[1] As indicated, discussions in this chapter will concentrate only on the specifics of domestic regulation of health services and will address the latter's interface with WTO rules. The chapter will not directly address other closely related areas, such as regulation of private health insurance, immigration laws, mutual recognition agreements, intellectual property protection, and so forth. In the context of future trade negotiations, it should be kept in mind, however, that trade in health services can be connected with all of these other issues (see Butkeviciene and Diaz 1998).

Regulatory Issues Related to the Provision of Health Services

Countries have engaged in different experiences to limit the costs of public health policies while maintaining quality standards and equal access to health services. Of course, considering the lack of clear-cut results and different political, institutional, and social realities within countries, no international harmonization of policies has yet taken place.

Certain common regulatory issues in the health sector can be identified and used as a possible analytical framework for the purposes of this chapter. Thus three key areas of regulation stand out: the production of health services, the supply of pharmaceuticals, and the financing of health services. In the first two areas, rules address three main issues: ensuring quality, guaranteeing universal and nondiscriminatory access to health services, and controlling public expenses. The third area, financing, clearly has a close connection with the previous two and when it affects them its regulation addresses similar concerns. It should be noted that public financing in the form of social security may operate both as a fiscal and as a subsidization mechanism.

The need to contain costs entails the adoption of many sorts of regulatory mechanisms, the most radical being central planning under a fixed budget.

Occasionally, limited market mechanisms are used in resource allocation, but that is not necessarily the case. It is difficult to predict which system will prevail in the future. The current trend would consist of variations of a system by which social security funds would be responsible for the distribution of social security contributions and would be financed according to the number of affiliates. They would purchase health services for the benefit of their affiliates and compete with each other for those services. A perceived domestic advantage to this mechanism is an increased cost efficiency because funds would develop a capacity to obtain the best offers for the supply of health services, under high-quality conditions. This mechanism also seems to have produced positive results in terms of trade in health services. Two possible shortcomings are the apparent incentive to select patients according to their perceived health risk and the possible development of anticompetitive clusters of service providers.

The Application of WTO Rules in the Health Services Sector

This section examines the current effect of WTO rules on the health services sector. The review will be limited to the first area of regulation, that is, the production of health services. The second area of regulation—provision of pharmaceuticals—mainly concerns trade in goods and the protection of intellectual property rights, and so falls outside the scope of the present work. The third area of regulation—financing of health services, particularly establishing and operating the social security system—will be covered only to the extent that WTO rules may affect the functioning of the mechanisms established or if those mechanisms may affect trade in health services as such.

Applicable Agreements

Generally speaking, although all WTO agreements are applicable, the most relevant one here is the General Agreement on Trade in Services. Regulating the production of health services indeed mostly affects trade in these services.

General Agreement on Tariffs and Trade (GATT) 1994 would also be relevant to the extent that trade in the goods needed to supply health services was affected. For instance, if a domestic regulation required the use of equipment of local origin as a condition on the financing of hospital services or the granting of operating licenses, then both trade in goods (that is, trade of the equipment concerned) and trade in services (that is, trade in hospital services) would be affected. As previously indicated, however, trade in goods is not covered by the present study, even if the goods concerned are necessary to supply a health service. Restrictions on trade in equipment will be addressed only to the extent they might adversely affect trade in health services.

The Government Procurement Agreement (GPA) might also be relevant. In several countries social security funds act as purchasers of health services for the benefit of their affiliates. The impact of this agreement, however, is still very theoretical, given that few countries agreed to be bound by its provisions,[2] only one of those countries has included the health services sector in its appendix attached to that agreement,[3] and none of them has included in such appendix social security funds as procuring entities to which the provisions of the agreement would apply.[4] At this stage it is only useful to bear in mind that any future inclusion of health services and of social security funds in the appendixes would oblige the countries concerned to respect the procedures and the nondiscrimination rules contained in the GPA whenever social security funds purchase health services for their affiliates.

Thus the GATS will be the focal point of the legal analysis below.

The GATS

The GATS, like the GATT, aims at protecting the equality of competitive opportunities for companies in domestic markets regardless of their origin and the origin of their services. It aims at facilitating progressive liberalization of services "*as a means of promoting the economic growth of all trading partners and the development of developing countries*" (GATS Preamble, para. 2).

The GATS also explicitly recognizes the rights of members to "regulate, and to introduce new regulations, on the supply of services within their territories in order to meet national policy objectives." It also underlines that, "given asymmetries existing with respect to the degree of development of ser-

vices regulations in different countries," the particular rights of developing countries to regulate must be preserved (GATS Preamble, para. 2).

The GATS is thus characterized by its flexibility and the regulatory freedom that is, in principle, recognized for members. Commitments under the GATS, however, might entail the search for least trade-restrictive regulatory solutions that can be a source of legal uncertainty.

In principle, the GATS constitutes the framework agreement relevant to all services and particularly those that have been or are being liberalized, but it does not apply to services that are supplied in the exercise of governmental authority (Article I.3[b] and Article 1.3[c]). Its structure also differs from that of the GATT. It contains a mix between horizontal commitments applicable to all services and service suppliers, and sectoral commitments applicable only to those sectors that have been explicitly open to trade by WTO members. In only the latter situation does it entail noticeable regulatory consequences in the health services sector.

Scope of the GATS with Respect to Health Services   We turn now to the central question of how some of the key provisions of GATS affect the regulation of health services when these are traded.

Exclusion of services supplied in the exercise of governmental authority.   Pursuant to GATS Article I.3(b), the GATS applies only to services that are not supplied in the exercise of governmental authority. This means it applies to services that are supplied either on a commercial basis or in competition with other service suppliers (Article I.3[c]). The GATS does not further define these notions.

Although developments below constitute my attempt to further clarify these concepts, it should be stressed that, in practice, this is not a key issue in relation to the regulation of health services. In most cases, health services are supplied in competition with one or more service suppliers. Furthermore, in the absence of any explicit opening of trade in a sector by members, the GATS is not particularly burdensome because it does not impose obligations other than the most-favored-nation (MFN) principle and a rule of transparency.

Before entering into some speculative considerations below, there is one situation in which the GATS would clearly not apply. This concerns health services that are supplied exclusively by the government, that is, in hospitals that are entirely dependent on the government and by doctors who are appointed by the government on a completely or nearly gratuitous basis, without allowing the patient to choose among the hospitals or doctors available.

- *Services supplied on a commercial basis:* The question of which services are supplied on a commercial basis remains unsettled. In many countries, the medical profession and the public do not consider health services to be commercial. Indeed, for ethical reasons health services cannot be dominated by the search for profit, as a typical business activity would be. Their provision is deemed to pursue by itself a public policy objective that is not commercial in nature. Thus, in the sector of health, commercial interests must be subject to higher values that impede the providers of health services from functioning as any other economic agent.

  The difficulty here lies with the different possible interpretations of the word "commercial." One could question whether the scope of this notion is confined to activities or undertakings that are profit seeking. It would be difficult to argue that the application of a provision in an agreement could vary according to the operators' subjective view of the purpose of their operations. Other subjective criteria such as the private character of an undertaking or the existence of a financial risk equally may not determine the commercial character of an activity. A more objective criterion based on the nature of the undertaking could prevail. Would the activity of those who have organized themselves "commercially" (i.e., those who must generate resources while controlling and recovering their costs) be "commercial" (see Van Ryn and Heenen 1976, pp. 15–23)? In other words, according to this interpretation (which is not official and is subject to questioning) and taking into account the constraints imposed on its provision and the cost of the resources necessary for its supply, would a service supplied for a price be commercial? Ownership of the undertaking supplying the service (public or private) or its final objectives would not matter in this context.

Concerning health services, by this view GATS would apply as long as

1. The service is supplied by doctors or hospitals who are organized as separate economic entities and financially structured according to economic criteria.
2. A price, reflecting the operating conditions of the supply of the service, is charged for it to a patient or a social security fund (or both).[5]

Those two elements generally are connected and it would be rather pointless to try to figure out whether the first element is really indispensable. Even if hospital or medical services are entirely supplied by the government and if a price is paid for them and reflects actual operating conditions, arguably a service is supplied on a commercial basis.

On the other hand, when a service is provided for free or at a price that is substantially below costs and is directly financed by the government,[6] it would not be supplied on a commercial basis. Direct financing by the government is intended financing through a fixed appropriation or, more generally, the absence of any direct connection between the amount and level of services supplied and the income of the service provider.

To establish the "commercial" basis of the supply of a service, a question could arise about whether the price paid for it should also reflect market conditions (i.e., whether, for instance, predefined price tables obligatory for all would remove the commercial basis of the supply of the service). This does not appear to be an appropriate test. It belongs more to the issue of whether there is competition among service suppliers. Indeed, to the extent that a service supplier organized as an autonomous undertaking receives sufficient payment for its services, whether or not such payment reflects a competitive market, it can be deemed to operate under conditions that are sustainable—that is, "commercial" in the sense described above.

It should be recalled that these developments are theoretical and still uncertain, and that in practice they are not essential in the health services sector. Arguably, according to the view expressed here, only medical services and not hospital services would be supplied on a commercial basis. In fact, the prices charged for hospital services seldom cover all costs, particularly fixed costs, and a governmental appropriation is needed to make up the difference.[7]

• *Services supplied in competition with other service suppliers.* The second criterion determining the applicability of GATS is the existence of competition among service suppliers. This requires the absence of special or exclusive rights granted to doctors or hospitals, or, where certain monopoly rights still exist, the establishment of rules that enable patients to choose among a certain number of hospitals or doctors.

Competition occurs when the patients have the choice of their service suppliers and when the supplier's income depends on the number of patients treated. This is the case when the services are paid by the patients themselves and prices are freely established by the service providers, notwithstanding reimbursement caps. But competition may also take place even if social security funds entirely pay for the services on the basis of set prices, whether those prices result from a mutual agreement with the medical profession or are fixed pursuant to unilateral regulation by the government. Thus to determine the existence of competition among service providers the market does not have to operate under perfect competitive conditions; it is sufficient that some rivalry exists among providers concerned.

In summary, it is the author's view that the GATS would apply to health services

- that can be supplied by several doctors or in several hospitals
- among which the patient can choose
- for which the income of the doctors or hospitals concerned depends on the number of patients treated.

For example, there would not be competition in central planning systems where each hospital is granted special or exclusive rights in a specific region and where patients are compelled to be treated in the hospital in their region. The same would be true for medical services supplied by doctors who are authorized exclusively to operate in a specific zone in each city.

Competition also would be lacking where patients had some choice of hospitals or doctors, but where the providers' income originated in the government regardless of the number of patients treated. In that case there would not be a particular incentive to draw new patients. Note also that services would not be supplied on a commercial basis in such a situation.

One question is whether competition can be assumed from the mere coexistence of governmental and private services in the health sector. In other words, would it be possible to shield from the scope of the GATS those services supplied and financed by the government even if private suppliers are admitted? It can be argued that those are two different sectors that deserve completely different treatments. Indeed, to the extent that services supplied by the government are not competing with services supplied under certain competitive conditions, they could be excluded from the scope of GATS pursuant to Article 1.3(c). However, the problem is wrongly phrased. The question is not whether the market is divided between public and private services, but whether a specific service is supplied in a country under certain competitive conditions. When independent operators are authorized to supply a service and some competition exists among them, arguably the GATS applies to the service concerned even if the service is also supplied by the government under certain privileged conditions. The applicability of GATS to a certain service does not affect the possibility of governments supplying the service or granting special or exclusive rights to certain undertakings. It should be noted in this regard that the issue of ownership (i.e., the question of whether a service provider is public or private) is irrelevant in this context. For the purpose of assessing the applicability of the GATS, it is the author's opinion that the only question to be asked concerning the criterion of competition is whether there is some financial rivalry among suppliers of the service concerned in the country, no matter how intense the competition or however imperfect the conditions of competition prevailing for that specific service.

- *Irrelevance of the exclusion contained in the Annex on Financial Services.* Article 1(b)(ii) of the Annex on Financial Services specifies that:

For the purpose of subparagraph 3(b) of Article I of [the GATS], "services supplied in the exercise of governmental authority" means the following

(ii) activities forming part of a statutory system of social security or public retirement plans.

A wrong interpretation of such exclusion would be that health services supplied under the conditions imposed by social security laws would be excluded from the scope of GATS. Indeed, such an exception is included in the Annex on Financial Services and thus only concerns these services, not health services as such. It means that the provision of financial services through a statutory system of social security (such as life insurance) is excluded from the scope of GATS. It is thus not relevant for our purposes.

- *Summary.* A health service would be excluded from the scope of the GATS if it was supplied neither on a commercial basis nor in competition with other service providers. This typically would be the case of health services that are supplied exclusively by the government, that is, in hospitals that are entirely dependent on the government and by doctors who are appointed by it and who serve on a completely or nearly gratuitous basis, without allowing the patient to choose among the hospitals or doctors available. This is seldom the case (see WTO Council for Trade in Services 1998, para. 38). Most situations are hybrid in nature, entailing a mix between commercial and noncommercial conditions as well as some competition among service providers, thereby justifying the applicability of GATS.

In an attempt to formulate positive rules, one could argue that the GATS would be relevant to all those health services

- That are supplied by doctors or in hospitals organized as economic undertakings, and
- For which a price reaching the level of costs is paid by the purchaser of the service (the patient himself or the social security/insurance fund), and/or

- When any form of competition exists among providers of health services, whether the competition takes place for patients or for obtaining public financing, and whether it takes place among independent providers alone or among public and private providers of like services.

It should be noted that the exclusion of a particular service from the GATS would not mean that the manner in which it is provided cannot affect another service supplied on a commercial or competitive basis. For instance, a public hospital operating under monopoly rights may refuse infrastructure access to certain doctors or members of any other medical profession. In that case, although the GATS would not apply to the hospital service as such, it would be fully applicable to protect the competitive position of the other medical services affected by the restrictive behavior.

Finally, the exclusion contained in Article 1(b)(ii) of the Annex on Financial Services relating to social security is not relevant as far as health services as such are concerned.

The modes of supply and health services. When services fall within its scope, the GATS (Article I.2) applies to measures affecting four modes of supply:

1. *The cross-border mode,* that is, from the territory of one member into the territory of any other member. This mode concerns the provision of health services from a distance, without the movement of doctors. This is now increasingly possible because of the recent development of telemedicine.

2. *The consumption abroad mode,* that is, in the territory of one member to the service consumer of any other member. This mode concerns the opportunity given to patients to be treated outside of their country by foreign doctors or in foreign hospitals.

3. *The commercial presence mode,* that is, by a service supplier of one member through commercial presence in the territory of any other member. This mode concerns the possibility for hospitals' operators to build hospitals in a foreign country.

4. *The physical presence mode,* that is, by a service supplier of one member through the presence of

natural persons of a member in the territory of any other member. This mode is the most relevant to doctors (or nurses or members of other medical professions) who wish to exercise their profession in a jurisdiction other than their own.

It is clear that to the extent that the health services concerned are not supplied in the exercise of governmental authority, measures that affect one of these four modes of supply can be assessed according to the GATS. An overview of current trade flows taking place under each mode can be found in the joint study of the UNCTAD and the WHO (UNCTAD/WHO 1998).

Horizontal disciplines that concern all services and service suppliers. This would generate clusters of service providers. To the extent that a service is covered by the GATS, horizontal rules apply to all measures by members affecting trade in this service (GATS Article I.1).[8]

It is useful to note at the outset that when there are no specific commitments under the GATS, few of the agreement's rules apply to measures affecting trade in covered services. The contents of rules that are applicable irrespective of commitments taken are as follows:

Most-favored-nation treatment. Article II of the GATS contains the obligation to grant most-favored-nation treatment to all services and service suppliers of any WTO ember. This obligation implies the prohibition of de facto as well as de jure discriminations between foreign services and service suppliers (see WTO Appellate Body Report 1997a, para. 234).

As an exception to this basic principle, however, a member may exempt itself from this obligation in a list of exemptions under GATS Article II. No special exemption seems to have been listed in the health services sector.[9] Consequently, should health services from certain third countries be authorized in a domestic market, such treatment should be extended to services and service suppliers from all other WTO members under similar conditions, whatever the commitments taken by a member with respect to the service concerned.[10]

Naturally, qualification requirements may be imposed but they should not be discriminatory or be applied in a discriminatory manner. Members are encouraged to recognize the education, experience, and authorization obtained in certain third countries with which they conclude bilateral recognition agreements. Mutual recognition is nevertheless subject to a number of conditions set forth in GATS Article VII and cannot constitute a means of discrimination between countries or a disguised restriction to trade.

Also, should patients be authorized to consume health services abroad or to receive reimbursement for such services, there should be no discrimination as to the country in which that is possible, without prejudice, of course, to certain objective conditions that may be imposed.

Transparency. GATS Article III contains an obligation of transparency, which obliges all WTO members to publish promptly all laws, regulations, or administrative guidelines that significantly affect the operation of the GATS. In the health services sector this provision compels WTO members to publish licensing conditions and procedures for hospitals, qualification requirements for doctors, the details of the social security system, bidding procedures when organized, ethical rules and their operation, and so forth.

The rule of transparency applies to doctors' professional organizations to the extent these have been delegated powers by the government, such as disciplinary powers or the capacity to determine and/or control the conditions of access to the profession (GATS Article I.3[a][ii]).

Monopoly suppliers. Pursuant to GATS Article VIII, the rules above, particularly the most-favored-nation obligation, apply to monopoly suppliers, that is, enterprises that have been granted special or exclusive

In the health sector this obligation is particularly relevant to all hospitals that have been granted special or exclusive rights to operate in a region or to provide certain services, such as those requiring huge investments. When providing their services, these hospitals cannot treat services or suppliers of health services (such as doctors) of different nationalities in a discriminatory manner. Should that be the case, their behavior would constitute a violation of the MFN rule by the state in which the hospitals are located.

In practice, an illicit discriminatory treatment could result from different conditions for using the hospital's infrastructure imposed on doctors or on cross-border medical services, such as telemedicine, according to their nationality. It could also result from different work conditions and remuneration applicable to doctors according to their nationality or from requirements to them to charge different tariffs to patients because of the patients' nationality, and the like.

It is important to clarify that, in the absence of any commitment on health services, there is no obligation to give to foreign doctors or foreign telemedicine services access to the local hospitals' infrastructure. However, if access to such infrastructure is granted to doctors or services from one country, it should be granted to those from all other countries under similar conditions.

This implies that the service supplied by the doctors concerned is distinct from the hospital service as such. Indeed, should the doctors be employed by a hospital only to handle hospital equipment, the discrimination is more a question of local labor law than one concerning international trade of medical services. The difficulty comes from the unclear distinction between hospital and medical services and from the many differences existing among countries in this regard. For instance, in certain countries, such as Belgium or the Netherlands, all services supplied by doctors are considered to be medical services, even if they can only be supplied in hospitals, such as surgery or complex medical work. In other countries these services would be classified as hospital services. Thus, for the purposes of determining the scope of obligations for hospitals that have been granted special or exclusive rights, it is important to have some clarity and common views concerning the classification of health services.

Subsidies. In contrast to trade in goods, there are currently no specific disciplines on subsidies for trade in services other than MFN treatment and transparency and a commitment under GATS Article XV to develop disciplines in future in response to the acknowledged possible distortive effect of subsidies on services trade. Therefore, subsidization originating from public resources, such as social security or other public financing mechanisms, is in principle authorized by the GATS,

except that in such cases governments are supposed to enter into consultations and accord each other "sympathetic consideration" (Article XV.2).

It should be noted that the conditions upon which subsidies are granted and the manner in which they are granted may be discriminatory and subject to the other GATS rules. For example, pursuant to Article II, if treatment in a third country is reimbursed by social security funds, reimbursement must be granted to similar treatment provided by all other WTO countries.

Disciplines that apply to sectors open to international trade. Obligations concerning services for which commitments have been made are much more stringent than those applicable to services for which no commitments were made. Making a commitment for a service results from its inclusion by WTO members in their individual Schedules of Commitments. Approximately 44 members have done so in relation to health services, all classifications included. The precise scope of the commitments depends on the limitations that may be included in each member's schedule. It also implies that the services concerned are appropriately defined and classified.

It should be stressed that the GATS does not function like the GATT. In contrast to the latter, GATS are subject to that agreement's more stringent provisions only to the extent indicated in their individual schedules. Another way to express this is that obligations under GATS can be limited to the extent described in individual Schedules of Commitments. In any event, limitations in schedules should not be perceived as exceptions to the GATS, but rather as rules specifying its scope and the scope of its provisions, and occasionally complementing it. This means that GATS's main characteristic is its flexibility, which enables members to tailor their schedules according to their national laws (subject, of course, to horizontal provisions).

Remember that the preamble to the GATS expressly recognizes the right of members to "regulate and to introduce new regulations in the supply of services within their territories in order to meet national policy objectives" (para. 4). In other words, none of the provisions of the GATS should be intended to undermine the right of members to pursue the regulatory objectives identified in the first section of this chapter.

Although possible shortcoming are possible, these considerations are essential in defining the margin of discretion currently left to members to regulate the provision of health services.

Definition and classification of health services in the GATS. Under the GATS, most commitments are made in relation to services according to a classification prepared by the WTO Secretariat during the Uruguay Round, on the basis of the United Nations Central Product Classification (CPC) list. Health services are classified in the sectors "Business Services" and "Health Related and Social Services." Definitions and classifications beyond four digits (except CPC No. 93191) are found only in the CPC list (see WTO Council for Trade in Services 1998, p. 22).

Health services are subdivided as follows in the CPC Classification system used by WTO members for purposes of scheduling commitments under the GATS:

Business Services
A. Professional services
  h. Medical and dental services (CPC No. 9312): Services chiefly aimed at preventing, diagnosing, and treating illness through consultation by individual patients without institutional nursing
  i. Services provided by midwives, nurses, physiotherapists, and paramedical personnel (CPC No. 93191)

Health Related and Social Services
  a. Hospital services (CPC No. 9311): Services delivered under the direction of medical doctors chiefly to in-patients aimed at curing, reactivating, and/or maintaining the health status
  b. Other human health services (CPC No. 9319): . . . residential health facilities services or clinics other than hospital services, . . . services in the field of: morphological or chemical pathology, bacteriology, virology, immunology, . . . blood collection services . . . private services of clinical laboratories auxiliary to medical diagnosis, etc.
  c. Social services (CPC No. 9333): Includes a variety of welfare services with and without accommodation, vocational rehabilitation services, etc.

Such a classification still raises a number of questions concerning health services. One incidental difficulty with the classification is that "medical and dental services" as well as "services provided by midwives, nurses, physiotherapists, and paramedical personnel" are classified as "professional services" within "business services." In French, "business services" is translated as "services provided to businesses." Thus, apparently, services provided to individuals are not addressed. This is rather surprising and results perhaps purely from a problem of translation.

A major difficulty, however, concerns the determination of the dividing line between hospital services and medical services. It is unclear whether services of doctors supplied in hospitals should be classified in one or the other category. As indicated above, this question among others is relevant when determining obligations of monopoly hospitals with respect to doctors needing to use their infrastructure. It is also relevant in evaluating the exact scope of the commitments made by members concerning hospitals or medical services.

From the CPC definitions, it would appear that all services of doctors aimed at curing, reactivating, and/or maintaining the health status of patients in hospitals are hospital services. The same services to outpatients could also be classified as hospital services because the CPC definition refers to services delivered "chiefly" to inpatients, thus arguably including all types of patients, provided that inpatients remain the majority. This would mean that the most relevant test would be whether services "aimed at curing, reactivating, and/or maintaining the health status" are supplied in hospitals.

The CPC definition of medical services refers to "services chiefly aimed at preventing, diagnosing, and treating illness through consultation by individual patients without institutional nursing." "Preventing, diagnosing, and treating illness" arguably means the same as "curing, reactivating, and/or maintaining the health status." There is thus some overlap with hospital services. The CPC definition of medical services only excludes services that do not require institutional nursing; it does not seem to exclude services supplied in hospitals. Thus, diagnosis, consultation, and treatment provided to outpatients by doctors in hospitals without nursing could be classified both as medical services and as hospital services.

Certain members' schedules also maintain the confusion. For instance, in medical services, Belize introduced a commitment on neurosurgery; Botswana introduced commitments in specialized medical services including forensic medicine, neurosurgery, cardiothoracic surgery, microvascular surgery, plastic surgery, geriatrics, traumatology, anesthesiology, clinical immunology and oncology, child psychiatry, physical medicine, and intensive care specialist; and Malaysia introduced commitments covering forensic medicine, nuclear medicine, geriatrics, microvascular surgery, neurosurgery, cardiothoracic surgery, plastic surgery, clinical immunology and oncology, traumatology, anesthesiology, intensive care specialist, child psychiatry, and physical medicine. None of these services can be provided outside hospitals with intensive institutional nursing. Apparently, according to the definitions above, they should be classified as "hospital services" and not as "medical services."

A clearer distinction between these services could be the one suggested in the first part of this chapter. Hospital services would be services that can be supplied only in hospitals—emergency services, surgery, and other heavy medical treatment or analysis. They also would include the provision of beds, space, and nursing necessary for patients to recover. Medical services would be those that can be supplied in places other than hospitals, such as diagnosis or light medical treatment. Alternatively, according to another classification, such as the one used in Belgium and the Netherlands, hospital services would be those supplied by hospitals themselves, such as the opportunity to use equipment, operating rooms, and the like, whereas medical services would be all the services provided by doctors to inpatients and outpatients. The current CPC corresponds more closely with the first of the two options proposed here, but the second option is more likely to avoid discriminatory treatment of doctors within hospitals resulting from special or exclusive rights.

Concerning certain other services that are ancillary to hospital or medical services, such as light diagnostic examinations and blood analysis, the current classification does not seem to pose problems because CPC No. 9319 appears to be the most relevant position. The other classifications do not seem to pose problems either.

Scheduling of health services.   Schedules of members determine the scope of their commitments. Services included in the schedules may be limited by certain qualifications or exclusions. For example, a member may introduce commitments for medical services, with the exception of pediatric services. When a service is covered by commitments, the extent of obligations applicable to it can also be limited by an explicit indication in the schedule describing the level of commitments made with respect to the market access (second column) and the national treatment obligations (third column). Scheduling is thus characterized by full flexibility for members. Scheduling, however, should be coherent with the rest of the GATS and limitations contained therein should be relevant. An overview of the members' Schedules of Commitments concerning health services reveals a number of difficulties in this regard. For instance, Poland and Slovenia introduced certain commitments concerning private hospital and sanatorium services, excluding services provided by the public sector. Malaysia and Mexico also introduced commitments for private hospital services only.[11] The exclusion of the public sector from the scope of commitments (i.e., as noted in the schedule's first column) does not make sense. Either a service is open to international trade or it is not. If a service is scheduled, foreign service suppliers can have access to the domestic market of the country making the commitment. Of course, this does not prevent the state from also supplying the service itself. It also may grant certain privileges to selected undertakings, whether public or private. Ownership of the undertaking is irrelevant in this regard. Therefore, if there are to be limitations to market access rights with respect to a scheduled service, in principle they cannot result from excluding an allegedly subordinate service from the scope of the commitments on the basis of its private or public nature. Pursuant to GATS Article XX.2, limitations to market access rights that result, for example, from the maintenance of certain special or exclusive rights must be the object of an explicit limitation in the second column of the schedules relating to Article XVI.

Another interpretation of the public sector exclusion above could be that the commitments do not cover the scheduled services to the extent they are provided by the public sector. This interpretation, however, would mean that the scope of commitments would continuously vary according to the level of services provided by the state. Such interpretation cannot be valid because it would be an easy way to modify the scope of commitments unilaterally and thus circumvent the procedure for the modification of schedules set forth in GATS Article XXI. If a government wants to reserve for itself the entire opportunity to provide a service, it should not insert that service in its Schedules of Commitments at all.

Market access commitments.   Subject to commitments made in individual schedules, GATS Article XVI (Market Access) requires members not to maintain national measures limiting the number of service suppliers in a domestic market, the value or quantity of services supplied, or the number of people authorized to supply a service.[12] It also requires them not to maintain limitations on the participation of foreign capital or restrictions on the legal entity under which a supplier is authorized to provide a service. Capital movements that are an essential part of the service must be authorized (see footnote 8 to para. 1 of GATS Article XVI and Article XI).

If fully applicable, Article XVI thus indirectly obliges WTO members to dismantle special or exclusive rights granted in their country to any provider of health services. It thus implies domestic liberalization of these services.[13] As indicated above, limitations to this principle are possible to the extent described in the Schedules of Commitments (see GATS Article XVI.1, footnote 8). Theoretically, states may maintain all special or exclusive rights as desired. In practice, however, it is doubtful that a member would schedule a service if it is to avoid the applicability of Article XVI.

In any event, in the health sector typical limitations might concern the possibility of countries to maintain some regional quotas of hospitals, or beds, or doctors, or quotas of services per doctor, as part of a public plan for allocating health resources. Limitations would also be expected either to maintain special or exclusive rights for certain hospitals requiring huge investments[14] or supplying a universal service or to impose universal service requirements on all new operators.[15] Additional

rules and commitments can be included in this regard in the Schedules of Commitments pursuant to GATS Article XVIII.

National treatment commitments.   GATS Article XVII contains the national treatment obligation. It has the same meaning as Article III of the GATT and implies the prohibition of de jure and de facto discrimination between domestic and foreign services and service suppliers (see WTO Appellate Body Report 1997a, paras. 233, 240, and foll.). Thus, by definition all domestic regulation that is not discriminatory by its effects is tolerated under Article XVII.

The national treatment obligation, the market access obligation, is subject to scheduling of the service concerned and may be limited by the contents of individual schedules (see footnote 8 to para. 1 of Article XVI and XI).

In the health services sector typical limitations inserted by members in their schedules could concern the possibility reserved by the states to maintain certain privileges to such public service providers as public hospitals. Indeed, without an explicit indication that these privileges can be maintained, Article XVII would require members to abolish them. Even if limited to public service providers, privileges would provide certain advantages to domestic services that foreign services would not have. Limitations could thus concern, for example, certain tax exemptions, social security reimbursements, regulatory facilities, or more lenient licensing or qualification requirements.[16]

It should be noted that in systems of organized competition, whereby the government is the buyer of hospital services and grants special or exclusive rights to hospitals making the best offer for each pathology or for the use of specific equipment, the national treatment obligation implies that every foreign service provider should have the same opportunities to bid as do domestic suppliers. If maintained, nonportability of private insurance should thus be subject to a specific limitation in column three of the schedule (assuming that the service concerned is bound).

Access to telecommunications infrastructure.   As a corollary to the national treatment obligation concerning services for which commitments were made, all existing public telecommunications infrastructure must be made available to these services pursuant to the GATS Annex on Telecommunications. This is particularly relevant to suppliers of telemedicine services. These suppliers must be able to use all public telecommunication services and networks (i.e., those offered to the public generally) on reasonable and nondiscriminatory terms and conditions (see Article 5[a] of the Annex on Telecommunications), They also have the right to purchase or lease terminal equipment or to interconnect private leased lines or owned circuits with the public network. They must be given the opportunity to use their own operating protocols and to have access to international communications and to information contained in databases (see Articles 5[b] and 5[c] of the Annex on Telecommunications).

Right to regulate services under conditions of objectivity, impartiality, and necessity to achieve the quality of the service.   Pursuant to GATS Article VI.5, read in conjunction with Article VI.4, measures relating to qualification requirements and procedures, technical standards, and licensing requirements can be adopted by WTO members even with respect to services for which they made commitments.

If these measures nullify or impair commitments of members,[17] they must be based on objective and transparent criteria, cannot be more burdensome than necessary to ensure the quality of the service, and must reasonably have been expected at the time the commitments were made. Licensing procedures themselves cannot be a restriction on the supply of services. Articles VI.4 and VI.5 do not further specify these rules, but negotiations are open on the subject.

This provision is obviously essential with respect to health services. In virtually all countries, the supply of hospital services or medical services is subject to rather severe requirements and authorization procedures. They generally create obstacles to trade by excluding or complicating entry of foreign services or service providers who do not comply with them. Depending on the commitments made, such obstacles to trade may nullify or impair commitments and thus be subject to the requirements of Article VI.5.

- *Scope of Article VI.5 of GATS*
  (i) Technical standards and licensing and qualification requirements
      Although it is not entirely clear what measures are covered by the phrase "licensing or qualification requirements," all rules relating to the opportunity for doctors or for hospitals to provide their services and the rules relating to technical standards seem to be caught by this provision.[18] This article has a very large potential scope that depends on the manner in which members organize their domestic regulation. If compliance with domestic rules is a condition for obtaining or keeping a license or an authorization to supply a service, then it can be argued that such rules are a licensing or a qualification requirement subject to the disciplines of Article VI.5.
  (ii) Nullification or impairment of commitments
      Article VI.5 only concerns standards and requirement that "nullify or impair . . . specific commitments." Arguably, this only covers measures that are adopted after commitments were made. The notion of nullification or impairment of commitments taken in the context of Article VI.5 is still unclear. Nullification or impairment of benefits accruing under the GATT has been interpreted by Panels in the context of Article XXIII of the GATT as an upsetting of improved market-access opportunities arising out of relevant tariff concessions. Thus nullification or impairment occurs, in the context of trade in goods, when a measure (whether or not consistent with the WTO) that was not reasonably anticipated affects the competitive position of the goods benefiting from the concession (see WTO Report of the Panel 1998, paras. 10.61, 10.82).
      It is unclear whether the same reasoning would apply to trade in services, but there are no obvious reasons why it should not. The concept of nullification or impairment covers measures that are consistent with GATS and those that are not. Under this interpretation, economic needs tests or other quantitative prescriptions possibly prohibited by Article XVI of GATS would be covered by Article VI.5 of the GATS licensing and qualification

requirements. The Working Party on Professional Services, however, excluded this possibility, considering that GATS Articles VI and XVI have a different scope and cover different categories of measures (see WTO Council for Trade in Services 1999a, paras. 9, 12). Thus according to the Working Party a measure that is contrary to a commitment cannot be justified under Article VI.5. By this interpretation, the article covers only standards or licensing and qualification requirements that, although consistent with commitments, would upset the competitive position of services subject to commitments in a manner that was unforeseeable at the time the commitments were made.

If this interpretation was officially recognized (for example, in the form of a WTO Council Decision), the rule would simply be another expression of the requirement that standards and licensing or qualification requirements be consistent with members' reasonable expectations. As indicated below, such interpretation would mean that all existing legislation as well as new rules that are equally or not more restrictive to trade would be excluded from the scope of Article VI.5.

- *Conditions imposed by GATS Article VI.5*
Article VI.5, read in conjunction with Article VI.4, states that qualification requirements and technical standards that nullify or impair commitments are based on objective and transparent criteria, that they could have been expected at the time commitments were made, and that they are not more burdensome than necessary to ensure the quality of the service.

(i) Objective and transparent criteria

This condition could be read first in light of the transparency requirement contained in GATS Article III. Concerning the objectivity of the criteria used, Article VI.4 refers, among other things, to the competence of the service supplier or the ability to supply the service. This would mean that qualification requirements and technical standards should not be based on subjective criteria unrelated to the provision of the services themselves. For example, they should not result simply from protectionist pressures of domestic doctors

or hospitals. The context of a case would provide all necessary elements in this regard.

(ii) The protection of reasonable expectations

The reasonable expectations of WTO members concerning the possible future domestic regulation of health services in the territory of their trade partners are not easy to define. Any regulation in place at the time of the commitments could satisfy this condition, and later rules would be satisfactory to the extent they are not more restrictive to trade than those they replace. It should be noted in this regard that the Preamble to the GATS (para. 4) recognizes the right to adopt new regulation in services in order to meet national policy objectives. Because this condition appears to reflect the limitation of the scope of Article VI.5 to measures that nullify or impair specific commitments, existing and new regulations that are not more trade restrictive would not even be covered by Article VI.5.

If new rules are more restrictive to trade, however, it would be more difficult to admit that they could reasonably have been expected at the time of commitments. One would have to find legislative proposals existing at the time of commitments or any other declaration to be able to argue the reasonableness of such expectations. This could be a source of concern for those countries that have not developed substantial regulation at the time of commitments (assuming commitments were made). And this condition seems to impede reforms in the health sector from systems of hybrid or organized competition to one of central planning.

(iii) Not more burdensome than necessary to ensure the quality of the service

The necessity test is not defined in the GATS, but one could refer to the interpretation given it in the context of GATT.[19] This is, uncertain, of course, and subject to formal clarification. Should this interpretation be confirmed in the context of GATS,[20] a trade-restrictive requirement would be necessary to the extent it represents the least trade-restrictive solution reasonably available to achieve the objective sought,[21] that is, in the context of Article VI, ensuring the quality of the service. To be more specific, according to this interpretation, to be necessary to ensure the quality of the service, a requirement must

- Relate to the quality of the service
- Be the least trade-restrictive measure reasonably available.
  (1) Relate to the quality of the service
      This test is extremely vague. The question is whether it refers to the intrinsic technical quality of the service only or if it also includes the overall economic quality of the service and the pursuit of the patients' satisfaction. According to the second view, the quality test would concern not only doctors' professional qualifications[22] and technical standards applicable to hospitals,[23] but also rules intended to make services available to all at reasonable prices.

      It remains to be seen whether this view could also justify measures intended to limit public spending and those that are connected with social security systems in general. These objectives should be covered to the extent they are part of the quality goals of ensuring a universal service or the affordability of the service for all. Furthermore, as indicated in the Preamble to the GATS, states should be able to determine for themselves the policy objectives they want to pursue and GATS Article VI should not constitute a limitation in that regard. In any event, whatever objective is included in the notion of quality of service, the level of quality sought remains a sovereign choice of each WTO member.

      All new requirements or standards that nullify or impair commitments of members and that would not be related to the quality of the service, whatever interpretation is given to this notion, would be illicit with regard to Article VI and would have to be justified according to one of the exceptions to the GATS, particularly those contained in Article XIV.

  (2) Be the least trade-restrictive measure reasonably available
      In the health sector this test, which is still speculative, is extremely difficult to apply. As a rule, new licensing and qualification requirements and technical standards are measures more restrictive to trade than the absence of requirements or standards. To evaluate the extent of trade restriction those requirements and standards entail, an analysis of the consequences of noncompliance with them could be made. For example, the lack of compliance may entail the prohibition of supply of a service or, alternatively, the imposition of an additional tax or adverse publicity for such noncompliance. Arguably, the first kind of measure would be more restrictive to trade than the second or third. The question would thus be whether enabling a noncompliant service to penetrate the market, while imposing an alternative least trade-restrictive measure, would affect the quality of the service. This is obviously a subjective determination that depends on the circumstances of the case and the concept of the quality of service used.

      Should the objective promoted by the new measure be to ensure that qualifications of doctors and technical standards of hospitals are of a certain level, a country legitimately could worry if services not meeting these requirements are supplied in its territory. This is particularly true in the health sector. So it would be more difficult to consider that measures less restrictive to trade than prohibition are reasonably available to achieve the level of quality sought.[24]

      As indicated above, new requirements that hospitals or doctors operate on a not-for-profit basis may also be in pursuance of quality objectives. These are based on the perception that a nonprofit activity may be less tempted to maximize profits to the detriment of the quality of the treatment. However, one may argue that alternative least trade-restrictive measures in this case could consist of the implementation of appropriate control mechanisms. Panels considered in the context of GATT that it is not because alternative measures are more difficult or more expensive to implement that they cannot reasonably be used (WTO Report of the Panel 1996; 2000b, para. 8.207). The difficulty lies in determining whether these alternative measures are actually less restrictive to trade and whether they are reasonable and as effective as the one adopted.

Should the quality objective pursued be the general availability of the service, then new universal service requirements such as those made to hospitals to accept all incoming patients seem to be justifiable. One could argue that less trade-restrictive measures in this regard could consist of incentives given to service providers to accept all patients rather than obligations imposed as a condition for pursuing an activity. For example, incentives could take the form of a mechanism of payment/reimbursement per service provided instead of payment per day or hour spent with a patient. An alternative measure could be an obligatory contribution to a public fund for public hospitals. But theoretically assessing here the effectiveness of these alternative measures, without considering the overall context of a case and the organization of the health system in a country, would not be appropriate. Furthermore, this determination would depend, in every case, on the level of risk tolerated by each country—arguably a sovereign choice.

Finally, if the quality objective pursued is the affordability of the service for patients, then new measures imposing maximum prices may appear to be justifiable. Again, one could argue that a less trade-restrictive measure would be the organization of an effective social security system whereby patients are reimbursed the cost of their care. In that context, if maximum prices are maintained, despite reimbursement rights, one could consider that they are intended not to guarantee the affordability of health services for patients but to ensure the sustainability of the entire social security system. The question would thus be whether the latter is a quality objective per se. As indicated above, such is the case. Otherwise all new measures imposing qualification requirements connected to social security systems would not be legal under GATS Article VI. One can argue that this would not be reasonable because these measures would be indefensible unless justified by one of the exceptions of GATS. This does not mean that these measures should not be the least trade-restrictive measures available (according to the speculative interpretation of the concept of "necessity"). Determining these measures, however, is extremely delicate and uncomfortable, considering that no optimal social security system has been found to date.

In all cases the appreciation of the degree of effectiveness of least trade-restrictive measures would have to be made in light of other countries' experiences, international standards, studies by the World Health Organization, declarations of intent of states, and so forth. Should a doubt remain as to the availability or effectiveness of a least trade-restrictive measure, it should benefit the member making the new measure. Indeed, an advantage of GATS Article VI, compared with Article XIV, is that

Article VI is not an exception to GATS. Thus the burden of proof lies on the petitioner and not on the defendant (see WTO Appellate Body Report 1997b, paras. 72–74).

In summary, determining whether *new* licensing and qualification requirements and technical standards meet the requirements of Articles VI.4 and VI.5 is rather complex and uncertain. It depends mostly on existing commitments and the status of legislation existing at the time those commitments were made. It also heavily depends on the interpretation given to the notions of "qualification requirements" and "quality of the service" and on the application that is made of the necessity test.

The only method to reach certainty in this regard would be to adopt a complete regulatory framework before commitments are made or to insert numerous limitations in the commitments. Or international agreement might be reached on a set of rules establishing the optimal regulation of the supply and consumption of health services in a domestic jurisdiction, as suggested by GATS Article VI.4 (see also Article VI:5[b]). As already noted, such international consensus seems beyond reach at this stage, not only from an economic point of view but also because of the varying perceptions that countries have of the level of social security they want to provide.

Reasonableness, objectivity, and impartiality in the administration of domestic regulation. GATS Article VI.1 imposes on governments a general obligation to be reasonable, objective, and impartial in administering domestic regulations that affect trade in services. This provision concerns all measures of general application affecting trade in health services, not only those imposing qualification requirements or technical standards. The issue here is not to check whether the measure itself is valid or necessary to achieve a specific objective, but whether its application is discriminatory or unreasonable. This rule is similar to GATT Article X.3 concerning trade in goods. Accordingly, WTO members must ensure that formalities imposed on foreign entrants are not more burdensome than necessary to achieve the objective sought, that those who are supposed to implement them are not themselves competitors of foreign service suppliers,

that they abide by minimum transparency requirements and a sense of equity, and that they provide justification for all their decisions that affect trade in health services.[25]

This provision is completed by GATS Article VI.2, which requires the implementation of judicial or administrative tribunals to review decisions affecting trade in services, and by Article VI.3, which imposes disciplines in the provision of authorizations and licenses. For instance, service suppliers applying for authorizations must be informed without delay about the status of their application and of the decision on their application.

Applying these provisions should not pose particular difficulties in the health services sector.

Activities of public monopolies. Pursuant to Article VIII, GATS rules apply to monopoly suppliers, that is, those who have been granted special or exclusive rights. As indicated above, this provision is more relevant to hospitals than to doctors. Concerning those medical services for which commitments were made (and to the extent provided for by those commitments), it requires that monopoly hospitals comply with the MFN obligation and grant access to their infrastructure to foreign doctors (without prejudice to possible qualification requirements meeting the conditions of GATS Article VI), and that they treat them as they would treat domestic doctors. These obligations imply that medical activities carried out in hospitals are classified differently than are hospital services. Otherwise, relations between hospitals and their personnel are only governed by domestic contractual laws.

Article VIII is also relevant for monopoly hospitals that supply both liberalized and reserved services.[26] It requires governments to ensure that they do not abuse their dominant position in the reserved services by acting in a manner inconsistent with their country's commitments relating to the liberalized services (Article VIII.2). The notion of "abuse of dominant position" is not explained in the GATS, and that leaves a wide margin of discretion to the legal interpreter. In practice, it could address the issue of cross-subsidization, that is, the practice of using the profits generated by the operation of the reserved service to finance the provision of the liberalized service. This could be the case of public hospitals supplying, for example, certain liberalized diagnostic services.

Restrictive business practices of private operators. Pursuant to Article IX of GATS, WTO members may find that certain business practices of doctors or independent hospitals that do not benefit from special or exclusive rights nevertheless may restrain competition and thereby restrain trade in services. Even though, strictly speaking, states are not obliged to combat such practices, at the request of any other member they must at least agree to enter into consultations with a view to eliminating those practices (Article IX.2).

This provision might be useful in those countries where hospital services recently have been liberalized but where incumbent hospitals remain de facto dominant in their market. It also could be relevant to price-fixing activities undertaken within the professional orders of doctors.

Additional commitments. As suggested by GATS Article VI.4, the rules described above may be completed by additional commitments regarding qualifications, standards, licensing requirements, and so forth. These commitments can be added to the members' Schedules of Commitments pursuant to GATS Article XVIII. As previously indicated, no such commitments have yet been made in the health sector.

Exceptions. Pursuant to Article XIV, WTO members may impose measures restricting trade in services in a manner inconsistent with their commitments under GATS if such measures are needed

- To maintain public order
- To protect human, animal, or plant life or health
- To secure compliance with laws or regulations that are not otherwise inconsistent with the provisions of the GATS,

and if those measures are not applied in a manner that would constitute a means of arbitrary or unjustifiable discrimination among countries where like conditions prevail, or would constitute a disguised restriction on trade in services.

The analysis under this provision is thus twofold. First, it is necessary to determine whether the objective of the measure concerned pursues one of the objectives indicated in Article XIV and, second, whether its application is made in good faith.[27]

Article XIV seems to complete Article VI, which relates to the conditions applicable to "new" qualification requirements and technical standards affecting trade in a scheduled service. It is different, however, in nature and scope. First, Article XIV is an exception to GATS and is relevant when other GATS obligations are not complied with. Consequently the burden of proof that the conditions of its application are met at first view shifts to the member taking the measure.[28] The doubt here benefits the petitioner, whereas in the case of Article VI it benefits the member taking the measure.

Second, Article XIV concerns all measures that are necessary to meet one of the objectives it protects. Article VI.5, instead, relates only to "new" technical standards and to "new" licensing and qualification requirements that are necessary to ensure the quality of the service. As indicated above, the notion of service quality requires clarification. It certainly includes the protection of human life and health, which is one of the objectives explicitly protected by GATS Article XIV, so several requirements or standards meeting the requirements of Article VI may not need to be scrutinized under Article XIV. Article XIV is relevant only to the extent that new qualification requirements or standards either are discriminatory or do not comply with the conditions of Article VI, among others.

It is difficult to identify in advance which measures would have to be scrutinized under Article XIV. Concerning "new" qualification requirements and standards, this would depend not only on the specific commitments made and the status of existing legislation, but also on the interpretation given to the notion of "quality of the service" in Article VI.4. If this notion corresponds only to the intrinsic technical quality of the service (i.e., doctors' professional qualifications and hospitals' technical characteristics), then "new" qualification requirements or standards pursuing the general availability of the service or the containment of public spending could be contrary to Article VI. In that case, they would have to be justified pursuant to Article XIV.

But if the notion of "quality of the service" includes requirements and standards intended to make services available to everyone at reasonable prices (as arguably it should), then Article XIV would be relevant only for those that, while being adopted after commitments were taken, are not more restrictive than existing legislation or are the least trade-restrictive measures available to ensure these objectives. Unless there is an international agreement on the optimal regulation of health services, it is extremely difficult to determine in advance the least trade-restrictive measures that are reasonably available.

Concerning measures that are not licensing or qualification requirements or technical standards, or that do not nullify or impair specific commitments, there are no specific conditions imposed on them by GATS Article VI.[29] Such measures must abide only by the commitments of members in their schedules concerning market access and national treatment and, in all cases, by the MFN principle. It is only when a violation of one of these rules is discovered that a justification under Article XIV is required. In the health sector, this would correspond to all domestic rules that affect the daily operations of doctors or hospitals but do not relate to their ability to deliver their services or to the granting of licenses or authorizations. Although, as indicated above, the dividing line between the two kinds of rules is difficult to determine, it would appear that certain aspects of the organization of the social security system,[30] or the degree of competition authorized,[31] or ethical rules or best practice recommendations[32] would fall under the second category not covered by GATS Article VI. Thus only if relevant measures are violating market access commitments[33] or are discriminatory would they have to be justified under Article XIV.

For a GATS-incompatible measure to be justified under Article XIV, it must pursue one of the objectives explicitly protected by it. In the health sector, three such objectives seem to be relevant:

1. **The protection of human life or health (Article XIV[b]).** In the health sector most domestic regulation can pretend to be connected to the appropriate organization of a country's health system. It could be argued that the lack of such regulation would constitute a risk to human life or health in that country—for example, when special or exclusive rights given to hospitals require huge investments and are connected to the financing of their fixed costs. Without these measures, there might be no investments for such hospitals.

Difficulties may arise, however, in relation to measures that are only intended to curtail public spending and that may have the effect of limiting the supply of health services. In that regard it would be difficult to pretend they are intended to protect human life or health as such.

Other difficulties concern the necessity test, which can be interpreted in the same manner as GATS Article VI or GATT Article XX. Thus only the least trade-restrictive measures that reasonably could be employed to meet stated objectives could be justified by this exception. If a less restrictive alternative measure be available and capable of providing the required level of protection, the necessity test would not be met.

With regard to the exception concerning human life or health, the Appellate Body admitted (in the context of GATT) that determining the availability of alternative measures should be very strict and that a strong degree of effectiveness should be required for a measure to be regarded as effectively meeting the objectives pursued (see WTO Appellate Body Report 2001a, paras. 172–74).

2. **The compliance with laws or regulations that are not inconsistent with the provisions of the GATS (Article XIV[c]).** This exception also exists in GATT with respect to trade in goods. In this context it has been interpreted by a GATT panel as applying to measures that actually implement laws or regulations that are GATT compatible, and not to those that pursue the same objectives of these laws or regulations.[34]

In the health services sector, this exception would be relevant for those measures that implement social security laws that are not otherwise inconsistent with the provisions of the GATS or with individual commitments. This concerns, for example, price-fixing arrangements, quotas of doctors or of services per doctor flowing from more general budgetary constraints relating to the financing of health services. Determining which measure implements the other would depend on the circumstances of the case. If appropriately drafted, much of the regulation intended to limit public spending could be caught by this exception.

The next step would be to check whether the necessity test has been met. Each specific measure would have to be the least trade-restrictive measure reasonably available to implement the main legislation. One could argue here that reimbursement limits would be less trade restrictive than, for example, quotas of doctors or quotas of services per doctor. But, considering the importance of the objective pursued by social security laws, it also could be argued that the necessity test should be interpreted rather flexibly because determining which measure would be more effective for its stated purpose would be extremely difficult.[35]

3. **The maintenance of public order (Article XIV[a]).** According to a footnote to Article XIV(a), this exception may justify measures intended to overcome a "genuine and sufficiently serious threat posed to one of the fundamental interests of society." It remains to be seen whether measures intended, for example, to maintain a social security system would qualify for this exception. Indeed, the absence of social security could constitute a genuine and serious threat to one of the fundamental interests of society.

The necessity test is applicable here. Considering the apparently broad and exceptional character of the public order exception, in this context this test will be interpreted rather strictly.

Good faith application. When a GATS-inconsistent measure pursues one of the objectives explicitly protected by GATS Article XIV, it must be applied in good faith to be entirely justified by Article XIV. The chapeau of Article XIV requires that these measures are not applied in a manner that would constitute a means of arbitrary or unjustifiable discrimination between countries where like conditions prevail, or constitute a disguised restriction on trade in services.

Developing here the meaning given by the jurisprudence to the same provision under the GATT would take too long. To summarize, even if a measure apparently satisfies the conditions imposed by one of the subparagraphs of GATS Article XIV, its actual application may reveal a disguised restriction to trade. For example, this would be the case if a measure were authorized that prohibited "foreign" hospitals from providing certain treatments because the results of those treatments are uncertain although competing treatments with equally uncertain outcomes traditionally would be

provided by national hospitals. Identification of a disguised restriction to trade obviously depends on the facts of each case and requires a proper understanding of the market concerned and of the economic interests in play.

Finally, the Appellate Body admitted that any measure that would implement an international agreement or would be the object of serious negotiations undertaken with trade partners while meeting the conditions of one of the subparagraphs of GATS Article XIV would meet the good-faith requirement contained in the chapeau of that article (see WTO Appellate Body Report 2001b, para. 119 and foll.).

In the health sector, as previously indicated, such international agreement has not yet been negotiated.

Summary Applying WTO rules to the regulation of the health services "production" is a rather complex exercise that requires careful attention, given the importance of the subject.

Although several WTO agreements could be relevant (particularly GATT 1994 and the GPA), the GATS is obviously the one that deserves the greatest attention.

The GATS concerns all measures that affect trade in services supplied either on a commercial basis or in competition with other service suppliers. In the health sector this means that almost all hospital and medical services supplied by systems other than pure central planning would be covered by GATS. The agreement is relevant anywhere that some form of competition for the supply of health services exists. Uncertainties concerning the commercial nature of the service are thus not particularly important.

One of the major characteristics of the GATS that is particularly important in the health sector is its flexibility. Depending on commitments made by member countries, virtually all domestic regulation of health services could be GATS compatible, except those that would discriminate against the services of foreign hospitals or doctors based on their nationality.

GATS's flexibility is revealed in three ways:

1. Countries first have the choice to decide whether they want to bind a specific service in their Schedules of Commitments. Should they

refuse to do so, they are bound mainly by the MFN rule and the transparency requirements. They would thus be compelled to treat services and service providers of different origin in a nondiscriminatory manner and to publish all laws and regulations that significantly affect trade in such services. Should they accept to open a service to international trade, they may limit their market access and national treatment commitments as much as needed to tailor them to their current laws.

2. In sectors in which commitments were made, technical standards and licensing and qualification requirements existing at the time of the commitments can be maintained. Countries may also impose new standards and requirements that are not more restrictive to trade than existing measures. They may finally impose new standards and requirements that are more restrictive to trade than existing measures[36] if these are necessary to ensure the quality of the services. In this situation, according to an interpretation of the concept of "necessity" that is consistent with the one developed under the GATT, they would be compelled to search for the least trade-restrictive measure reasonably available to meet stated objectives. In the health sector this may be a difficult test to apply in practice, considering the myriad possible interpretations of "quality of health services" and uncertainty regarding the effectiveness of alternative least trade-restrictive measures. In addition to standards and qualification requirements, countries may impose any conditions on the ways in which doctors or hospitals conduct business, to the extent that the conditions are compatible with their commitments and are not discriminatory.

3. Should a domestic regulation eventually be found to be incompatible with one of the provisions of GATS, it may be justified by one of the exceptions included in GATS Article XIV if it is necessary to pursue a public health objective, the application of a GATS-consistent law, such as one organizing the fiscal and budgetary aspects of the social security system, or a fundamental interest of society.

Notwithstanding this flexibility, *full commitments* in health services may require profound changes in the health systems of many countries. For example, in principle, special or exclusive rights given to hospitals or doctors must be eliminated[37] and all quantitative regulations aimed at curtailing supply of these services for the purpose of cost containment must be repealed, unless justified by one of the exceptions to the GATS (and that is unlikely).[38] Furthermore, foreign service providers must be treated the same as domestic providers. This means, among other things, that reimbursement for their services by social security funds must be done in a manner that is equitable.

In addition, if new qualification requirements and technical standards de facto nullify or impair the expectations of foreign doctors or hospital operators that accrue from commitments made, the requirements and standards must be limited to those necessary to ensure the quality of the service. So this rule, which might be relevant for countries whose domestic legislation is not particularly developed at the time when commitments are made, functions both as an element of flexibility in GATS and as a limitation on the regulatory freedom of WTO members. The limitation can be tempered by admitting that the concept of "quality of the service" incorporates whatever policy objective is connected to the service concerned and whatever objective a member decides to pursue.

Concerning measures intended to ensure the viability of the social security system, these can be tolerated if they are not discriminatory or if they do not contain quantitative limitations or economic needs tests.[39] They also can be accepted if they are existing measures or are not more trade restrictive than are existing measures. Should they take the form of licensing or qualification requirements and should they be new measures or more trade restrictive than existing ones, they could be admitted pursuant to GATS Article VI if they are necessary to ensure the quality of health services. As an alternative, if one of these measures violates a GATS provision it can be admitted pursuant to one of the exceptions contained in Article XIV if it is necessary to secure compliance with budget limitations or to maintain public order.

Finally, depending on commitments made and on the classifications and definitions given to different health services, monopoly hospitals themselves must treat the doctors working on their premises in a nondiscriminatory manner.

In conclusion, in the health services sector, the provisions that require the most delicate interpretative exercise seem to be the following:

– GATS Article VI, particularly the notions of "qualification requirements," "quality of a service," and "necessity"
– GATS Article XIV, particularly the notions of "necessity" and "public order."

Considering that these provisions are mostly relevant if the services concerned have been subject to commitments in members' schedules, a proper classification and an understanding of the scope of the services concerned are equally essential.

Assessment of the Adequacy of WTO Rules in the Health Services Sector

The final section of this chapter examines what may be the shortcomings of GATS if trade opens in the health services sector. The section reviews the regulatory issues identified in the first section of the chapter and assumes that all GATS provisions are fully applicable (i.e., that commitments were made in all sectors concerned). As was noted earlier, a trade agreement such as the GATS is most appropriately tested by assuming that all its provisions are applicable rather than by admitting that members may unilaterally limit its application.

Because this section is more prospective in nature and stretches the rules to their full potential, it may not correspond to the views currently prevailing among most WTO members. Although it is unlikely that limitations will disappear from schedules when commitments are made by members, this chapter offers an opportunity to test the horizontal provisions of the GATS to see if eventually more reliance could be placed on them rather than on individual schedules. Whenever possible, suggestions for new rules are offered.

Hospital Services

The title of this section raises the question, What services are included? This question is important if we hope to understand the level of obligations of hospitals benefiting from special or exclusive rights to the doctors working on their premises. I suggest again that hospital services are those that can be supplied only in hospitals—that is, emergency services, surgery, and other complex medical treatment or analysis. Hospital services also would include the provision of beds and space necessary for patients to recover. Such definition maintains some flexibility for monopoly hospitals with respect to the selection of their personnel. On the other hand, should a less open definition be adopted, such as the one applicable in Belgium or the Netherlands, all GATS rules would benefit all doctors, irrespective of where they work. Members should thus ensure consistency in the manner in which they define the scope of their commitments in their schedules.

Quality of the service New technical standards and licensing and qualifications requirements that relate to the hygiene of the premises, the equipment available, the qualification of personnel, and so forth, are needed to ensure the quality of the service. Although applying the necessity test depends on the circumstances of each case, it should not pose major problems with respect to requirements generally applicable in most countries.

The necessity test would pose difficulties with regard to any new obligation that hospitals operate on a not-for-profit basis. Some could argue that other requirements such as management of hospitals by doctors or reliance on ethical rules might be less restrictive to trade,[40] but the effectiveness of those alternatives remains uncertain.

Other rules, such as warranty systems undertaken by hospitals to treat patients within a certain deadline, should not pose difficulties if those systems are applied on a nondiscriminatory basis.

Universal and nondiscriminatory access to hospital services Assessing the GATS consistency of new universal service requirements (assuming that full commitments are made), such as the prohibition against hospitals refusing to admit a patient because of the seriousness of his or her condition or because of the costs of the cure or mandated contributions to a public fund, is not an easy exercise. First one must determine such licensing or qualification requirements fall within the scope of Article VI.5 of the GATS. That would be the case if they were applied as conditions imposed at the time of the licensing or the authorization procedure. The second difficulty would be determining whether universal service is part of the notion of the quality of the service in the context of Article VI.4. If the response to the first two questions is positive, then universal service requirements would fall within the scope of Articles VI.4 and VI.5. Otherwise such requirements may not be subject to a GATS discipline unless they are discriminatory or restrictive to trade in a manner incompatible with Articles XVI and XVII or with obligations assumed under Article XVIII. In that case, they would have to be justified under Article XIV of GATS.[41] The third difficulty lies in applying the necessity test in the context of Articles VI and XIV. For example, it could be argued that incentive mechanisms are less trade restrictive and could be as effective in achieving universal service as are admissibility requirements imposed on hospitals. There remains, however, a high degree of uncertainty about that. If Article VI is applicable, the doubt benefits the member taking the measure. This would be in line with the express admission of universal service requirements in the context of telecommunications services.[42] If Article XIV is applicable, however, the doubt would benefit the member challenging the measure, and thereby reduce the chances that "new" universal service requirements would be considered GATS consistent. Clarification would thus be welcome in this regard.

Rules that limit patients' choice of hospitals through reimbursement conditions often imply that special or exclusive rights are granted to hospitals per region. If that is the case, such rules might be contrary to Article XVI (assuming that full commitments have been made) and would have to be reviewed according to Article XIV. It seems unlikely that they could meet the applicable necessity test, even if their objective was to organize the general availability of hospital services.

Rules imposing a minimum number of hospitals per region do not appear to pose problems with respect to the GATS. It should only be noted that if the government itself provides public hospitals and confers on them certain privileges, such as reimbursement facilities, tax exemptions, and the like, the hospitals themselves should behave in a GATS-compatible manner toward doctors supplying distinct medical services on their premises. Furthermore, privileges granted in this context would be contrary to the national treatment principle because they would not be available to foreign hospitals' operators. Limitations to the national treatment obligation, however, could be inserted very appropriately in Schedules of Commitments, and such limitations could be justified under GATS Article XIV as necessary to protect human health. Indeed, the argument could be made that human health would be endangered in the absence of any such hospitals. Considering the remaining uncertainty in this regard, formal clarifications would be welcome.

Economic regulation and control of public expenditure Regulation of the economic aspects of the supply of hospital services is delicate and no optimal models have been found to date. It should be recalled that one of the main objectives of such regulation is to limit public spending while maintaining the quality of the service and its availability and affordability for all people. Different systems that may be adopted in this context may contain a mix of licensing requirements, limits on the number of services provided, exclusive rights granted to certain operators, and internal regulation concerning conditions for the reimbursement of hospital services or the manner in which the services should be supplied.

Assuming no discrimination among services and service suppliers according to their nationality,[43] different aspects of the systems implemented by states may fall either within the scope of Article XVI (Market Access), Article VI (Licensing Requirements), or Article XIV (Exceptions to Illicit Trade Restrictions). Parts of the system may be tolerated whereas other parts will be considered illicit, thus dismantling the system entirely.

Measures aimed at directly controlling the supply of hospital services, such as limits on the number of hospitals or hospital beds, would be contrary to GATS Article XVI in the absence of any such limits included in the schedule of the member taking the measure (assuming that full commitments are made).[44] Measures limiting the number of doctors per hospital either would be contrary to Article XVI (concerning medical services that are not hospital services supplied by doctors in hospitals) or would be considered licensing requirements imposed on hospitals (which would fall under Article VI). In any case, these measures would be needed either to ensure the quality of the service (Article VI of GATS) or to protect public order or secure compliance with a social security system that is not otherwise inconsistent with the GATS (Article XIV).

There is no obvious evidence that these measures would comply with the necessity test. One could argue that least trade-restrictive measures could consist of incentives given to hospitals to limit the number of treatments they supply to patients or of incentives given to patients to consume fewer hospital services. But the effectiveness of these alternative measures is uncertain. Empirical evidence is needed. On the other hand, the GATS could provide a more flexible rule indicating conditions on which measures directly limiting supply of hospital services would be tolerated, in light of the need to ensure the viability of a social security system. A suggestion could be to admit all such measures to the extent they are *related to* the maintenance of a social security system. The test of the existence of a "relation" rather than a "necessity" arguably would be more in line with the existing uncertainty about managing social security in health economy. This test is also used in GATT Article XX, the provision corresponding to GATS Article XIV with respect to the conservation of exhaustible natural resources. It has been interpreted in this context as requiring a "*close and real*" connection between the measure and the objective pursued.[45]

It should be recalled that if measures limiting the number of doctors per hospital fall within the scope of GATS Article VI, only new measures that are more restrictive to trade than those existing at the time of commitments would be subject to the necessity test. By contrast, if Article XIV were applicable, all measures would have to be scrutinized under this test. Formal clarifications of the provisions applicable to these measures would be welcome. The issue is clearly linked to the need for coherent definitions of hospital services and medical services.

Cost control mechanisms also have an unclear status in the GATS. In principle, full commitments in the health services sector would render untenable those systems that require the granting of special or exclusive rights to hospitals. Under certain conditions, those rights could be justified pursuant to Article XIV if access to those rights results from nondiscriminatory procedures and the rights are necessary to protect human life or health or one of the "fundamental interests of society," or to secure

compliance with a social security system that is not otherwise inconsistent with the GATS.

Central planning systems would be subject to the necessity test. Central appropriations to hospitals in a region might be considered necessary to cover hospitals' fixed costs. In such a case, the selection of the authorized hospitals and the allocation techniques should be entirely transparent and based on objective criteria related to the objective pursued. Varieties of such systems, which could be more easily defended, would require that the allocation of appropriations be made on the basis of transparent and nondiscriminatory procedures, such as bidding, handled by the state (or public social security funds) acting as purchasers of hospital services.

Systems of hybrid competition whereby hospitals are paid for services provided on the basis of prices uniformly fixed in advance do not necessarily entail the granting of special or exclusive rights. They also enable some form of competition among hospitals. Thus, to the extent no privileges are granted, such systems would have more chances to be GATS consistent than would centrally planned systems (assuming that full commitments have been made). It is doubtful that price fixing by the government would pose particular problems under GATS, unless the low level of prices, coupled with subsidies to local operators, resulted in market access restrictions.

If systems of hybrid competition nevertheless included the granting of special or exclusive rights to operators, they would obviously have less chance of being GATS consistent. Special or exclusive rights could be justified only if they were necessary, for example, to enable hospital investments in a region. In that case, these systems arguably should be structured as systems of organized competition; that is, special or exclusive rights would be granted to hospitals making the best offer for each illness or for the use of specific equipment. It might be argued that granting privileges in the form of reimbursement limited to services supplied by the selected hospitals instead of formal exclusivity might be a less trade-restrictive option.

I doubt that systems of additional competition, in which the mechanism of organized competition is completed by the patient's choice of the procuring entity of hospital services, would increase chances of being GATS consistent. In fact, although these systems obviously increase the level of competition in domestic markets, the GATS is not directly concerned with this aspect because it is not its purpose to impose the most efficient domestic regulatory models.

Mixtures of the various systems, such as central budgetary planning (for fixed costs) and hybrid or additional competition (for variable costs), are likely to become the more common regulatory frameworks. The difficulty with them lies in their central planning component, which inevitably entails the granting of special or exclusive rights associated with financing the fixed costs of the hospitals concerned, especially if prices for the services rendered are not sufficient to cover them. Given the usually high level of fixed costs, however, these systems may be the only ones enabling some form of competition in the market while maintaining social security. Furthermore, maintaining special or exclusive rights may be necessary to provide certain services that require huge investments and that are arguably natural monopolies, such as emergency services or highly sophisticated equipment. Unless already excluded from commitments in schedules, the market access limitations resulting from those rights could be justified by the exception clause Article XIV that relates to human life or health.

Medical Services

As I have noted, the definition of medical services remains unsettled, particularly regarding services that doctors supply in hospitals. If all of these services are qualified as medical services, then commitments made with respect to them must be applied by hospitals that have been granted special or exclusive rights pursuant to GATS Article VIII. Furthermore, those hospitals cannot use the financing they receive through the operation of the services for which they benefit from special or exclusive rights to cross-subsidize medical services for which commitments have been made.

Quality of the services Requirements of diplomas, technical qualifications, experience, and the like are fully justifiable under Article VI because they are necessary to ensure the quality of the services provided. It is important, however, that these requirements be related to the quality of the service. That would not be the case with requirements that have a protectionist nature intended to benefit established doctors—for example, a requirement that foreign doctors repeat a course of medical education. Defining the appropriate boundary between normal and excessive requirements may not always be easy and would depend on the circumstances of the case. The necessity test seems appropriate here and there is not much more that current rules could (and should) achieve in this regard. Remember that the necessity test can be interpreted rather flexibly when human life or health considerations are at stake.

State formulation of good practices in medical treatment, as well as ethical rules, arguably are merely internal regulations subject to nondiscrimination rules. Should they be implemented as licensing conditions, Article VI.5 would apply if they nullified or impaired commitments made. This would be the case if the new rules were more restrictive to trade than were any existing measures, such as membership in a professional organization becoming obligatory or new sanctions being imposed against those who did not comply with the new measures. In such situations, rules intended only to protect the economic interests of local doctors would not be justifiable; the new rules would have to be necessary to ensure the quality of the service.

Finally, rules establishing professional liability of doctors would not pose particular problems because they are merely internal regulations subject to the nondiscrimination rules.

Universal and nondiscriminatory access to medical services Requiring a minimum number of doctors may oblige the state to provide its own doctors. In that case the doctors could be employed by public hospitals and could benefit de facto from exclusive rights in those hospitals. Such exclusive rights could be justified under GATS Article XIV by the need to protect human health or to ensure compliance with rules that require the supply of a universal service.

However, it is unlikely that denying patients the freedom to choose their doctors could be accepted under GATS (assuming that full commitments are made). Restrictions along those lines normally are accompanied by special or exclusive rights granted to doctors per zone of habitation and result in market access restrictions. As with hospital services, the need for such measures to ensure universal service is highly questionable.

Control of public expenditure The application of GATS to the different techniques aimed at limiting public spending for medical services may be as delicate as it is for hospital services. The difficulty also derives from the lack of any agreed optimal solution.

Quantitative limits on the number of services provided—for example, limits on the number of graduated doctors admissible in a country or regional limits on the number of established doctors—may be contrary to Article XVI. Justification for these restrictions would depend on their being necessary to maintain a viable social security system in the context of Article XIV. It is doubtful that such measures, which would require the granting of special or exclusive rights, would pass the necessity test. It could be argued that incentives to reduce the supply of medical services by doctors, implemented through social security regulations, might be less trade-restrictive measures.[46] The effectiveness of these alternative measures is uncertain, however, and it would be necessary to clarify which quantitative limitations intended to reduce social security costs would be admissible under the GATS. Alternatively, a new test requiring a "real and close" relationship between the measure and the objective pursued could be established.

Other limitations, such as a fixed number of services per illness, quotas of services per doctor, or prohibition of direct access to specialist doctors or hospitals, would also be contrary to either Article VI.5 or Article XVI. This means that these limits also may have to be reviewed in light of the necessity test in the context of Article XIV. It is extremely difficult, of course, to make such an evaluation at this stage and, as is the case with the more direct quantitative limitations addressed in the previous paragraph, a clarification would be welcome here.

New and complex qualifications requirements for doctors unrelated to medical skills arguably would nullify or impair commitments made and would be contrary to GATS Article VI. They probably would be unjustifiable under Article XIV as well, unless they are needed to maintain public order or ensure compliance with social security

laws that are GATS consistent. This remains uncertain, although these measures appear to be less restrictive to trade than do more direct limitations imposed on the supply of medical services.

Including certain services that are eligible for reimbursement in a limited list of items defined by the state does not alone constitute a limit on the number of services authorized, so it would be difficult to consider it a violation of Article XVI. Therefore this kind of measure could be authorized, unless it operates de facto as a means to discriminate against foreign doctors, in which case it would be contrary to GATS Article XVII.[47]

Cost limitation systems can be reviewed according to the same principles as those applicable to hospital services. A system of pure central planning does not seem to be acceptable (assuming that full commitments have been made). In the context of hospital services, such a system might be accepted as necessary to finance high fixed costs, but that argument does not pertain to medical service whose fixed costs are rather limited. In systems of hybrid competition, price-fixing arrangements among doctors may raise competition concerns that justify the states' entry into consultations with each other in the context of GATS Article IX. It may be less trade restrictive merely to accept complete liberalization of prices of medical services applicable to patients, even if caps are established for the reimbursed portion of the honoraria.

Generally speaking, granting special or exclusive rights in the context of medical services appears to be less justifiable than in the case of hospital services because of the more limited fixed costs of doctors and the absence of natural monopolies.

Access to infrastructure by doctors As previously indicated, doctors' access to hospital infrastructure depends on the classification given to their services. If their services are not classified as hospital services, then arguably they should benefit from the infrastructure of hospitals that have been granted special or exclusive rights, in accordance with GATS Article VIII. Those hospitals cannot take advantage of their regionally dominant positions to adversely affect the competitive positions of doctors who are not connected with them. Finally, access of telemedicine services to the existing public telecommunications infrastructure should not pose particular difficulties because of the provisions of the Annex on Telecommunications (assuming full commitments have been made).

Conclusion

Although it appears that the GATS is sufficiently flexible to support almost all regulatory systems for the provision of health services—except those that would discriminate among foreign services and service suppliers—its application in a number of cases still raises several uncertainties. These increase with the level of commitments made.

The higher degree of legal certainty currently derives from the absence of any commitments at all. If commitments are made, the lack of clarity in applicable horizontal rules (particularly those pertaining to domestic regulation) will encourage members to limit the scope of those commitments in their schedules. Members may consider it important to maintain certain special or exclusive rights or other trade-restrictive measures that are associated with public spending reductions and other objectives.

Without limitations described in schedules, trade-restrictive domestic regulations may have to be shown necessary either to ensure the quality of health service or to protect one of the nontrade objectives covered by the exception clause of GATS Article XIV. Uncertainty in this respect, especially in relation to such important notions as "licensing or qualification requirements," "quality of service," "necessity," or "public order," as well as rules governing the burden of proof that depend on the applicability of either Article VI or Article XIV, inevitably discourage members from relying on general rules in the absence of individual limits.

Inserting limits in schedules is another source of difficulties. Individual schedules are not always legally consistent or relevant. In addition to the recurring problem of defining terms, limiting the scope of commitments to private services only at best is useless and at worst enables the unilateral reduction of commitments in a manner incompatible with GATS Article XXI. Furthermore, the possible variety of commitments and limits that reflect the diversity and spread of regulatory models may complicate matters and, in fact, may disorganize

trade in health services more than they open it. (Such a situation calls to mind the circumstances existing in trade in goods before the Uruguay Round.) Furthermore, in the practice of negotiations, the possibility of imposing unilateral limitations may be restricted.

It thus appears necessary to clarify a number of concepts before any general opening to trade can be encouraged in the health sector. States must be aware of the precise consequences that such opening would entail. Full commitments in health services may have a profound effect on the organization of their health systems. States that have been trying to achieve a delicate balance among a number of objectives—the inherent quality of the services, universal access to them at affordable prices, and the maintenance of a viable social security system—must understand precisely how each objective would be affected by regulation under GATS. Indeed, uncertainty concerning any one component of the system may affect the entire system, especially if budget considerations and delicate political balancing enter into play. It is understandable that states would be reluctant to accept the right of panels to judge the GATS consistency of their legislation after the fact. This is especially true if applying provisions that pose problems requires an important level of discretionary appreciation. For example, the necessity test could entail determining the effectiveness of least trade-restrictive measures that might be available. Clearly, because no optimal regulatory system has been found to date, such a determination would have a regulatory effect it might be inappropriate to permit a panel to define.

In summary, the following clarifications are most necessary:

- First, concerning the definitions and classification of health services, a clear distinction should be made between hospital services and medical services, at the least. Beyond that, the more subclassifications that can be drawn, the better. For the purpose of consistency with the rest of GATS, classification criteria should not be based on ownership of the undertakings that provide the services.
- Second, concerning Articles VI.4 and VI.5, the main technical standards and licensing or qualification requirements should be specified. They

should correspond to qualitative conditions that are imposed on service providers to enable them to provide their services. These specifications obviously should rely on the work undertaken within the Working Party on Domestic Regulation. Then, because GATS Articles VI.4 and VI.5 require these measures, if new, to be necessary to ensure the quality of the services, the notions of "quality of health services" and "necessity" should be defined. "Quality of health services" could incorporate not only technical considerations, but also the need to make health services available to all people at reasonable prices. The necessity test also could explicitly incorporate a flexible criterion of proportionality that, arguably, would be more appropriate than the search for the least trade-restrictive measure available and the determination of its effectiveness to meet the objective pursued.

- Third, the importance of the exceptions contained in Article XIV should not be underestimated. In particular, they are relevant to most trade-restrictive rules aimed at curtailing public spending, such as quotas of hospitals or doctors or of services per hospital or doctor, and the like—that is, all rules that formally limit the supply of health services. Budgetary considerations relating to the financing of health services are essential for finding the balance between universal access to health services and reasonable cost, and the circumstances under which these trade-restrictive rules could be justified under Article XIV should be specified. Because there is no agreed optimal system concerning the economic aspects of health services regulation, perhaps the necessity test could be replaced by a requirement of a "real and close" connection between the measures employed and the objective of achieving a complete and sustainable financing of health services. Also, Article XIV would be relevant in assessing the admissibility of special or exclusive rights that are connected to the financing of fixed costs of hospitals that need significant investments. It can be argued that these rights are justifiable pursuant to GATS Article XIV(b), but this could be made explicit.

The question is then how to insert these clarifications in the WTO regulatory system. Perhaps the most appropriate method would be to negotiate outside the WTO an international agreement that addresses the profoundly technical and political character of the issues raised. Furthermore, both Article VI and Article XIV are crafted to take into account international agreements that would satisfy, for example, the necessity test. In Article VI this is made explicit with respect to international standards of relevant international organizations (Article XV.5[b]). In Article XIV the jurisprudence of the Appellate Body related to GATT Article XX admits that, to the extent they meet one of the objectives covered by this provision, regulations complying with international instruments may not constitute a means of arbitrary or unjustifiable discrimination among countries where like conditions prevail.

Alternatively, a possible solution within the WTO system would be to negotiate a kind of Reference Paper, like those created for basic telecommunications[48] or accountancy (WTO Council for Trade in Services 1998), which would clarify all provisions whose application in the sector is still uncertain. Such reference paper would then be included in Schedules of Commitments pursuant to GATS Article XVIII and would accompany any new commitments made in the health services sector, and clearly would be supported by the work carried out within the Working Party on Domestic Regulation.

In the health services sector, given the importance of the objectives pursued by domestic regulation and the interdependence of each regulatory element, the clearer and more thorough the GATS rules are, the better. Thus, to the extent possible, opening debate on this issue may be more appropriate than relying exclusively on horizontal rules, even if the latter are substantially improved and completed. Trade negotiations could provide an additional step toward the definition of well-balanced health systems.

Endnotes

1. Readers are referred to a comprehensive study conducted in 1998 under the auspices of the United Nations Conference on Trade and Development (UNCTAD) and the World Health Organization, which describes existing trade flows and addresses the regulatory barriers that need to be overcome to facilitate such trade for the benefit of developing countries (UNCTAD/WHO 1998).

2. Twelve WTO members plus the 15 members of the European Community have agreed to be bound by the Government Procurement Agreement.

3. See Annex 4 and Note 1 to Article I:1 of the GPA. The country concerned is the United States. This is of little practical importance, however, because of the predominance of the private sector there (WTO Council for Trade in Services 1998, para. 41).

4. See Annexes 1 to 3 and Article I:1 of the GPA.

5. Arguably, a service can be supplied below cost *and* on a commercial basis. Indeed, it may be cross-subsidized by revenues generated by another service of the same operator. This is why the proposed test looks at the manner in which the supplier of the service is organized and not at the manner or the conditions under which the specific service is supplied.

6. There is a difference between the financing of a service and its acquisition by a social security fund for the benefit of its affiliates. In the first case, there is no commercial relationship. In the second case, arguably, the commercial relationship exists between the service provider and the social security fund.

7. This should be distinguished from the situation in which the government itself acts as an "investor."

8. See Article I.1 of the GATS. In accordance with Article I.3, GATS rules apply to central, regional, or local public authorities and to nongovernmental bodies in the exercise of powers delegated by the above-cited public authorities.

9. Horizontal exemptions applicable to all service sectors, however, could be relevant—for example, limitations to land ownership, participation in the equity of domestic service providers, free movement of persons, and the like.

10. It should be noted that, under certain conditions set forth in GATS Article V, members may conclude preferential regional trade agreements.

11. It should be noted that the public sector exclusion is found in several other schedules and is not limited to the countries above and to the health services sector.

12. These measures can take the form of quotas or economic needs tests. Article XVI applies to market access through the modes of supply identified in Article I. The restrictions that are prohibited by Article XVI, to the extent indicated in schedules, are explicitly formulated in paragraphs (a) to (f) of GATS Article XVI.2. Again, it should be stressed that members prefer that the actual structure of the GATS is reflected in the terminology used; what is not explicitly included in commitments is permitted. It should be noted, however, that if a service is scheduled, then the "prohibitions" contained in Articles XVI and XVII are fully applicable to that service, unless limitations are expressly mentioned in the second or third column of individual schedules.

13. This means opening the sector concerned to competition in the national territory.

14. Such rights could be conferred, for instance, in the context of build-operate-transfer arrangements whereby private investors agree to build a hospital in exchange for a certain period of exclusivity.

15. The imposition of such requirements could be subject to economic needs tests that are, in principle, prohibited in paragraphs (a) to (d) of GATS Article XVI.2.

16. If the services concerned are scheduled, such limitations must be explicitly included in the third column of members' Schedules of Commitments relating to Article XVII. If these limitations also affect market access rights of members, then their indication in the second column suffices because it remains valid for the third column as well (Article XX.2).

17. Arguably, this could include requirements and standards that violate Article XVI of GATS. The Working Party on Professional Services excluded this possibility, maintaining that Articles VI and XVI have a different scope and cover different categories of measures (see WTO Council for Trade in Services 1999a, paras. 9 and 12).

18. These have been defined by the Working Party on Domestic Regulation in the following manner: ". . . qualification requirements, that is to say substantive requirements which a professional service supplier is required to fulfil in order to obtain certification or a licence; qualification procedures, administrative or procedural rules relating to the administration of qualification requirements; licensing requirements, comprising substantive requirements other than qualification requirements, which a service supplier is required to comply with in order to obtain a formal permission to supply a service; licensing procedures, administrative procedures relating to the submission and processing of an application for a licence; and technical standards, requirements which may apply both to the characteristics or definition of the service and to the manner in which it is performed" (WTO Council for Trade in Services 1999a, para. 4).

19. See WTO Council for Trade in Services (1999a, para. 19 and foll.). It should be noted that there is no agreement on this interpretation of the necessity test for the future. The European Communities propose in this regard a proportionality test (see WTO Working Party on Domestic Regulation 2001; see also WTO Working Party on Domestic Regulation 2000).

20. If a panel or the Appellate Body is requested to arbitrate a dispute concerning GATS, it is likely that they would confirm this interpretation in order to maintain consistency across WTO agreements. In fact, to interpret their provisions in accordance with Article 31.2 of the Vienna Convention on the Law of Treaties, all WTO agreements are considered one unique international treaty (see WTO Appellate Body Report 1999, para. 81; WTO Report of the Panel 2001, paras. 7.46, 7.47, and 7.128).

21. See WTO Appellate Body Report 2001a, paragraph 170 and following; GATT 1947 Panel Report 1990b, paragraph 75; and WTO Report of the Panel 1996, paragraph 6.24. This definition of the term "necessary" was adopted for the first time in the context of GATT Article XX(d) (GATT 1947 Panel Report 1989, para. 5.26).

22. Note in this regard that Article VI.6 of GATS specifies "[i]n sectors where specific commitments regarding professional services are undertaken, each Member shall provide for adequate procedures to verify the competence of professionals of any other Member."

23. Quality standards applicable to hospitals typically include standards related to the hygiene of the premises, the equipment available, the qualification of personnel, architectural requirements, and so forth.

24. The Appellate Body admitted that, in the context of GATT Article XX(b), in which the necessity test is also used, the severity of the review of an alternative measure's effectiveness must equal the importance of the objective pursued. Protecting human health has been considered to be of vital importance in this context (WTO Appellate Body Report 2001a, paras. 172–74).

25. Concerning GATT Article X.3 see WTO Appellate Body Report 1998, paragraph 182 and following; WTO Report of the Panel 2000a, paragraph 11.80 and following; and WTO Report of the Panel 2000c, paragraph 6.51.

26. Reserved services are those that are subject to special or exclusive rights and that are unbound in Schedules of Commitments.

27. This sequence of the analysis has been established by the Appellate Body with regard to GATT Article XX, the provision corresponding to GATS Article XIV (see WTO Appellate Body Report 1996, section IV, para. 1; WTO Appellate Body Report 1998, paras. 115 and 157; and WTO Appellate Body Report 2000, para. 156).

28. Concerning GATT Article XX see WTO Appellate Body Report 1996, section III.A; WTO Report of the Panel 2000b, paragraph 8.166; and GATT 1947 Panel Report 1989, paragraph 5.9.

29. All of these measures would be subject to Article VI.1, requiring that they be administered in a reasonable, objective, and impartial manner.

30. This would concern the fiscal aspects of the social security system, or rules aimed at limiting expenses, such as the prohibition of direct access to specialist doctors or hospitals or the inclusion of services eligible for reimbursement in a limited list of items defined by the state.

31. This would concern, for example, rules governing the ability of patients to choose their doctors or hospitals or price-fixing arrangements among doctors, hospitals, and the government.

32. This would also arguably cover warranties imposed to treat patients within certain deadlines, additional liabilities for doctors, and the like.

33. This could be the case, for example, if rules maintaining special or exclusive rights were connected to the financing of hospitals.

34. WTO Report of the Panel 1997, paragraphs 5.9–5.11; GATT 1947 Panel Report 1990a, paragraphs 5.16–5.18.

35. The Appellate Body admitted, in the context of GATT Article XX(d), that the necessity test could be applied in a more flexible manner according to such issues as the relative importance of the common interests or the common values that the legislation seeks to protect (WTO Appellate Body Report 2000, paras. 162–64).

36. Arguably, such standards and requirements would nullify and impair existing commitments. This, however, must be demonstrated by the claimant (GATS Article VI.5).

37. Exceptions can be tolerated if special or exclusive rights are connected to the financing of certain hospitals' fixed costs and if it can be demonstrated that there would be no hospitals without such financing. In such a case, GATS Article XIV(b) relative to the protection of human life or health could apply.

38. Other measures aimed at containing public costs may be authorized, such as reimbursement caps, obligations to consult a general practitioner before having access to specialist doctors, and so forth.

39. It is assumed that commitments are made with respect to the health services that benefit from social security reimbursements.

40. Throughout this section it is assumed that the necessity test is interpreted in a manner consistent with the GATT, that is, requiring that recourse is made to the least trade-restrictive measure that reasonably can be used. See endnote 21.

41. An alternative, of course, is to introduce a request to modify a schedule, pursuant to GATS Article XXI, to include limitations concerning new universal service requirements that would be contrary to Articles XVI or XVII. This possibility is limited, however, to a period of three years after the entering into force of the commitments and it requires the negotiation of compensatory adjustments. In addition, remember that the methodological assumption underlying this section of the chapter is that full commitments have been made so that the adequacy of horizontal provisions in the GATS can be assessed.

42. See Article 3 of the "Reference Paper" annexed to commitments made by most members on basic telecommunications services.

43. Rules prohibiting portability of insurance (whether public or private) would be discriminatory and contrary to GATS Article XVII. If full commitments are made in relation to hospital services, it is unlikely that they could be justified according to one of the subparagraphs of Article XIV.

44. Measures limiting the supply of heavy equipment to specific hospitals could be contrary to GATT Article XI, but that issue falls outside the scope of this chapter.

45. WTO Appellate Body Report 1998, paragraphs 136–37 and 140–41. To avoid the uncomfortable character of the necessity test, a proportionality test has been suggested by the European Communities (see WTO Working Party on Domestic Regulation 2001).

46. This could be the case, for example, when reimbursement by social security funds is limited to a specific number of consultations per day per doctor.

47. This would be the case of prohibition of insurance portability for medical services supplied abroad (affecting the supply of these services under Mode 2).

48. See Fourth Protocol to the GATS, S/L/20, 30 April 1996, WTO. See also WTO Negotiating Group on Basic Telecommunications 1996.

References

Adams, O., and C. Kinnon. 1998. "A Public Health Perspective." In *International Trade in Health Services—A Development Perspective*. Geneva: UNCTAD/WHO.

Adlung, R. 2000. "Service Trade Liberalisation from Developed and Developing Country Perspectives." In Pierre Sauvé and Robert M. Stern, eds., *GATS 2000: New Directions in Services Trade Liberalization*. Washington, D.C.: Brookings Institution Press.

Adlung, R., and A. Carzaniga. 2001. "Health Services under the General Agreement on Trade in Services." *Bulletin of the WHO*, No. 79.

Butkeviciene J., and D. Diaz. 1998. "GATS Commitments in the Health Service Sector and the Scope for Future Negotiations." In *International Trade in Health Services—A Development Perspective*. Geneva: UNCTAD/WHO.

Detels, R., W. Holland, J. McEwen, and G. S. Omenn, eds. 1996. *Oxford Textbook of Public Health*, 3rd ed., vol. 1. Oxford, U.K.: Oxford University Press.

Duriez, M., and D. Lequet-Slama. 1998. "Health Systems in Europe." *Que sais-je?* 3343. (In French)

Feketekuty, G. 2000. "Regulatory Reform and Trade Liberalization in Services." In Pierre Sauvé and Robert M. Stern, eds., *GATS 2000: New Directions in Services Trade Liberalization*. Washington, D.C.: Brookings Institution Press.

GATT (General Agreement on Tariffs and Trade). 1989. *1947 Panel Report. United States—Section 337 of the Tariff Act of 1930.* Adopted November 7. L/6439, *BISD* 36S/386.

————. 1990a. 1947 Panel Report. *EEC—Regulation on Imports of Parts and Components.* Adopted May 16. L/6657. *BISD* 37S/142.

————. 1990b. 1947 Panel Report. *Thailand—Restrictions on Importation of and Internal Taxes on Cigarettes.* Adopted November 7. DS10/R. *BISD* 37S/214.

Hoekman B. M., and P. A. Messerlin. 2000. "Liberalising Trade in Services: Reciprocal Negotiations and Regulatory Reform." In Pierre Sauvé and Robert M. Stern, eds., *GATS 2000: New Directions in Services Trade Liberalization.* Washington, D.C.: Brookings Institution Press.

Holland, W., and E. Mossialos. 1999. *Public Health Policies in the European Union.* London: Aldershot.

Lambert, Denis-Clair. 2000. *Les systèmes de santé. Analyse et évaluation comparée dans les grands pays industriels,* Paris: Economie humaine, Editions du Seuil. (In French)

Low, P., and A. Mattoo. 2000. "Is There a Better Way? Alternative Approaches to Liberalization under GATS." In Pierre Sauvé and Robert M. Stern, eds., *GATS 2000: New Directions in Services Trade Liberalization.* Washington, D.C.: Brookings Institution Press.

Mandil, S. H. 1998. "TeleHealth. What Is it? Will It Propel Cross-Border Trade in Health Services?" In *International Trade in Health Services—A Development Perspective.* Geneva: UNCTAD/WHO.

Mossialos, E., and J. Legrand, eds. 1999. *Health Care and Cost Containment in the European Union.* London: Aldershot.

Nicolaïdis, K., and J. Trachtman. 2000. "From Policed Regulation to Managed Recognition in GATS." In Pierre Sauvé and Robert M. Stern, eds., *GATS 2000: New Directions in Services Trade Liberalization.* Washington, D.C.: Brookings Institution Press.

OECD (Organisation for Economic Co-operation and Development). 1994. *La réforme des systèmes de santé—Etude de dix-sept pays de l'OCDE,* Paris. (In French)

————. 1996. *La réforme des systèmes de santé. La volonté de changement.* Paris. (In French)

Pierre Sauvé and Robert M. Stern, eds. 2000. *GATS 2000: New Directions in Services Trade Liberalization.* Washington, D.C.: Brookings Institution Press.

UNCTAD (United Nations Conference on Trade and Development. 1998. "International Trade in Health Services: Difficulties and Opportunities for Developing Countries" In *International Trade in Health Services—A Development Perspective.* Geneva: UNCTAD/WHO.

UNCTAD/WHO (World Health Organization), eds. 1998. *International Trade in Health Services—A Development Perspective."* Geneva.

Van Ryn, J., and J. Heenen. 1976. *"Principes de droit commercial,"* Vol. 1, 2nd ed. Brussels: Bruylant. (In French)

WTO (World Trade Organization). 1998. *Disciplines on Domestic Regulation in the Accountancy Sector.* S/L/64, December 17.

WTO Appellate Body Report. 1996. *United States—Standards for Reformulated and Conventional Gasoline.* WT/DS2/AB/R, April 29.

————. 1997a. *European Communities—Regime for the Importation, Sale, and Distribution of Bananas.* WT/DS27/AB/R, AB 1997-3, September 9.

————. 1997b. *India—Patent Protection for Pharmaceuticals and Agricultural Chemical Components.* WT/DS50/AB/R, December 19.

————. 1998. *United States—Import Prohibition of Certain Shrimp and Shrimp Products.* WT/DS58/AB/R, October 12.

————. 1999. *Korea—Definitive Safeguard Measure on Imports of Certain Dairy Products.* WT/DS98/AB/R, December 14.

————. 2000. *Korea—Measures Affecting Imports of Fresh, Chilled, and Frozen Beef.* WT/DS161/AB/R, WT/DS169/AB/R, December 11.

————. 2001a. *European Communities—Measures Affecting Asbestos and Asbestos-Containing Products.* WT/DS135/AB/R, March 12.

————. 2001b. *United States—Import Prohibition of Certain Shrimp and Shrimp Products.* WT/DS58/AB/R, November 6. Recourse to Article 21:5 of the Dispute Settlement Understanding by Malaysia. WT/DS58/AB/RW, October 22.

WTO Council for Trade in Services. 1998. "Health and Social Services." Background Note by the Secretariat. S/C/W/50, September 18.

————. 1999a. "Article VI:4 of GATS: Disciplines on Domestic Regulation Applicable to All Services." Note by the Secretariat. S/C/W/96, March 1.

————. 1999b. "International Regulatory Initiatives in Services." Background Note by the Secretariat. S/C/W/97, March 1.

WTO Negotiating Group on Basic Telecommunications. 1996. *Definitions and Principles on the Regulatory Framework for the Basic Telecommunications Services* (the "Reference Paper"). April 24.

WTO Report of the Panel. 1996. *United States—Standards for Reformulated and Conventional Gasoline.* WT/DS2/R, January 29.

————. 1997. *Canada—Certain Measures Concerning Periodicals.* WT/DS31/R, March 14.

————. 1998. *Japan—Measures Affecting Consumer Photographic Film and Paper.* WT/DS44/R, March 31.

————. 2000a. *Argentina—Measures Affecting the Export of Bovine Hides and the Import of Finished Leather.* WT/DS155/R, December 19.

————. 2000b. *European Communities—Measures Affecting Asbestos and Asbestos-Containing Products.* WT/DS135/R, September 18.

————. 2000c. *United States—Antidumping Measures on Stainless Steel Plate in Coils and Stainless Steel Sheets and Strip from Korea.* WT/DS179/R, December 22.

————. 2001. *United States—Transitional Safeguard Measure on Combed Cotton Yarn from Pakistan.* WT/DS192/R, May 31.

WTO Working Party on Domestic Regulation. 2000. "The Necessity Test." Communication from the Republic of Korea. S/WPDR/W/9, September 28.

————. 2001. "Domestic Regulation: Necessity and Transparency." Communication from the European Communities and Their Member States. S/WPDR/W/14, May 1.

12

DOMESTIC REGULATION AND TRADE IN SERVICES: LOOKING AHEAD

Aaditya Mattoo
Pierre Sauvé

Background Considerations

This volume of essays has explored one of the most important and difficult issues in international trade today: the relationship between trade and investment liberalization and domestic regulatory autonomy. Although regulatory autonomy is required to enable domestic rules to respond to local conditions, there may be times when such autonomy leads to trade friction, either unintentionally or as disguised protectionism.

The interface between international trade and domestic regulatory conduct has been the object of a growing body of rules and jurisprudence in relation to trade in goods but is new in the realm of services. Given the pervasive influence that domestic regulatory conduct exerts on trade and investment conditions, it is no surprise that the above tensions, and the attendant policy sensitivities to which they give rise, have become so prominent in General Agreement on Trade in Services (GATS) negotiating circles.

A paradox of the body of rules governing trade in services at the multilateral level is that the disciplines dealing with the centrally important issue of

domestic regulation and the disciplines' effect on market access rank among the weakest elements in the body of rules. GATS Article VI remains provisional in nature. A central question confronting the multilateral community—and one to which the contributors to this volume have tried to provide some answers—is how best to strengthen GATS disciplines without unduly curtailing national regulatory freedom. Of related interest are the questions of how to determine the extent to which government regulations in the services field can be based on principles of economic efficiency and good governance; and to what degree, amid considerable sectoral diversity, regulatory principles can be pursued through the creation of meaningful horizontal (i.e., non–sector-specific) disciplines.

This concluding chapter draws on the body of analysis contained in this volume to identify a set of issues to which services negotiators and regulators will need to devote closer attention in the coming years. From a forward-looking perspective, six key themes appear to warrant closer analytical scrutiny.

First, the rationales for regulation and the reasons for collective action at the multilateral level are similar across service sectors. Further experimentation on this policy interface along sectoral lines certainly is needed—to nurture greater GATS "buy-in" on the part of sectoral regulators, among other reasons. The argument can be made, however, that a horizontal approach to disciplines on domestic regulation is possible under the GATS. Horizontal rules may emerge (in the future) from sectoral experimentation.

Second, before new disciplines on domestic regulation can be contemplated a fuller understanding of the scope of existing GATS disciplines must be achieved. This concerns most centrally Articles III (Transparency) and XVII (National Treatment). As it happens, much can be achieved by making the process of rulemaking more transparent and striving for nondiscrimination in rule design and enforcement. This is a centrally important conclusion presented in the chapters by Keiya Iida and Julia Nielson and by David Leebron.

Although strengthened transparency disciplines beyond those currently found in Article III may be desirable as a means to promote good governance and efficient regulation, however, the design of any new disciplines in this area must be informed by a careful assessment of potential benefits and costs, particularly enforcement costs. The latter may be nontrivial in developing-country settings.

Meanwhile, there can be little doubt that the nondiscrimination (both de jure and de facto) disciplines found in GATS Articles II (Most-Favored Nation [MFN]) and XVII (National Treatment) already exert powerful discipline on domestic regulatory conduct in the services area. But, as several of the essays in this volume suggest, there may be a variety of reasons to create deeper disciplines to protect the rights of foreign producers and consumers.

Third, insofar as nondiscriminatory access to or control of essential facilities is a problem, market-opening commitments on trade and investment will typically have to be complimented by procompetitive regulatory disciplines. This fact emerges in the chapters on telecommunications by Daniel Roseman, on transportation by Richard Janda, on energy by Peter Evans, and (somewhat surprisingly, given his characterization of the industry's increasing "commoditization"), in the chapter on financial services by Stijn Claessens.

Fourth, insofar as regulations such as licensing and qualification requirements are impediments to trade, market-opening commitments may need to be supported by the right to challenge trade-impeding or needlessly burdensome regulation. This need emerges most clearly in the chapters on accountancy by Claude Trolliet and John Hegarty and on health services by David Luff, as well as in the chapter on financial services standards by Joel Trachtman. Recognizing this challenge lies behind the Article VI.4 work program on the development of possible new disciplines on regulatory conduct (beyond those already agreed for accountancy services). However, as we discuss in greater detail below, opinions diverge quite significantly on the form any new disciplines might take—indeed, they diverge over the very feasibility of reaching agreement on such disciplines.

Fifth, regarding the promotion of regulatory harmonization (or, at the very least, greater doses of regulatory convergence) and the conclusion of mutual recognition agreements (MRAs), greater participation by developing countries is clearly desirable in the development of international standards in services. Where such standards do exist, the likelihood of disguised or needlessly restrictive impediments to trade and investment may be significantly lower, to the extent that such standards reflect best practice policies. Multilateral disciplines under the GATS should, accordingly, create a stronger presumption in favor of genuinely international standards in services trade. Moreover, because of the potential of MRAs to create trade and investment distortions, bilateral or plurilateral recognition agreements should respect the nondiscrimination principle, as mandated by GATS Article VII. As a rule, such agreements should not be notified under Article V of GATS (Economic Integration) but rather be open to all eligible participants under the potentially less trade-restrictive terms of Article VII.

Sixth, developing countries have much to gain from strengthened multilateral disciplines on domestic regulation. This is so for two important reasons. First, the development of such disciplines can play a significant role in promoting and consolidating domestic regulatory reform efforts. Second, such disciplines can help developing country exporters address potential regulatory barriers to their exports in foreign markets. A central challenge confronting developing countries is thus how best to harness multilateral rulemaking efforts with a view to promoting sound regulatory institutions and practices at the national level.

Understanding the Rationales for and Possible Trade Effects of Domestic Regulation

The service economy comprises an extraordinarily rich variety of economic activities. Such diversity—and the rulemaking challenges it poses in international negotiations—are defining characteristics of the GATS. Are services sectors so different that each will need a distinct approach? Or are there certain basic general principles that can be applied across sectors—and that will remain relevant over time in a world of changing technology and policy?[1]

The great diversity of services sectors, the difficulty of making policy-relevant generalizations in the midst of rapidly changing regulatory environments, and the regulatory precaution associated with the sheer novelty of trade negotiations in the services field have all tended so far to impart a certain degree of sectoral specificity to discussions of the GATS–domestic regulation interface. However, as several of the chapters in this volume bring out

quite vividly, even though services sectors differ greatly, there is considerable similarity in the underlying economic and social reasons for regulatory intervention: monopolies in network-based services (e.g., telecommunications, transportation, and energy services), externalities and asymmetric information in knowledge and intermediation-based services (e.g., financial and professional services), and the desire to ensure universal access in essential services (e.g., health and education services). These rationales and a range of possible GATS- and domestic policy–based responses thereto, are presented in Table 12.1. Focusing on these rationales may provide the basis for determining the desirability and feasibility of answering one of the key issues confronting services negotiators under the Article VI.4 work program: choosing between horizontal and sectoral disciplines.

In the current GATS talks, negotiators will be considering whether and how such disciplines could be applied to a variety of other network services, including transport (terminals and infrastructure), environmental services (sewerage), and energy services (distribution networks), with a view to ensuring, among other things, that any major supplier of

TABLE 12.1 Dealing with Domestic Regulations at the Multilateral and National Levels

Market failures	Services sectors	Possible GATS responses	Possible national policy responses
Monopoly/oligopoly	Network services: telecommunications; transport (terminals and infrastructure), environmental services (sewerage) and energy services (distribution networks)	Generalizing key disciplines in telecommunications reference paper to ensure cost-based access to essential facilities, such as roads, rail tracks, terminals, sewers, networks, or pipelines Strengthened disciplines to deal with anticompetitive conduct	Developing procompetitive regulation to protect consumer interests where competitive market structures do not exist
Asymmetric information	Intermediation and knowledge based services: financial services, professional services, and so forth	Nondiscrimination and possible application of a necessity test	Strengthening domestic regulation to remedy market failure in an economically efficient manner
Externalities	Transport, tourism, and so forth		Devising economically efficient means of achieving social objectives in competitive markets
Social objectives: universal service	Transport, telecommunications, financial, education, health		

essential facilities provides access to all national and foreign suppliers at cost-based rates and does not abuse its dominant position in markets.

Transparency

The chapter by Keiya Iida and Julia Nielson provides a comprehensive review of existing transparency provisions in national, regional, and World Trade Organization (WTO) agreements, and the options for enhancing transparency under the GATS. Transparency is, however, rather like the trade policy equivalent to motherhood and apple pie. Few would question its innate desirability. Two issues arise, however, in the context of strengthening transparency disciplines. First, although transparency can help reduce concealed protectionism, it alone cannot eliminate the more persistent and the more deeply embedded inefficiencies. Second, although it is important to recognize the many benefits of enhanced transparency, it is also important to acknowledge that its pursuit in greater quantities may also be costly. Accordingly, any new multilateral disciplines on transparency must be based on a careful assessment of the benefits and costs, both globally and nationally.

For instance, ex ante transparency in the form of obligations providing for consultations with all interested parties before the enactment of a new law or regulation will almost certainly have a higher administrative cost than ex post transparency, whereby new regulations and regulatory decisions are made public after they have been made. Proponents of strengthened transparency disciplines—strengthened notably through prior notification requirements—point to the greater political legitimacy likely to be attached to laws and regulations deriving from broad public consultations, and the attendant scope for lessening protectionist capture and the risk of inefficient regulatory design.

Nonetheless, it is plausible to assume that greater transparency can be associated with diminishing marginal benefits and increasing marginal costs, and that there is an optimal level of transparency that equates the two at the national level. The question then is why the national optimal level may not necessarily be the global optimal. Simply put, why are multilateral rules on transparency needed? One possibility is that domestic transparency may not translate into transparency for foreign providers—for example, calls for tender in the local-language press or consultations with local suppliers do not engage foreign providers. More generally, national transparency may be a global public good but the full benefits of it are not fully internalized by each national government. In any case, if multilateral rules do create deeper transparency obligations, there must be some way to ensure that these rules do not place an excessively costly administrative burden, especially on poorer countries. There is, accordingly, a great need for empirical investigation of the costs and benefits of increased transparency disciplines and of how the choice of optimal levels is today made at the national level.

Monopoly

The problem of monopoly has two dimensions in services trade: the effect on conditions of access to markets and essential facilities for foreign producers and the effect on consumers. The chapters in this volume have focused for the most part on the former issue, but we also make some comments about the latter problem.

Market failure resulting from natural monopoly or oligopoly may create trade problems because dominant incumbents can impede access to markets through their control of essential facilities. Because of its direct effect on trade, this form of market failure typically will have to be addressed directly by multilateral disciplines so that market-opening commitments are not nullified or impaired.

The relevant GATS provision, Article VIII dealing with monopolies and exclusive service providers, is in its current shape fairly limited in scope. As a consequence, and as the essay by Daniel Roseman describes, a reference paper featuring a number of procompetitive regulatory principles was developed in the context of the telecommunications negotiations to ensure that monopolistic or dominant suppliers would not undermine market access commitments. A number of chapters in this volume conclude that in the current set of GATS talks negotiators should consider whether and how such disciplines could be usefully applied to a variety of other network services, including transport (terminals and infrastructure), energy services (distribution networks), and financial services (payment systems) with a view to ensuring, among other things, that any major supplier of "essential facilities" provides nondiscriminatory conditions of access and use to all national and foreign suppliers.

The effects of rules dealing with issues such as "reasonable" and "cost-oriented" conditions of access to networks and pricing of services are considerably more complex and will require more careful consideration. They also are likely to show considerable variance and raise highly technical issues across various sectors. In such situations generic disciplines may prove inadequate, a conclusion drawn by both Daniel Roseman (telecommunications) and Peter Evans (energy).

One possibly important issue that the chapters in this volume do not deal with concerns the potential need for international rules to protect consumers. Market power can be an issue even in the absence of government restrictions on entry. Despite changes in technology, it is far from clear that consumers in small markets necessarily will secure access to competitively priced supplies of telecommunications, transport, and financial services even if all barriers to entry are eliminated.

In some sectors, anticompetitive practices are likely to be a problem. Two considerations would seem relevant in determining whether a regulatory response may be necessary and, if so, what form it should take. One such consideration derives from whether the national market is segmented from the international market. If cross-border delivery is feasible then services trade resembles goods trade and the size of the national market may be largely irrelevant in determining competitive conditions. In many cases, however, the cross-border delivery of services will be difficult, either for technological reasons or because of the nature of consumer and/or regulatory preferences. For example, fixed-line local telecommunications services may be difficult to supply without some form of commercial presence, and consumers will often be reluctant to buy life insurance or enter into other types of retail financial services transactions with overseas firms. In these cases, national market structures assume critical importance.

A second consideration is whether the minimum efficient scale of operation is large relative to the size of the market—or whether sunk costs are important, if market contestability (i.e., the credible threat of new entry) is deemed to be the relevant benchmark. Despite changing technologies

that have greatly reduced both the optimal scale of operation and the importance of sunk costs, in basic telecommunications, banking, and air and maritime transportation services the answer to both questions is likely to be positive for some time.

Concerns about consumer interests and how they may be affected by monopolistic and other anticompetitive types of behavior are addressed in principle by GATS Articles VII and IX, but these articles provide only for information exchange and consultation. Strengthened multilateral rules may be needed to reassure small countries with weak enforcement capacity that the gains from liberalization will not be appropriated by international cartels.[2]

Regulatory Impediments to Trade: Is a Necessity Test Necessary?

When market failure is attributable to informational problems or externalities, multilateral trade disciplines need not address the problem per se but rather ensure that domestic measures to deal with the market failure do not unduly restrict trade. The same may be said of measures designed to achieve social objectives to the extent that they may be covered by GATS rules and subject to scheduled commitments. Such trade-restrictive effects can arise from a variety of technical standards, prudential regulations, and qualification requirements in professional, financial, and numerous other services, and from the granting of monopoly rights to complement universal service obligations in services such as health, transport, and telecommunications.

One means that has been suggested for disciplining the trade- and investment-inhibiting effects of this entire class of regulations is to complement the national treatment and market access obligations with the development of a "necessity" test. Such a test essentially leaves governments free to deal with domestic economic and social objectives, provided that any measures taken are no more burdensome than necessary to achieve the relevant objective. Such a test, for which a trade in goods equivalent is found in the Agreement on Technical Barriers to Trade (TBT) and the Agreement on Sanitary and Phytosanitary (SPS) measures, has long been in use as a legal standard within the European Community. A necessity test also forms part of the accountancy disciplines agreed to by WTO members in 1998 and described by Trolliet and Hegarty in this volume.

In principle, a necessity test could be used to encourage the adoption of economically efficient policy choices in remedying market failures and in pursuing noneconomic objectives. For example, in the case of professional licensing a requirement to requalify could be deemed unnecessarily burdensome because the problem—inadequate information about whether individual practitioners possess the required skills—could be remedied by a less burdensome test of competence (which is—and should be—the main rationale of professional licensing regimes).

Important unanswered questions remain about the feasibility and desirability of embedding a necessity test for services trade under the GATS. These questions include how might "necessity" be defined—or whether further definition is necessary; whether "necessary to ensure the quality of the service" is sufficiently broad to allow for a host of regulatory objectives; and how other elements, such as the reasonable availability of alternative measures (or the lack of them), should be taken into account in resolving possible trade disputes.

It is difficult, however, to see how even the basic GATS disciplines of MFN and national treatment can be enforced without the application of some similar test. In such situations a necessity test may be more than a mere Article VI add-on.

Consider first the national treatment obligation, which requires that foreign services and service suppliers receive no less favorable treatment than the equivalent national services and suppliers. In applying the traditional GATT/WTO two-step approach of first establishing likeness and then determining whether "like" foreign suppliers are receiving less favorable treatment, one can easily end up in a legal cul-de-sac.

For example, consider the hypothetical case of a medical doctor from Greece arriving in Canada with a view to practicing medicine there. Imagine that the Canadian licensing authorities ask him to requalify fully in his new country of adoption. Would such a requirement be inconsistent with national treatment? The Canadian licensing authorities could legitimately allege that a doctor trained in Greece is not "like" a doctor trained in Canada. What would a WTO panel say? If it said that a Greek medical doctor was like a Canadian doctor, then Canada would not have the right to impose even a slightly greater burden on the Greek doctor. This is

hardly sustainable and with some justification could be seen as a threat to regulatory autonomy. If, on the other hand, a Greek doctor is not deemed to be "like" a Canadian doctor, the national treatment discipline simply does not apply, and the Canadian (provincial) licensing authorities are given a free rein to do whatever they want. This is also likely to be an unsatisfactory outcome.

The most reasonable argument would be to ask, What is it that the Canadian licensing authorities really need to do to ensure that foreign doctors do not constitute a threat to the health of Canadian citizens? Under such an approach, anything that strayed unduly from competence-based reasons for licensing (which quite legitimately can include a demonstrable command of local languages) should be deemed inconsistent with national treatment. But this is precisely a variant of the necessity test.

Some WTO members have raised the fundamental question of whether a necessity test is itself "necessary," given the scope for addressing problems via other means (such as transparency) and the concerns raised about the potential for such a test to limit the full scope of possible government action to regulate service sectors. Indeed the very discussion of this issue has generated considerable controversy in regulatory and civil society circles, particularly in the Organisation for Economic Co-operation and Development (OECD) area.[3] As intractable and politically sensitive as these questions may be, it is doubtful that WTO members will be able to reach closure (in one way or another) on the Article VI.4 work program without a more thorough airing of the challenges posed by the possible adoption of a necessity test for services trade.

If policy sensitivities arise when necessity-type arguments are invoked in dealing with overtly discriminatory (i.e., national treatment–inconsistent) regulatory measures, the application of a necessity test to measures that satisfy nondiscrimination disciplines tends to be even more controversial. This is so because under such circumstances a necessity test could be seen as suggesting that domestic regulatory conduct should somehow be subordinated to trade policy imperatives in light of its possible trade- or investment-impairing effects.

The possible new disciplines called for under the Article VI.4 work program are to deal with regulatory measures not addressed by Articles II (MFN), XVI (Market Access), and XVII (National Treatment) of GATS. Identifying the specific types of measures to which Article VI.4 disciplines would apply has long bedeviled WTO members. Indeed, the empirical (and commercial) significance of strictly nondiscriminatory trade-impeding measures has yet to be established satisfactorily. Moreover, even if such measures do matter, how they should be dealt with under the GATS remains quite unclear.

A deliberately far-fetched example helps to highlight some of the challenges negotiators would need to contend with in developing a necessity test applicable to nondiscriminatory regulatory measures. Imagine that a WTO member required that all taxi drivers be certified cardiologists because it is simply socially unacceptable in that country for people to die of heart attacks while trapped in traffic jams. On its face, this would seem to be an excessively burdensome regulatory requirement. It is, however, strictly nondiscriminatory and so the question is, should WTO rules prohibit it? Would such a prohibition not be considered unduly intrusive? David Leebron's depiction of the tentativeness of U.S. judicial rulings on challenges to nondiscriminatory measures is a sobering reminder of the political difficulties encountered in making rules in this area. Moreover, it remains unclear that nondiscriminatory measures other than quantitative restrictions (i.e., other than those addressed by GATS Article XVI in scheduled sectors) are important sources of trade or investment friction, or that they are comparable in economic significance to de facto discriminatory measures.

A central challenge facing those WTO members who favor embedding a necessity test in the GATS will be to give more precise meaning to the notion of necessity and to the conditions under which such a discipline would be triggered. At a minimum it would seem necessary to err on the side of permissiveness to make any such new disciplines politically acceptable. A balance would need to be struck between political concerns about the intrusiveness of multilateral rules and the need to ensure that protectionist or needlessly burdensome regulation does not undermine market access commitments.

Several existing models could serve as a starting point for discussions along these lines in a GATS setting. One such model is offered by the wording of necessity tests already found in the General Agreement on Tariffs and Trade's (GATT) TBT and SPS

Agreements as well as in Article XX (Exceptions), which draw attention to the need for regulatory measures to be "the least trade restrictive alternative reasonably available to achieve the regulatory goal." A second model comes from the proportionality tests codified under European Union law and applied in a number of rulings by the European Court of Justice on the internal trade effects of regulatory measures maintained by European Community member countries. Proportionality has tended to include least trade-restrictive analysis and other tests, notably with regard to desirability (means–end rationality), cost-benefit analysis, and feasibility. A third model stems from proposals calling for the development of necessity-based criteria creating a presumption in favor of economically "efficient" regulations and regulatory outcomes (Gamberale and Mattoo 2002). Whatever model (if any) is ultimately adopted in the GATS, one rule of thumb may well be to avoid creating rules whose enforcement would require judicial decisions to be rendered on highly delicate policy matters. Rather, the rules should serve mainly to target truly egregious regulatory measures. Perhaps it would be sufficient to ensure that a nondiscriminatory measure is "not obviously unnecessary" to secure compliance with a legitimate public policy objective. Following the example of the accountancy disciplines, it may also be desirable to provide guidance to prospective WTO panelists by drawing up an illustrative list of legitimate public policy objectives to which presumptions of regulatory immunity would apply at first view.

Harmonization And Recognition

Harmonization and mutual recognition can be seen as complements of rather than substitutes for multilateral rules on domestic regulation. Three core questions arise under this cluster of issues. First, where is it feasible and desirable to develop international standards for services trade? Second, what should be the link between the GATS and international standards? And, third, how should the GATS deal with plurilateral or bilateral mutual recognition?

The pessimism that calls for regulatory harmonization typically generate is based on the absence of widely accepted international standards in services. Where such standards do exist, as in financial services (banking, securities, and insurance) or maritime transport, meeting them often tends to be seen as a first step toward acceptability rather than as a sufficient condition for market access. The GATS, like the GATT, does not specifically require the use of international standards. It generally provides weaker incentives for the use of such standards than do the SPS or the TBT Agreements, and it does not provide a presumption of compliance as do those other two agreements.[4]

It is unlikely that meaningful international standards for most services will be developed any time soon, but it bears noting that in those areas where global standards do exist, the likelihood of disguised or needlessly restrictive impediments to trade and investment may be significantly lower. This may in part occur because internationally agreed norms can more easily reflect best-practice regulatory policy. The existence of such standards also may significantly facilitate trade and investment, particularly in the case of cross-border trade where international standards may help overcome the various forms of information asymmetries that hold back such trade—and its commensurate liberalization under the GATS.

Accordingly, efforts should be directed to ensure that the GATS creates a stronger presumption in favor of genuinely international standards in services trade. As with recognition agreements (see below), efforts at developing international standards for services trade are likely to require greater doses of technical assistance and capacity building. This may be done usefully at the national and regional levels (particularly because geographic and historical/cultural proximity may be expected to ease regulatory convergence).

At the multilateral level, efforts to promote the adoption of international standards invariably will be made outside the WTO framework. The WTO is not in the business of making regulatory standards. Rather, its remit lies in how such standards are formulated and implemented if and when they affect trade. The relevant institutions for promoting international standards for services are to be found in various specialized regulatory institutions, such as the Bank for International Settlements for banking standards, the International Telecommunications Union for telecommunications, the International Civil Aviation Organization for air transport services, and the International Standardization

Organization for various categories of services (including the means of producing and supplying them).

Another concrete example of forward movement in international standardization involving developing countries is provided by the International Monetary Fund/World Bank Financial Sector Assessment Programs, which are helping many jurisdictions assess their compliance with international standards in the financial sector with the aim of addressing any underlying weaknesses. Carried out in a voluntary and participative manner outside the trade policy framework, such regulatory cooperation may nonetheless be expected to assist the progressive, orderly pursuit of liberalization of trade and investment in financial services.

With regard to mutual recognition agreements, three observations seem in order. First, such agreements cannot be made to happen. Second, they do not seem to be happening—at least not on any major trade-influencing scale. Often touted as a desirable alternative to regulatory harmonization for reducing transaction costs, in practice there are relatively few examples of successful, operative MRAs in services trade (see Beviglia-Zampetti 2000 and Nicolaidis and Trachtman 2000). Third, even if MRAs were to happen in greater numbers, it is unclear whether they would always be desirable.

A multilateral agreement like the GATS cannot require countries to conclude MRAs—just as any provision such as GATS Article V (Economic Integration) or GATT Article XXIV cannot make regional integration agreements happen. As in the case of regional agreements, multilateral disciplines can be more or less permissive with regard to mutual recognition.

This in turn raises a key question: where and how strong are the incentives to conclude MRAs? The practice of MRAs suggests that their scope is quite limited; they are invariably concluded between very similar countries. Even in a region with as strong an integrationist dynamic as the European Union, and despite a significant level of prior and/or complimentary (minimal) regulatory harmonization, the effect of MRAs has been limited by the unwillingness of many host country regulators to cede full control (see Commission of the European Communities 2002). It should come as no surprise that MRAs have yet to exert significant effects on services trade.

Such an outcome in turn raises the question of the benefits and costs of MRAs. The analogy with regional integration agreements is useful here again because MRAs can be likened to sector-specific preferential arrangements. In circumstances where regulatory barriers are prohibitively high—one can imagine autarchy as the ultimate example—recognition can only create trade. But if the barriers are not that high, selective recognition can have discriminatory effects and lead to trade diversion. The result may well be to create trade according to a pattern of mutual trust rather than on the basis of the forces of comparative advantage. For instance, one can readily observe OECD countries making progress (albeit limited) toward MRAs in professional services but avoiding those agreements with countries such as the Arab Republic of Egypt, India, or the Philippines.

GATS Article VII (Recognition) strikes a delicate balance by allowing such agreements, provided that third countries have the opportunity to accede or demonstrate equivalence. Thus, Article VII has a desirable open-ended aspect that Article V (dealing with integration agreements) does not have. This makes it particularly worrisome that many MRAs require notification by WTO members under Article V rather than under Article VII.

The key concern for any multilateral agreement should not be how those who enjoy preferential access are treated, but how those who do *not* enjoy such access are treated. Somewhat ironically, the only line of defense on the rights of third countries could well come from a necessity test aimed at ensuring that such countries would not be subject to unnecessarily burdensome regulation even if they were not parties to an MRA.

Because of the potential of MRAs to create trade and investment distortions, bilateral or plurilateral recognition agreements should respect the nondiscrimination principle mandated by GATS Article VII. As a rule, such agreements should not be notified under GATS Article V (Economic Integration) but rather be open to all eligible participants under the terms of Article VII.

Regulatory Reform and Development

Developing countries have much to gain from strengthened multilateral disciplines on domestic regulation for two main reasons. First, the development of such disciplines can play a significant role in promoting and consolidating domestic regulatory reform efforts. The experience in telecommunications in many developing countries is a powerful example of this possibility (see Roseman 2001).

Secondly, such disciplines can help exporters in developing countries address potential regulatory barriers to their exports in foreign markets. For example, unless disciplines are developed to deal with potentially restrictive licensing and qualification requirements for professionals, market access commitments on the movement of natural persons may have limited commercial meaning. Adopting best regulatory practices or adhering to international standards similarly may help developing countries overcome regulatory hurdles in foreign markets.

It is important to note that there are limits to what can be achieved at the multilateral level because many key regulatory challenges must still be addressed at the national level, particularly in the realm of building credible and independent regulatory institutions. This is so because multilateral trade rules are often primarily designed to ensure market access and not directly to promote economic efficiency or social welfare.

For developing country negotiators, an important question is how best to harness multilateral rulemaking efforts with a view to promoting sound regulatory institutions and practices at the national level. Attention must be given in this context to the need for a proper sequencing of regulatory reform and liberalization efforts. Technical assistance for the development of regulatory capacity in developing countries is bound to be a crucial accompaniment to future services trade liberalization.

Advancing our understanding of the interface between domestic regulation and services trade remains critically dependent on the quality of policy dialogue between the trade and regulatory communities. The GATS has been instrumental in prompting a much needed *rapprochement* between these two communities, promoting mutual learning and helping dispel misunderstandings. Much remains to be done to enhance the quality and depth of such a dialogue, which in today's more politically charged negotiating environment must also involve broad participation by civil society organizations, but without such dialogue it will be difficult to make much headway on this difficult policy interface. Although probably more acute in the OECD area, such a challenge is equally important for developing countries as they acquire a greater stake in services liberalization and the multilateral trading system more generally.

Endnotes

1. The existence under GATS of a multilateral framework of disciplines of generic application, coupled with a series of annexes addressing sectoral specificities, suggests that no single answer can be given to the above tensions. The policy tensions arising from sectoral diversity appear to require flexible (and dual) rulemaking responses.
2. An important reason for developing a first-best international response to these practices is to prevent recourse to an inferior national response. It bears recalling in this regard that the costly cargo-sharing schemes imposed by many developing countries in the maritime sector were primarily a reaction to the perceived power of maritime conferences.
3. See OECD (2002) for a further depiction of the public policy controversy surrounding the GATS and its alleged effects on the right to regulate the supply of services.
4. Such a presumption can be found in Article 2.5 of the TBT Agreement and Article 3.2 of the SPS Agreement.

References

The word "processed" describes informally produced works that may not be available commonly through libraries.

Beviglia-Zampetti, Americo. 2000. "Market Access through Mutual recognition: The Promise and Limits of GATS Article VII." In Pierre Sauvé and Robert M. Stern, eds., *GATS 2000: New Directions in Services Trade Liberalization*. Washington, D.C.: Brookings Institution Press.

Commission of the European Communities. 2002. "Report from the Commission to the Council and the European Parliament on the State of the Internal Market for Services." COM(2002)441. Brussels, July 30.

Gamberale, Carlo, and Aaditya Mattoo. 2002. "Domestic Regulations and Liberalization of Trade in Services." In Bernard Hoekman, Aaditya Mattoo, and Philip English, eds., *Development, Trade, and the WTO*. Washington, D.C.: World Bank.

Nicolaidis, Kalypso, and Joel Trachtman. 2000. "From Policed Regulation to Managed Recognition in GATS." In Pierre Sauvé and Robert M. Stern, eds., *GATS 2000: New Directions in Services Trade Liberalization*. Washington, D.C.: Brookings Institution Press.

OECD (Organisation for Economic Co-operation and Development). 2002. *GATS: The Case for Open Services Markets*. Paris.

Roseman, Daniel. 2001. *Economic Impact of Trade and Investment Liberalization in the Telecommunications Sector—A Review of the Literature for Selected Countries*. Ottawa: Department of Foreign Affairs and International Trade. Processed.

Authors and Their Affiliations

Aaditya Mattoo
The World Bank

Pierre Sauvé
Groupe d'Economie Mondiale,
Institut d'Etudes Politiques de Paris

Keiya Iida and Julia Nielson
Trade Directorate, Organisation for Economic
Co-operation and Development, Paris

Joel P. Trachtman
The Fletcher School of Law and Diplomacy,
Tufts University

David W. Leebron
Dean and Lucy G. Moses Professor of Law,
Columbia University School of Law

Daniel Roseman
Roseman Associates, Ottawa, Canada

Richard Janda
McGill University, Montreal

Stijn Claessons
University of Amsterdam

Claude Trolliet
World Trade Organization

John Hegarty
The World Bank

Peter C. Evans
Center for International Studies,
Massachusetts Institute of Technology

David Luff
University of Liége, Belgium

INDEX